Black English
and the Mass Media

Walter M. Brasch

|||

University of Massachusetts Press, Amherst
1981

Copyright © 1981 by
The University of Massachusetts Press
All rights reserved
Printed in the United States of America
LC 81-2762   ISBN 0-87023-335-1
Library of Congress Cataloging in Publication Data
Brasch, Walter M., 1945–
Black English and the mass media.
Includes index.
1. Black English in mass media—United States—
History.   I. Title.
P96.B532U52   302.2′3   81-2762
ISBN 0-87023-335-1   AACR2

Acknowledgments made to publishers for permission
to reprint selections from copyrighted materials are
listed in the "Selected List of Works Cited" on
page 321 of this book.

To Milton Brasch. May his generosity and wisdom be a source of strength for others.

And to Helen Haskin Brasch, Fannie Haskin Friedin, Morris Haskin, and Samuel Friedin. Although they will never be able to read this book, let it be known that their wisdom and teachings, along with those of Milton Brasch, helped shape my life and expand my mind.

Contents

Acknowledgments   vii

Introduction   ix

1 The Colonial-Revolutionary Cycle   1

2 The Antebellum Cycle   23

3 The Reconstruction Cycle   59

4 The Negro Renaissance Cycle   147

5 The Civil Rights Cycle   227

Appendix: General Language Observations   291

Notes   301

Selected List of Works Cited   321

Index   327

Acknowledgments

Nothing exists in isolation. We who help create our environment are, in fact, a product of that environment. It is impossible for any person to know or fully understand all the forces that help shape attitudes and scholarship. And so it is with the development of this book. Past comments and suggestions of others, now probably buried within my subconscious, may have been forces that helped create this book. To those who helped, but who are not acknowledged, my subconscious and I apologize. However, a number of persons who contributed much to the development of this book can be acknowledged. They have given valuable time and assistance over a long period of time, and deserve special credit.

The advice, assistance, and encouragement of Drs. Norman H. Dohn and Karlen Mooradian, both of whom are very close personal friends, are deeply appreciated. Their backgrounds as leading journalists and mass communications scholars, and their active participation in my scholarly development, enabled me to understand and develop new concepts about the nature of our profession.

During the past few years, primarily because of the influence of Dr. Gilbert D. Schneider, I developed an interest in linguistics, especially in language and culture studies. Dr. Schneider spent countless hours helping me understand relationships not only between journalism and linguistics, but between man and his world. As one of the leading authorities in West African languages, Dr. Schneider helped draw together important comparisons between the West African languages and American Black English. He, like Drs. Dohn and Mooradian, presented me with new challenges and new insights into a complex phenomenon.

I have also benefited from discussions with Drs. Richard W. Bailey, Hugh Culbertson, Ian Hancock, Ralph Izard, John C. Merrill, Ernie Smith, Riley B. Smith, John H. Timmis III, and Colston Westbrook.

Throughout my research I was assisted and encouraged by Vivian M. Laughrey. Her conscientious sensitivity to detail was most helpful.

I am especially thankful to librarians James R. Housel, Barbara Flynn, Gary Friedman, Bertha Makow, Vicki Myers, Kay Pearlman, Diane Perry, Ed Templeton, and Leonard Wheeler at the Ontario (California) City Library; and to librarians at Ohio University, Ohio State University, Temple University, and the Claremont colleges.

I also extend my appreciation to Leone Stein, director of the University of Massachusetts Press, who served as my editor; Dr. Carroll E. Reed, consulting editor; Carol G. Schoen, copyeditor; Mary Mendell, design and production manager; and Ralph Kaplan, sales and marketing director.

To my parents, Milton and Helen Brasch, I can only express deepest appreciation for helping to provide an intellectual and social environment that allowed the development and completion of the work.

Finally, several publishers and authors have permitted me to take small sections from their works to illustrate certain aspects of this study; they are acknowledged here and in footnotes with my appreciation for their assistance.

Walter M. Brasch, Ph.D.
Ontario, California

Introduction

In the spring of 1971, I began compiling what was to become *A Comprehensive Annotated Bibliography of American Black English,* dubbed *Acababe* for short. It was a project that would last three years, with publication in the summer of 1974. *Acababe,* unlike some scholarly bibliographies, does not focus entirely upon scholarly research. As its name suggests it is a comprehensive bibliography, and as such, it represents the integration of both academic scholarship and popular studies or reports, many of which appeared in the mass media. The 2,300-item bibliography, which was long overdue in the rapidly expanding field of American Black English studies, served as a basis of this book, for without the bibliography, this as well as many other studies of Black English and its relationships within society—both historical and contemporary—could never have been accomplished or brought to completion.

In August 1973, Dr. Gilbert D. Schneider and I presented joint professional papers to the Midwest regional meeting of the American Dialect Society. Dr. Schneider focused upon the use of the nineteenth-century mass media—everything from advertising postcards to general circulation magazines—as sources of primary research into ethnolinguistic studies of American Black English. He concluded that many of the structures—syntactic, phonological, ideophonic, nonverbal, and paralinguistic—which were present in nineteenth-century Black Americana, are also present in a number of West African languages, notably Wes-Kos, the West African Pidgin English.

For my paper, which became the skeleton for this book, I reviewed the historical development of Black English literature from the seventeenth through the twentieth centuries. It was while preparing this paper that I became acutely aware, like Dr. Schneider, that the mass media serve as a basis of research into American Black English. Historically, the mass media provided a forum for debate about validity and theoretical interpretations of Black English, and served to popularize, occasionally quite erroneously, studies about the language. And equally important, the mass media served as the vehicles for presenting both fiction and nonfiction stories, poems, articles, and novels that included Black English in either narration or dialogue.

While reading and rereading, evaluating and analyzing many of the items from the mass media which became entries in *Acababe,* and from an extensive analysis of *Acababe* itself, a startling, though yet embryonic pattern, began to emerge. It appeared that there were periods in which American Black English in the mass media peaked, and periods in which there was almost a dearth of activity. Due to lack of time, I could only present these observations as a tentative hypothesis to the 1973 meeting of the American Dialect Society. Yet the idea of a cyclical theory so intrigued me that a few weeks after the professional meeting, I began to develop a formal methodology to explore the possibility further. As in the preliminary study, I established the hypothesis that the only strong evidence available as to the existence of Black English historically in America is what appeared in the mass media, for until recently relatively few academic publications included discussions of American Black English.

The second major hypothesis is that the mass media reflect the state of knowledge, concern, and awareness of Black English. Extensive analysis of the mass media from a historical perspective justifies the validity of the "five-cycle" theory of American Black English which is presented here, formally, for the first time. It has been determined that Black English concern historically has fallen within separate and distinct cycles, that each cycle lasted between twenty-five and forty years, and that each cycle was followed by an intercycle lasting between ten and twenty years. The lone exception was the Civil War intercycle of about seven years, the explanation being that war, at any moment in history, changes and accelerates the process of society.

The cycles and their approximate dates are: the Colonial-Revolutionary Cycle (about 1765–about 1800); the Antebellum Cycle (about 1820–about 1860); the Reconstruction Cycle (about 1867–about 1902); the Negro Renaissance Cycle (about 1915–about 1940); and the Civil Rights Cycle (about 1958–the present). Each cycle is characterized by a peak at least ten years before the end of the cycle, and by the fact that in quantity of materials available, it is larger and more substantive than the cycle that preceded it. And, most important, each cycle can be distinguished not only by volume (or quantity) and chronology, but by genre. Further, the nature of American society and of its mass media indicates that there will continue to be cycles; that each future cycle will not only have the same time frame as the preceding cycles, but that each future cycle will be represented by its own distinctive genre; that this is true whether it is American Black English being discussed and analyzed, or any field integrated within mass communications.

Chapter 1 discusses the Colonial-Revolutionary Cycle of American Black English, which did not begin until about 1765, and was preceded by a precycle of about eighty-five to one hundred years. During this precycle, several items in the mass media reflected the colonists' concern for Black English, but these items were so few and so chronologically distant that it could neither be considered a separate cycle nor part of the first cycle.

The Colonial-Revolutionary Cycle is distinguished by certain "feelers" into the nature of Black English. A number of "travelers' comments" by the English who visited the colonies were published, and several of these comments reflected on the nonstandard English in the colonies. Many of these observations resulted from perceptions which themselves were based on error. On another level, classified advertisements in newspapers provided a primary source for determining English language proficiency of runaway slaves. Drama also formed a major part of the cycle. During the country's early years, drama was part of the mass media, and served not only to entertain, but to persuade as well. As with newspapers, drama was often written to exploit political beliefs. Most drama was not written to be produced, but to be read—to be distributed and sold like books or newspapers. The circulation of drama was often far greater than that of local newspapers. The first cycle reached its peak about 1785–90, and was drawn to its natural conclusions about 1800.

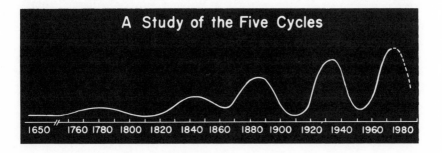

A Study of the Five Cycles

1650 1760 1780 1800 1820 1840 1860 1880 1900 1920 1940 1960 1980

Chapter 2 focuses on the Antebellum Cycle. In drama, the presence of Black English became almost nonexistent. Drama itself had changed, becoming less political and more superficially entertaining. The minstrelsy, with its black-faced Whites using stereotyped costume and language, was another major development of the cycle—theatrical presentation for the masses.

The novel began to assume its place in literary history during the Antebellum era, and the Black English of the period reflected this change. The works of both James Fenimore Cooper and William Gilmore Simms included Black English; Cooper and Simms actually pioneered better representations of Black speech. Nevertheless, the Black, with rare exceptions, was but a minor character in the literature. If he appeared, it was only as a filler or to reflect humor. The few studies made about Black speech during this cycle were only minor probes in comparison to what followed.

Travelers' comments, prevalent during the first cycle, diminished in the Antebellum cycle. When they did appear, they were usually comments by an American who traveled to another part of America, or by persons whose job it was to report on the language and culture around them. Slave narratives, written by escaped or recently freed slaves, were a major literary genre of this cycle. Although many narratives were ghosted by White abolitionists, they provide a major source to document Black speech during the Antebellum cycle.

The Reconstruction Cycle of American Black English is discussed in Chapter 3. In the mass media, the novel was now becoming secondary to the short story, a change reflected by the media and Black English in the media. Newspapers and magazines became dominant, reflecting the changing tastes of a nation. Within the pages of the most widely circulated magazines—among them *Appleton's, Century, Harper's Weekly, Lippincott's, Munsey's,* and *Scribner's*—appeared a literal flood of Black dialect verse, Black ethnic humor, and stories that included Black speech, or added insights into the nature of that speech. During the Reconstruction cycle, the names of William Francis Allen, Thomas Wentworth Higginson, Irwin Russell, Thomas Nelson Page, Eugene Zimmerman, Mark Twain, Joel Chandler Harris, Paul Laurence Dunbar, and Charles Waddell Chesnutt became known throughout the country.

Philology, the study of language (it would be many decades before linguistics, the science of language, was developed) began exploring the nature of nonstandard English. Many of the inquiries into and observations of American Black English, whether written by philologists, philosophers, sociologists, or laymen, were published in the newspapers and magazines that dominated the era.

The Negro Renaissance Cycle of American Black English, which spanned the years between the two world wars, was a continuation of the Reconstruction Cycle. After twenty years of almost nonexistent literature in Black English, the Black was again "in vogue," and once again the subject of ridicule. The 1920s were an unsettling time for Blacks; the Ku Klux Klan was still strong, and its view of "inferior races" more often than not was reflective of society. The "inferior Black," the shuffling, happy-go-lucky, mush-mouthed, watermelon-stealing, lustful Black was the stereotype, as it had been for so many decades. But the 1920s also witnessed a reawakening to a new literature that now allowed Blacks to become a part of the American creative arts—a segregated part, perhaps, but a part, nevertheless. From Arna Bontemps, Countee Cullen, Langston Hughes, Jean Toomer and others came a new literature; from W.E.B. Du Bois, Marcus Garvey, and James Weldon Johnson came a new militancy; from Scott Joplin, Blind Lemon Jefferson, W. C. Handy, Eubie Blake, and Huddie Ledbetter came a new music; from Charles Gilpin, Paul Robeson, and Bill Robinson came new interpretations in the theatre.

America had become enamoured with Blacks, and with Black-oriented themes, as evidenced by the mass media's unprecedented outpouring of Black-oriented short stories and novels. Most literary representations of Blacks were distortions of reality, butchered by incompetent writers.

However, many writers began to develop Black-oriented themes in order to better understand and explain the nature of society. Eugene O'Neill, who earned four Pulitzer Prizes and the Nobel Prize, wrote several dramas focusing on Blacks; Paul Green, a writer and philosophy professor, earned a Pulitzer Prize for *In Abraham's Bosom,* a study of a Black trying to gain freedom of the soul by gaining freedom of the mind; and Marc Connelly, adapting the stories of Roark Bradford, earned a Pulitzer Prize for *The Green Pastures,* an interpretation, in Black English, of Black worldviews of the Bible. In literature, William Faulkner, who earned the Nobel Prize in 1949, created a semifictional county to serve as the background for a series of novels which included in-depth studies of the role of Blacks in the South. Other novels, insightful and deeply moving, came from DuBose Heyward, Julia Mood Peterkin, and Margaret Mitchell. The short story, which had emerged as a dominant art form in the Reconstruction Cycle, achieved its greatest popularity during the Negro Renaissance Cycle, as Octavus Roy Cohen and others began to dominate the media; Cohen, himself, wrote more than 1,000 stories, a large portion of which involved Blacks speaking Black English.

It was during the Negro Renaissance Cycle that the electronics media began to develop. *Hallelujah,* directed by King Vidor, and featuring an all-Black cast, was one of the better films from the infancy of "talkies." Other films included *Porgy and Bess* and *Gone With the Wind.* At one time it seemed as if most films included a dialect-speaking Black. And on radio—which began as a channel for distress calls—*Amos 'n' Andy* was the highest-rated program, listened to by more than 40 million people.

During the Negro Renaissance Cycle, a number of studies were made into the nature of Black English. Most concluded that Black English, including Gullah, was derived from seventeenth-century British English. A few disagreed, citing possible African origins. Melville Herskovits pointed to African cultural origins, and Lorenzo Dow Turner emphasized African linguistic origins. But the world was not yet ready to fully comprehend the scope of their investigations or to accept their findings. And so the cycle ended, sometime around World War II.

A newer awareness of the Black as a human, with the same needs, feelings, and rights as any person, ushered in the civil rights era, and with it the Civil Rights Cycle of American Black English. A number of writers began using Black English as the language of the narrator, not strictly of the characters. Now, instead of reading the works of Paul Laurence Dunbar and Charles Waddell Chesnutt, or Langston Hughes and Countee Cullen, the American public was reading the stories of Richard Wright, Ralph Ellison, James Baldwin, Claude Brown, and LeRoi Jones, all of whom used Black English in their stories of Black life. Soon, Black English extended into childrens' stories as publishers became aware of a new audience.

The mass media, especially newspapers, extended their reporting about the nature of Black English. The expansion of specialized media—the academic and specialized journals—served as the forum for extensive linguistic and sociocultural studies of Black English. During this cycle, major studies of the nature of the language were published, attacked, and defended, and numerous educators began flooding the media—popular and specialized—with studies, opinions, essays, and overt vitriolic attacks on Black English.

Throughout the civil rights era, the significant writings about Black English have appeared in the largely unavailable academic journals, presumably because most of the original research into Black English is currently done by persons associated with higher education, a significant number of whom see the academic journal as the proper forum for such studies. A few researchers have found the doors of the mass media closed to studies of Black English. Some are afraid to test the doors; others are unable. Still others have been unwilling to write for the mass media and have maintained a very elitist or paternalistic attitude about Black English scholarship. This had not been true in the past. During the four previous cycles of Black English interest, the media had been used extensively to discuss and present this variety of speech. Each of these cycles is rich in written evidence of the development and spread of Black English.

To fully understand the representation of Black English in the mass media, it is necessary to understand some of the distinguishing features which describe Black English as a separate dialect based primarily upon African linguistic influence. The appendix presents many of the distinguishing features that set American Black English apart historically as a separate dialect/language in the written media, and not as a poor or sloppy English, as claimed in the Deficit Theory. The presentation of these features serves four very distinct purposes. First, it serves to explain complex linguistic terminology which appears throughout the book. Second, it serves as an index to distinguish some of the major features of Black English as represented within the mass media. These features comprise a list of those Black English features which regularly appeared in the mass media and, more important, which are consistently observed in a large volume of evidence. The language characteristics represent only features appearing in the written language, and are not fully reflective of the spoken language. Third, the list itself prevents lengthy and often unnecessary elaboration or explanation of distinguishing linguistic characteristics in selected literary passages. And fourth, the list is a "how to" for journalists and other writers. It accurately sets forth Black English features of which the careful journalist or writer must be aware if he or she wishes to write in Black English. Whereas not all features are present, and although there are many Black English dialects rather than just one Standard Black English, the person who refers to the list will have at least a basic working knowledge for accurate representation, rather than distortion based upon incorrect perception.

The linguistic features described in the appendix are not all-inclusive, but they do represent most of the major features of the dialect as represented historically in the American print media. As such, they differ from the rules described by present-day dialectologists and linguists who are armed with tape recorders and intricate research methodologies. The features are merely simplified general descriptions of the speech in the mass media identified as Black English, and are not meant to identify a "standard" Black English, nor are they meant to imply a thorough descriptive or contrastive analysis of the speech. Further, the list reflects Black English only in comparison to American Standard English. Thus, for descriptive reasons, it becomes necessary to include such words as "loss of" or "deletion of" when comparing Black English. In reality, as the ebonics theorists point out, there is no "loss of" anything and it might be assumed that it is the American language that has rules that could be interpreted as "addition of."

Many of the rules of Black English have their basis in African languages, notably Wes-Kos, the West African Pidgin English (WAPE).[1] Therefore, it is theorized that because American mass media writers of the eighteenth and nineteenth centuries had virtually no formal knowledge of African languages and were recording the language of the American Black as they heard it, any linguistic similarities of phonological and syntactic rules, as well as lexicon, between American Black English—as represented in the media—and the West African languages—notably WAPE —provide in effect a major source of data to justify the creolist theory.

HISTORICAL CONCEPTS

The Greek philosopher Heraclitus argued that no one can step into the same river twice, that everything is in a constant change. And so it is with historical data. Time alone will change not only the data itself, but the observations, interpretations, perceptions, and conclusions about that data. Time alone modifies changes and selects data. Primary sources are lost in history, and each apparent void changes interpretations of what remains, for even the most careful reconstruction can never restore the whole in its original state.

Any historical analysis of American Black English must, by necessity, depend upon historical, written documentation. The task is difficult for several reasons. There is no assurance that all the data, or even a significant portion, is available; there can be no guarantee that the historical reconstruction adequately represents all available data; and, it is impossible for the researcher of the present to interpret the primary source data in the same light in which the original authors saw that data and so entered it into history.

With American Black English, the task has been magnified, but not to such a degree as to render historical analysis impossible. It is from historical written documentation, especially in the mass media, that it has been possible to determine the development of five separate and distinct cycles of American Black English, each followed by an intercycle, and to draw a number of conclusions about each cycle in isolation, and about each cycle as part of a greater sociological-literary pattern. The wealth of dialect material available from each of these five cycles is a largely untapped resource that is unknown or, in a few instances, unacceptable to persons working in the field of Black English.

An overwhelming number of contemporary researchers have concentrated on the spoken language and on contemporary attitudes, but have neglected the written language (including illustrations, cartoons, and wood-types) and its importance in historical analysis and development. By concentrating solely on the synchronic analysis of Black English, researchers can only establish a frame of reference, but are unable to connect the important points of Black English study. It was the written language, perhaps more than the spoken, that helped establish attitudes and beliefs not only about language, but of the people as well. In the North during the nineteenth century, impressions about Blacks came from the written language and gross distortions within the mass media. Because of the absence of recording instruments in those days, the only way to analyze the spoken language is by examining the written language. Such evidence is also useful in drawing correlates between the language as spoken now and the language spoken at an earlier time, with the goal of determining the possible origins of present-day Black English.

Without a historical analysis of Black English, based upon the mass media, we are unable to fully determine whether Black English was a separate language, whether it was a creole or is becoming decreolized, or whether it merely reflected the language and dialect of a geographical region. This analysis may also answer the question of whether Black English is becoming more similar to, or different from, Standard English in the United States. Without the media, we are unable to measure past public attitudes about Black English—attitudes that may have influenced, and been influenced by, the media itself. The mass media can be a valuable resource, both primary and secondary, for the language scholar. It can also be used to enlighten and inform the public about Black English studies now being conducted and evaluated. To understand Black English and its role in our culture, we must look to the historical development within the media and its place in each of the five cycles.

HISTORIC VISIBILITY

By tracing a historical development of almost three hundred years, as reflected within the literature of the mass media, it becomes obvious that the visibility and importance of the Black increased in literature as the years progressed. In the Colonial-Revolutionary Cycle, the Black was present only as a servant or slave, often to utter a few comic lines and then depart. By the end of the Reconstruction Cycle, the Black was a major literary character. His visibility in many instances literally dominated plot or character development, as in Mark Twain's "Pudd'n-head Wilson." This increased visibility, though not always honest or sympathetic, would continue into the Civil Rights Cycle of the mid-twentieth century.

As the visibility of the Black increased, Black language in the mass media became more readable. There are two, though not necessarily conflicting, reasons for this. It is possible in some instances that the speech of the Black, as represented in the Colonial-Revolutionary Cycle, was a more separate, distinct speech, whereas the speech of the Black during Reconstruction reflects a continuing process of decreolization. It is possible that as the years progressed, the speech became easier to read and understand because it was in fact becoming more assimilated into, and by, Standard English.

Another explanation is equally possible. Although there are distinct creole evidences of Black English in the Colonial-Revolutionary Cycle, it is also clear that representation of Black speech was inconsistent at best, abysmal at worst. It is probably that the early writers of Black English, who were just beginning to work with the language, were not aware of the subtle nuances of language that distinguished Black English or Gullah from Standard English. The obvious distinctions, such as the replacement of the *th* by the *d* were regularly included in the mass media, but the subtle distinctions were not. And surprisingly, syntax—a stronger and more obvious difference—was often quite similar to Standard English in its presentation by the mass media. It is possible that the writers were aware of differences but defined those differences as the "natural result" of Blacks speaking "baby talk" or "debased English." In attempts to record Black speech, it is possible that the early writers overcorrected. They knew there were differences, but unsure about what those differences were, they inserted whatever happened to be handy, assuming possibly that "debased speech" was not consistent anyway. And, even those skilled writers who were able to transcribe the language accurately, probably had difficulty understanding the context and semantic field of what they heard and eventually wrote. But as more and more writers became aware of Black English, whether they called it that or not, the recording of the language improved, for each writer was now able to draw upon the literary productivity of every other writer. Thus, it would be expected that the language of the Black, as reflected in the mass media of the Reconstruction Cycle, would have been easier to read because it was more consistent, and took into account a natural rhythm of language which few earlier writers considered. The early writers, rather than record Black speech, may have written White speech, then attempted to translate it into Black English forms. What resulted was often bastardized English that had some appearance of Black language, but which was merely a hodgepodge of sounds and phrases that would take many extensive linguistic analyses to unravel.

METHODOLOGY

To understand the nature of the Black English theory, it is important to understand the methodology used for the presentation of data. Through an extensive and painstaking process of historical research and documentation, it has been possible to present most of the major items of Black English interest in the Colonial-Revolutionary Cycle, taking into account of course the probability that the farther back one delves into historical documentation, the less is available. As the country developed, more studies of Black English, and more stories that included Black English, reached the market; the theory accounts for an increased quantity of items for each cycle. Thus, whereas it may have been possible to include a greater percentage of items containing Black English elements in the Colonial-Revolutionary Cycle, it would have been overwhelming and impossible to use the same percentages for the Civil Rights Cycle.

Items presented as part of the primary source justification of the theory represent particular points that need to be explained to emphasize particular aspects of the media of that cycle. Items that significantly advance or retard the development of any particular cycle are included, as are a number of items that because of other factors—such as popular interest at the time—serve to illuminate the cycle. The individual selection of passages and excerpts for discussion and analysis was by no means a random selection. Each passage and excerpt represents a logical and rational decision. If, for example, a certain rule or feature needs to be emphasized, a passage was selected that contains that particular rule or language feature, usually more than once. Thus, the passages were selected to emphasize or allow discussion of selected features of Black English in the mass media.

A careful, analytic study of Black English and its relationships to the mass media enables the researcher to understand the development not only of Black English, but also of the media, themselves. It allows for a better understanding of forces that influenced population and the media, and has shed light on journalistic and literary trends.

INTERRELATIONSHIPS WITH THE EPS CURVE

The primary data that serve as the foundation for the presentation of the five-cycle theory of American Black English, and the theory itself, also serve to document and justify a theory of the historical development of the mass media. The EPS (Elite-Popular-Specialized) theory was developed by Dr. Ralph L. Lowenstein and presented formally in *Media, Messages, and Men* (1971), a book he and Dr. John C. Merrill co-authored.[2] According to Lowenstein, in the beginning of a nation's history, its mass media are elitist; illiteracy and poverty are determinants that force the media to appeal to society's elite. A careful analysis of the "five-cycle" theory indicates that the elitist stage existed primarily during the Colonial-Revolutionary Cycle.

The second stage in media development, according to Lowenstein, is the "popular" stage. Circulation rises and the mass media reflect a different kind of genre. The Antebellum Cycle may be viewed as the transition from an elitist to a popular orientation in mass media. The Reconstruction Cycle falls within the "popular" stage. The Negro Renaissance Cycle also represents a "popular" stage in media development, but the final years of that cycle show a transition to the third stage.

The third stage is the "specialized" stage. Lowenstein points out that higher education, affluence, leisure time, and population of at least 10 to 15 million are the four factors leading to a specialized press. It is important to note that the development of the specialized press, notably the academic journal, permitted the Black English media of the Civil Rights Cycle to reach a peak greater than the peak of the previous cycle. In essence, there are two subcycles working together. Quantification and separation of the studies in either the popular mass media or the specialized academic media would result in peaks in the Civil Rights Cycle below that of any previous cycle. But when both elements of the mass media are considered, then the peak, in line with the theory, does indeed exceed that of previous cycles.

Through an analysis of the five identified cycles of American Black English, it is also possible to determine that not only does the EPS curve affect the historical process, but it also applies to the development of individual media within the process. As an example, although television was developed as a mass medium during the latter years of the Negro Renaissance Cycle—itself part of the "popular" stage—television began as an "elite," moving into the area of "popular" only during the intercycle between the Negro Renaissance and Civil Rights cycles.

A study of both the cyclical theory of Black English and the EPS Theory reveals that peaks in the five already-identified cycles of Black English productivity tend to loosely parallel peaks in media productivity; likewise, the intercycles in Black English tend to reflect moments of low or nonlasting productivity in the mass media. Thus, the first peak occurs shortly after the American Revolution, perhaps 1785–90. This Black English peak parallels a peak in newspaper production in the country. There were more newspapers, and each newspaper had, if not a large circulation, then certainly a literate one. The newspapers were elitist; those which included studies of Black English were also elitist. The intercycle of 1800–1820 shows a decreased activity not only in Black English study, but in the media itself.

The development of the "penny press" era, beginning in the early 1830s, spurred an increase in circulation and a change in emphasis of the American media. This led to the beginning of the "popular" stage in the EPS model. And not so surprisingly, the increased circulation in newspapers, reflecting greater literacy, was paralleled by an increase in books for a nonelite, general audience. The peak of the Antebellum Cycle of Black English was about 1840–45, about the time that the Antebellum period of the American media was peaking. This was not coincidental.

Following the Civil War, about the time that William Randolph Hearst and Joseph Pulitzer were beginning their circulation wars, the Reconstruction Cycle of American Black English was also reaching a peak. This, too, was not a coincidence.

Media activity in the twentieth century closely paralleled studies and primary source documentation of Black English in the mass media. Each peak in Black English activity reflected similar peaks in mass media activity.

THE CONCEPT OF "MASS"

To better understand how Black English and the mass media are so closely integrated, it is necessary to understand what is meant by "mass," "mass communication," and "mass media." *Mass* is a heterogeneous population spatially separated and composed of individuals with loose ties to each other.[3] The term "mass communication" means any type of communication directed at a mass audience, in which feedback is often minimal or delayed. Defining what is meant by "mass media" is a task that may never fully be accomplished, for it reflects each definer's prejudices and biases. Some persons have placed a very narrow band around mass media; others have given it wide latitude. The mass media are the offspring of mass communication; they are a communication of any type directed to a mass audience (though not necessarily a large audience) through the media. The media, themselves, serve as the vehicles of communication. I give both mass communication and mass media a wide latitude, for the reason that both are products of the society in which they exist, and that society must by its own definition be given breadth to enable a comprehensive and often complex study of the process of society.

Mass communication is the process; mass communications can be the message on a billboard or advertising flyer; it can be the sensory impulses from a multimedia light-show with psychedelic lights and acid music; or it can be articles in newspapers or magazines. The mass media would be the billboards and advertising flyers, the technical equipment for the multimedia show, or the newspaper and magazine.

Some persons would limit the definition of mass media to indicate that there is a "periodicity" that distinguishes them. This is a "crutch definition," an attempt to define without really defining; it served the profession well at one time, but newer theoretical insights have rendered it obsolete. The medium, itself, as Marshall McLuhan and others theorized, is the message; each message that appears to a mass audience is shaped by the medium in which it is presented.

A number of other "definers" describe the mass media in traditional terms: it (1) informs, (2) persuades, (3) entertains, and (4) sells. But all four elements are rarely present within any one story, editorial, feature, or advertisement. And although two or three of the elements are, on occasion present, it is still important to remember that the medium itself is the vehicle, and if the medium itself allows the publication or dissemination of all four elements, whether or not present in any one item, then the medium must be part of the definition of a mass medium.

THE LINGUISTIC THEORIES OF BLACK ENGLISH

Just as the mass media do not exist in isolation, neither does Black English. The same society which determines the nature of the media also determines perceptions and attitudes of language. To understand perceptions and attitudes, it becomes necessary to understand the major theories enveloping Black English study.[4]

The basic tenet of the Deficit Theory, which is occasionally known as the Theory of Verbal (or language) Deficiency, claims that because of cultural deprivation, the Black English speaker not only has linguistic deficiencies, but also cognitive deficiencies. The theorists of this school of thought believe that cognition is restricted because Black English is a deficient language; not only is it *not* a complete language, but it is substandard as well. Deficit theorists often falsely equate Black English with low-class status, and claim that for Blacks to advance in society, they must "cast off" the shackles of Black English. Many deficit theorists believe there is only one correct and acceptable language, and that the "proper" language for Americans is Standard English. Black English, as well as any nonstandard dialect, is therefore considered to be "poor," "sloppy," or "substandard" English.

The Deficit Theory has received its strongest support within the education profession, as teachers on all levels, their own training molded by concepts of what is "right" and what is "wrong," attempt to impose that "correct language" upon their students. Attitudinal change within the education profession comes slow, but it does come. And many of the leading studies into the nature of American Black English have been undertaken by educators. Psychologists, many of whom have never studied linguistics, also tend as a group to advance the concepts of the Deficit Theory, arguing that language "deficiency"—as determined by not being able to speak Standard English—is a result of a cognitive deficiency. And, not surprisingly, journalists become involved in advancing the Deficit Theory—although many who have studied linguistics are seeing the merits of other theories. Most will agree that journalists, when dealing with mass audiences, must write in Standard English; it is imperative that for the written message to be communicated, a common language—in this case Standard English—must be employed. The use of written dialect, even when employed by the best dialect writers—such as Joel Chandler Harris, himself a professional journalist—often create *noise,* a barrier between the communicator and the receiver. Nevertheless, many editors have extended this belief to areas that have reflected or brought about a distinct bias, whether intentional or not. Attitudes, originated within society and reflected within the journalism profession, have often led journalists to believe that because Standard English is the medium of expression in the written word, it must also be the expression for the spoken word.

During the 1960s, editors, suddenly becoming aware of a newer Black militancy, began hiring "token" Blacks for the news staffs—Blacks who would sit near the door or who would be assigned to cover the "Black ghetto." Few of these "tokens" spoke Black English; often they were from middle- or upper-class neighborhoods, and knew little of the "urban beat" they were assigned to cover. Few were trained in journalism. And, more sadly, those Blacks who were competent journalists were seldom allowed to cover beats other than the urban or Black beat. Editors, trapped by events progressing faster than they were able to cope with, were forced into actions which they thought beneficial at the time to both the profession of journalism and to their readers.

Black reporters—with closely cropped hair, dark business suits, and Standard English—soon found that being the same color as their news sources wasn't really the panacea that their editors had hoped for. Black reporters who spoke Standard English found Black English-speaking sources just as closed to them as to the White reporters. There was no special communication; the language and meanings were different. But those reporters who were able to code-switch, disguising their knowledge of Black English to their editors, soon found that communication developed; language itself was the factor, not the color or the beliefs. Black English became the medium of communication. The reporter would write his story in acceptable Standard English, but his primary contacts were made in "the language of the street." A common bond, a bond forged by language, had developed.

Nevertheless, the stigma remains, a stigma shared equally by Black and White journalists. Whether subconscious or not, to speak Black English is perceived as a failure in a profession that values the word and its place within a structured pattern. Black English is regarded as "unacceptable," "sloppy," or "poor" English, an "inferior" language in the same sense as are the varieties of Southern English, Yiddish English, Irish brogue, or any other dialect. Those who speak it are perceived, again perhaps subconsciously by some, as being inferior to those who do not speak it. This problem is not unique to journalism but is advanced by educators, psychologists, and others; it is a problem shared by society.

Although a major part of the Deficit Theory is based upon cultural mores, another though not as prevalent part is based upon racial distinction. Proponents of this argument claim that the Black is genetically inferior to the White; any deficiencies in language or cognition are, therefore, based not upon culture, but upon genetics. The "theory of the thick lips," which linguists had hoped to bury several years ago, also falls into this classification. Whereas the eradicationist position argues for the abolition of Black English, and assumes that Blacks can be forced to learn Standard English, proponents of the "thick lips theory" claim Blacks are incapable of learning Standard English because of genetic and anatomic differences. On the surface, the partially educated layman can argue that it seems obvious that because the nose and lips, as well as teeth, gums, and larynx, are articulators of speech, any anatomical differences would change sound. This false argument still occurs frequently in the popular media, and linguists have proven that such arguments have no basis in fact. The easiest rebuttal the linguist can direct to the noninformed layman is that despite the anatomical features, Blacks can and do speak Standard English. The entire Deficit Theory, with its many subtheories and hypotheses, is often advanced by educators, social scientists, and, to a certain extent, by journalists. It is not a linguistic theory of language, and not based upon hard language data.

In contrast, both the creolist theories of Black English and those of the dialect geographers are based on a detailed analysis of the language. Both theories argue that the language is not substandard or "sloppy" English; Black English is an acceptable dialect or variety of speech with its own well-defined set of linguistic rules. They also account for the fact that Black English is not one, but many varieties of language, that not all Blacks speak Black English, and that some Whites also speak it.

Roger D. Abrahams, a leading folklorist and Black English scholar, points out that:

> In the controversy over the "legitimacy" of the speech of Afro-Americans in the United States we tend to forget that a person's image of himself is intimately bound up with ways in which he chooses to talk. To criticize a way of speaking, or to denigrate it any way, is to attack the image a person has of himself.[5]

The primary difference between the theories of the dialect geographers and creolists lies in the interpretations of the origins and subsequent development of Black English, as well as in interpretation of the linguistic rules.

Dialect geographers often argue that to understand the status of Black English today, which they identify as a variety of speech rather than a separate dialect or language, it is necessary to look to Elizabethan English. They maintain that the English migration to the United States brought about a divergence of dialects, that as sociocultural groups were separated by geography, dialects were formed. For that reason, they claim that what is identified as Black English by others is in reality a reflection not of race, but of geographical areas in which the Black lives. They argue that the Black slaves, or their descendants, essentially took on the linguistic characteristics of the geographical region in which they lived; Black English, therefore, is similar to White Southern dialects, as well as to various British dialects.

In contrast, the creolists point to certain types of linguistic rules and to historical development in West African languages to support the argument that Black English is, or has been at one time, a separate language in the United States. A major corollary to this position is that Black English, which was once a creole, is becoming decreolized. The creolists turn to history as part of the justification of their theory. In order to prevent revolt, slavetraders broke up groups of Blacks from the same cultures and language groups, believing that if the Blacks were unable to communicate with each other, it would be impossible for them to plan revolt against their White "owners." *A New Voyage to Guinea* (1744), written by William Smith, documents this philosophy:

> As for the language of *Gambia,* they are so many and so different, that the Natives, on either Side of the River, cannot understand each other; which, if rightly consider'd, is no small Happiness to the *Europeans* who go thither to trade for slaves. . . .
>
> I have known some melancholy Instances of whole Ship Crews being surpriz'd, and cut off by them. But the safest Way is to trade with the different Nations, on either Side of the River, and having some of every Sort on board, there will be no more likelihood of their succeeding than of finishing the Tower of Babel.[6]

In principle, this was a good hypothesis, but what most traders did not understand was that at the time the Blacks were forcibly taken from their homes in West Africa, a significant number spoke a pidgin English, a trade language derived from the assimilation of English and a number of West African languages.[7] Thus the Blacks spoke not only their own native language, but, in essence, a common trade language. The creolist theory maintains that while in the United States, Black slaves by necessity developed regional variations of a creole, possibly as early as the seventeenth century, and that the creole had its basis not in Elizabethan English but in West African languages. They argue that although surface structure may seem similar to various American dialects, the deep structure is different and based on West African languages. The dialect geographers counter this argument by maintaining:

> In the last decade . . . the most sweeping generalizations have been drawn by those who would assert African or creole substrata and deny that features of British or Irish dialects of the Seventeenth Century might be better preserved among American Negroes than

among their white counterparts, or indeed among Southern Americans of all races than among speakers of other regional varieties of American English. . . .

A person would need a detailed knowledge, not only of African languages and creoles and pidgins, but synchronic and diachronic variations of English and several Romance languages as well. And one cannot overlook the definite evidence from Early Modern English, from more recent Irish English, and from other dialects (such as Newfoundland and upland American South) where creole influence is improbable.[8]

However, analysis of Black English in the mass media, when compared and contrasted with studies of West African languages, reveals strong similarities in a number of important areas, including syntax, semantics, phonology, lexical items, ideophonics, morphology, paralinguistics, and in various nonverbal systems. These similarities, which could only have been determined by a close analysis of the American mass media and a synchronic analysis of West African languages, show that Black English may have in fact been closer to West African Pidgin English—itself composed of elements of many West African languages—than to Standard American English.

During the past decade, a variation of the creolist theory has developed. Known as a "transformational theory" of Black English, this variation argues that the surface structure similarities and differences between American Black English and Standard English and West African languages are superficial and not conclusive. It is in the deep structure and only in the deep structure, they argue, that evidence as to the existence and nature of American Black English can be determined.

Another major theory which began developing in the mid-1970s, is the Ebonics Theory. The proponents of ebonics argue that Black English—identified as ebonics (ebony + phonics, *i.e.,* Black Sounds)—did not develop from either a pidgin or a creole, but is a linguistic system that is a continuation of the African Hamito-Bantu language families. They further argue that to identify American Black English on the basis of comparison to Standard English is neither valid nor acceptable linguistic practice. According to Mervyn Alleyne, "To relate non-standard dialects of Black American urban communities to a pidgin would lead to the inference that there has been discontinuity, as far as the transmission of an African cultural item is concerned, and would in fact support the deficiency hypothesis."[9]

Thus, according to Ernie A. Smith, one of the major developers of the theory, they "reject the Caucasio-centric inference that there has been an African language linguistic discontinuity in the deep structure."[10] Smith further argues that:

[T]he question of linguistic genesis cannot be explained by merely using phrase structure rules, tree diagrams, and transformational rules synchronically on contemporary linguistic events . . .

[E]ven if transformationalists can by ex post facto examinations and analysis derive closely approximating deep structures for some sociolects or varieties of ebonics and the so-called Standard English of Anglo-American speakers, this does not in any way negate the well-established historical fact that the autochthonous African ancestors and antecedents of the Slave Descendants of African Origin did not originally speak English.

Therefore, when transformationalists *synchronically* employ the use of the generative transformational model for descriptive analysis of Afro- and Euro-American speech, and then conclude that contemporary varieties and dialects of Ebonics are merely nonstandard social dialects of English, they are actually ignoring the question of linguistic genesis; for if the notion of the deep and surface structure in language is valid, then African languages (morphological systems) had deep structures also. And, if indeed African languages had deep structures, the mere intrusion of European lexicons would not alter the basic structure of African languages.[11]

It is doubtful that many persons understand these important concepts about language. Their reactions and opinions about Black English are often based on nonlinguistic, often emotional evidence. The controversy in Black English is not likely to subside in the future. There are no "right" or "wrong" theories. The development of linguistics as a science has brought clarification, but it has not yet provided definitive answers to a very complex language which, like all languages, carries within it a history, an anthropology, a sociology, a psychology and, in the case of Black English more so than any other American language or dialect, an emotion.

All that remains now is to predict the conclusion of the Civil Rights Cycle of American Black English. The cycle began in the late 1950s. If, as determined historically, each cycle is at least twenty-five years—taking into account that the nature of time, itself, accelerates historical development—then it would appear that the cycle would conclude about the mid-1980s. Under those limits, the peak of the cycle—that time when more about Black English appeared in the mass media than at any other time—was in the late 1960s and early to mid-1970s. The next major change in the nature of the mass media—that element which unifies and directs—will influence the conclusion of the fifth cycle . . . and the development of a sixth cycle, beginning, perhaps, with the emergence of the twenty-first century. Time, the fourth dimension—and perception, which transcends all other dimensions—determined the nature of the media; it determined the nature of American Black English.

1. The Colonial-Revolutionary Cycle

The year was 1607. The place, a swampy inlet protected by a peninsula on the southeastern coast of the North American continent. From England, 105 persons embarked in three small wooden boats, under charter granted by James I, landing in a place they would soon name James Towne.

Almost fourteen years later, one hundred more settlers came to Plymouth, about 500 miles northeast of James Towne. They had fled England to escape religious persecution. In this new land, a land of exile, they too hoped to build, colonize, and practice their religion. For the settlers at Plymouth and James Towne, this new land, a barbarian wilderness by European standards, would hold their future.

Basic to the survival of the colonists was a need for an adequate communications system. The development of communications in the American colonies closely paralleled the development of mass communications in any developing nation. More than 3,500 years earlier, the American Indians had undergone the same process that the colonists would go through in the seventeenth century. At first the settlers of James Towne and Plymouth needed only a simple system; interpersonal communication, one person talking to another, was sufficient. The social order of the community determined the dissemination of news as well as distribution of responsibilities. News that affected the welfare of the community—whether a ship's arrival or warnings of approaching danger—followed a definite communication process established by the society. As the population grew and groups of settlers established new communities, the communications systems expanded. Letters written from individuals to individuals filled the void. The writer included news of the community as well as personal news; the recipient passed the letter on to his friends.

Along with the continual growth of the settlements came the need for more systematic dissemination of news. The first reporters in the colonies were professional letter writers who collected the news, and then wrote letters to be read in other communities.

With the introduction of the first printing press in the Colonies in 1636, mass communications again reached out. The press, shipped from England, was used to print religious tracts, as well as flyers announcing proclamations, edicts, and notices of meetings. Yet, it wasn't until 1690, eighty-three years after the first European settlers arrived in James Towne, that a newspaper was published. The first issue became its last—the paper was so scandalous that the publisher was ordered to suspend publication. A second effort to begin a mass-circulated printed newspaper in the New World was successful in 1704 when John Campbell established the *Boston News-Letter*.

In 1619, only twelve years after the founding of James Towne, the first twenty slaves from West Africa arrived in the American colonies. These slaves undoubtedly had at least a minimal knowledge of one of the pidgin languages of the Central Atlantic area being developed in the wake of increased British trading along the West Coast of Africa. It was these pidgin languages, notably West African Pidgin English (WAPE), which served as the base for a creole that would later be named Black English.[1]

Because much of the evidence, if such evidence ever existed, has been lost in the catacombs of history, it is virtually impossible to determine when the Colonial-Revolutionary Cycle of American Black English began.

Although the documentary evidence of the seventeenth- and eighteenth-century mass media is too scanty to justify the parameters of the Colonial-Revolutionary Cycle, it is sufficient to draw a number of sociohistorical observations. Actually, it is only by looking back more than three hundred years, from our contemporary vantage point, and attempting to reconstruct certain trends in light of theoretical evidence and field techniques developed within the past three decades, that we can even determine that a cycle, based upon media evidence, did in fact exist; that this cycle, like each of the four succeeding cycles, lasted between twenty-five and forty years; and that it, like each of the other cycles, was followed by an intercycle of about ten to twenty years in which little about Black English entered the mass media, either as primary or secondary reporting, or as part of the literature.

One cannot establish definite parameters for two major reasons. First, the further into history one delves, the less primary evidence is available; thus, more evidence would most likely be available in the more recent cycles than in the first cycle. Second, licensing and other varieties of censorship existed during America's colonial years. It is possible that many varieties of Black speech, if included in those publications deemed by various colonial governments to be in violation of existing laws or beliefs did not enter into the mass media, but were suppressed before publication or shortly thereafter; any surviving evidence would be extremely rare.

EARLY REFERENCES

One of the first printed references to Black English in the American colonies appeared not in the mass media but in the court transcripts of the notorious Salem witch trials of 1692. The testimony of the slave Tituba, as recorded by Magistrate John Hathorne, and published almost two hundred years later in Samuel G. Drake's *The Witchcraft Delusion in New England* (1866), reveals a number of West African Pidgin-English constructions. Tituba, a major witness for the prosecution, proclaims, "He tell me he God," thus signaling the deep structure copula, a common feature in both West African Pidgin English and American Black English. Hathorne also recorded Tituba as saying, "I no hurt them . . ."[2] Because of Magistrate Hathorne's lack of familiarity with linguistic transcription, it is probable that Tituba did not say, "I no hurt them" but rather, "Ah no hotem," a distinct West African Pidgin-English phrase. Almost three hundred years later, Arthur Miller reintroduced Tituba in his powerful drama, *The Crucible* (1953), a semi-fictional dramatization of the Salem trials. Although some pidgin English constructions are present, most of Tituba's dialogue is a modified Black English, a near approximation of Standard English.

Another early reference to Black English in the colonies appeared in a private journal written in 1704 by Sarah Kemble Knight. Unpublished until 1858, the *Journal* includes some evidence that both Black and Indian pidgin were known to the colonists.

Cotton Mather attempted to record the speech of American Blacks in 1721, during the height of controversy over smallpox inoculation.[3] In an unpublished medical treatise, Mather wrote:

I have since mett with a considerable number of these *Africans,* who all agree in One Story: That in their countrey *grandy-many* dy of the *Small-Pox:* But now they learn this way: People take

Juice of Small-Pox; and *cutty-skin,* and Putt in a Drop; then by 'nd by a little *sicky, sicky:* then very few things like *Small-Pox* any more. Thus, in *Africa* where the poor creatures dy of the *Small-Pox* like rotten sheep, a merciful GOD has taught them an infallible preservative. Tis a common practice, and is attended with common success.[4]

It is possible that Mather may have, in his own mind, heard or perceived the phrase "by 'nd by" which he indirectly quoted. But internal linguistic evidence suggests that what was said probably wasn't "by 'nd by" but "by m by," pronounced as one word, *baimbai.*[5] *Baimbai,* often spelled other ways, is part of the lexicon of numerous ethnic groups in many diverse areas of the world, although it probably originated in parts of West Africa. Persons living in the American colonies who spoke what was identified as Standard English at that time, subconsciously aware of the rules present in Standard English but not pidgin English, undoubtedly incorrectly perceived *baimbai,* spoken by Blacks, as "by 'nd by," or "by and by."

The words *grandy-many* ("very many"), *sicky, sicky* (reduplicated form of "sick," indicating "very sick"), and *cutty-skin* ("to cut, or incise, the skin") are all present in West African Pidgin English. Although Mather may have heard *cutty-skin,* what was said was undoubtedly "cut i sikin," a pidgin English phrase that translates literally as "cut his skin (body)." The Standard English speaker, however, hears "cut i sikin" as *cutty-skin.*[6]

TRAVELERS' COMMENTARIES

During the eighteenth century, the American colonies became less forbidding and more "exotic" in the eyes of the British. More and more British visitors crossed the Atlantic to see the New World, their reports becoming popular reading material in England. Unfortunately, although the visitors to the colonies commented widely upon colonial language and customs, they usually overlooked—whether deliberately or subconsciously—Black language and Black contributions to colonial life. What was recorded usually reflected their ethnocentric world views.

In the July 1746 issue of *London Magazine,* G. L. Campbell noted: "One thing they [the colonists] are very faulty in, with regard to their Children, which is, that when young, they suffer them too much to prowl amongst the young Negroes, which insensibly causes them to imbibe their Manners and broken Speech."[7]

During the Revolutionary War, J. F. D. Smyth made a number of interesting observations. Smyth mentioned that a slave he had purchased was useless because "he scarcely understood a single word that I said to him, nor did I know one syllable of the language." Representing a racist, as well as a popular misconception, Smyth also said: "You can not understand all of them, as great numbers, being Africans, are incapable of acquiring our language, and at best but very imperfectly, if at all; many of the others also speak a mixed dialect between the Guinea and English."[8]

Smyth, nevertheless, did present the rudiments of American Black speech in a number of brief anecdotes. In one, he re-created a story told to him by a slave who was caught sleeping while supposed to be fishing:

> Kay, massa (says he), you just leave me, me sit here, great fish jump up into de canoe; here he be, massa, fine fish, massa; me den very grad; den me sit very still, until another great fish jump into de canoe; but me fall asleep, massa, and no wake till you come; now, massa, me know me deserve flogging, cause if great fish did jump into de canoe, he see me asleep, den he jump out again, and I no catch him; so, massa, me willing to take good flogging.[9]

Although the passage is riddled with linguistic inconsistencies, a number of items have significance. *Kay* (or *ki*), for example, is an exclamation in many West African languages, including West African Pidgin English, and is similar to the American English *O!* The omission of past-tense markers is also notable in the passage.

Although many writers allowed their prejudices to dictate their impressions, a few observers tried to understand the Black slave and his language. In *The Present State of Virginia,* published in London in 1724, the Rev. Hugh Jones claimed that slaves "that are born there [in the colonies] talk *good English,* and reflect our Language, Habits, and Customs."[10] John Leland also presented a kinder view of the slave than did Campbell or Smyth. In *The Virginia Chronicle* (1790), Leland wrote, "Their language is broken, but they understand each other and the whites may gain their ideas."[11]

Even Benjamin Franklin had some observations about Black English. In a travelogue article written about America and directed to British travelers in the latter part of the eighteenth century, Franklin observed:

> They [the Americans] are pleased with the observations of a negro, and frequently mention it, that Boccarorra (meaning the white man) make de black man workee, make de horse workee, make

ebery ting workee; only de hog. He de hog, no workee; he eat, he drink, he walk about, he go to sleep when he please, he lib like a gentleman.[12]

Franklin's recording of Black dialect shows that he was, if not an expert recorder of the language, then certainly a capable one.

In 1785, a number of phrases attributed to "the negroe language" appeared in *The Classical Dictionary of the Vulgar Tongue,* compiled by Francis Grose. The book, first published in England, later became popular in the United States. Black English and West African Pidgin English were still considered inferior languages, vulgar at best.

THE CLASSIFIED AD

Newspaper classified advertising is an excellent source of data for understanding the approximate level of standard English spoken by slaves during the Colonial-Revolutionary Cycle. During the eighteenth century and the early nineteenth century, it was common for owners of runaway slaves to place classified advertisements in newspapers, both local and regional, in much the same style as ads for "lost" items are placed in newspapers today; the missing "article" was described, and a reward offered for his return. Southern slaveowners knew that, probably more than anything else, a reward would usually guarantee return of the slave —provided, of course, that the reward far exceeded the costs of returning the slaves.

Northern residents often became bounty hunters. Many ads contained references to the speech of the slaves, for speech was considered one of the distinguishing features of the individual:[13]

> . . . Ran away . . . the following negroe's *viz.* Sambo, a small, thin visaged Fellow, about 30 years of age, speaks *English* so as to be understood . . . Aron . . . can't even speak *English* . . . Berwick . . . can't speak English. They have been in above 8 months in the country.
>
> —*Virginia Gazette*
> August 24, 1751, p. 3

> . . . speaks broken English.
>
> —*The American Weekly Mercury*
> September 14–21, 1721, p. 2

. . . he can't scarce speak a word of English.
—New York Evening Post
December 17, 1744, p. 4

. . . can speak but a few words in *English*.
—Virginia Gazette
January 30, 1752, p. 3

. . . speaks fast and bad English.
—Maryland Gazette
September 21, 1752, p. 3

. . . they speak no English.
—South-Carolina Gazette (Charleston)
November 8–15, 1760, p. 3

. . . speaks no English
—American Weekly Mercury
October 7–14, 1742, p. 3

. . . he don't speak *English* enough to tell his master's name.
—Georgia Gazette
January 24, 1766, p. 1

. . . speaks very good English.
—Weekly News-Letter (Boston)
April 25–May 2, 1728, p. 2

. . . as he was imported very young he speaks very good English. . .
—Virginia Gazette
Dec. 12, 1755, p. 4

. . . speaks pretty good English.
—Virginia Gazette
May 30–June 6, 1745, p. 4

. . . speaks English tolerable well.
—Georgia Gazette
August 4, 1763, p. 3

. . . speaks plain for an *African* born, but avoids looking in the face of them he is speaking to as much as possible.
—Rind's Virginia Gazette
August 8, 1766, p. 3

. . . remarkable for being well spoken.
>   —*Pennsylvania Packett* (Philadelphia)
>   January 4, 1733, p. 2

. . . He is of Dutch descent, but speaks tolerable good English.
>   —*Pennsylvania Gazette*
>   January 22, 1783, p. 3

. . . speaks proper English.
>   —*South Carolina Gazette*
>   *and Weekly Advertiser*
>   January 10, 1784

. . . speaks exceedingly good English.
>   —*State Gazette of South Carolina*
>   April 20, 1797

. . . speaks very proper.
>   —*City Gazette and Daily Advertiser*
>   June 22, 1799

Those slaves who were born in the colonies and who spoke what the colonists called "good English" were more valuable than those born in Africa who spoke only African languages; the rewards to bounty hunters, and the "market price" of a slave reflected this.

COLONIAL DRAMA

Nonfiction and documentary evidences alone are not sufficient to justify a description of a separate Colonial-Revolutionary Cycle of American Black English as reflected within the mass media. But when viewed in relation to the fiction of the era, a distinct pattern emerges. It becomes evident that when the fiction (primarily drama) is added to the non-fiction, there is sufficient clustering of evidence to claim the existence of a cycle during the last three decades of the eighteenth century. During this period, the mass media itself also showed remarkable growth.

The pioneering efforts to identify Black speech in eighteenth-century fiction were made by Richard Walser (drama) and Tremaine McDowell (novels). According to Walser: "There can be little doubt that most of the Negro characters were drawn from life and that their speech is a crude, if occasionally distorted, duplication of the sounds which the playwrights thought they heard. . . . Spelling is capricious, even within one play; and syntax is widely variable."[14] Nevertheless, there are enough consistencies of language in the drama to suggest that Black speech in the eighteenth century had a possible African language substratum. A number of British plays which included West Indies Black speech—and were available in the colonies in the latter eighteenth century—showed many distinct Africanisms.

Advertisements in the *Pennsylvania Chronicle* of March 30–April 6, 1767, and April 6–13, 1767, announced that *The Disappointment,* a drama by Andrew Barton—pseudonym of either Thomas Forrest or John Leacock—would be published. However, the *Pennsylvania Gazette* of April 16, 1767, printed the announcement, ". . . as it contains personal reflections, is unfit for the stage."[15] Four days later, *The Prince of Parthia* became the first play written in the American colonies to be produced. Nevertheless, *The Disappointment* did prove to be a first in one respect. The character of Raccoon spoke what may be identified as a variety of Black speech. A number of scholars have suggested that the character of Raccoon was meant to grossly ridicule not Blacks but the American Southern dialect. Walser, however, believes that Raccoon was a White who lived in Jamaica at one time.[16] During the colonial era, vitriolic attacks against individuals literally flooded the mass media in the eighteenth century. It is quite possible that Barton deliberately meant to ridicule one person, whom Barton loosely disguised as Raccoon, someone who, by speaking a variety of Black English, would appear even more ludicrous. Raccoon, for example, says: "But now I hab seen my folly and former bickedness . . . I bill hab noting more to say to de banities, bexationis, and alewments of dis world."[17]

Although there are a number of linguistic inconsistencies,[18] there are also a number of rules which reflect possible African influence. Both the voiced bilabial semivowel [w] and the voiced labiodental fricative [v] become a voiced bilabial plosive [b]: *have* becomes *hab, wickedness* becomes *bickedness, will* becomes *bill, vanities* becomes *banities,* and *vexations* becomes *bexationis.* However, *of* does not become *ob* as would be expected in an accurate representation. "Sweet talk," an integral part of many African languages, is also in evidence in the phrase, "de banities, bexationis, and alewments of dis world."[19]

The second play in the American colonies to include Black speech was Robert Munford's *The Candidates; Or, The Humoris of a Virginia Election,* written in 1770, but not published until 1798. The servant Ralpho speaks an "overcorrect" standard English through much of the play; his announcement of a guest is a typical example: "Sir John Toddy is below, and if your honour is at leisure, would beg to speak to you." However, Munford did give Ralpho his "relapses":

But e'gad, it's time to think of my new clothes; I'll go and try them on. Gadso! this figure of mine is not reconsiderable in its delurements, and when I'm dressed out like a gentlemen, the girls, I'm a thinking, will find me desistible.[20]

The only Black English in that passage is the use of "sweet talk," a distinct African language trait. The rest of the passage is essentially standard English written to appear to be Black English.

The third surviving play to include Black English was *The Trial of Atticus Before Justice Beau, For a Rape,* written anonymously in 1771. At a trial, the slave Caesar is called before the stand to testify about the slave Atticus who is on trial:

> *Justice.* Well, *Caesar,* did Mrs. *Chuckle* ever tell you anything about Atticus' abusing of her.
> *Caesar.* Yesa, Maser, *he* tell me that *Atticus* he went to bus 'em one day, and shilde cry, and so he let 'em alone.
> *Justice.* How came she to tell you of this.
> *Caesar.* Cause, Maser, I bus him myself.[21]

Because few African languages have the glottal fricative [h] in word-initial position, it is probable that Caesar really said /i/ (pronounced as the vowel in *beet*) instead of /hi/, *i* being an undifferentiated pronoun meant to substitute for all nominals. Caesar probably said /i/ or /am/ rather than /hɪm/. And it is probable that he didn't say /mæsər/, but the more common /masə/ or /mæsə/, written *Mahsuh* or *Massa*. *Bus* is probably the believed Black English equivalent of the Standard English *əbuse*.

The first major scene that included significant Black dialogue was in John Leacock's *The Fall of British Tyranny; Or, American Liberty Triumphant,* published in 1776, but unlike most other plays of that era, never produced. The setting is a ship. A number of Blacks, having experienced the cruelty of slavery and having escaped, enlist in the British Navy. Several African language constructions are evident in their speech:

> *Lord Kidnapper.* Well, my brave blacks, are you come to list?
> *Cudjo.* Eas, massa Lord, you preazee.
> *Kidnapper.* How many are there of you?
> *Cudjo.* Twenty-two, massa.
> *Kidnapper.* Very well, did you all run away from your masters?
> *Cudjo.* Eas, massa Lord, eb'ry one, me too.
> *Kidnapper.* That's clever; they have no right to make you slaves. I

wish all the Negroes would do the same, I'll make 'em free—what part did you come from?

Cudjo. Disse brack man, disse one, disse one, disse one, disse one, come from Hamton, disse one, disse one, disse one, come from Nawfok, me come from Nawfok too.

Kidnapper. Very well, what was your master's name?

Cudjo. Me massa name Cunney Tomsee.

Kidnapper. Colonel Thompson—eigh?

Cudjo. Eas, massa, Cunney Tomsee.

Kidnapper. Well, then I'll make you a major—and what's your name?

Cudjo. Me massa cawra me Cudjo.

Kidnapper. Cudjo?—very good—was you ever christened, Cudjo?

Cudjo. No massa, me no crissen.

Kidnapper. Well then I'll christen you—you shall be called major Cudjo Thompson, and if you behave well, I'll soon make you a greater man than your master, and if I find the rest of you behave well, I'll make you all officers, and after you have serv'd Lord Paramount a while, you shall have money in your pockets, good cloaths on your backs, and be free as them white men there. (*Pointing forward to a parcel of Tories.*)

Cudjo. Tankee, massa, gaw bresse, massa Kidnap . . .

Kidnapper. Tomorrow you shall have guns like them white men. Can you shoot some of them rebels ashore, Major Cudjo?

Cudjo. Eas, massa, me try.

Kidnapper. Wou'd you shoot your old master, the Colonel, if you could see him?

Cudjo. Eas, massa, you terra me, me shoot him down dead.[22]

The word *Cunney,* meaning "Colonel," is consistent with a West African Pidgin-English rule where syllabic lateral *l* is a vocalic sound; and the rule for the deletion of the postvocalic [r]. The substitution of the [r] for the [l] as in *terra,* does not appear to be linguistically valid, but the substitution of the [r] for the [l] in *bresse,* the *r* not being postvocalic, appears to have some justification. Orthographically, both *Lord* and *Kidnap,* spoken by Cudjo, should have been represented as *Lo'd* (or *Lawd*) and *Ki'nap* to better represent the phonology of the language.

In Samuel Low's *The Politician Out-Witted,* published anonymously in 1789, Cuffy's speech bears distinct African language characteristics. If one considers that Gullah (a creole spoken by Blacks on the Sea Islands off South Carolina and Georgia) and varieties of Black English both are based in West African Pidgin English, itself the fusion of Western European languages and West African languages, and assuming that Low was at least partially accurate in his writing, then it appears that there might have been common elements present in both Gullah and Black English. Cuffy, when faced with having to carry a heavy trunk, says:

> Tankee, massa buckaraw; you gi me lilly lif, me bery glad;—disa ting damma heby (*Puts down the trunk*). An de debelis crooka tone in a treet more worsa naw pricka pear for poor son a bitch foot; an de cole pinch um so too![23]

A number of rules are present in Cuffy's speech: the replacement of the voiced *th* by *d* (*de, disa*); replacement of the unvoiced *th* by *t* (*Tankee*); consonant cluster reduction (*lift* becomes *lif; stone* becomes *tone; street* becomes *treet; cold* becomes *cole*); and external sandhi ("gi me"). The word *lilly* ("little") is consistent with a West African Pidgin-English phonological rule for adjective base forms having a CVCV (consonant, vowel, consonant, vowel) structure; thus *lilly*, which is phonologically represented as /lɪli/, has the CVCV form. The speech of Cuffy also contains a number of nonlinguistic evidences; for example, *for* should have been *fo';* and *glad* would probably be replaced by *glat* (a devoicing).

The same year *The Politician Out-Witted* was published, a playwright destined to remain anonymous contributed *Occurrences of the Times; Or, a Transaction of Four Days,* a two-act farce. Linguistically, the play is distinguished because of the language of Debauchee, a house slave. In one scene, Debauchee tells his mistress about a duel that never happened:

> *Debau.* Ah—Missy Marta.—Here is terrible tings—did you eber see de like—My massa and I went to fite.
> *Mar.* What—say—what do you mean.
> *Debau.* Ah! dat is—we didn't fite—Twixt you and I massa he no courage. Misser Harcourt he say—shentlemen you no de law . . . Well and so we didn't do any ting—and so he was beat, I tink, and den we come home.[24]

Later, Debauchee says:

> Yes, Sir, me be in a great flury; my masser is in shuch a passion, dat I run very hard to fine you, Sir, for I tink, may be you will be able to pease him. . . .
> Yes, Sir, I stand you; but masser made me take an oaf; I don't

know what that is; masser say "Me don't know any ting;" now so I forget all bout it . . .[25]

Although there are many inconsistencies of language (especially the phrase "I don't know what that is"), a number of African language elements are present, such as "massa he no courage," and the omission of the unstressed word-initial syllables: *about* becomes *bout, appease* becomes *pease,* and *understand* becomes *stand* (though it should have been further reduced to *sitan* or *tan*).

In 1792, the Old American Company of Comedians produced, in New York City, J. Robinson's farce, *The Yorker's Strategem; Or, Banana's Wedding*. The play entered the printed media that year when it was published by T. & J. Swords. There is some question as to whether the Black speech is reflective of American Black speech or West Indies speech, since the setting is in the West Indies. Nevertheless, there are a number of distinct Africanisms in the speech of the servant. In Act 1, the servant informs his master about the visit of three gentlemen:

Servant. Masa Acid dere want for see you, he hab two Yankey wid he.
Mr. Fingercash. How do you know they are Yankeys?
Servant. Dem tan so, dem hab salt fish in one hand, and trokey in todder.

Later in the play, the servant uses a distinct African syntactic construction: "he no fill he belly."[26] The word *trokey* (also spelled *troki* elsewhere in literature) is pidgin English for "turtle." The word *tan* is the Black English equivalent of "stand."

The first extensive speech, in reality a soliloquy, by an American Black on stage was that of Sambo in John Murdock's *The Triumph of Love; Or, Happy Reconciliation* (1795). The four-act comedy was first produced in 1795 at Philadelphia's New Theatre, and had a subscription list of seven hundred, larger than most newspapers.

The soliloquy of Sambo, although surrounded by robust comedy, is especially tragic when one considers that he reflects not only upon himself, as it appears, but upon the institution of slavery:

Sambo, what a gal call a pretty fellow. (*Sings and dances—tol lol de rol lol—goes again to the glass.*) Dis woll of mine will curlee up so, can't get him trait—dat all de fashion among gemmen. Sambo tink himself handsome. He berry complish'd to; he sing well; he dance well; he play fiddle well. Can tink so, so, pretty well. He tink; he berry often tink why he slave to white man? Why black foke sold like cow or horse. He tink de great somebody above, no order tings so. —Sometime he tink dis way—he got bess massa in e world. He gib him fine clothes for dress—he gib him plenty money for pend; and for a little while, he tink himself berry happy. Afterwards he tink anoder way. He pose massa George die; den he sold to some oder massa. May be he no use him well. When Sambo tink so, it most broke he heart.[27]

Shortly thereafter, Sambo, having just gained his freedom, expands upon his earlier soliloquy:

When massa George ax me how I like go free, I tink he joke; but when he tell me so for true, it make much water come in my eye for joy. I could hardly peke a word, and I tink he look like an angel. God bress him. Sambo hope he no be sorry for make him he own massa. I sabe all my wages for buy my Sue free, and make her my wife . . .[28]

A number of West African Pidgin-English constructions are present in Sambo's two soliloquies, including "broke he heart," "he tell me so for true," "it make much water come in my eye for joy," and "no be sorry." Sambo's speech also includes serial phrasing, a West African language feature—"he sing well; he dance well; he play fiddle well." Also distinguished in this speech is the dropping of the unstressed word-initial syllable; *pose* ("suppose"), and consonant cluster reduction (*trait, peke,* and *pend*—although in Black English, *spend* would have been further reduced to *pen* or *sipen*), and the replacement of the voiced *th* [ð] by the [d] (*dis, dat, de*). The word *ax* (ask), a common English dialect variant, shows metathesis—the reversing of phonological sounds—and is consistent with rules in West African Pidgin English.

Both Robinson's *The Yorker's Strategem* and Murdock's *The Triumph of Love* were performed. However, *The Politicians; Or, A State of Things,* written anonymously by Murdock in 1798, wasn't. The noted drama historian Arthur Hobson Quinn suggests that "the negro characters are . . . drawn with such a skill in which Murdock surpassed anyone else for many a year."[29] The drama, a political vehicle, became part of an era in which political invective spewed forth from virtually all media. The opening lines of *The Politicians* are spoken by Cato, a house slave who reflects upon the constant gossip between his mistress and one of her friends:

I wonder what e debil woman have do we poletic, dere my misse and misse Violet, talke, talke, talke, bout trety, bout Massa Jay,

bout president, bout congree, bout English, bout French, it mak me
sick, dere two tongue go like mill clap.[30]

Murdock was probably the first American dramatist to use the word
e to represent the West African Pidgin-English /i/. Also prominent are
the words *bout* (deletion of the unstressed word-initial schwa) and *dere*
(replacement of the voiced *th* with *d*). In Standard English, the lack of
the plural marker *-s* on *tongue* would be incorrect; in West African
Pidgin English, the word *two* indicates plural, and "two tongues" in
pidgin would be redundant. The Pidgin-English word *wati* loosely translates to English as "what the"; Murdock, like many others, probably
perceived the word *wati* as being "what e."

A dialogue later in the play gives some clues not only to Black language, but also to the political situation at the end of the eighteenth
century:

Caesar. Citizen Pompey, how you do, to-day, Sir?
Pompey. Tank you, citizen Caesar, berry well; I hope you and you
lady enjoy good health.
Caesar. Berry good! I gib you tank, Sir.
Pompey. Here cum citizen Sambo, twig he pig cu. Since he get free,
how he wag he tail.

(Enter Sambo.)

Gemmen, it gib me extreme pleasure to see you bote: I hope you
are bote well, citizens.
Omnes. Tank you, Sir, bery will.
Sambo. Any ting new to day, gemmem?
Pompey. Trong talks French war.
Caesar. Dam French.
Pompey. Dam English.
Caesar. Why you dam English, for?
Pompey. Why e debil you dam French, for?
Caesar. Cause I don't like 'em.
Pompey. Why you no like 'em?
Caesar. Cause massa no like 'em.
Pompey. My massa no like English—I hate 'em too-drom proud—
so conceit coxcomb—look like ebery body tunk in e nose.
Caesar. Ten hundred time better den French, drom fribble, buf-
foon, ape, monkey; English, fine, manly fellow, besides French
come cut out troat, I like English: English, for eber!
Pompey. France for eber! France git liberty to slave liberty; and,

France, for eber! my massa for France—so I, who you for, Sambo?
Sambo. I go we massa, too.
Pompey. He for France.
Sambo. No.
Pompey. For English.
Sambo. No.
Caesar. Who debil he for den?
Sambo. He for he country.
Pompey. For he country![31]

Later, Pompey and Caesar again argue about the French and English;
someone has "slandered" the French:

Pompey. He don't peak true, damme, he don't peak true, he tell lie
bout French.
Caesar. He do peak true, I say, he can't tell lie bout French, he
can't make em too bad.
Pompey. Take care what you say Caesar, you and I are friends, but
I bedam if I hear my friends abuse.
Caesar. Pompey I no fraid you, I say, I no fraid you, Pompey, I
hate e French.
Sambo. He, he, he! Two black fool go fight . . .
Cato. Caesar and Pompey, take advice of an old man, neber quarrel bout politic, it bring too much trouble, what you do wid such
tings? it seem to me, Negro head got quite a wrong now-a-day, you
must all be gemmem, must dress in fashion, talk high flow, must
have cue and wool powder, dat foolish, only make your face look
more black, howeber, let me advise you no quarrel bout politic, I
wish all e world like my massa, Conciliate; he good man, he seek
how he do good; if any body be in distress, he help em, he neber
quarrel bout politic—if a man be an aristocrat, and for English, he
no fight him, if he democrat and for French, he no quarrel wid
him, he no angry wid any body, for what day tink, he ebery body
friend, and no body enemy, he so good, he no hurt cockroach.
Sambo. I suppose he no kill a fly when he bite im.
Pompey. No, I see him many time brush a fly off he leg when he
bite him.
Sambo. He no shoot a bird.
Cato. No, he tink dat cruel.
Sambo. He eat him when he shot?
Cato. O yes, he eat him when he shot.
Sambo. Ha, ha, ha! dat make me a laught, dat put me in mind of a

person who preach against eating good tings, afterwards go home
and tuff e gut like e debel.

Cato. Ah! you young fool, Sambo.

Pompey. Massa Conciliate a bery good man, but I like a man take
some part for all dat.

Sambo. Oh! dram me, I sick of politic, let us go.[32]

The overpoliteness of Caesar, Pompey, and Sambo in the first scene
undoubtedly is meant to satirize, perhaps even ridicule, the customs of
a White citizenry, the language serving as a convention of society. There
are many inconsistencies in the language of the four Blacks, but it is
possible to discover a number of rules—the replacement of the *v* by the
b (*bery* and *berry; debil* and *dibel; eber, ebery, haweber,* and *neber*);
the replacement of the unvoiced *th* by a *d* (*dat, day, wid*); the reduction
of consonant clusters (*strong* becomes *trong; stuff* becomes *tuff; speak*
becomes *peak*); and the omission of the unstressed word-initial syllable
(*about* becomes *bout; afraid* becomes *fraid; because* becomes *cause*).
The word *cum* (for "come") is eye dialect, the deliberate misspelling
of a word to make it appear to be a dialect item consistent with other
lexical items in the sentence. There is no difference in pronunciation,
and the use of the misspelling is often intended to show "dialect inferiority" as well as a language and culture "inferiority." The use of eye
dialect was infrequent during the Colonial-Revolutionary Cycle, but
increased significantly during the latter half of the nineteenth century
and the early twentieth century. In dialect writing, the words *come, was,*
and *says,* often became *cum, wuz,* and *sez.*

A number of syntactic phrases are present that also reflect an African
language base, such as "you lady," "how you do," "what e debil," "for
e country," "you no like em," and "I go we massa." It is virtually impossible to determine if *drom* and *dram* are indeed the same word, different only because of a typographical or writer's error, or whether two
such words—with different pronunciations—were in fact part of the Black
speech of the time. Nevertheless, the other two words that reflect "ob-
scenity"—*bedam* and *damme*—were part of the White colonial lexicon.

COLONIAL NOVELS

In England, a number of Black English constructions appeared in
novels that became available to, and reprinted by, the American colonists. In *The History and Remarkable Life of the Truely Honorable
Colonel Jacque* (1722), Daniel Defoe included several passages in a

Negro dialect that was later identified as that from Virginia. However, Defoe himself did not distinguish geographical variation in American Black speech. Although two of his earlier novels—*The Family Instructor* (1715), and *The Life and Surprising Adventure of Robinson Crusoe* (1719)—included passages of Black speech, neither was Black speech in the colonies; none of Defoe's novels was written in the American colonies.

Although the novel had been an established literary form in many parts of the world for several centuries, it wasn't until late in the eighteenth century that the first novel was published in the United States. William Hill Brown's *The Power of Sympathy,* published in 1789 by Isaiah Thomas, is believed to have been not only the first novel published in the United States, but also the first American novel to include a Black character. However, the slave, a field laborer, spoke perfect Colonial English.

Modern Chivalry; Containing the Adventures of Captain John Farrago, and Teague Oregon, His Servant is believed to be the only satirical novel of the colonial eighteenth century. Written by H. H. Brackenridge, and published in 1792, *Modern Chivalry* attacks a number of American institutions. In one section, the pompous American Philosophical Society comes under attack. A slave, Cuff, has found a petrified moccasin. The society is so enthused by this "scientific discovery" that it has not only made Cuff an honorary member, but has also asked him to deliver a major address. The speech Cuff gives to the society includes a number of linguistic inconsistencies, but also a number of linguistic rules:

"Massa shentimen; I be cash crab in de Wye river; find ting in de mud; tone big a man's foot: holes like to he; fetch massa: massa say, it be de Indian moccasin . . . O! fat de call it; all tone. He say, you be filasafa, Cuff: I say, O no, Massa, you filasafa. Wel; two tree monts afta, Massa calle me and say, *You* be a filasafa, Cuff fo' sartan: Getta ready, and go dis city, and make grate peech for shentima filasafa. I say, fat say, Massa? Massa say, somebody say dat de first man was de fite man: but you say dat de first man was de black-a-man. Vel, I set out: cam along: Massa gi me pass. Some say, where you go Cuff? I say, dis city, be a filasafa. Oh no Cuff, you no be filasafa: call me fool, gi me kick i' de backside; fall down, get up again, and come to dis city.

"Now, shentima, I say dat de *first* man was de black-a-man, and de first woman was de black a woman: and get two tree *children;*

de rain vasha dese, and de snow pleach, and de coula come brown, yella, coppa coula, and, at the last, quite fite; and de hair long: and de fal out vid anoder; and van cash by de nose, an pull so the nose come long, sharp nose.

"Now I go home, Massa shentima; and tel grate Massa, dat make peech, and ibedy body vas da; an den Cuff fin a more tings . . . cabs, oysta, cat-fish, bones, tones, ibedy ting . . . sen to you, shentima."[33]

Brackenridge used a number of words that are virtually unintelligible without a broad knowledge of Black speech—*cash* (from WAPE *kas,* "to catch"), *tone* ("stone"), *peech* ("speech"), *tree* ("three"), *pleach* ("bleaches"), *ibedy body* ("everybody, everyone"), *cabs* ("crabs"), and *sen* ("send"). The replacement of the bilabial semivowel [w] by the voiced labiodental fricative [v] and the unvoiced labiodental fricative [f] (as in *vel* for *well, vid* for *with, van* for *one, fat* for *what,* and *fite* for *white*) may have some basis in Dutch or some other Germanic languages. Richard Walser suggests that Brackenridge was influenced by his knowledge of European immigrants, many of whom spoke Dutch.[34] There is another possibility. Blacks who were the slaves of Dutch masters were exposed, not infrequently, to the Dutch language. Many learned a pidgin English with many Dutch lexical items assimilated into the linguistic system. Thus, although Brackenridge probably was influenced by his own knowledge of Dutch, it is also possible that his fictionalized slave, Cuff, was also so affected; Brackenridge heard Dutch elements in language from the slaves he knew personally.[35]

Tabitha Tenney's *Female Quixoticism,* published in 1801, belongs to the last days of the Colonial-Revolutionary Cycle of American Black English. In one scene from the novel, the slave, Scipio, had teased a naive Betty so that she believed the purpose of a visit of a handsome gentleman was to court her. Scipio's master became angry at the ruse, and Scipio pleaded, trying to keep a straight face: "I ask pardon massa, I no mean treat massa Cumberland ill. In only in fun with Betty, and no tink she fool enough to breve me."[36]

In another section, Scipio becomes upset that Dorcasina would become degraded by marrying a man named John Brown:

"Debil! . . . what you tell me, Betty? Missy lub John? John go marry missy? Den he be massa, pose. No, Betty; this muss not be; dis sall not be. Massa Brown, ha! No, no Betty. John Brown no be massa here, I send him to debil fuss. Massa Brown, ha!"[37]

A more accurate phonological/orthographic representation might have been:

> "Ah ax pahdon massa. Ah no mean fo' massa Cumuhlan be sicky. Ah on'y be fun wif Be'y, an' no tink i be fool 'nough fo' breve me."
>
>   "Debil! Wha' fo' you di teh me? Missy lub John? John go fo' meh'y missy? Den he be massa, pose. Dis no be so; dis muss *no* be so! Massa B'own, ha! Massa B'own no be massa heuh. Ah sen' i fo' debil fuss! Massa B'own, ha!"

Nevertheless, for its period of time, Tenney's representations of Black speech were commendable.

BLACK ENGLISH SCHOLARSHIP

It was not unusual that during the Colonial-Revolutionary Cycle virtually all Black English in the media was written by Whites. Most publishers would not publish the writings of Blacks, no matter what the literary merits. What was written by Blacks was usually written in Standard English, and often left unpublished. It would be several decades before Black writers would have the courage to write in Black English without the fear of being called "illiterate." There was, however, one major exception. During the late eighteenth century, a Mandingo slave in Georgia contributed one of the outstanding works of scholarship to Black English study. The slave, identified only as "London," owned by a man named Maxwell, researched and wrote *The Gospels Written in the Negro Patois of English, With Arabic Characters*. That document is lost in history, and only external evidence allows us even to know of its existence. On October 13, 1857—long after London died—W. B. Hodgson presented London's document to the Ethnological Society of New York. Only Hodgson's published comments, themselves extremely rare, are left for the Black English scholar. According to Hodgson: "With my present information, it is the only attempt ever made by a native African Mohammedan, to use the letters of the Koran, the first book of his religious instruction, in transcribing the Gospel, the book of his second instruction and conversion, and in the adopted dialect of his land of captivity." Hodgson also pointed out in his speech that London "had written a book of hymns, with Arabic letters which has not been preserved."[38]

The Colonial-Revolutionary Cycle ended about the turn of the century. Like each of the subsequent cycles, it was distinguished not only by

chronology, but also by genre, both elements being central to the identification of a cycle. The precycle may have spanned more than a century. The actual cycle began in the mid-1760s, possibly sooner. It was
characterized by foreign travelers' reports on American speech, by observations about Black English, and by the drama and novels that reflected the embryonic stages of a developing and emerging nation. And
most important, like each of the cycles, it served as a base for the
next one.

2. The Antebellum Cycle

The United States, which was just beginning to recover from a bloody revolution and assume its role as an emerging nation, underwent radical changes in the first half of the nineteenth century. The nation was still largely agricultural and rural, but cities grew along the Eastern seaboard as the Industrial Revolution created jobs for more and more people. Farmers whose crops had failed, who were left with little but untillable soil and a windswept cabin, migrated to the cities, found factory jobs, and became part of a new class of Americans, one neither wealthy nor poor; it was a working class, a middle class.

The members of this new class saw in the cities opportunities for a better life for themselves and their children. The steppingstones to that better life were schooling and hard work, often twelve to sixteen hours a day. Children who once would have gone to work before completing elementary school now attended school until they were twelve or thirteen years old. In those families that could afford it, children were encouraged to complete high school.

The increased emphasis on literacy ushered in a change in the mass media, giving rise to a uniquely American product, the "penny press." The rise of the middle class—coupled with the technological advancements in printing—saw an increase in advertising from businesses in the city and provided the base for inexpensive newspapers in the metropolitan areas of the East and Northeast. These mass-circulation newspapers, often scandalous yet entertaining, were sold for a penny apiece on the street corners. They provided direct competition for the more elite "six-cent" daily newspapers which catered to the upper classes and often could be purchased only by a yearly subscription.

The first successful penny paper, the *New York Sun,* copublished by Benjamin H. Day and George Wisner, made its appearance on September 3, 1833. Within a decade, James Gordon Bennett's *New York Herald,* and Horace Greeley's *New York Tribune* also appeared and provided direct competition to the *Sun.* Soon, instead of circulations of 1,000–4,000, America's major newspapers could boast of circulations of more than 30,000. By the Civil War, circulations of 80,000–90,000 would be reached.

The six-cent newspapers persevered, clinging to the upper class for continued support. But the upper class, with more time for leisure, began to turn to books. Once, America's book production had been largely nonfiction, or pirated European editions. Now, American publishers, in response to an increased demand for reading material, began to publish fiction by American authors, much of which first appeared in newspapers.

Magazines, numbering about one hundred in 1825, found a growing market between the penny press newspapers and the still-expensive books. Oriented to the "common man," and often printing poetry, critical essays, short stories, and serialized novels, magazines began to blanket the country, their regional and national focus and distribution giving a common bond to the people. By the end of the nineteenth century, there would be more than 4,000 different magazines in circulation.

Throughout the nineteenth century, there was a strong interest in the plantation slaves. Their presumed happiness, evidenced by singing and dancing under the greatest of hardships, fascinated White Americans. Publishers of newspapers, magazines, and books were quick to note this interest; as the industry grew, so did media interest in the Black. The abolition movement, the Civil War, and Reconstruction all occurred in the nineteenth century and, coupled with the natural curiosity about the unusual, placed the Black in the center of media attention.

THE FIRST INTERCYCLE

For some reason, a number of evidences of Black speech cluster in the intercycle during 1807. Many writings record the spread of West African Pidgin English, the base of American Black English, both in the United States and throughout the Central Atlantic area.

From 1802 to 1806, C. C. Robin toured Louisiana. His *Voyages Dans L'Interview de la Louisiane* (1807), written in French and published in Paris, presented a number of observations about Black speech, but with a concentration on the Black-French creole.

In *Stranger in America* (1807), Charles William Janson quoted a slave who "received the punishment due for his abuse and insulting of White women": "Tank ye, massa doctor, you did me much great good; white or blackee woman, I care not for."[1] The slave was castrated.

Caesar's opening speech—in reality a prologue to L. Beach's fictitious *Jonathan Postfree; Or, The Honest Yankee* (1807)—is virtually standard English, and shows no improvement in recording over previous efforts of the Colonial-Revolutionary Cycle: "I no like this massa Fopling—I don't know what ole misse can see in him to make her likee him so much:—he no half so good as Jemmy Seamore,—and young misse Maria she know it;—she love one little finger of Jemmy more better than Fopling's whole body—but I must holee my tongue—here he come."[2]

Henry Bolingbroke's *A Voyage to Demarary* (1813), documented the spread of West African Pidgin English into northern parts of South America. According to Bolingbroke: "It is curious that the talkee-talkee, or patois of the blacks, though it includes many African words, should have for its basis the English language, pared of inflections, and softened by a multitude of vowel terminations." Bolingbroke also presented a glossary of selected Africanisms which he defined as a "specimen of negro English, or talkee-talkee . . . which is spoken by the creole ladies in preference to any other dialect."[3] Among the words Bolingbroke identified were *Matie* ("a friend"), *Onofo* ("enough"), *Loeke deeja* ("look here"), *tantiere* ("stand still"), and *mekie jesoe* ("make haste").

THE AMERICAN NOVEL

The studies of Black speech published in 1807 were chronological exceptions to the Antebellum Cycle of American Black English, having fallen during the intercycle which lasted about twenty years. During these first two decades of the nineteenth century, the American media were in transition. Drama and travelers' commentaries would soon cease to dominate the media, and would be replaced by the novel and the popular mass-market newspaper.

The first major American novelist was James Fenimore Cooper, and it is his writings that form the base of the Antebellum Cycle. The language of Caesar Thompson in Cooper's epic of the emerging nation, *The Spy; A Tale of the Neutral Ground* (1821), is inconsistent, probably reflecting inaccurate recording of language, not diglossia. Yet it represented one of the first major attempts to include Blacks and their language within literary works. According to literary critic Tremaine

McDowell: "Most significant . . . is Caesar's place in the plot, for he is allowed to assist substantially in the action, recognition not previously given a negro in American fiction nor again granted before the work of [William Gilmore] Simms."[4]

Nevertheless, Cooper, America's first novelist to gain worldwide attention, firmly believed that the slave, as a slave, had an important role to fulfill in the developing American nation. Like Aristotle more than 2,000 years earlier, Cooper believed that it was "as much to the slaves' interest to be ruled as it is to the masters' interest to rule them." From Euripides, he learned that "only one thing disgraces a slave, and that is the name. In all other respects a slave, if he be good, is no worse than a freeman." Freedom for the slave, said Cooper, could never come by laws or proclamations, but only when all citizens accepted the slave—now forced into slavery by color and not geography as was the case with the Greeks—as an equal. These beliefs were transformed into the character of Caesar Thompson, the first Black to be given a major role in an American novel. Caesar's speech is distinguished by a number of syntactic and phonological rules. Viewed solely from the perspective of Standard English, there are often no tenses, no possessives, few plurals, and no gender. Changing of the consonants ([ð] to [d], and [v] to [b]) is frequent, as is the change from the unvoiced *th* [θ] to [t]. However, Caesar switches from Standard English forms to Black English forms within the same passage or scene, such as using the words *gentleman* and *gemman, very* and *bery.* Cooper, however, was probably the first writer to use the apostrophe regularly as an indicator of omitted letters or sounds within a word, such as *p'r'aps, rig'lar,* and *s'pose.* Although not frequently, he also dropped the unstressed word-initial syllable, as in *'baccy* for *tobacco.*

The Spy established Cooper as America's leading novelist.[5] During the next two decades, he would write some of the nation's outstanding historical fiction: *The Pioneers,* and *The Pilot* (both 1823), *The Last of the Mohicans* (1826), *The Prairie* (1827), *The Red Rover* (1828), *The Pathfinder* (1840), and *The Deerslayer* (1841). But always he was the journalist, the writer who sifted through the facts of a people's life, then tried to report, interpret, and analyze them, to describe life as it is, or once was.

In *Satanstoe; Or, The Littlepage Manuscripts* (1845), the first volume of a trilogy, Cooper looked back to colonial America and to the internal problems that had to be solved within a peoples' collective consciousness before a nation could come into being. Almost twenty-five years earlier, Cooper had created Caesar Thompson. Now, for his final major literary effort, he created Jaap, a house servant quite similar to Caesar. The recording of the language in *Satanstoe* shows a distinct improvement over that in *The Spy,* but is still far from being an accurate recording of Black speech. In one scene, Jaap and his young master, Cornelius Littlepage, discuss the "upper counties" they are visiting:

"[Jaap], how do you like the upper counties?"

"Lor', Massa Corny, how you t'ink I know, when dere not'in but snow to be seen?"

"There was plenty of snow in Westchester; yet, I dare say you could give some opinion of our own county!"

"Cause I know him, sah; inside and out, and all above, Massa Corny."

"Well; but you can see the houses and orchards, and barns, and fences, and other things of that sort."

"Em pretty much like our'n, Massa Corny; why do you bother nigger with sich question?"

Here another burst of hearty "yah—yah—yahs" succeeded; and Jaap had his laugh out before another word could be got out of him, when I put the question a third time.

"Well, den, Massa Corny, sir, you will know, dis is my mind. Dis country is oncomparable with our ole country, sah. De houses seem mean, de barn look empty, de fences be low, and de niggers, ebery one of 'em, look cold, sah—yes, sah, 'ey look berry cold!"[6]

A number of dialect-writing errors are present in Jaap's answers. Although Jaap says *t'ink* and *not'in,* he also says *with.* He says *inside* rather than *i'side, mind* rather than *min', cold* rather than *col', barn* rather than *ba'n* or *bahn, of* rather than *ob,* and *above* rather than *'bove.* Syntactically, it would have been expected that Jaap, although a house slave who would have been expected to have learned elements of Standard English, would nevertheless have said "dis be min' fo' me" or "dis be my min' " rather than "dis is my mind." (The West African Pidgin English is "my sens tok say" or "my sens tok fo me.") It is also doubtful that Jaap would have used the copula in the phrase, "not'in but snow to be seen." Nevertheless, even with these inconsistencies, the Black language as represented in Cooper's stories shows a marked improvement over the speech presented in the previous cycle.

In *Redskins; Or, Indians and Injins* (1846), the last book of the Satanstoe trilogy, Cooper shows a familiarity with the process of pidginization: "The Colonists caught a great many words from the Indians they first knew, and used them to all other Indians, though not belonging to their language; and these other tribes used them as English, a sort of *lingua franca* has grown up in the country that everybody understands."[7] Internal analysis of the language Cooper ascribed to the Indians and the Black in *Redskins* show that the surface structure copula was not present in either's speech.

Cooper believed that his literary purpose was to use the novel to help Americans achieve a *"mental* independence" in the growth of the country. In his later novels, written as America was beginning a period of terror it had never before known, Cooper tried through his writings to restore what others had called "an American ideal." And while others had systematically excluded the Black from their own writings, Cooper included the Black, whom he saw as contributing to the growth of the country. To *not* include the Black's role would have been to have overlooked a part of the nation's history. The language and culture of the Black, and their impact upon America, were so intertwined that Cooper *had* to include Black English in his stories. Through the language of the Black, Cooper could describe and explain not only the slave culture, but the life of a people. He could no more have his field slaves speak standard English than he could have eliminated them entirely. And if there were imperfections in Cooper's recording of the language, they were not deliberate imperfections; within his own perception of language, Cooper had tried to understand the race called Negro, and the language that was called Black English.

Anne Newport Royall, although less known than Cooper, contributed much to the development of journalism and the recording of Black English during the Antebellum Cycle. Although she was a newspaper publisher and author of several regional documentary books about the American people, her fame came from her only romantic novel, *The Tennessean,* published privately in 1827. It was in this novel that she introduced the character Sambo, a body servant, who told about a slave uprising:

> "Oh, massa, he go away to Englan'—to 'long to ole massa, he wife fadda. Dis here massa he stay so long de nigger rise—kill ebery body, burn house—ole massa he lib close to de sea, he talk bout takin' ship—Before dat, by blood! One night here cum great many niggers; ole misse she tell me, Sambo run tell youn' masse—youn' misse she run to one house, tay all night—I run all my might knock at de doa to tell um all will be kill'd—call youn' misse, yerk de chile out he arms, tell him run arter me so hard he can."[8]

There is significant inconsistency in Royall's recording of Black English. Although she writes *'long* and *'bout,* thus illustrating the rule of the elision or loss of the unstressed word-initial syllable, she also writes *away* and *Before.* In one sentence she writes *stay;* in another, *tay,* illustrating consonant cluster reduction. The zero possessive ("he wife fadda" and "out he arms") and the pronominal cross-reference markers ("mass, he," "massa he," "Misse she") are apparent, but Royall did not acknowledge plural markers, as in "great many niggers." It is difficult, by internal analysis of the writing, to determine why she, like H. H. Brackenridge thirty-five years earlier, chose to modify the verb *jerk* into the Dutch-sounding *yerk.*

Nathaniel Beverly Tucker was a contemporary of both Cooper and Royall. Under the pseudonym of Edward William Sidney he wrote *The Partisan Leader; A Tale of the Future.* The novel was published in 1836, the year Martin Van Buren was running for the presidency, but the book carried the publication date of 1856. It was meant to reflect back on events of 1849—Van Buren had become dictator of the United States; he and his machine politics were determined to crush the South in order to protect Northern business and political interests. South Carolina had already seceded from the Union; Virginia, which was about to declare its independence, had been invaded by the Army of the North. The Northern soldiers had correctly guessed that the field slaves, who spoke Black English, would be disloyal to their masters; the house slaves, who spoke standard Southern English, would be loyal. The soldiers approached a loyal house slave who, switching to the dialect of a field slave, led them into a linguistic trap: "Who?—I, Massa? My name Jack, sir . . . What I love him [his master] for? Hard work, and little bread, and no meat? No, Massa, I love soldier; 'cause I hear 'em say soldier come after a while, set poor niggur free."[9] To counter anticipated questions from readers about why the slave, Tom, usually spoke a standard Southern English, and why he did not speak the same variety of Black English as did the characters of other novels of the era, Tucker, writing as Sidney, added a footnote:

I crave the forebearance of all critics who have taken their ideas of a Virginia house servant from Caesar Thompson, or any such caricatures, for giving Tom's own words, and his own pronunciation of them. It is not my fault if there is but little peculiarity in his phraseology. His language was never eloquent, and frequently ungrammatical. But he spoke better than the peasantry of most countries, though he said some things a white man would not say.[10]

The Knights of the Horse-Shoe, by William Alexander Caruthers, first appeared serially in several issues of *The Magnolia* in 1841, then was published in book form in 1845. Caruthers included several passages in Black English; certain phrases are distinctively Pidgin English in origin. A saddened slave, for example, says:

"De spirits [music] make June feel berry happy misses long as he last, but no bring back miss Kate, and all de fine young gentlemen, and de ladies, and de carriages, and de horses . . ."

". . . frog hab all de fun to heself, and de whooperwill, he sing so solemn, he make poor nigger cry for true."

"Good night, and tankey missus, June gwine to broke he eye [cry]."[11]

"The Black Saxons," a tale in Lydia Maria Child's book, *Fact and Fiction* (1847), includes a few lines and lexical items of Black English, but the dialogue is quite inconsistent, and the recording of the speech makes no advancement over earlier works.

Two of Captain Ahab's crew of the Pequod in *Moby-Dick* (1851), Herman Melville's epic allegory of the sea and the human spirit, were Blacks. Daggoo—"Third among the harpooners . . . a gigantic coal-black negro-savage, with a lion-like tread"[12]—spoke Standard English. Fleece, the old cook, spoke a curious mixture of Standard and Black English. In his one major scene, Fleece is ordered by Stubb, Ahab's second mate, to quiet the sharks snapping at the Pequod's side, waiting for a dinner of whale. "Now then," commanded Stubb, "go preach to em."[13] Fleece's "preaching" presents a number of insights into the human condition, although the recording of Black speech is inconsistent:

"Fellow-critters: I'se ordered here to say dat you must stop dat dam noise dare. You hear? Stop dat dam smackin' ob de lip! Massa Stubb say dat you can fill your dam bellies up to de hatchings, but by Gor! you must stop dat dam racket . . .

"Do you is all sharks, and by natur wery woracious, yet I zay to you, fellow-critters, dat dat woraciousness—'top dat dam slappin' ob de tail! How you tink to hear, 'spose you keep up such a dam slappin' and bitin' dare? . . .

"Your woraciousness, fellow-critters, I don't blame ye so much for; dat is natur, and can't be helped; but to gobern dat wicked natur, dat is de pint. You is sharks, sartin; but if you gobern de shark in you, why den you be angel; for all angel is not'in more dan de shark well goberned. Now, look, here, bred'ren, just try wonst to be cibil, a helping yourselbs from dat whale. Don't be tearin' de blubber out your neighbor's mout, I say. Is not one shark dood right as toder to dat whale? And, by Gor, none of you has de right to dat whale; dat whale belong to some one else. I know some o you has berry brig mout, bigger dan oders; but den de brig mouts sometimes has de small bellies; so dat de brigness ob de mout is not to swaller wid; but to bite off de blubber for de small fry ob sharks, dat can't get into de scourge to help demselves."[14]

The sharks don't respond; they continue to snap for the whale meat on board the Pequod:

"No use goin' on; de dam willains will keep a scroungin' and slappin' to each oder, Mass Stubb; dey don't hear one word; no use a-preachin' to such dam g'uttons as you call 'em, till dare bellies is full, and dare bellies is bottomless; and when dey do get em full, dey wont hear you den; for den dey sink in de sea, go fast to sleep on de coral and can't hear not'in at all, no more, for eber and eber . . .

"Cussed fellow-critters! Kick up de damnest row as ever you can; fill your dam bellies 'till dey bust—and den die!"[15]

THE AMERICAN SHORT STORY

During the Antebellum Cycle, the American short story became a dominant genre in the media, existing because of the development of the mass-circulation newspapers and magazines. The writer most often credited with developing the American short story into a literary art form was Edgar Allan Poe.

By the time of his death at the age of forty, Poe had established an international reputation for his meticulously plotted short stories and for his haunting poetry. As vehicles for his fiction and social commentary, he was editor of the *Southern Literary Messenger* (1835), *Gentleman's Magazine* (1839–40), *Graham's Magazine* (1840–41), and *The Broadway Journal* (1844), all of them highly prestigious popular magazines.

Between the time he edited *Graham's Magazine,* until the time he assumed the editorship of *The Broadway Journal,* Poe wrote "The Gold Bug," a seriocomical story containing none of the morbid tone he had become identified with in his earlier fiction, but which still retained the charm and careful finesse that was distinctively his. The story of a man who had succumbed to "gold fever" was immediately popular. The *Philadelphia Dollar Newspaper* published the first part on June 21, 1843, and the second, one week later on June 28. The *Philadelphia Sunday Courier,* with simultaneous publication rights, ran it as a three-part series on June 24, placing the first part on page 3 of the four-page newspaper. The story's popularity, however, forced the editors to move it to page 1 for the remaining installments. The *Dollar Newspaper,* in response to a continuing demand, reprinted the entire story in its July 12 issue.

The language of Jupiter, a freed slave who chose to remain with and to protect his gold-fevered master, is Poe's only use of Black speech, yet remains important to the historical understanding of Black English. Although some scholars have attacked Jupiter's dialect as being contrived and inconsistent, internal linguistic evidence—when combined with the linguistic analysis of the recordings of Black speech present in other stories of the period—strongly suggests that Jupiter's language, though flawed in places, is a far more accurate representation of one variety of Black speech than that recorded by any previous other author, including Cooper. And equally important is the place of "The Gold Bug" in linguistic literature, for just as the story itself influenced public attitudes, so did the speech of Jupiter. So popular had been the story that readers, whether conscious of it or not, undoubtedly accepted Jupiter's speech as representative of all Black speech.

In one representative scene, the narrator of the tale asks Jupiter about his master's health:

"Well, Jup," said I, "what is the matter now?—how is your master?"

"Why, to speak the troof, massa, him not so berry well as mought be."

"Not well! I am truly sorry to hear it. What does he complain of?"

"Dar! dat's it!—him neber 'plain of notin'—but him berry sick for all dat."

"*Very* sick, Jupiter!—why didn't you say so at once? Is he confined to bed?"

"No, dat he ain't—he ain't 'fin'd nowhat—dat's just whar de show pinch—my mind is got to be berry hebby 'bout poor Massa Will."

"Jupiter, I should like to understand what it is you are talking about. You say your master is sick. Hasn't he told you what ails him?"

"Why, massa, 'taint worf while for to get mad about de matter—Massa Will say noffin at all aint de matter wid him—but den what make him go about looking dis way, wid he head down and he soldiers [shoulders] up, and as white as a goose [ghost]? And den he keep a syphon [keeps figuring] all de time—"

"Keeps a what, Jupiter?"

"Keeps a syphon wid de figgurs ob de slate—de queerest figgurs I eber did see. Ise gettin' to be skeered, I tell you. Hab for to keep mighty tight eye 'pon him 'noovers. Todder day he gib me slip 'fore de sun up and was gone de whole ob de blessed day. I had a big stick ready cut for gib him deuced good beating when he did come—but Ise sich a fool dat I hadn't de heart arter all—he looked so berry poorly."

"Eh?—what?—ah yes!—upon the whole I think you had better not be too severe with the poor fellow—don't flog him, Jupiter—he can't very well stand it—but can you form no idea of what has occasioned this illness, or rather this change of conduct? Has anything unpleasant happened since I saw you?"

"No, massa, dey aint bin noffin onpleasant *since* den—'twas 'fore den I'm feared—'twas de berry day you was dare."

"How? what do you mean?"

"Why, massa, I mean de bug—dare now."

"The what?"

"De bug—I'm berry sartin dat Massa Will bin bit somewhere 'bout de head by dat goole-bug."

"And what cause have you, Jupiter, for such supposition?"

"Claws enuff, massa, and mouff, too. I nebber did see sich a deuced bug—he kick and he bit ebery ting what cum near him. Massa Will cotch him fuss, but had for to let him go 'gin mighty quick, I tell you—den was de time he must ha' got de bite. I didn't like de look ob de bug mouff, myself, nowhow, so I wouldn't take hold ob him wid my finger, but I cotch him wid a piece ob paper dat I found. I rap him up in de paper and stuffa piece of it in de mouff—dat was de way."

"And you think, then, that your master was really bitten by the beetle, and that the bite made him sick?"

"I don't tink noffin about it—I nose it. What make him dream 'bout des goole so much, if 'taint cause he bit by the goole-bug? Ise heered 'bout dem goole-bugs 'fore dis."

"But how do you know he dreams about gold?"

"How I know? why, 'cause he talk about it in he sleep—dat's how I nose."[16]

Shortly after that, Will Legrand, Jupiter's master, decided to explore for the gold. He apparently had decoded the strange markings on a treasure map. The narrator asked Jupiter why there were a scythe and three spades in the boat:

"Him de syfe and de spade what Massa Will sis pon [insisted upon] my buying for him in de town, and de debbil's own lot of money I had to gib for 'em."

"But what, in the name of all that's mysterious, is your 'Massa Will' going to do with the scythes and spades?"

"Dat's more dan *I* know, and de debbil take me if I don't b'lieve 'tis more dan he know, too. But, it's all cum ob de bug."[17]

On the island, which was believed to contain the gold, Legrand had Jupiter climb a tree to search for a marker:

"Mos feered for to ventur pon dis limb berry far—'tis dead limb putty much all de way."

"Did you say it was a *dead* limb, Jupiter?" cried Legrand in a quavering voice.

"Yess, massa, him dead as de door-nail—done up for sartain—done departed dis here life."[18]

After a near miss—on a critical instruction, Jupiter had confused his right eye with his left eye—the three-man party finally located the treasure. Jupiter, perhaps the most amazed of all, says: "And dis all cum ob de goole-bug! de putty goole-bug! de poor little goole-bug, what I boosed [abused] in that sabage kind ob style! Aint you shamed ob yourself, nigger?—answer me that!"[19]

A number of linguistic rules of Black English are present in Jupiter's speech. Phonologically, there are shifts from the voiced labiodental fricative [v] to the voiced bilabial stop [b] (*berry, debbil, ebber, ebery, gib, hab, hebby, neber, ob, sabage*); from the voiced alveolar fricative [ə] to the voiced alveolar stop [d] (*dar, dare, de, den, dis, wid*); from the unvoiced alveolar fricative [θ] to the unvoiced labiodental fricative [f] (*mouff, noffin, syfe, troof*); and consonant cluster reduction (*goole, mos*). The dropping of the unstressed word-initial syllable is also present (*boosed, 'bove, 'fin'd, 'fore, 'noovers, 'plain, 'pon* and *pon, shamed, sis, 'taint*). A number of syntactic rules are also evident—"he de syfe and spade what Mass Will sis pon my buying," "in he sleep," "wid he head down," and "ob de bug mouff." However, a number of orthographic errors are also present, such as *hadn't* rather than *ha'n; buying* rather than *buyin'; yourself* rather than *you'se'f; of* rather than *ob* in a few places, although *ob* is used also; and *most* rather than *mos*. The words *rap, nose, cum,* and *ventur* are eye dialect. Some linguistic scholars have suggested that the consistent inclusion of the postvocalic [r] is another error. However, by taking into account Poe's own Virginia dialect, this apparent anomaly is cleared up. Orthographically, the postvocalic [r] would be included in written language, but would be omitted in spoken language, with a possible change in the sound of the preceding vowel. Although Poe wrote the word *heart,* he, like Jupiter, undoubtedly pronounced it /hat/ (*haht*).

Only in "The Gold Bug" did Poe record Black speech, but it was far more accurate a recording than previously available, one that influenced reader perceptions of Black language for several years.

William Gilmore Simms (1806–1870) has been relegated to the backshops of journalism history. He and his writings remain largely unknown and unexamined by contemporary journalists. Yet, within his novels and short stories, there breathed the life of what was to become part of a journalistic-literary tradition that would serve as part of the roots for the "new journalism," the combining of the talents and styles of the journalist with those of the novelist. As vehicles for his talent, Simms edited several magazines, including *The Magnolia* (1842–43), *The Southern and Western Monthly Magazine and Review* (1845), and *The Southern Quarterly Review* (1856–57). His magazines included both fiction and nonfiction.

Simms spent much of his life in Charleston, South Carolina, and although he tried to be accepted into the Southern aristocratic society, his birth as the son of a poor shopkeeper was never forgotten by those who established the rules and taboos of social acceptability. Yet Simms understood this and defended the aristocracy, plantation life, and Southern slavery. Like Cooper, he believed that slavery was part of the natural order of the universe, sanctioned by God. He glorified and embellished the "virtues" of slavery, and used Black characters in his stories to express his own ideas about slavery. He believed the Black to be an inferior human being in all ways possible—morally, intellectually, and physically. Slavery for the Black, said Simms, elevated his mind and morals; it improved and prolonged his life. Yet Simms had great compassion for the seventy to eighty slaves he kept on his plantation; he thought of the slaves as children who must be cared for by others, for they were unable to care for themselves. There is no evidence that his slaves did not return his paternal love.

Five of Simms's fifty-nine major short stories, and nine of his sixteen novels include Gullah or Black English in dialogue. J. Allen Morris, writing almost a century after Simms's first major efforts in dialect were published, praised the accuracy of the recording:

> The Negro dialect used in Simms's stories to add verisimilitude, color, and realism to his characters, is a remarkably accurate and authentic reproduction of the Carolina Gullah dialect. . . .
>
> The Gullah dialect in Simms's stories is not a haphazard attempt by a white man to represent the strange-sounding dialect of the Negro but is a consistent, unusually accurate reproduction of the actual sounds and words of the Carolina Negro dialect, in so far as their peculiar dialect can ever be reproduced in print.[20]

The distinguished dialectologist Raven I. McDavid, Jr., writing sixteen years after Morris, also praised Simms's recording of the language: "[Simms] is seriously interested in the speech of his characters, and generally effective in representing [the dialect of] Negroes, poor whites, and mountaineers."[21]

"The Lazy Crow," which appeared in *The Wigwam and the Cabin* (1845), is one of Simms's better short stories, and is based upon Black superstition. Scipio, a field slave, is constantly plagued by a crow. His reasoning is that Gullah Sam, a field slave from a neighboring plantation, has turned himself into a crow to bewitch him. Scipio tries to shoot the crow, misses, and becomes very ill. Attempts are made to convince Scipio, who had been converted to Christianity, that devilry has no power over those who don't believe in it. Scipio replies:

> "I can't help it, mossa—de ting's de ting, and you can't change 'um. Dis Gullah Sam—he wus more nor ten debble—I jis' laugh at 'um t'oder day—tree week 'go, when he tumble in de hoss pond, and he shake he finger at me, and ebber since he put bad mout' 'pon me. Ebber sence dattime, dat ugly crow bin stand in my eyes, which eber way I tu'un. He habe gray dirt on he wing, and enty dere's a gray patch on Gullah Sam jacket? Gullah Sam hab close 'quaintan' wid day same lazy crow da's walk 'roun me in de cornfield, mossa.

I bin tink so from de fuss; and when he 'tan and le' me shoot at 'um and no 'fraid, den I sartin."[22]

Scipio's master suggests that Gullah Sam be punished. Scipio replies:

"You lick Gullah Sam, den you lose Scipio for eber and eber, amen. Gullah Sam nebber guine take off de bad mout' he put on Scip, once you lick em. De pains will keep in de bones—de leg will dead, fuss de right leg, den de lef, one arter t'oder, and you nigger will be dea, up and up, till noting lef for dead but he head. He head hab life, when you kin put he body in de hole, and cubber um up wid du't."[23]

The solution is an exorcist—Methuselah, identified as 'Tuselah (the dropping of the word-initial unstressed syllable). 'Tuselah—"a witch he self, worse more nor Gullah Sam"—frees Scipio from his psychosomatic bondage.[24]

"The Loves of the Driver" was published in the May, June, and July 1841, issues of *The Magnolia*. The central character is Mingo, a Black driver[25] whose amorous ways are known throughout the region. His wife, Diana, tells the plantation owner, who is looking for Mingo:

"Mingo, mossa? Whey him dey? Ha! mossa, you bes' ax ebbry woman on de plantation 'fore you come to he own wife. I bin marry to Mingo by Parson Buckhorn, and de Parson bin make Mingo promis' for lub and 'bey me, but he forgot all he promise tree day after we bin man and wife. He nebber bin lub 't all and as for 'bey,—lor' ha' massy 'pon me, mossa, I speak noting but de trute when I tell you,—he 'bey ebbry woman from yer to town 'fore he 'bey he own dear wife. Der's not a woman, mossa, 'pon de tree plantation, he ain't lub more dan Di. Sometime he gone to Misser Jacks place—he hab wife dere! Nex' time, he gone to Squar Collins, —he hab wife dere! Why he no hab wife, mossa? Who can tell? He hab wife ebbry which way, and now, he no *sacrify,* he gone—you aint gwine to bleeb me, mossa, I know you aint—he gone and look for wife at Indian camp, wha's down by the 'Red Gulley.' De trute is, mossa, Mingo is a mos' powerful black rascal of a nigger as ebber lib on a gentleman plantation."[26]

Most of the inconsistencies of Diana's language reflect the rules of either the loss of the postvocalic [r] or the replacement of the postvocalic [r] by the schwa [ə] (*powerful, after, dear, ebber, Misser, nigger*). Like Poe, Simms probably did not pronounce a postvocalic [r]; thus, these instances may not have been errors of transcription. There are, however, a few syntactic errors of transcription, as in "I bin marry to Mingo."

Mingo's chief antagonist in the drama is Richard Knuckles, a Catawba Indian whose wife Mingo is attempting to seduce. As opposed to the speech of Diana, the speech of Mingo is a mixture of Standard and Black English; perhaps it was Simms's technique of leading the reader to believe that Mingo was educated. Mingo's language is also a clue to his character, as when he confronts Knuckles who has just pulled a knife on him:

"Whor' afeard! . . . Look you, my friend: 'taint your knife, let me tell you, that's gwine to make me turn tail on any chicken of your breed. You tried it and what did you git? Why, look you, if it hadn't been for the gripe of gal—maybe she's your daughter, mount be your sister?—but it's all one—ef it hadn't been her gripe which fastened my arm, the butt of my whip would have flattened you, until your best friend couldn't ha' said where to look for your nose. You'd ha' been all face after that, smooth as bottom land, without e'er a snag or stump; and you'd have passed among old acquaintance for any body sooner than yourself. But I'm no bragdog—nor I don't want to be a biting dog, nother; when there's nothing to fight for. Let's be easy. P'rhaps you don't feel certain whose plantation you're on here. Mout be if you know'd you find out it won'nt altogether the best sense to draw knife on Mingo Gillison.—Why, look you, my old boy, I'm able to say what I please here—I make's the law for this plantation—all round about, so far as you can see from the top of the tallest of them e're pine trees, I'm the master! I look 'pon the pine land field and I say, 'Tom, Peter, Ned, Dick, Jack, Ben, Teney, Sam—boys—you must 'tack that field to-morrow.' I look 'pon the swamp field and I say to 'nother ten, 'boys, go there!'—high and low land, upland and swamp, corn and cotton, rice and rye, all 'pen' 'pon me for order; and jist as Mingo say, jist so they do. Well, wha' after that! It stands clear to the leetlest eye, that 'taint the best sense to draw knife on Mingo Gillison; here, on he own ground. 'Spose my whip can't do the mischief, it's a needcessity only to draw a blast out of this 'ere horn, and there'll be twenty niggers 'pon you at once, and ebery one of dem would go off with he limb. But I ain't a hard man my fren, ef you treat me softly. You come here to make your clay pots and pans. Your people bin used for make 'em here from sebenty nine [1779]—mout-be forty seben year—who knows? Well, you can make 'em

here, same as you usen to make 'em, so long as you 'habe you'self
like a gentleman. But not none of your knife-work, le' me tell
you. I'll come ebery day and look 'pon you. 'Moughtbe, I'll trade
with you for some of your pots. Clay pot is always best for bile
hom'ny."[27]

Apparent in the language of Mingo is his mastery of "sounding"—the
Black verbal insult game in which language is used to establish superiority. It is a mental debunking by use of language, a verbal squalling that
can be more effective than fighting. Like "sweet talk" and hypercorrection, sounding is part of both African and American Black language
norms.[28]

"The Snake of the Cabin" appeared in the July 1845 issue of *The
Southern and Western Monthly Magazine and Review;* "The Bride of
the Battle" appeared in the July, August, and September 1850, issues of
Graham's Magazine, and was the last short story Simms wrote that included Black language.

In Simms' second novel, *Guy Rivers; A Tale of Georgia* (1834),
Caesar, a slave, lectures a Yankee traveling salesman, who is attempting
to flim-flam a mentally retarded man: "Always 'member, ef you wants
to be a gempleman's, dat you kaint take no money from nigger and poor
buckrah. You kin gib um wha' you please, but you mustn't 'speck dem
to be gibbing you."[29]

The Yemassee (1835) is one of Simms's better novels. Hector, like
slaves in many of Simms's stories, is content with his role in life, secure
in his bondage, and terrified of freedom. Hector existed as the vehicle
that allowed Simms to argue the South's case for slavery. When faced by
the possibility of freedom, Hector argues:

"I d—n to h—ll, maussa, ef I guine to be free! . . . I can't loss you
company, and who de debble Dugdale guine let feed him like
Hector? 'Tis onpossible, maussa, and dere's no use for talk 'bout it.
De ting aint right; and enty I know wha' kind of ting freedom is
wid black man? Ha! you make Hector free, he turn wuss more nor
poor buckrah—he tief out of de shop—he git drunk and lie in de
ditch—den, if sick' come, he roll, he toss in de wet grass of de
stable. You come in de morning, Hector dead—and, who knows—
he no take physic, he no hab parson—who know, I say, maussa, but
debble fine 'em 'fore anybody else. No, maussa—you and Dugdale
berry good company for Hector. I tank God he so good—I no want
any better."[30]

A number of Black English rules are present in Hector's speech, but it is doubtful that the slave of the time period of the book (1715) would have used the contractions *can't, aint* (rather than "no be"), and *dere's.*

The character of Tom appears in both *The Partisan; A Romance of the Revolution* (1835) and *The Sword and the Distaff* (1853), which was revised as *Woodcraft* the following year. A number of Tom's lines reflect Black English constructions:

> "Ki! Maussa, you no lub sleep you'self, da's no reason why he no good for udder people."
>
> "He feel so, maussa. He berry much as if he been brack [broken]."[31]
>
> "I yer dat noise too, but he's fur away on de road."[32]
>
> "Ki! wha' for you do such t'ing."
>
> "Miss Ebleigh! He's a bressed woman for sartin for sen' we all mich good t'ings."
>
> "Cha'lot, my biggest da'ter;—he marry Cromanty Ben."
>
> "But nigger wha' got he two arm, and he two leg, he kin dance an' feel he sperrit joyful."
>
> "How kin he see ole woman in my room, ef me, Tom, no bin see 'em?"[33]

A number of passages in Black English are present in the 1856 novel, *Eutaw:*

> "Dey lock me up in house with Cato, and Cato's mos' go made, kaise he ain't le' em see to he hoss."
>
> "I jes' been wait for you done talk, maussa."
>
> "I day look for young maussa."[34]

The word *day* (*de* or *di* in West African Pidgin English) is an imperfect aspect marker. *Ki* is a common exclamation in many West African languages, including pidgin English.

In dealing with the literary representations of the Blacks within Simms's novels, critic Elizabeth McClellan Fleming noted: ". . . Simms did not consistently increase his use of the Negro as a character. However, although irregular, there is a progression toward the last-portrayed Tom. Tom of *Woodcraft* is Simms's ultimate achievement in that he is a product of the most nearly perfect combination of all the author's purposes for including the Negro in his fiction."[35] The same description could also be applied to Simms's use of dialect; he established his standards of transcription and changed little during the two decades he wrote fiction. The exception would be the Tom of three separate novels whose speech showed greater traces of African origins and linguistic consistency than Simms's other characters. Yet if Simms is to be faulted, it can be neither for his dialect-writing nor for the quality of his short stories and novels; rather, it must be for his being an apologist for the forced slavery of a race of people.

BLACK ENGLISH OBSERVATIONS

The increase in population—which led to an increase in business and the expansion in newspapers and magazines—led to an increase in nonfiction and the development of nonfiction books. Nonfiction works published during the Antebellum Cycle included several references to the nature of Black speech, as well as numerous observations reflective of commonly held attitudes.

Caroline Howard Gilmore's *Recollections of a Southern Matron* (1828), includes numerous references to Black speech—both direct quotes and observations. In discussing Black English, she noted: "I have never felt any more apprehension at having my children associate with the negroes, lest their dialect should be permanently injured, than I should have at listening to the broken English of a foreigner; and though at the time of which I speak, I preferred to talk to the negroes in their dialect, I never used it to the whites."[36]

Although she may have thought of Black English as "broken English," there is little doubt that she recognized it to be a separate dialect from what she spoke. Her recording of Black speech shows a strong acquaintance with the language. Although there are a number of phonological inconsistencies, as might be expected, Gilmore nevertheless recorded a number of syntactic constructions that paralleled West African Pidgin English:

". . . wid he head to de east, and he limb straight, and he eye shut."

"Maussa send me for de key for get four quart o' corn for him bay horse."

"Tank you much, my missis . . . Jacque hab everything him want in dis world 'cept he shroud, praise God."

"He berry awful for true."

"He eye clean" [He is watchful].

"Something bad gwine for happen."

"He bery dirty, for true, Miss Neely."[37]

Gilmore also used footnotes to explain language which might have been unfamiliar to the reader. To a direct quote in the text—"keep straight, my young massa, walk close"—she footnoted: "These expressions are very common among negroes, and signify, be correct, be pious." A few pages later, she footnoted: "The terms daddy, maumer, uncle, aunty, broder and titter (brother and sister) are not confined to connexions among blacks, they seem rather to spring from age."[38]

Joseph Holt Ingraham's *The South-West by a Yankee* (1835), includes a number of observations on Black English. Upon arriving at the Port of Natchez, Ingraham reported that two Blacks approached him:

"I'm de gemman, massa, what care de trunk."
"Dis nigger, him no noffing, massa—I'm what's always waits on um gentlemans from de boats."[39]

Since one Black says *gemman,* and the other says *gentlemans,* it is possible that this reflected not an error in writing or transcription, but the actual lexicon of the individuals involved.

Ingraham also discussed "sweet talk," a distinct African language characteristic, although he undoubtedly did not understand the sociolinguistic connotations:

The [Blacks] prefer collecting [on Sunday] in little knots in the streets, where, imitating the manners, bearing, and language of their masters, they converse with grave faces and in pompous language, selecting hard high-sounding words, which are almost universally misapplied, and distorted, from their original sound as well as sense to a most ridiculous degree—astounding their groping auditors 'ob de field nigger class' who cannot boast of such enviable accomplishments.[40]

Ingraham, a clergyman, also recorded a brief conversation he had with a Black following church services:

"Ben, how did you like the sermon to-day?" I once inquired of one, who, for pompous language and high-sounding epithets, was the Johnson of negroes.—"Mighty obligated wid it, master, de 'clusive 'flections very distructive to de ignorum."[41]

The "sweet-talking" Black had used the White language rules to create rhythm and words where none previously existed; he was praising the sermon by disregarding the "exact" language and creating a new language to express his admiration.

Ingraham's romantic history, *Lafitte, the Pirate of the Gulf* (1836), included a number of passages in Black English, including: "Ol' Juana tink Doly better wait till morning come [to leave]; cause if massa Lafitte sa' he let lilly lady and buckra gemman go free—dey sure go as Juana 'tan here. But den, if lilly Missy 'fraid, Juana go 'long wid her."[42]

The Journal of a Residence on a Georgian Plantation, written by Frances Anne Kemble during the winter of 1838–39, was apparently privately circulated prior to its publication in 1863 as a tract meant to influence British opinion against the South and slavery. Kemble, a well-known British actress, spent two years in America before marrying a Southern aristocrat in 1834. Although she was empathetic to the struggles of the Southern Black, she also maintained many of the stereotypes about language:

> The children of the owners, brought up among [the slaves] acquire their Negro mode of talking—slavish speech surely it is—and it is distinctly perceptible in the utterance of all Southerners, particularly of the women, whose avocations, taking them less from home, are less favorable to their throwing off this ignoble trick of pronunciation than the varied occupation and the more extended and promiscuous business relations of men. The Yankee twang of the regular down home Easter is not any more easily detected by an ear, nice in enunciation and accent than the thick Negro speech of the Southerners.[43]

Kemble was especially upset that her daughter, Sally, had acquired elements of Black English:

> I am amused, but by no means pleased, at an entirely new mode of pronouncing which S—— had adopted. Apparently the Negro jargon has commended itself as euphonious to her infantile ears, and she is now treating me to the most ludicrous and accurate imitations of it every time she opens her mouth. Of course I shall not allow this to become a habit. This is the way Southern ladies acquire the thick and inelegant pronunciation which distinguishes their utterances from the Northern snuffle, and I have no desire that S—— should adorn her mother tongue with either peculiarity.[44]

It is not surprising that Kemble maintained such attitudes about Black English or, for that matter, Southern English. The language she spoke was standard British English—the language of the British upper class and well educated, the language of the theatre. All other dialects of English were considered inferior. And certainly this belief was extended into America, whose people tended to view standard British English as the "pure" language.[45]

Charles Lyell, a British geologist, also thought Black English was an inferior language. His *Second Visit to the United States of America* (1849), reflected the prejudices of language which he shared with most his contemporaries, British as well as American: "Already their [the slaves'] task-masters have taught them to speak, with more or less accuracy, one of the noblest of languages."[46] But, according to Lyell, the Black would never acquire the "pure" language. To affirm his position, he recorded a Black prayer which he called "ungrammatical":

> Make he good, like he say
> Make he say, like he good
> Make he say, make he good, like he God.[47]

Ungrammatical it may have been to someone familiar only with standard British English, but grammatical it was in West African Pidgin English. And, more important, the prayer contained a world of meaning that would have lost its impact and exact meaning had it been translated into standard British English.

Lyell's unfamiliarity with African naming practices also reflected his ethnocentricism: "The parents indulge their own fancies in naming their children . . . one is called January, another April, a third Monday, and a fourth Hard Times."[48] Although Lyell, with a distinct air of superiority, was smiling at African naming practices, it is quite likely that the Blacks were smiling right back at the unusual naming practices among the British and Americans.[49]

The Rev. Charles Colcock Jones also had prejudices about Black English. But, unlike many of his contemporaries, he believed that the Black could become an equal—if only he could be "Christianized." *Religious Instruction of the Negroes* (1842) was his attempt to provide instruction in proselytizing; it was a "how-to" manual for preachers, and, as such, received wide distribution in the South. Jones was known for his compassion and humanitarianism toward the Black, but he warned his preachers that they must not, even when speaking to all-Black congregations, speak "their broken English." It was his belief that the Black must be strongly encouraged to speak only Standard English. However, Jones also recognized that the Blacks spoke an identifiable and common language; he realized that those Blacks who were brought over from the West Coast of Africa knew this common language, in all probability West African Pidgin English, although he never identified it by name. Among the clues are: "But a further difficulty is, that they are *utter strangers to our language* and *we* to *theirs*," and, "Many of the Negroes . . . do of themselves attain so much of our languages as enables them to understand and to be understood in the things which concern the ordinary business of life."[50]

James Redpath, a correspondent and editor for Horace Greeley's *New York Tribune,* conducted a number of in-depth interviews of slaves throughout the South. *The Roving Editor; Or, Talks With Slaves in the Southern States* (1859), is distinguished not only because of Redpath's transcriptions of Black speech, but also because his interviewing ability revealed the innermost thoughts and observations of the people called "niggers." Redpath, an abolitionist deeply concerned about the plight of man, dug into the souls of the people he interviewed and, through the language, brought forth example after example of man's cruelty to man:

"Yes, mass'r . . . I had twelve [children] by my firs' wife. I got her when she was seventeen, and I lived wid her twenty-four years. *Den da sold her and all de chil'ren.* I married anoder wife, 'bout nine years since; but I had her little mor dan tree years. *Da sold her too.*"

"Yes, massa . . . we goes to de church; we's not members ob de church, kase we's colored people, and dey won't let us be.

"I's a slave, massa; dat's what I is, and I neber 'specks to be free."[51]

It is possible that the phonological/orthographic inconsistencies of language reflect actual usage, rather than errors of transcription; for example, *twelve* rather than *twe'f, children* rather than *chillun or chill'un, seventeen* rather than *seb'teen, lived* rather than *libbed, church* rather than *chu'ch* or *chuhch*. However, one slave, as Redpath transcribed, probably would not have said both *belieb* and *bliev,* or *children* and *chil'ren.* It is also probable that the Black did not use a surface structure copula syntactic construction; "and I never 'specks to be free," was probably an error in transcription. Redpath—who would two years later become a battlefield correspondent for the *New York Tribune*—presented an interesting observation about freedom, and man's interpretation of freedom: "I did not know then, what I soon learned, that the Press [in

the South] is a greater slave than the negro, and is treated by the planters and politicians who rule it, exactly as it deserves to be—like a serf.[52]

THE AMERICAN MINSTREL

In a small, elite theatre in colonial America, an actor smeared his white
face and hands with burnt cork, covered his hair with a sheep's-wool
wig, exaggerated the language and mannerisms of the American Black,
and entertained his audience with speeches, songs, and dances. This
black-faced actor, who had learned his act from similar performances
in England, became America's first minstrel. Today, his name remains
unknown; where and when he performed can only be estimated. But,
he was to set the base for a new form of American entertainment—
entertainment by and for one race of people that mocked and ridiculed
another race; entertainment that would remain popular for more than a
century.

After the War of 1812—when the nation was searching for distinctively American roots, and theatrical performances were aimed at the
"common man" rather than society's elite—the minstrel shows became
popular. From the barrooms on showboats to 2,500-seat auditoriums,
from the rural areas of the South to the urban centers of the North and
East, minstrelsy was sweeping the nation, becoming in the 1840s and
1850s the most popular stage entertainment in America.

The burnt-cork actors, speaking thick and exaggerated dialect, reduced the Black to absurdity and portrayed him as irresponsible and
immature, as lazy, frivolous, and foolish—all the characteristics that
White audiences, both North and South, wanted to believe the Black
possessed. For the White audiences, the minstrel shows also provided a
joyful release of tension, a chance to laugh at the foibles of others.
They could laugh and enjoy themselves and leave the performance secure in the belief that although they had their own problems, there were
others who looked, acted, and talked different than they did, who were
even more pretentious and stupid than they could ever be. As long as
the Black was portrayed in grotesque and distorted terms, the White
could be secure in his own insecurity. And, if the "Black" on stage
could dance better than the White, it was not because the Black was
better, and the White less capable, but because the Black had a "natural rhythm" which he inherited from his African heritage. In all other
attributes, especially intelligence and industrious labor—traits valued by
White Americans—Blacks were seen as inferior and incapable of ra-

tional thought. The fact that the "Black" on stage was white underneath the burnt cork did not diminish the stereotype.

To emphasize the "inferiority" of Blacks, the minstrels used variations of Black speech, for the nuances of what was believed to be degenerate English spoken by the Blacks were the White-perceived clues to inherent Black inferiority. The provincial attitudes of White Americans about their language allowed no substantial deviation. As Americans split from England, they retained much that was English. In America's collective subconsciousness, there were still many things English that were "better"—the standard British English was better, for it was a "pure" language. And if Americans could not speak English as well as their English cousins, at least they could speak it better than "foreigners" and slaves. The dialects of the European immigrants, however, were received with moderate toleration, for European languages were somewhat related to English; and European immigrants were the same color as Americans. But the African roots of Black English were in stark contrast to the Indo-European languages; it suited White ethnocentrism to believe that Blacks were incapable of even forming the sounds of Standard English. The speech of slaves, therefore, was represented on the level of untutored children—attempts to speak Standard English would always be doomed to fail. It was this need of Americans to establish themselves in both language and culture that allowed minstrelsy to flourish.

In January 1843, the proprietor of a billiard room in New York City's Bowery reluctantly allowed a group of four White musicians to stage an impromptu concert. So popular was their form of entertainment that when the musicians moved back across the street to the North American Hotel where they were staying, many in the audience followed, and the concert continued in the hotel lobby. The group, which called itself the Virginia Minstrels, would change the concepts of minstrelsy for decades to come. Playing the banjo was Bill Whitlock, a former compositor for *The New York Herald,* and a protégé of P. T. Barnum. Shaking and pounding the tambourine was Richard Ward Pelham, an agile imitator of Black dances. The "bones," a relatively new instrument created to appear to have originated in Africa, were knocked together by Frank Brower who, like Pelham, was one of the outstanding imitators of Black dance. The group's fiddler was twenty-seven-year-old Daniel Decatur Emmett, a veteran minstrel who would achieve musical immortality sixteen years later with "Dixie," a dialect song he composed for

Bryant's Minstrels as part of a musical walk-around. (Emmett would later say that he never intended "Dixie" to be anything more than a minstrel song; he would claim that the overwhelming popularity of "Dixie," which was first sung by both the North and South before becoming the rallying song of the Confederacy, was an embarrassment. But of the hundreds of dialect songs he composed, of all the Black speeches and sermons, walk-arounds, and sketches he wrote, it was "Dixie" for which he would be remembered.)

Within two weeks of their founding, the Virginia Minstrels performed to overwhelming applause at the famous Bowery Amphitheatre. During the next two months, they were enthusiastically received in Boston and other major Eastern cities. In the spring, so great had become their fame that they were invited to London; the British crowded the theatre to see this "new" American entertainment that portrayed the American slaves as happy, ignorant fools who, when not in the fields under benevolent masters, spent their time singing and dancing. By the end of the decade there were a number of professional minstrel troupes; each troupe had different characteristics, actors, and acts, but all included the same basic elements of buffoonery and joyful stupidity believed to be typical Black characteristics. The full minstrel show, developed by the Virginia Minstrels and expanded by the Christy Minstrels and others, all included humorous stump speeches, solo and duet dances, short humorous skits, one-act comedies, and numerous dialect songs.

The stump speeches, emphasizing the dialect and religious "quirks" of the Blacks, usually featured the minstrel as a Black preacher unsuccessfully trying to imitate the White speech of his master by inserting long and important-sounding words as often as possible, and disregarding all meaning in favor of the rhythm of the language. Among the passages of "sweet talk" and hypercorrection contributed by Dan Emmett to minstrelsy were:

"I jis tole yoa now, dat de hegeniture ob my connuberalness substancherates its own casloozens . . ."

"De quinin ob my 'scoas, dis ebenin, am tended to sessiate de sessity ob yoa own mine being kept cool, same like de mud turkle on de driff log . . ."

"De heeven 'lossifer Harry Stottle, sez nuttin 'tall 'bout it; Jo Seefus dat set on 'top ob Gurusalemm, an wrote nigga songs couldn't tole ye: Antony Hannibal an Julycum Sezar had to gub it up, an I myseff froes it clarr under de table."[53]

The Whites "knew" that the Black would "never get it straight," and was thus doomed to a fate of never reaching the level of linguistic superiority achieved by the White. The speeches, themselves, were commentaries on everything from the grossest absurdities to profound social comment to pseudoscientific explanations of the universe.

The one-act plays, often called Ethiopian operas, and the short skits present in most minstrel shows were carefully scripted to include a variety of theatrical devices, everything from soliloquies and verbal squalling to dances, songs, and slapstick. And although the dialogue reeked with stereotypes of the Black, even the strongest abolitionists, those who would have been expected to have had the most compassion and understanding for the Black slave, found themselves laughing and enjoying the jokes and absurdities presented in the minstrel shows.

By the end of the 1850s, the minstrels' attitudes toward slavery began to change. Once they had opposed the abolition movement, but public sentiment in the North, where most of their performances took place, had slowly grown to a point that suggested a division in the nation was quickly becoming inevitable. The traveling minstrels, aware of the grassroots feelings of the people, but still believing that Abraham Lincoln and the abolitionists would divide, not preserve, the Union, noted the trend and reacted accordingly. Those who could not bring themselves to support abolition, at least did not openly oppose it on the stage, although they did retain many of the Black stereotypes.

By the end of the decade, freed slaves began to enter minstrelsy—some hoping to change White concepts about Blacks, others because it was the only thing they could do or were allowed to do. But with few exceptions, Black minstrels—no matter what their language—were usually rejected by the audiences. Audiences that reacted with enthusiasm to the *portrayal* of Blacks on the minstrel stage, were hushed by the appearance of Black minstrels. Replacing a stereotyped image with a flesh-and-blood person brought reality too near.

Many elements of minstrelsy had become so popular that publishers, recognizing a public demand that meant significant income possibilities, began printing and distributing stump speeches, one-act plays, and song sheets. Printed by the thousands, these items soon began to saturate the country. On their covers, many printed in color, were usually illustrations of Blacks in grotesque and humanly impossible contortions; there were drawings of the elements of minstrelsy—the banjo and bones; and if the composer or author were well known, his picture was placed on the cover. Often, if a famous minstrel group were identified with a song or skit, that fact would be emblazoned on the cover, for publishers knew that name identification was an important part of sales. Knowing this human foible, publishers often attributed songs to famous composers who had never written them, and famous musicians and groups who had never performed them; it made little difference whether the group had actually performed the song, skit, or speech as long as the impressionable readers would think it was so. That's all it took to sell much of what was printed.

Once there were millions of song sheets, printed dialect stump speeches, and dialect plays in circulation throughout the country. Once they were almost as proliferous as the daily newspapers. Now, a hundred years later, little remains from the early decades of minstrelsy; what does remain is often locked away in little-remembered manuscript collections, or is rotting in attics and basements. But for more than a half-century, minstrelsy was the "king of verbal entertainment"; for more than a century, it entertained the masses of the American public.

THE SLAVE NARRATIVES

The Antebellum period, which had seen the rise of the minstrel shows and the growth of Southern plantation life, also saw the cruelty of human bondage. It was from the deepest human emotions that men like John Brown, whom some called a religious fanatic and others called a martyr, fought and died for what they believed. And if their methods had been at times savage, they were fighting in savage times. Slavery had finally awakened a public consciousness to the misery of human life; part of that awakening resulted from, and was reflected within, the mass media.

From the language of their masters and the languages of their African heritage, slaves took their oral traditions and molded them into written accounts of their own lives that told not of the mint julep and magnolia portraits of slavery painted by Simms and numerous others, not the grotesque distortions and stereotypes portrayed by the minstrels. Instead they bespoke of the brutality and horror that bondage plays upon the human soul.

On January 27, 1837, in the Twenty-fourth Congress of the United States, Sen. John C. Calhoun of South Carolina, one of the nation's most brilliant politicians and orators, rose to defend slavery. Slavery, said Calhoun, had civilized the Black. A "divine Providence," he said, had brought the two races together—the White, or European race, to be the masters, the Black, or African race, to be the slaves. Slavery, said Calhoun, was not an evil. The slave narratives disputed his claim.

The first slave narrative was published in 1705; a few more were published during the remainder of the eighteenth century. But it was not until the first half of the nineteenth century that the narratives, which were beginning to flood the Northern markets, began to make their greatest impact upon the Northern conscience. Throughout the country, slave narratives written by former and runaway slaves, unceasingly hammered out their messages of the human spirit unchained. The fiery speeches of the White abolitionists became more meaningful, and slowly began to influence a nation. Here, in the words of the slaves, was testimony to the cruelty of slavery, testimony to the horror and brutality of bondage. At abolitionist meetings, the narratives were hawked to finance the cause of freedom; from bookstores and newsstands they were sold, some for twenty-five cents, the better ones for as much as a dollar and a half. Some narratives were privately printed on presses more than fifty years old, others on modern presses; some narratives had sales of only a handful of copies, others had sales into the thousands. *The Narrative of William Wells Brown* quickly reached sales of eight thousand copies. Two years after its publication in 1851, *The Narrative of Solomon Northrup* had sales of more than 27,000 copies. The narratives of Moses Roper and Frederick Douglass each went into more than ten editions.

In the decades before the Civil War, the narratives established a new literary form in America, a genre that became so popular that it rivaled the most popular novels of the day, so popular that almost any slave could get his story published. So influential were these tales of human misery that Frederick Law Olmstead, a distinguished Northern scholar during the Antebellum Cycle, could suggest that the Northern views of slavery were based not upon newspaper and magazine accounts, not upon abolitionist claims, but upon the narratives themselves. Indeed, Ephraim Peabody, writing in the July 1849 issue of *The Christian Examiner,* was not overstating the case when he claimed, "The narratives are the most remarkable productions of the age."

Although the slave narratives served as personal commentaries on an American socioeconomic system, they also served as primary evidence of the existence of a language system—in this case, Black English. It was a common belief, and not an incorrect one at that time, that publishing the narratives wholly in Black English would strengthen the antiabolitionist claim that Blacks were inferior. Thus, no matter what dialect or language the Black spoke, his narrative was usually in Standard English, although many phrases, as well as direct quotes of field slaves, might be in Black English.

Those slaves, like Frederick Douglass, who spoke Standard English usually wrote their own narratives. Those slaves who spoke Black English usually dictated their stories to White abolitionists, some of whom faithfully translated the stories into Standard English, others of whom embellished the conditions of slavery to make the stories seem more like White evangelical perceptions of slavery than what really existed. Many narratives, moreover, were wholly written by Whites eager to "cash in" on the popularity of the slave narratives. Nevertheless, many passages in Black English provide sufficient evidence for study and analysis.

The Autobiography of a Female Slave (1857), written by Mattie Griffith (also known as Martha Griffith Browney) includes several extensive passages in Black English, virtually all in direct quotation. A number of language rules are remarkably consistent throughout the narrative; a number of other rules are noticeably inconsistent. One thing, though, is striking: the text itself is written in a formal Standard English, whereas the direct quotes of the other slaves are usually in Black English. If the author, a house slave, learned and spoke only Standard Southern English, it would explain some of the inconsistencies in recording the Black English of the field slaves. But it is also possible that the narrative was not written by a Black, and may have actually been a composite sketch written either by abolitionists or, not inconceivably, a writer/publisher team hoping to profit from the North's almost complete acceptance of the slave narratives. The many linguistic inconsistencies that the author attributes to Aunt Polly suggest that the writer was not familiar with Black speech. Nevertheless, whoever the author— Black or White—he or she was familiar enough with some of the rules of Black English. The narrative, which sold very well, undoubtedly influenced many Northerners not only about the conditions of slavery, but also about Black speech. For that reason the narrative, whether real or fraudulent, is important.

In an early chapter of the book, the author, recovering from a severe beating at the hands of the overseer, recalls the words of Aunt Polly:

"Oh, chile, when Masser Jones was done a-beatin' ob yer, dey all tought you was dead; den Masser [the owner] got ortful skeard. He cussed and swore, and shook his fist in de obserseer's face, an sed he had kilt you, and dat he was gwine to law wid him 'bout de 'struction ob his property. Den Masser Jones he swar a mighty heap, and tell Masser he dar' him to go to law 'bout it. Den Miss Jane and Tilda kum out, and commenced cryin', and fell to 'busin' Masser Jones, kase Miss Jane say she want to go de big town, and take you long wid her for lady's maid. Den Mr. Jones fell to busen ob her, and den Masser and him clinched, and fought, and fought like two big black dogs. Den Masser Jones sticked his great big knife in Masser's side, and Masser fell down, and den we all tought he was clar gone. Den away Masser Jones did run, and nobody dared take arter him, for he had a loaded pistol and a big knife."[54]

Aunt Polly then recounts how, when the other folks went to take care of the owner, she stayed behind to take care of Mattie who was believed to be dead, but was only unconscious from the beating given her by the overseer. After Aunt Polly tells her tale of human misery, Mattie puts herself back into the narrative as she talks to, and about, Aunt Polly:

I threw my arms around her again, and imprinted kisses upon her rugged brow; for, though her skin was sooty and her face worn with care, I believed that somewhere in a silent corner of her tired heart, there was a ray of warm, loving, human feeling.

"Oh, child," she began, "can you wid yer pretty yellow face kiss an old pitch-black nigger like me?"

"Why, yes, Aunt Polly, and love you too; if your face is dark I am sure your heart is fair."

"Well, I don't know 'bout dat, chile; once 'twas far, but I tink all de white man done made it black as my face."

"Oh no, I can't believe that, Aunt Polly," I replied.

"Wal, I always hab said dat if dey would cut my finger and cut a white woman's, dey would find de blood ob de very same color," and the old woman laughed exultingly.

"Yes, but, Aunt Polly, if you were to go before a magistrate with a case to be decided, he would give it against you, no matter how just were your claims."

"To be sartin, de white folks allers gwine to do every ting in favor ob dar own color."

"But, Aunt Polly," interposed I, "there is a God above, who disregards color."

"Sure dare is, and dar we will all ob us git our dues, and den de white folks will roast in de flames ob old Nick."

I saw, from a furtive flash of her eye, that all the malignity and revenge of her outraged nature were becoming excited, and I endeavored to change the conversation.

"Is master getting well?"

"Why, yes chile, de debbil can't kill him. He is 'termined to live just as long as dare is a nigger to torment. All de time he was crazy wid de fever, he was fightin' wid de niggers—'pears like he don't dream 'bout nothin' else."[55]

The blunt language in *The Autobiography of a Female Slave* was unusual for the slave narratives. Most narratives were free of gross exaggeration; the Black saw his enemy not as the White, but as the White's system. The writers of the narratives, whether Black or White, believed that exaggeration would do more to hurt than help the cause of abolition. However, there was another exception.

UNCLE TOM'S CABIN

Harriet Beecher Stowe's *Uncle Tom's Cabin; Or, Life Among the Lowly* is regarded as the most immediately influential of any novel published in nineteenth-century America. The powerful, though grossly exaggerated and often distorted view of plantation life and the effects of slavery, was first serialized in *The National Era,* a four-page abolitionist weekly newspaper with an influential readership. The first part of the serial appeared on June 5, 1851; and with only two exceptions—when copy was received after the deadline—the subsequent chapters appeared in every issue, usually on page 1, until its conclusion on April 1, 1852.

The slave narratives had awakened a nation's conscience and served as the base that allowed *Uncle Tom's Cabin* to dominate both Northern beliefs and American literature. So powerful had been Stowe's highly personal tale of human misery that within eight weeks of its publication in book form, in late March 1852, by John P. Jewett & Co., 50,000 copies of the two-volume set had been sold. By the end of September, more than 150,000 copies were sold; the January 1853 issue of *Putnam's Monthly* reported that more than 200,000 copies had been sold in the United States alone. By the end of the following year, more than a half-million copies were in circulation as numerous publishers began reprinting for the European markets. Eventually, there would be twenty-five separate translations, and more than a million copies in print. Throughout the world, leading newspapers were serializing *Uncle Tom's Cabin.*

In the United States, so dangerous had *Uncle Tom's Cabin* become that the entire South suppressed it. An 1852 novel by Mary Eastman, *Aunt Phillis's Cabin; Or, So Life As It Is,* was written to counter the sympathy aroused by *Uncle Tom's Cabin.* Although it contained dialect and was highly popular in the South, it did little to diminish the impact of Stowe's tale which had brought the nation's division to the surface. From New York City, *The Journal of Commerce,* one of the nation's most influential daily newspapers, led the fight against *Uncle Tom's Cabin,* only to have its influence blunted by Horace Greeley's *New York Tribune,* a newspaper with even greater influence, and long recognized as one of the nation's leading voices against slavery.

Uncle Tom's Cabin solidified Northern opinion and gave its people an honorable and righteous crusade against the South. Rather than citing regional, economic, and political differences, the North could now use the morality of slavery as a cause for a split among people. Without *Uncle Tom's Cabin,* said William A. Seward, secretary of state from 1861 to 1869, Abraham Lincoln would never have become president. And Lincoln, himself, meeting Harriet Beecher Stowe for the first time on November 25, 1862, shortly before the Battle of Fredericksburg, and feeling the weight of the presidency during a civil war, remarked. "So you're the little woman who wrote the book that made this great war."

In the United States, an entire Uncle Tom cult had arisen. By the end of 1852, the dramatization of Stowe's now-classic tale had premiered in both the Museum Theatre in Boston and the prestigious National Theatre in New York City. For the next eighty years, *Uncle Tom's Cabin* was never "off the boards." The novel had also spawned numerous "Uncle Tom" novels and "Uncle Tom" songs, most of them using Black speech, or what the authors thought was Black speech; and, it had spawned the "Tom Show," a parade of Negro and White minstrel bands, with hunting dogs and characters dressed to resemble those of the novel.

The dialect of *Uncle Tom's Cabin,* like the dialect that was passed off as Black speech in the "Uncle Tom" cult media, is linguistically inconsistent and reveals either Stowe's unfamiliarity with the mechanics of Black English, or her inability to accurately record what she heard. Most of the syntactic rules that distinguished Black speech in the Antebellum Cycle are either poorly recorded or omitted entirely. Phonologically, she recognized the shift from the voiced interdental fricative [ð] to the voiced alveolar stop [d] (e.g., *that → dat*), although her recording of that shift was by no means systematic. She failed to recognize the shift from the unvoiced interdental fricative [θ] to the unvoiced alveolar stop [t] (e.g., *cloth* → *clot'*). Only occasionally did she record the shift from the voiced labiodental fricative [v] to the voiced bilabial stop [b] (e.g., *very* → *bery*), one of the major phonological rules in Black English. Other phonological rules of Black English, like the syntactic rules, were either poorly recorded or omitted entirely. As literary critic Tremaine McDowell pointed out: "The very core of authentic negro dialect [is] slighted or ignored, until much of the speech of Uncle Tom and his contemporaries might come from the lips of semi-literate European immigrants. . . . A very few touches of revision would make such a harangue appropriate not to the Southern negro but to one of the characters of Artemus Ward."[56]

Stowe did not improve her representation of Black English in her next novel, *Dred; A Tale of the Great Dismal Swamp.* However, a surprising number of improvements are present in *The Minister's Wooing,* a romance set shortly after the American Revolution, and first serialized in *The Atlantic Monthly* (December 1858–December 1859) before being published in book form. Although improved, the dialect is still unconvincing and inconsistent:

> "When Gineral Washington was here, I heard 'em read de Declaration ob Independence and Bill o' Rights; an I tole Cato den says I 'Ef dat ar' true, you an' I are as free as anybody.' It stands to reason. Why, look at me,—I a'n't a critter. I's neider huffs nor horns. I's a reasonable bein',—a woman,—as much a woman as anybody," she said, holding up her head with an air as majestic as a palm-tree;—"an' Cato,—he's a man, born free an' equal, ef dar's any truth in what you read,—dat's all."
>
> "But, Candace, you've always been contented and happy with us, have you not?" said Mr. Marvyn.
>
> "Yes, Mass'r,—I ha'n't got nuffin to complain ob in dat matter. I couldn't hab no better friends 'n you an' Missis."
>
> "Would you like your liberty, if you could get it, though?" said Mr. Marvyn. "Answer me honestly."
>
> "Why, to be sure I should! Who wouldn't? Me ye," she said, earnestly raising her black, heavy hand, "ta'n't dat I want to go off, or want to shirk work; but I want to *feel free.* Dem dat isn't free has nuffin to gib to nobody;—dey can't show what dey would do."[57]

Candace is given her freedom, then Marvyn indicates he will ask Cato, her husband, if he also wishes his freedom—"when he returns home from work tonight." Candace's response, and Stowe's careful writing, may be an unknown classic in American literature:

> "Laus, Mass'r,—why Cato, he'll do jes' as I do,—dere a'n't no kind o' need o' askin' him. 'Course he will."
>
> A smile passed round the circle, because between Candace and her husband there existed one of those whimsical contrasts which one sometimes sees in married life. Cato was a small-built, thin, softly-spoken negro, addicted to a gentle chronic cough; and, though, a faithful and skilled servant, seemed, in relation to his better half, much like a hill of potatoes under a spreading apple-tree. Candace held to him with a vehemence and patronizing fondness, so devoid of conjugal reverence as to excite the comments of her friends.
>
> "You must remember, Candace," said a good deacon to her one day, when she was ordering him about at a catechizing, "you ought to give honor to your husband; the wife is the weaker vessel."
>
> "*I* de weaker vessel?" said Candace, looking down from the tower of her ample corpulence on the small, quiet man whom she had been fledging with the ample folds of a worsted comforter, out of which his little head and shining bead-eyes looked, most like a blackbird in a nest, "*I* de weaker vessel? Umph!"
>
> A whole women's-rights convention could not have expressed more in a day than was given in that single look and word. . .[58]

Stowe's later writings show only an occasional use of dialect, none of it any better than in *The Minister's Wooing*. Tremaine McDowell sums up Stowe's handling of dialect:

> No historically-minded reader will condemn her because she lacked, in the 1850's, the instincts of a twentieth-century realist, or because she was unable . . . to preserve a correct phonetic record of ante-bellum negro speech. But it is permissible to compare her work with that of her predecessors; and the result is not credible to Mrs. Stowe . . . Coming into the field after [the] preliminary work had been accomplished [by Tenney, Cooper, and Simms], Mrs. Stowe not only made no improvement over her predecessors, but actually fell below them. Convincing effects could no longer be produced by a liberal sprinkling of *dat's, dere's,* and *dem's,* interspersed with a few familiar colloquialisms and barbarisms. Mrs. Stowe's negro dialect, therefore, whether it is judged relatively or abso-

lutely is only a makeshift in *Uncle Tom's Cabin,* and, in *The Minister's Wooing,* only an approximation.[59]

Harriet Beecher Stowe died at the age of eighty-five in 1896, forty-five years after her first novel shook the foundations of a country. As the decade of the 1860s approached, the country was a pressure cooker, and its people were rushing forth to meet a destiny more bloody than they had ever known. The prophecy of Nathaniel Beverly Tucker, who more than two decades earlier had written about a civil war among America's people, would soon become a nightmare of reality.

3. The Reconstruction Cycle

The war was over. A war that tore at the heart and guts of the country. A war that saw brother fight brother, father fight son. Its brutality and horror would never again be matched in the history of the American people. The prosperity of the South and the awareness of the human condition had set the tone of the Antebellum Cycle; it was a foundation that led to a civil war among a people just reaching maturity. And when that war was over, and more than 200,000 Americans lay dead on the fields of battle that soldiers call "honor," there emerged a different country. It was a country that had changed more rapidly than at any other time since the Revolutionary War. The ironclad philosophies of the North had changed; the heart of the South was devastated. No longer was the South prosperous. Where once there was happiness and contentment, there now existed only misery; where once palatial estates marked a beautiful land and a proud people, there now was but cinder.

During the decade following the Civil War, the South would be occupied territory; federal troops and military governors would dictate its policies. And, for the first time, Blacks would be given the vote—guaranteed of their rights by the thirteenth, fourteenth, and fifteenth amendments to the Constitution, all passed between 1865 and 1870, and enforced by the military. During the decade that would be known as Reconstruction, there would be Black senators and representatives to the U.S. Congress, Black mayors, assemblymen, state senators, and even governors in the Southern states. But, as a result of the presidential election of 1876, it would soon end.

Governor Samuel J. Tilden, a Democrat from New York, with over 200,000 more votes than Governor Rutherford B. Hayes, Republican from Ohio, appeared to have won the election. In the electoral college however, Tilden had only 184 votes, one short of a majority; Hayes had 165 votes. Twenty votes—nineteen from three Southern states, and one from Oregon—were still outstanding. Following lengthy bargaining, Hayes agreed that in exchange for the needed twenty electoral votes he would, when he became president, pull federal troops out of the South. On March 5, 1877, Rutherford B. Hayes became the nineteenth president of the United States; in May, federal troops began to leave the South. Few in either the North or the South complained—both sides were tired of the political battles that had to be fought to give even token equality to the Black. But with the pullout of federal troops, segregation, in forms more ugly and more vengeful than much of what had existed during the years of slavery, began to dominate the South and the mind of the South. Jim Crow laws, passed by all-White legislatures, again forced a second-class citizenship upon a race of people who were under the impression that they were not only free, but equal as well. And in 1896, the Supreme Court of the United States, in the landmark *Plessy v. Ferguson* decision, sanctioned the separation of the races, although ordering that public facilities be "separate but equal." And through it all, the tortures, the murders, and the lynchings continued.

In the three decades before the Civil War, the "penny press" had ushered in a changing culture. The war, as do all wars, accelerated time and destroyed the natural progression of events; it accelerated the patterns that were determining America's course for the rest of the century. As the number of Americans who could read and write nearly tripled, and the population more than doubled in the four decades following the Civil War, the nation's newspapers extended the concepts of the "penny press" to virtually all the people of the country. In New York City, Joseph Pulitzer and William Randolph Hearst were building newspaper empires that would dominate America's life and conscience. By the end of the century, mass-circulation newspapers, many with circulations well over 400,000—more than ten times that of most of the penny papers—were leading one of the most significant journalistic changes in America's history. It was a change that would see the newspaper expand its role as a medium of expression for all the people, that would make the newspaper one *of* the people, rather than *for* the people.

To fill part of the void left by the newspapers, magazines arose, some to last only a couple issues, others to extend well into the twentieth century. The year the Civil War ended, there were 700 magazines in the country. By the end of the century, there would be more than 4,000.

The magazines would proliferate and profit as they published the essays, short stories, and nonfiction articles that newspapers were forced to give up in order to fulfill their newer, more specialized role. In less than thirty years the nation was blanketed by *Appleton's, Graham's, Scribner's, Century, Harper's, Lippincott's, Putnam's, Everybody's, McClure's, Munsey's, The Atlantic Monthly, Cosmopolitan, The Literary Messenger,* and many others, magazines of great influence that, as World War I approached, went into decline and were lost in history; a few to be resurrected later under different circumstances, in a different time.

THE FIRST MAJOR STUDIES

The Reconstruction era in American history, originally political, had set the stage for a different American lifestyle in the last third of the nineteenth century. By presidential proclamation the Black was no longer a slave, but by the common consensus of many Americans, North as well as South, he was not yet free. It would be many years, and many trials and battles, before the Black could gain even the most basic of human rights.

Dialect verse, short stories, and novels in those years often portrayed the Black in stereotyped images as a lazy, ignorant, irresponsible, immature, sloppy-talking fool. A few, though relatively very few, authors and journalists portrayed the Black as a human being with the wants and needs of any human being. A number of pioneering studies into the nature of Black English were completed during the Reconstruction Cycle, and through the mass media, the people became more aware of a variety of speech they usually thought of as being sloppy or substandard English.

The first major study of Black speech during the Civil War-Reconstruction years appeared in the December 1865 issue of *The Nation,* soon to become one of the most influential magazines in the country.[1] The author, Marcel, was later identified as William Francis Allen who would two years later begin a distinguished twenty-two-year career as a professor of ancient languages and history at the University of Wisconsin. Allen not only indicated reasons to study the language, but also defined the geographical parameters—information seldom given prior to this time:

Fearing, however, that in the progress of civilization among these people these curious features will vanish, I wish to put them on record before they fade from my memory. Ordinary negro-talk,

such as we find in books, has very little resemblance to that of the
negroes of Port Royal, who were so isolated that they seem to have
formed a dialect of their own. Indeed, the different plantations
have their own peculiarities, and . . . profess to be able to determine by the speech of a negro what part of an island he belongs to,
or even, in some cases, his plantation. My observations were confined to a few plantations at the northern end of St. Helena Island.[2]

Thus, Allen not only described part of the process of the creolization
of a language, but may have been the first person to use the medium of
the popular magazine to define and explain a language that was to be
known, and identified by others, as Gullah. His observations of Gullah
represent a "mixed bag" as far as the language scholar is concerned. He
presents a number of valid observations, although calling the language,
"[the result of] phonetic decay [which has] gone as far, perhaps, as possible, and with it the extremest simplification of etymology and syntax."[3]

Allen's conclusions about grammar were as naïve as they were incorrect, but they were, nevertheless, the commonly believed attitudes about
nonstandard language:

I come now to the subject of grammar, upon which I might almost
be entitled to repeat a very old joke, and say that there is no grammar; for there probably is no speech that has less inflection than
that of these negroes. There is no distinction of case, number,
tense, or voice—hardly of gender. Perhaps I am wrong in saying
that there is no number, for this distinction is made in pronouns,
and some of the most intelligent will, perhaps, occasionally make
it in nouns. But "Sandy hat" would generally mean indifferently
Sandy's hat or hats; "dem cow" is plural, "dat cow" singular;
"nigger house" means the collection of negro houses. . . . As to
cases, I do not know that I ever heard a regular possessive, but
they have begun to develop one of their own, which is a very curious illustration of the way inflectional forms have probably grown
up in other languages. If they wish to make the fact of possession
at all emphatic or distinct, they use the whole word "own." Thus,
they will say "Mosey house," but if asked whose house that is, the
answer is "Mosey own." . . .

Verbs have no inflection; but it is true that these have nearly
disappeared . . . Present time is made definite by the auxiliary do
or da, as in the refrains "Bell da ring," "Jericho da worry me." Past
tense is expressed by done, as in other parts of the South. The pas-

sive is rarely, if ever used. "Ole man call John" is the answer when you ask who is such and such a person.[4]

Do, da, and *done,* as Allen described them, are distinct grammatical features in West African Pidgin English, as is the lack of a passive.

His section on the lexicon of the Gullah Black could easily have been included in the section on grammar since many of his observations were not about lexicon, but of West African syntactic rules, a distinction Allen undoubtedly was unaware of:

> *Both* they seldom use; generally "all-two," or emphatically "all-two boff togedder." *One* for alone. "Me one an' God," was the answer of an old man in Charleston when I asked him whether he escaped alone from his plantation. "Heaben 'nuff for me one." [i.e., I suppose, "for my part"], says one of their songs. *Talk* is one of their most common words, where we should use *speak* or *mean.* "Talk me, sir?" asks a boy who is not sure whether you mean him or his comrade. "Talk lick, sir! nuffin but lick," was the answer to the question whether a particular master used to whip his slaves.[5]

The use of the word *talk* in the context mentioned by Allen is a distinct Africanism, an all-pervasive word that takes on different semantic fields depending upon context. It is also probable that the Gullah Black said *suh* rather than *sir;* *fo'* or *foh* rather than *for.*

In the section on phonology, Allen noted:

> The usual softening of *th* and *v* into *d* and *b* is observed among them; likewise a frequent interchange of *v* and *w:* as *veeds* and *vell* for *weeds* and *well;* "De wile' sinner may return" (for *vilest*). This last illustrates also the habit of clipping syllables, which they do constantly: as *lee'* for *little; plant'shun* for *plantation.* The lengthening of short vowels is illustrated in both these words—*a,* for instance, never has our short sound, but always the European sound.[6]

Allen also discussed the use of language as part of a socioeconomic system:

> It is well known that the negroes all through the South speak of their elders as 'uncle' and 'aunt;' from a feeling of politeness, I do not doubt—it seemed disrespectful to use the bare name, and from *Mr.* and *Mrs.* they were barred. On the Sea Islands similar feeling has led to the use of *cousin* towards their equals. Abbreviating this after their fashion, they get co'n or co' (the vowel sound *u* of

cousin) as the common title when they speak of one another. C'Abram, Co'Robin, Co'n Emma, C'Issac, Co'Bob, are specimens of what one hears every day.[7]

Two years later, Allen expanded his study of the Port Royal Gullah. In the introduction to *Slave Songs of the United States,* compiled by Allen, Charles Pickard Ware, and Lucy McKim Garrison, Allen included an analysis of Black speech "as taken down by the editors from the lips of the colored people themselves."[8] Elaborating on the concept of Gullah being "foreign," Allen wrote:

> The strange words and pronunciations, and frequent abbreviations, disguise the familiar features of one's native tongue, while the rhythmical modulations, so characteristic of certain European languages, give it an utterly un-English sound. After six months' residence among them, there were scholars in my school, among the most constant in attendance, whom I could not understand at all, unless they happened to speak very slowly.[9]

Even when speaking very slowly, the Gullah boys might have been unable to communicate with Allen; speaking a foreign language slower does little to increase comprehension.

Allen also made a very interesting observation about language, culture, and the educational process, although it is doubtful that he fully understood all the connotations and ramifications:

> I asked a group of boys one day the color of the sky. Nobody could tell me. Presently the father of one of them came by, and I told him their ignorance, repeating my question with the same result as before. He grinned: "Tom, how sky stan?" "Blue," promptly shouted Tom.[10]

Allen also pointed out that the Gullah Black used *for* in place of *to,* citing the example, "Unky Taff call Co'Flora for drop tater." Although it appears that *for* replaces *to,* in the deep structure of West African Pidgin English the word *fo* has a broader grammatical meaning that is untranslatable in any literal interpretation.

Although Allen thought of Gullah as "phonetic decay," and undoubtedly harbored numerous prejudices about not only the people, but also their language, he nevertheless did contribute the first major analysis of the speech of one of the Sea Islands. Some of his analysis and conclusions may have been in error, but his observations have provided a valuable base of data.

Another of the major studies dealing with Black life, customs, and language was begun on a battlefield during the Civil War, and published in 1870. The book, *Army Life in a Black Regiment,* written by Col. Thomas Wentworth Higginson, was a historical description of the First South Carolina Volunteers, the first regiment of Black soldiers in the history of the United States. Higginson, a White (as were all officers), was a keen observer of human nature, interaction, and language, traits that aided him in his chosen professions of journalism and literature. It was this journalistic ability to observe and analyze society, coupled with his understanding of the Black, that allowed Higginson to avoid many of the stereotypes and prejudices presented as facts by many Reconstruction-era writers.

Discussing his transcriptions of the language of Black soldiers, Higginson pointed out, "The words will be here given, as nearly as possible, in the original dialect; and if the spelling seems sometimes inconsistent, or the misspelling insufficient, it is because I could get no nearer." He also noted that, in his transcriptions of Black speech, he wished to avoid eye dialect—"the occasional use of extreme misspelling, which merely confuse the eye, without taking us any closer to the peculiarity of the sound."[11]

Throughout the book, Higginson brings in the speech of Blacks, at times quoting his soldiers extensively, at other times including only a phrase, a few words, or a sentence or two. Nevertheless, what is included is a major source of data for understanding both the Black and his language during the Civil War and Reconstruction eras:

"Our mas'rs dey hab lib under de [U.S.] flag, dey got dere wealth under it, and eberyting beautiful for dere children. Under it dey hab grind us up, and put us in dere pocket for money. But de fus' minute dey tink dat ole flag mean freedom for we colored people, dey pull it right down again, and run up de rag ob dere own . . . But we'll neber desert de ole flag, boys, neber; we hab lib under it for *eighteen hundred and sixty-two years* and we'll die for it now."[12]

A Black soldier, describing how to investigate a suspicious dugout believed to contain the enemy, says:

"Fus' ting I shoot, and den I shoot again. Den I creep-creep up near de boat, and see who dey 'in 'em; and s'pose anybody pop up he head, den I shoot again. S'pose, I fire my forty rounds. I tink he hear at de [Rebel] camp and send more mans."[13]

A slave, who has just been freed by Black soldiers, explains what happened:

"De people was all a hoein', mas'r . . . Dey was a hoein' in de rice field, when de gunboats came. Den ebry man drap dem hoe, and leff de rice. De mas'r he stand and call 'Run to de wood for hide! Yankee come, sell you to Cuba! Run for hide!' Ebery man he run, and, my God! run all toder way!

"Mas'r stand in de wood, peep, peep, fraid for truss [afraid to trust]. He say 'Run to de wood!' and ebry man run by him, straight to de boat.

"De brack sojer so presumptious, dey come right ahore, hold up dere head. Fus' ting I know, dere was a barn, ten tousand bushel rough rice, all in a blaze, den mas'r's great house, all cracklin' up de roof. Didn't I keer to see 'em blaze? Lor', mas'r, didn't care notin' at all; I was gwine to de boat."[14]

Higginson also included a chapter on the Black spirituals, carefully detailing many of the language features in the lyrics. In one of the spirituals, for example, appeared the phrase "the mighty Myo." According to Higginson: "I could get no explanation of 'the mighty myo' except that one of the old men thought it meant river of death. Perhaps it is an African word. In the Cameroon dialect 'mawa' signified 'to die.' "[15]

Another of his observations from spirituals was that, " '[d]one' is a Virginia shibboleth, quite distinct from 'been' which replaces it in South Carolina. Yet one of their best choruses, without any fixed words, was 'De bell done ringing,' for which in proper South Carolina dialect would have been substituted 'De bell been a-ring.' "[16]

In general, Higginson's recording of the phonological rules is good, and those few rules which he undoubtedly knew but did not include may be attributed to his desire to increase readability. The more important syntactic rules are retained and serve as a major source of data to justify an African language base in American Black English.

BLACK MUSIC

Like folktales and sermons, music is part of the oral tradition of the American Black. It is not an inferior tradition that reflects illiteracy, but a different tradition, one with well-defined roots in tribal Africa. For the American Blacks, their music was more than just a catchy tune, the lyrics more than just pleasant-sounding words. This was their history; a history of a people and their struggles. It was an oral history, to be told in their own language, embellished, changed with the time, and passed on to their children and their children's children. It was music of the human struggle, of life, religion, and customs; it was a history of fear, frustration, joy and hope. Of the music of an earlier period, Frederick Douglass had written:

> I have sometimes thought that the mere hearing of those songs would do more to impress some minds with the horrible character of slavery, than the reading of whole volumes of philosophy on the subject could do. . . . They told a tale of woe which was then altogether beyond my feeble comprehension; they were tones loud, long, and deep; they breathed the prayer and complaint of soul boiling over with the bitterest anguish. Every tone was a testimony against slavery, and a prayer to God for deliverance from chains. The hearing of those wild notes always depressed my spirit, and filled me with ineffable sadness.[17]

By the standards of the White American, the Blacks who had not been exposed to the formal system of American education were illiterate, for they were unable to read and write in the graphemic system that put Standard American English onto paper. But by all other standards, the Blacks were not illiterate, for they did not need pen and paper to record the history of their lives. Their history was recorded in their minds and in the verbal expression of song and folklore; it was an oral medium more expressive and more powerful than the written word could ever be; it was a verbal medium that changed as the people changed, to better meet their needs. The two-dimensional writing could never adequately express the paralinguistic and kinesic language that became so important in the history of the people. And it could never explain the suprasegmental aspects of language.

The music itself became part of the mass media of the era. It was a medium all its own. The music and lyrics bore all the characteristics that distinguish and identify a mass medium: it entertained; it persuaded; it informed. And it sold. Often all four elements were present in one song, as in "Steal Away," a powerful song in which each characteristic was present on two separate levels. On the surface, "Steal Away" was a song of religion, a song that told about Christianity, and which appeared to convince a Black population to become Christian and "steal away to Jesus." It was sung in churches, in meeting halls, and on the plantations. And no White ever protested, for it was "a good and noble thing" that the "immoral and uncivilized savages," as many thought of them, would so wish to be civilized that they would try to become a Christian. On a

deeper level, however, "Steal Away" became the code-song of the in-
famous Underground Railroad; the same words, interpreted differently,
first persuaded Blacks to "steal away home," then informed them when
all preparations were ready to move on to another station on the Railroad.

The medium of music, although passed to generation after generation,
did not seem to be permanent enough for the White person. It seemed
to pass all too quickly. The three-dimensional language of music had to
be reduced to the two-dimensional language of the written word. A
number of writers, such as Allen and Higginson, with great skill froze
Black music at one particular moment in time and preserved it for a
people who were often ignorant about it. But much was lost by taking
the three-dimensional music of the Black and transcribing it into the
two-dimensional world of the White. The third dimension—paralan-
guage, idiophonics, tone, pitch, and nonverbal language—the suprasegmentals, could not be described; the two-dimensional world of writing had made provisions, at that time, only for words. Nevertheless with
words alone, new insights appeared, a new world opened. The language
and culture, as reflected within the music, seemed to be African; it
seemed to have been influenced by the African language and culture.

The nature of Black English and Gullah as separate languages not based
upon English, was recognized by a number of compilers of Black music.
Both Thomas Wentworth Higginson and William Francis Allen, in their
pioneering studies of gospel music, had presented evidence that Black
music, arising from an oral tradition, was not English—certainly not
Standard English. In the introduction to *Cabin and Plantation Songs*
(1874), Thomas Fenner who, with Frederick Rathbun and Bessie
Cleaveland compiled the music for the book, wrote: "It is of course
impossible to explain them [spirituals] in words, and to those who wish
to sing them, the best advice is that most useful in learning to pronounce
a foreign language: study all the rules you please; then—go listen to a
native."[18]

Although there were many reasons to compile and publish Black folk
music, Fenner presented, perhaps, the best reason when he argued:

> It is rapidly passing away. It may be that this people which has de-
> veloped such a wonderful musical sense in its degradation will, in
> its maturity, produce a composer who could bring a music of the
> future out of the music of the past. At present, however, the freed
> men have an unfortunate inclination to despise it, as a vestige of
> slavery; those who learned it in the old time, when it was a natural

outpouring of their sorrows and longings, are dying off, and if efforts are not made for its preservation, the country will soon have lost this wonderful music of bondage.[19]

By the time *Cabin and Plantation Songs* reached its third edition in 1901, at the end of the Reconstruction Cycle, Fenner's fears were beginning to come true.

DIALECT SERMONS

Sermons preached to all-Black congregations by Black preachers inevitably were different from those preached to all-White congregations by White preachers. The "brotherhood of man"—expounded and embellished almost every Sunday in White Christian churches—was a brotherhood of, and for, White men . . . and a separate brotherhood for Black men. The slave was now free; the churches were segregated.

Each race saw life differently. Each had a different history, a different background; each had accepted its own values and worldviews as being different from the other; each had experienced and understood the pains, frustrations, hardships, and even joys of life differently. Perhaps, in the late twentieth century, the language, customs, and beliefs of the two races have become closer, for time alone will allow the merging of beliefs. But in the late nineteenth century, after emancipation, the Black was still considered "different" in the eyes of the White who, just a few years before, had been master and not a legal equal. The Black was still African, not European. His folk tales, sermons, and music reflected an African heritage. It was all he had to hold on to.

Because the religions of the Blacks were "different"—African—the Whites became interested. A few, though very few, looked to the many African-based religions of the American Black to try to understand his soul. Others, with good intentions in their hearts and stereotypes in their minds, set about to convert the Blacks to Christianity—to make them "civilized." Many, however, looked at the religions that had originated in Africa and changed in America, then put them all together, distorted what they saw or heard, and reinforced their own stereotypes about primitive savages practicing a quaint but heathen religion.

During the Antebellum Cycle, the dialect sermons and stump speeches of the burnt-cork minstrels had enthralled the North. Now, during Reconstruction, those same sermons—modified to reflect a changing political climate—would be reduced to print and published in the mass-circulation newspapers, magazines, and dime novels that were blanketing the country. Most of the dialect sermons, like most of what passed as Black English in the mass media, were written by Whites; many writers either did not understand or were incapable of accurately recording Black speech. Some of the dialect sermon writers, however, were quite accurate in reproducing Black speech. Not surprisingly, several of the better dialect sermons were written by Dan Emmett. Some of his sermons were printed on flyers distributed in the 1840s and 1850s, only to be destroyed or lost by time. Still, there remain about forty unpublished sermons in manuscript form—on now-yellowed envelopes and pieces of paper—most which were written in the decade following the Civil War. All show Emmett's mastery of the Black speech of the time, as well as a knowledge of the use of "sweet talk" and other distinctly African syntactic and language characteristics. Apparently, only one of Emmett's sermons, simply titled "Negro Sermon," was published in a general circulation newspaper. It was printed in the *New York Clipper,* a theatre-oriented newspaper which often published much from minstrelsy. Despite some significant internal inconsistency, especially in the phonology, "Negro Sermon" illustrates Emmett's basic awareness of Black religion and language:

> "Bredren an' Sistars—I'm gwine to preach, I is: an' spose dis am de fust time, tho' I come berry nigh it once 'afoa when I swept out de chuch. I'ze gwine to 'splain de troof to de nebberlastin' bressin' ob yoa poar souls. I doesn't mean de soles on yoa foot, de soles ob yoa boots, nor de corns on yoa heels; but, as de pote sez, 'de soul dat lies widin de sarkumdicklar ob de human frame.' Fust ob all, I'm a rale true beleaber; dat is to say, I lubs de wimmin an' hate snakes; an' I can't let dis 'casion slip widout spreadin' myseff 'fore you like a coon-skin on de gable end ob a barn; an' if I was a big bladder blowed full of wind an' stretched wid a blacksniff's bellus, I couldn't feel puffed up wid pride any moa dan I now duz to see myself confruntin' so much speckability.
>
> "Bredren, de text am foun' in de inside ob Job, what Paul draw'd him pistol on 'Feesians, sebenteenth chapter, an' no 'ticklar verse: 'Brezzed am dem dat 'spects nutin', kaze dey aint gwine to get nuttin'!" Dem's em![20]

THE EMERGENCE OF REGIONAL FICTION

The American people following the Civil War had developed an almost insatiable demand for magazine fiction. The war had brought with it a new realization that no longer could any part of the country exist in isolation. Americans began to turn their natural curiosity to regional fiction. It was this curiosity, bolstered by developing mass-circulation magazine markets, that led to a newer awareness of the South and its people—both Black and White.

From the tradition of minstrelsy had come a new genre in American literature, the dialect verse. But it was not until shortly after the Civil War that dialect verse first appeared in the major Northern periodicals.

Although Thomas Dunn English (1819–1902) a lawyer-physician, was White, he was able to capture, through dialect verse, many of the deepest human emotions of the Black. And although his fame never approached his abilities, he was nevertheless a brilliant writer who may have contributed the first major Black English poems to the media. The first of his dialect verses was "Mahs' Lewis's Ride," which appeared in the May 8, 1871, issue of *Lippincott's Magazine*. During that year, three more of English's dialect verses appeared in the popular magazines of the era—*Scribner's Monthly* (July and November), and *Lippincott's Magazine* (September).[21]

The sixteen-verse "Momma Phoebe," may be an unknown classic in American literature. Using the language of the Black, English tore at the soul of his reader as he told about Momma Phoebe and how she lost her two sons—one White, one Black:

Er my hah is de colo' o' sillbah,
    I ain't no mo' d'n fifty yea' ole;
It tuck all dat whiteness f'om mo'nin',
    An weepin', an' tawtah o' soul.
Faw I los' bofe my dahlin' men-child'en—
    De two heve done gone to deh res'—
My Jim, an' my mist'ess' Mahs' William,
    De pah [pair] dat heve nussed at my breas'.

Miss' Lucy she mawied in Ap'il,
    An' I done got mawied in May;
An' bofe o' ow beautiful child'en
    Wah bo'n de same time to a day.
But while I got bettah an' strongah,
    Miss Lucy got weakuh an' wuss;
Den she died, an' dey guv me de baby,
    De leetle Mahs' William to nuss.

De two boys weh fotch up togeddah,
    Miss' Lucy's alongside o' mine;

Ef one got his se'f into mischief,
    De uddah wah not fuh behine.
When Mahs' William he went to de college,
    Why nuffin on ahf den won' do,
But Jeemes, his milk-bruddah, faw sahb
    Mus' git, an' mus' go wid him too.

Dey come back in fo' yea' faw to stay yeh—
    I allow 'twas de makin' o' Jim;
Setch a gemplum, de young colo'd women
    Got pullin' deh caps dah faw him.
But he wasn't a patch to Mahs' William,
    Who'd grown up so gran' an' so tall;
An' he hadn't fo'got his ole momma,
    Faw he hugged me, he did, fo' dem all.

Den Mahs' Dudley was tuck wid de fevah,
    An' I nussed him, po' man, to de las';
An' my husban', Ben Prossah, he cotch it;
    An' bofe from dis life dey done pas'.
Mahs' William, he run de plantation,
    But de niggahs could easy fool him;
An' de place would hev all come to nuffin'.
    Ef 'twant faw ole momma an' Jim.

Well, at las'—I dunno how dey done it—
    Aw Jes' what de fightin' was faw;
But de No'f an' de Souf got a quawlin,
    An' Mahs' William 'd go to de waw.
De folks roun' about, raised a squad'on,
    An' faw cap'en de boys 'lected him'
I prayed he'd stay home wid his people,
    But he went, an' o' co'se he tuck Jim.

It was gran' faw to see all dem hossmen
    Dat numbah'd a hund'ed an' fo',
As dey sot up so straight in deh saddles,
    An' rid in fo' rows by de do'!
An' Mahs' William he sed as he pas' me,
    An' me a'most ready to cry—
'Take good cah o'yourse'f, Momma Phoebe—
    Jim an' I'll be along yeh, bime-by!'

We hea' bout dem two sets a fightin',
    I reckon faw mo' d'n fo' yea';
An' bime-by we la'nt dat de Yankees
    Wid deh ahmy was comin' quite nea'.
An' den deh was fit a great battle,
    Jes' ovah dat hill dat you sees;
We could hea' all deh cannons a boomin',
    An' see de smoke obah dem trees.

I sot in my cabin a prayin'—
    I tought o' my two boys dat day—
An' de noise it went fudda an' fudda,
    'Tell all o' it melted away.
An' de sun it sot awful an' bloody,
    An' a great pile o' fi' in de sky;
An' beyond was de dead men a lyin,
    An' de wounded agwine faw to die.

Den I riz, an' I called faw ole Lem'el;
    An' a couple o' mo' o' de boys;
An' s'I—"Now you saddle de hosses,
    An' be kehful an' don't make no noise.
An' we'll go to de fiel' o' de battle,
    Afo' de las' bit o' de beams
O' daylight is gone, an' we'll look dah
    Faw ow young Mahs' William an' Jeems."

An' dey say—'Dey aint dah, faw sahtin;
    Deh's niffin de mattah, faw sho'!
But seein' it's you, Momma Phoebe,
    O' co'se all de boys yah'll go.
An' dey saddled an' bridled de hosses—
    De bes' had been all tuck away—
An' we retched to de place o' de fightin',
    Jes' on de heels o' de day.

An' oh! what a sight deh wah, honey!
    A sight you could nevvah fo'git;
De piles o' de dead an' de dyin'—
    I see um afo' me eyes yit.
An' de blood an' de gashes was ghas'ly,
    An' shibbed de soul to see,

Like de fiel' o' de big Ahmageddon,
   Which yit is agwine faw to be.

Den I hea'd a woice crying faw 'watah!'
   An' I toted de gode to de place,
An' den, as I guv him de drink dah
   My teahs dey fell obah his face.
Faw he was shot right froo de middle,
   An' his mastah lay dead dah by him;
An' he sed, s'e, "Is dat you dah, momma?"
   An' I sed, s'I, "Is dat you dah, Jim?"

"It's what deh is lef' o' me, momma"
   An' young Mahs' William's done gone;
But I foun' de chap dat had killed him,
   An' he lies dah, clove to de bone.
An' po' young Mahs' William, in dyin',
   Dese wah de words dat he sed:
"Jes you tell you' momma, Mom' Phoebe"—
   Den I scream, faw de dahlin fell dead.

All batte'd an shatte'd and bullets,
   An' hacked wid de bayonet an' swo'd;
An' bleedin', an' cut up, an' mangled,
   An' dead on de meadow so broad.
But what dah was lef' o' de bodies,
   I tuck um, an' washed um, an' dres';
Faw I membe'd de deah blessed babies
   Dat once drawed de milk f'om my breas'.

Den on to de ole plantation
   We toted de cawpses dat night,
An' we guv um a beautiful beryum,
   De colo'd as well as de white.
An' I shall be jined to dem child'en,
   When de jedgmen'-day comes on;
Faw God'll be good to Mom' Phoebe
   When Gab'el is blowin' his ho'n.[22]

The sound and rhythm of the words virtually dominate the poem, as English skillfully wove harsh and soft sounds together to lead the reader to experience the very emotions of Momma Phoebe.

    Although poets of the past may have been subconsciously aware of the psycholinguistic elements present in language, English may have been the first poet to include those elements in Black dialect speech. His deliberate avoidance of the harsh postvocalic /r/ almost dominates his poetry in places; and, it often seems that English included words with the *r* in word-medial or word-final position so that he could deliberately substitute the softer schwa sound. English also has Momma Phoebe say *ovah* and *obah* within two lines of each other; both words occur during a battle scene—the movement (*v* becomes *b*) serves as a partial transition to the following verse of sorrow. Other rules that are readily apparent in the poem are the replacement of the unvoiced *th* by the *f* (*bofe, froo, No'f, nuffin, Souf*); the replacement of the voiced *th* by the *d* (*dey, dis, wid*); consonant cluster reduction (*behine, bes', fiel', jedmen', las', pas'*); and nasalization reduction (*dahlin',* and *fightin'*). The word *sed* is the only eye dialect in the poem.

In 1897, the Frederick A. Stokes Co. published *Fairy Stories and Wonder Tales,* an anthology of many of English's better dialect poems. Seven years later, a more complete 694-page anthology, edited by his daughter, was published. Although English wrote numerous poems, many in Black English, and fifty plays, if he is remembered at all, it is usually for "Ben Bolt," a popular Civil War song which first appeared in the *New York New Mirror,* and was set to music twenty-six different times.

Sidney Lanier, who was to become one of the nation's outstanding poets, teamed with his brother, Clifford, to write "The Power of Prayer; Or, the first Steamboat Up the Alabama." The twenty-verse poem, each verse with twenty lines, became an immediate success shortly after its publication in the May 26, 1875, issue of *The Macon* (Georgia) *Daily Telegraph and Messenger.* Its reprinting in the June 1875 issue of *Scribner's Monthly* brought it national attention. But the publication of dialect verse was still controversial. Lanier, himself, lamented the literary attacks on dialect verse:

> . . . *'ought* one to be a little ashamed of writing a dialect poem,— as at least one newspaper has hinted? And did Robert Burns prove himself no poet by writing mostly in dialect? And is Tennyson's "Death of the North Country Farmer"—certainly one of the very strongest things he ever wrote—not a poem, really?[23]

Nevertheless, apparently encouraged by the success of "The Power of Prayer," the Laniers again teamed up to write "Uncle Jim's Baptist Revival Hymn," which appeared in the May 1876 issue of *Scribner's*

Monthly. Neither Sidney nor Clifford Lanier ever again wrote Black dialect poetry, although they later gave serious consideration to compiling a book-length anthology of Black poetry for Scribner's.

Between the time that "The Power of Prayer" and "Uncle Jim's Baptist Revival Hymn" appeared, *Scribner's Monthly* published a dialect poem written by Irwin Russell, a twenty-two-year-old Mississippi poet who would die just four years later. "Uncle Cap Interviewed" is an eleven-verse poem which, although humorous on the surface, is nevertheless a deeply touching tragedy of what slavery had done for one man. Among the verses is:

> What do I t'ink of freedom? I dunno; it's true I's free;
> But now I's got so awful ole, what good is 'at to me?
> I nebber bodders 'bout it much—to tell de troof, my min'
> Is tuk up now in t'inkin' 'bout de place whar I's a-gwine.[24]

A few inconsistencies in parts of the poem make it appear to be warmed-over Standard English, and the Black English of the poem is distinguished more by phonology than by syntax. Russell probably felt that his reader would be lost in the tangles of dialect and thus lose the musical rhythm he had created.

Through the eyes of "Uncle Caleb," Russell presented some interesting opinions of one element of the mass media, the newspaper:

> I ain't no hand for readin', so ob co'se, it's hardly squar'
> When bus'ness comes to writin', for to 'spect me to be dar—
> But I kin tell repo'tahs all de wisdom dat dey please,
> 'Kase wisdom don't depend upon yo' knowin' abycees.

> You're one de gemmen' writin' fo' de independent press—
> It ain't mo' independent dan yo'sef, sah! So I guess—
> And dem ar kind o' papers needs dey items bol' and free,
> An' so I sees de reason why you's come to talk wid me.

> I allus tells my min' stret out, no mattah what I think,
> As nateral as "Tank you, sah," when asked to take a drink.
> So, now, des ax me questions, an' I'll gib you solid news.
> 'Bout any kin' ob subject you is pleasin' for to choose.

> Dis trade of yours? Well, hit, sah, is a berry gallus-trade,
> Hit's dis a way an' dat a way, accordin' as you's paid.
> You has to do yo' bus'ness on the profitable plan—
> Dey ain't no room for conscience in a daily papah man.

I knows; I swep' an office out for more 'a seben years,
An' mixed de paste, and sharpened up de aidges of de shears,
An' all dat time, dem editors, I'm tellin' you for shore,
Was nebber men enough to lose two bits upon de floor.

But you, sah! Laws a mussy, you's a 'ception to de rule—
I nebber seed no 'potah yit so little like a fool,
An' if you keeps a marchin' on, who knows but what yo' course
Mought bring you up to wear a unicorn upon de force?

Well, mash'r, as you say so, I believe I will take in
A little ob de 'rig'nal—see here, Johnny, gib me gin!
Ahoomh! dat's hot an' hearty! When you wants to know some mo'
Just come to Uncle Caleb, an' he'll gib it to you, sho![25]

A year before he died, Russell wrote "Christmas-Night in the Quarters," perhaps his finest poem. The poem, in reality a poetic operetta, is the story of Black life and culture. In one scene, a Black, just prior to imbibing for the holidays, asks God:

O Mahsr! let dis gath'rin' fin' a blessin' in yo' sight!
Don't jedge us hard fur what we does—you know it's Christmas-
    night;
An' all de balunce ob de yeah we does as right's we kin—
Ef dancin's wrong—Oh, Mahsr! let de time excuse de sin!

We labors in de vineya'd, workin' hard and workin' true—
Now, shorely you won't notus, ef we eats a grape or two,
An' takes a leetle holiday—a leetle restin'-spell—
Bekase, nex' week, we'll start in fresh, and labor twicet as well.

Remember, Mahsr—min' dis now—de sinfulness ob sin
Is 'pendin' 'pon de sperrit what we goes an' does it in:
An' in a righchis frame ob min' we's gwine to dance an' sing;
A-feelin' like King David, when he cut de pigeon-wing.

It seems to me—indeed it do—I mebbe mout be wrong—
That people raly *ought* to dance, when Chrismus comes along;
Des dance bekase dey's happy—like de birds hops in de trees:
De pine-top fiddle soundin' to de bowin' ob de breeze.

We has no ark to dance afore, like Isrul's prophet king;
We has no harp to soun' de chords, to holp us out to sing;
But 'cordin' to de gif's we has we does de bes' we knows—
An' folks don't 'spise the vi'let-flow'r bekase it aint de rose.

You bless us, please sah, eben ef we's doin' wrong to-night;
Kase den we'll need de blessin' more'n ef we's doin' right;
An' let de blessin' stay wid us, untell we comes to die,
An' goes to keep our Chrismus wid dem sheriffs in de sky!

Yes, tell dem preshis anjuls we's a-gwine to jine 'em soon;
We's ready when you wants us, an' it aint no matter when—
O Mahsr! call yo' chillen soon, an' take 'em home! Amen.[26]

In the introduction to *Poems by Irwin Russell,* published posthumously in 1888, Joel Chandler Harris praised Russell:

> Irwin Russell was among the first . . . of Southern writers to appreciate the literary possibilities of the negro character, and of the unique relations existing between the two races before the war, and was among the first to develop them. . . . It seems to me that some of Irwin Russell's negro-character studies rise to the level of what, in a large way we term literature. His negro operetta, "Chrismas-Night in the Quarters," is inimitable. It combines the features of a character study with a series of bold and striking plantation pictures that have never been surpassed. In this remarkable group, —if I may so term it,—the old life before the war is reproduced with a fidelity that is marvelous.
>
> But the most wonderful thing about the dialect poetry of Irwin Russell is his accurate conception of the negro character. The dialect is not always the best,—it is often carelessly written,—but the negro is there, the old-fashioned, unadulterated negro, who is still dear to the Southern heart. There is no straining after effect—indeed, the poems produce their result by indirection; but I do not know where could be found to-day a happier or a more perfect representation of negro character.[27]

More than twenty-five dialect verse poems, most of which appeared in *Appleton's Journal, Puck,* or the *Popular Science Monthly,* are attributed to Russell. However, he wrote many more dialect poems which remain unattributed since he often used pen-names or did not sign his works. He also attempted a dialect verse play and a novel in Black English. However, the play was cancelled in rehearsal when a yellow fever epidemic swept through the area; the novel was never published. In 1879, ten days after *The New Orleans Item* published his poem about where he wished his final resting spot to be, Irwin Russell died in a cheap boarding house in New Orleans. His insights into man and his environment were brilliant. For a few years he would be remembered;

for a few more, his poems, popularized in the mass media, would be read. And then, silence.

Sometime about 1860, in rural Putnam County, Georgia, a twelve-year-old boy began writing for *The Countryman,* a newspaper modelled upon *The Spectator,* one of England's outstanding literary newspapers. Although young, the boy was already familiar with the literature of eighteenth-century England, literature that he had first read in *The Spectator.* For him, it was a pleasure and an honor to be working for *The Countryman,* if only as an office boy. The editor of the newspaper was Joseph Addison Turner, owner of a large plantation with many slaves. Though the young office boy was worked long and hard, he still found time to go to his publisher's plantation, to talk with the slaves, and listen to their stories about animals and people. He talked; he listened; he learned.

A few years later, after having written several articles for *The Countryman,* he became a reporter/printer, first in Macon, then New Orleans, then as an associate editor in Savannah. At the age of twenty-eight, when he began working for *The Atlanta Constitution,* Joel Chandler Harris, destined to become the greatest of all dialect-writers, and one of the nation's most beloved and respected folklorists, was already a veteran journalist. It was at the *Constitution,* where Harris spent more than thirty years, most of them as a senior editor, that he earned his greatest fame.

For several years, Sam W. Small, an excellent observer of people and their customs, had been writing a column of anecdotes and sketches of Black life. As a literary device, he had created an elderly Black, Uncle Si. When the *Constitution* was sold in 1878, Small resigned from the newspaper. The new owner, realizing the popularity of Small's columns, and aware that Harris had written several dialect poems for the *Constitution,*[28] asked Harris to take over the column in addition to his other responsibilities as editorial assistant. At first reluctant, Harris later agreed. His daughter-in-law, Julia Collier Harris, later recalled that Small's resignation "became the means of releasing this rich store of myths and legends which had slumbered for years in an obscure compartment of [my father's] memory."[29] Sam Small's Uncle Si was transformed into Uncle Remus, and a written folk history was born.[30]

In the January 1877 issue of *The Arena,* a popular magazine, W. S. Scarborough had brought to public attention the importance of Black folklore and language within folk tales. However, it was not until the stories of Joel Chandler Harris proved successful that others realized the wealth of available material. The Uncle Remus tales would appear regularly in *The Atlanta Constitution*—as well as in the widely read *Scribner's Monthly* and *The Century Illustrated Monthly Magazine*—until shortly after the turn of the century. The public was enchanted by Harris's mastery of language, and by his stories of life as seen through the eyes of Uncle Remus, the respected former slave who lived through the Antebellum, Civil War, and Reconstruction eras.

The stories of rabbits and turtles, and bears and tarbabies are, themselves, interesting and enjoyable; on their surface merit alone, the Uncle Remus stories may have endured and become part of the great literary folk history of the people. Yet, when the surface is peeled away, there emerges a more powerful tale, allegories of human life with all its frustrations, joys, and sorrows. In these tales are African perspectives on life and its consequences. As was the custom with African stories, in each succeeding generation the tales were told, then retold, embellished and modified. From the folk tales of Uncle Remus we realize, perhaps for the first time, that the life, culture, and languages of the American Black were African in origin.

The process of storytelling doesn't belong exclusively to Uncle Remus. Both Uncle Remus, a middle-Georgia Black, and Daddy Jack, a Gullah Black, are woven into many of the tales. Both characters appear in "Why the Alligator's Back is Rough," published in *Century Magazine;* Harris introduces the story; Daddy Jack tells the tale:

> The night after the violent flirtation between Daddy Jack and 'Tildy, the latter coaxed and bribed the little boy to wait until she had finished her work about the house. After she had set things to rights in the dining-room and elsewhere, she took the child by the hand, and together they went to Uncle Remus's cabin. The old man was making a doormat of shucks and grass and white oak splits, and Daddy Jack was dozing in the corner.
>
> "W'at I tell you, Brer Jack?" said Uncle Remus, as 'Tildy came in. " 'Dat gal atter you, mon!"
>
> " 'Fer de Lord sake, Unk' Remus [said 'Tildy], don't start dat ole nigger. I done promise Miss Sally dat I wont kill 'im, en I like ter be good ez my word; but ef he come foolin' 'longer me I'm des gwine ter enj'in [injure] 'im. Now you year me say de word."
>
> But Daddy Jack made no demonstration. He sat with his eyes closed, and paid no attention to 'Tildy. After awhile the little boy grew restless and presently he said:
>
> "Daddy Jack, you know you promised to tell me a story to-night."

"He wukkin wid it now, honey," said Uncle Remus, soothingly. "B'er Jack," he continued, "wa'n't dey sump'n n'er 'bout ole man Yalligator?"

"Hi!" exclaimed Daddy Jack, arousing himself, " 'e 'bout B'er 'Gator fer true. Oona no bin see da' B'er Gator?"

The child had seen one, but it was such a very little one, he hardly knew whether to claim an acquaintance with Daddy Jack's 'Gator.

" 'Dem all sem," continued Daddy Jack. "Big mout', pop-eye, walk on 'e belly; 'e is bin got bump, bump, bump 'pon 'e tail. 'E dif 'neat' de water, 'e do lif 'pon de lan'."

" 'One tam Dog is bin run B'er Rabbit, tel 'e do get tire; da' Dog is bin run 'im tell him ent mos' hab no bre't' in 'e body; 'e hide 'ese'f by de crik side. 'E come close 'pon B'er 'Gator, en B'er 'Gator, 'e do say:

"Ki, B'er Rabbit! wut dis is mek you blow so? Wut mekky you' bre't' come so?"

"Eh-eh! B'er 'Gator, I hab bin come 'pon trouble. Dog, 'e do run un-a run me."

"Wey you no fetch 'im 'long, B'er Rabbit? I is bin git fat on all da' trouble lak dem. I proud fer yeddy Dog bark, ef 'e is bin fetch-a me trouble like dem."

"Wait, B'er 'Gator! Trouble come bisitin' way you lif; 'e mekky you' side puff; 'e mekky you' bre't' come so."

" 'Gator he do flup 'e tail un 'tretch 'ese'f, un lahff. 'E say:

"I lak fer see dem trouble. Nuddin' no bodder me. I ketch-a dem swimp, I ketch-a dem crahb, I makky my bed wey de sun shiun hot, un I do 'joy mese'f. I proud fer see dem trouble."

" 'E come 'pon you, B'er 'Gator, wun you bin hab you' eye shed; 'e come 'pon you fum de turrer side. Ef 'e no come 'pon you in da crik, dun 'e come 'pon you in da broom-grass."

" 'Dun I shekky um by de han', B'er Rabbit; I ahx um howdy."

" 'Eh-eh, B'er 'Gator! you bin-a lahff at me; you no lahff wun dem trouble come. Dem trouble bin ketch-a you yit."

Daddy Jack paused to wipe his face. He had reported the dialogue between Brother Rabbit and Brother Alligator with considerable animation, and had illustrated it as he went along with many curious inflections of the voice, and many queer gestures of head and hands impossible to describe here, but which added picturesqueness to the story. After awhile, he went on:

"B'er Rabbit, 'e do blow un 'e do ketch um bre't'. 'E pit one

year wey Dog is bin-a bark; 'e pit one eye 'pon B'er 'Gator. 'E
lissen, 'e look; 'e look, 'e lissen. 'E no yeddy Dog, un 'e comforts
come back. Bumbye B'er 'Gator, 'e come drowsy; 'e do nod, nod,
un 'e head sway down tel ma'sh-grass tickle 'e nose, un 'e do cough
sem lak 'e teer up da crik by 'e root. 'E no lak dis place fer sleep at,
un 'e is crawl troo da ma'sh 'pon dry lan'; 'e is mek fer da broom-
grass fiel'. 'E mek 'e bed wid 'e long tail, un 'e is 'tretch 'ese'f out at
'e lenk. 'E is shed 'e y-eye, un opun 'e mout', un tek 'e nap.

"B'er Rabbit, 'e do hol' 'e y-eye 'pon B'er 'Gator. Him talk no
wud; him wullup 'e cud; him stan' still. B'er 'Gator, 'e do tek 'e
nap; B'er Rabbit 'e do watch. Bumbye, B'er 'Gator bre't, 'e do
come *loud;* 'e is bin sno' *hard!* 'E dream lilly dreams; 'e wuk 'e fut
un shek 'e tail in 'e dream. B'er Rabbit wink 'e y-eye, un 'e do
watch. B'er 'Gator, he do leaf 'e dream bahine, un 'e sleep soun'.
B'er Rabbit watch lil, wait lil. Bumbye, 'e do go wey fier bu'n in
da' stump, un 'e is fetch some. 'E say, 'Dis day I is mek you know
dem trouble; I is mek you know dem well.' 'E hop 'roun' dey-dey,
un 'e do light da' broom-grass; 'e bu'n, bu'n—bu'n, bu'n; 'e do bu'n
smaht.

"B'er 'Gator, 'e is dream some mo' lilly dream. 'E do wuk 'e fut,
'e do shek 'e tail. Broom-grass bu'n, bu'n; B'er 'Gator dream. 'E
dream da'sun is shiun' hot; 'e wom 'e back, 'e wom 'e belly; 'e wuk
'e fut, 'e shek 'e tail. Broom-grass bu'n high, 'e bu'n low; 'e bu'n
smaht, 'e bu'n hot. Bumbye, B'er 'Gator is wek fum 'e dream; 'e
smell-a da' smoke, 'e feel-a da' fier. 'E run dis way, 'e run turrer
way; no diffran' wey 'e is run, dey da' smoke, dey da' fier. *Bu'n,
bu'n, bu'n!* B'er 'Gator lash 'e tail, un grine 'e toof. Bumbye, 'e do
roll un holler:

" 'Trouble, trouble, trouble! *Trouble, trouble!'* "

"B'er Rabbit, 'e is stan' pas' da' fier, un 'e do say:

" 'Ki! B'er 'Gator! Wey you fer l'arn-a dis talk 'bout dem
trouble?"

"B'er 'Gator, 'e lash 'e tail, 'e fair teer da' ye't' [tear at the earth],
un 'e do holler:

" 'Ow, ma Lord! *Trouble, trouble, trouble!'*

" 'Shekky um by de han', B'er 'Gator. Ahx um howdy!'

" ' 'Ow, ma Lord! *Trouble, trouble, trouble!'*

" 'Lahff wit' dem trouble, B'er 'Gator, lahff wit' dem! Ahx dem
is dey he'lt' bin well! You bin-a cry fer dey 'wuaintun', B'er 'Gator;
now you mus' beer wit' dem trouble!'

"B'er 'Gator come so mad, tel 'e mek dash troo da' broom-grass; 'e fair teer um down. 'E bin scatter da' fier wide 'part, un 'e do run un dife in da' crik fer squinch da' fier 'pon 'e bahk. 'E bahk swivel, 'e tail swivel wit' da' fier, un fum dat dey is bin stan' so. Bump, bump 'pon 'e tail; bump, bump 'pon 'e bahk, wey da' fier bu'n." . . .[31]

The Gullah spoken by Daddy Jack, like the Middle-Georgia Black English spoken by Uncle Remus, is a creole; it is his first language. In the folk tale about the rabbit and the alligator, the difference in the two languages becomes apparent. Prominent in the Gullah of Daddy Jack are numerous syntactical constructions that reflect a West African language base, such as serial phrasing (" 'e bu'n bu'n—bu'n, bu'n; 'e do bu'n smaht"); the frequent use of a pronominal cross-reference marker (B'er Rabbit, 'e do hab 'e y-eye 'pon B'er 'Gator"); and West African language tense construction ("you bin hab," "hab bin," "I is bin git," "no bin see," "is bin run"). Phonologically, there is a consistent shift between the voiced labiodental fricative [v] to the unvoiced labiodental fricative [f], as in *dife* and *lif*. Daddy Jack also uses the enclitic vowel, as in *shekky* and *mekky*. The lexical item *bumbye* is the Gullah for *baimbai*. The words *w'en* and *w'at*, which may seem to be merely eye dialect, reflect that Black English, Gullah, and many West African languages do not have the aspirated [h] following the [w]. Thus, *when* and *w'en* are pronounced differently.

In the introduction to *Nights With Uncle Remus,* Harris briefly discussed the Gullah language of Daddy Jack. And, if some of Harris's assumptions about Gullah were later shown to be incorrect, it must be remembered that it was not until the mid-twentieth century that there was any extensive linguistic analysis of the language:

The dialect of Daddy Jack . . . is the negro dialect in its most primitive state—the "Gullah" talk of some of the negroes on the Sea Islands, being merely a confused and untranslatable mixture of English and African words. In the introductory notes to "Slave Songs of the United States" [1867], may be found an exposition of Daddy Jack's dialect as complete as any that can be given here. A key to the dialect may be given very briefly. The vocabulary is not an extensive one—more depending upon the manner, the form of expression, and the inflection, than upon the words employed. It is thus an admirable vehicle for story-telling. It recognizes no gender, and scorns the use of plural number except accidentally. "E" stands for "he" "she" or "it," and "dem" may allude to one thing or may include a thousand. The dialect is laconic and yet rambling, full of repetitions, and abounding in curious elisions, that give an unexpected quaintness to the simplest statements. . . .

The trick of adding a vowel to sound words is not unpleasing to the ear. Thus: "I bin-a wait fer you; com-a ring-a dem bell. Wut mek-a (or mekky) you stay so?" "Yeddy," "verry," and probably "churry" are the result of this—heard-a, yeard-a, yeddy; hear-a, year-a, yerry; chur-a, churray. When "eye" is written "y-eye," it is to be pronounced "yi." In such words as "back," "ax," *a* has the sound of *ah*. They are written "bahk," "ahx."[32]

In 1881, D. Appleton & Co. published *Uncle Remus, His Songs and His Sayings; the Folk-Lore of the Old Plantation.* The compilation of thirty-four legends, nine songs, twenty-one sayings, and one story—many which first appeared in *The Atlanta Constitution*—became a best seller. The publication of the Uncle Remus tales in a major New York newspaper established Harris as a leading writer of dialect folklore, and led to a book publishing contract. In a letter to the *New York Evening Post,* which had reprinted many of the tales that first appeared in the *Constitution,* Harris noted, "I feel that if the 'Evening Post' had not taken up Uncle Remus, his legends would have attracted little or no attention."[33]

Harris's introduction to his first book provides a number of interesting observations:

> I am advised by my publishers that this book is to be included in their catalogue of humorous publications, and this friendly warning gives me an opportunity to say that however humorous it may be in effect, its intention is perfectly serious; and, even if it were otherwise, it seems to me that a volume written wholly in dialect must have its solemn, not to say melancholy, features. With respect to the Folk-Lore series, my purpose is to present the legends themselves in their original simplicity, and to preserve them permanently to the quaint dialect—if, indeed, it can be called a dialect—through the medium of which they here become a part of the domestic history of every Southern family; and I have endeavored to give it to the whole a genuine flavor of the old plantation.
>
> Each legend has its variants, but in every instance I have retained that particular version which seemed to me to be the most characteristic, and have given it without embellishment and without exaggeration. The dialect, it will be observed, is wholly different from that [in most literature and] the intolerable misrepresentations of the minstrel stage, but it is at least phonetically genuine.

Nevertheless, if the language of Uncle Remus fails to give vivid hints of the really poetic imagination of the negro; if it fails to embody the quaint and homely humor which was his most prominent characteristic; if it does not suggest a certain picturesque sensitiveness—a curious exaltation of mind and temperament not to be defined by words—then I have reproduced the form of the dialect merely, and not the essence, and my attempt may be accounted a failure. At any rate, I trust I have been successful in presenting what must be, at least to a large portion of American readers, a new and by no means an unattractive phase of negro character.[34]

Harris then discussed the presence of tales similar to those told by Uncle Remus among the cultures of many people throughout the world, and gave hints that the Uncle Remus tales may have been originally African. In the conclusion of his ten-page introduction, Harris noted:

The difference between the dialect of the legends and that of the character-sketches, slight as it is, marks the modifications which the speech of the negro has undergone even where education has played no part in reforming it. Indeed, save in the remote country districts, the dialect of the legends has nearly disappeared.[35]

The second compilation of the Uncle Remus stories, *Nights With Uncle Remus,* proved just as popular as the first collection. However, Harris was still concerned about public acceptance of a book of dialect:

In the Introduction to the first volume of Uncle Remus, a lame apology was made for inflicting a book of dialect upon the public. Perhaps a similar apology should be made here; but the discriminating reader does not need to be told that it would be impossible to separate these stories from the idiom in which they have been recited for generations. The dialect is a part of the legends themselves, and to present them in any other way would be to rob them of everything that gives them vitality.[36]

The introduction of *Uncle Remus and His Friends* (1892) shows Harris still concerned about acceptance of Black English:

Naturally, these stories are written in what is called negro dialect. It seemed to be unavoidable. I sympathize deeply and heartily with the protest that has been made against the abuse of dialect. It is painful, indeed, when the form of the lingo trails on the earth, and the thought flies in the air. I had intended to apologize for the plantation dialect, but a valued correspondent in "The Flatwoods" assures me that "old man Chaucer was one of the earliest dialect writers," and I have recently seen (in the "New York Independent") an essay by Professor March, in which there is a perfectly serious effort to rival the phonetics employed by Uncle Remus.

The student of English, if he be willing to search so near the ground, will find matter to interest him in the homely dialect of Uncle Remus, and if his intentions run towards philological investigations, he will pause before he has gone far and ask himself whether this negro dialect is what it purports to be, or whether it is not simply the language of the white people of three hundred years ago twisted and modified a little to fit the lingual peculiarities of the negro. Dozens of words, such as *hit* for *it, ax,* for *ask, whiles* for *wiles,* and *heap* for a large number of people, will open before him the whole field of the philology of the English tongue. He will discover that, when Uncle Remus tells the little boy that he has a "monstus weakness fer cake what's got *reezins* in it," the pronunciation of *reezins* uncovers and rescues from oblivion Shakespeare's pun on *raisins,* where Falstaff tells the Prince, "If reasons were as plentiful as blackberries, I would give no man a reason on compulsion.[37]

Harris's concern about the acceptability of his dialect-writing may have forced him to be more accurate than his contemporaries in order to avoid negative comments about him, the dialect of the stories, or the Blacks, themselves. However, few persons thought of Harris as just a hack writer trying to be funny by using someone else. From throughout the nation, there came praise for his accurate and honest recordings of Black life and language. Shortly after the first Uncle Remus tales were published in *The Atlanta Constitution,* Sidney Lanier wrote, "It is real negro talk, and not that supositions [sic] negro-minstrel talk which so often goes for the original. It is as nearly perfect as any dialect can well be."[38] Author-critic James Wood Davidson, in a letter to Harris dated December 14, 1880, noted of the Uncle Remus tales:

It is the only *true* negro dialect I ever saw printed. It marks an era in its line—the first successful attempt to write what the negro has actually said, and in his own peculiar way. After so many dead failures by a hundred authors to write thus, and after the pitiful *niaiseries* of the so-called negro minstrels, "Uncle Remus" is a revelation.

Thomas Nelson Page, one of the nation's outstanding regional fiction writers who often used Black English in his stories, also praised Harris:

No man who has ever written has known one-tenth part about the negro that Mr. Harris knows, and for those who hereafter shall wish to find not merely the words, but the real language of the negro of that section, and the habits and mind of all American negroes of the old time, his works will prove the best thesaurus.[39]

J. P. Fruit, in an article for the 1896 volume of *Dialect Notes,* pointed out: "It represents the negro dialect that has most influenced the speech of the South. It is the language of the negroes when they were part and parcel of our households. Then the negro was a great factor in forming our spoken language."[40]

C. Alphonso Smith, a distinguished literary scholar, noted in 1918:

. . . the language of Uncle Remus is more interesting than his philosophy. In the picturesqueness of his phrases, in the unexpectedness of his comparisons, in the variety of his figures of speech, in the perfect harmony between the thing said and the way of saying it, the reader finds not only a keen aesthetic delight but even an intellectual satisfaction. . . . He leaves the impression not of weakness but of strength, not of contractedness but of freedom. What he says he has not only been through but seen through and felt through.[41]

Stella Brewer Brooks, one of the biographers of the life and writings of Joel Chandler Harris, concluded:

[He] stands among the greatest writers of dialect in the world. He developed to the utmost the gift of recording the speech of the plantation Negro. So accurately and fully has he reproduced the dialect that persons in Georgia who have heard the speech of some of the ante-bellum Negroes can almost hear them speaking, through Uncle Remus. In many sections of the country people who were not familiar with his biography thought he was a Negro. Once when he was visiting in New Orleans a large number of citizens turned out to meet him, and when he appeared there were whispers throughout the crowd, "Look, he's white."[42]

The most complete linguistic analysis of the Uncle Remus language was by Sumner Ives as a 1952 doctoral dissertation at the University of Texas. Ives concluded that based upon linguistic investigation and testing, the dialect of Uncle Remus was accurate and reflective of the language of the people of mid-Georgia in the post-Civil War period. However, in an article based upon his dissertation, Ives wrote:

> Actually the field records of the Linguistic Atlas, aside from a very few Gullah records, show hardly any usages in Negro speech which cannot also be found in rustic white speech. And there are many similarities in usage as Harris wrote the dialects. However, the peculiarity of his Negro speech, in addition to the features already listed, consists in the greater density of nonstandard forms, and in the fact that the nonstandard items include, in greater number, features which are associated with Southern plantation speech rather than with Southern mountain speech. Since the same features can actually be found in the speech of both Negro and rustic white, Harris could more justly be accused of exaggerating the actual difference than of failing to indicate it. One additional point should, however, be mentioned. Some of the Atlas field records of rustic white speech show much closer agreement with the Uncle Remus dialect than do others. These other records show features which are neither in the records of cultured informants of the region nor in the records of Negro speech. Instead, they show characteristics of South Midland or Southern mountain speech, and in this respect, their usage agrees substantially with that of the "poor white" as Harris wrote it.[43]

Linguists Richard L. Long and Gilbert D. Schneider have, independently, conducted significant research into the Black language of the Joel Chandler Harris stories. They, like Ives, agree that the dialects presented by Harris were accurate representations of the speech during the post-Civil War era. However, Long and Schneider disagree with Ives on possible origins. While conceding that elements of Black speech may be present in the speech of the "rustic white," both argue that the dialects are more African in origin than American. Schneider, who spent fourteen years in Africa researching and studying West African languages, especially West African Pidgin English, argues:

> There can be little doubt that the language of Uncle Remus is uniquely West African—everything from the obvious phonological constructions, to the less obvious syntactical, ideophonic, and ideolectal constructions. The phrasing and use of African language structures reflect a strong West African, not an American, language base.[44]

During the hundred years following the first dialect tales by Harris, such characters as Brer Rabbit and the Turtle (the classic African tricksters), Daddy Jack, Uncle Remus, and the Tar Baby became entrenched in American folklore. In 1946, the Uncle Remus tales were adapted to yet another medium, the motion picture. *Song of the South,* produced by Walt Disney, became one of the most popular feature films of all time. It was re-released in 1956, 1972, and 1980. Coinciding with the release of the film, Walt Disney Productions produced, in cooperation with the *Western Publishing Co.,* an illustrated *Uncle Remus Stories* for children. By 1975, it had reached its thirty-seventh printing. The foreword of that book offers an explanation for the modified orthography:

> To those few persons who are familiar with the dialect of the Georgia Negro at the time of the Civil War, it may seem an affront to change in any way the speech of Uncle Remus. Unquestionably the dialect is a living part of the legends themselves. But after much consideration, we have been forced to conclude that this dialect is much too difficult for the majority of modern, young readers. For this reason, we have greatly simplified it, although with regret that we had to alter it at all. . . .
>
> We do not expect that the stories in this book can take the place of the original Uncle Remus legends. Perhaps, however, they can help to introduce new readers to these legends. There, in the more archaic but picturesque language of the Old Negro himself, one may enjoy more fully the rhythm and the poetic fantasy that have made these stories classic.[45]

In 1907, Harris and his son, Julian, founded *Uncle Remus's Magazine,* a popular literary magazine that included Black English tales. Within a year, it reached a circulation of 240,000. Harris did not confine the Black languages to his Uncle Remus tales. Had he chosen only to write these tales, his fame would have been assured. But Harris, who was able to combine the style of the literary writer with the observations and talents of the journalist, chose to record stories and histories of the people of the South—Black and White, rich and poor. His expert use of Black language gave his stories an authenticity lacking in stories written by many, if not most, of his contemporaries. Four of his extended short stories of the South were collected in *Mingo, and Other Sketches in Black and White* (1884). Among his other collections of short stories are *Free Joe, and Other Georgian Sketches* (1887), *Tales of the Home Folks in Peace and War* (1898), and *The Making of a Statesman* (1902). His two historical novels—*Sister Jane: Her Friends and Acquaintances*

(1896) and *Gabriel Tolliver: A Story of Reconstruction* (1902)—added
to his reputation as one of the nation's greatest journalist-writers.

Harris had once written that "humor is an excellent thing to live by,
and all things being equal, an excellent thing to die by." A year after he
founded *Uncle Remus's Magazine,* Joel Chandler Harris, who had
brought happiness to so many, died.

Acknowledging the contributions of Joel Chandler Harris, Charles
Colcock Jones, Jr., compiled sixty-one folk tales from the Georgia
swampland for his book, *Negro Myths From the Georgia Coast, Written in the Vernacular.* The language of the folk tales, as Jones indicated in his introduction, is different from that of Uncle Remus or
Daddy Jack. Because the language is internally consistent, Jones's stories
are valuable to compare, in language as well as plot, with those of
Harris, as exemplified in the opening lines of the tale of the rabbit and
the alligator:

> One time Buh Rabbit, him meet Buh Alligator, an eh ax um:
> "Brudder, you tek life berry onconsarne. Enty [Haven't] you come
> pon trouble sometime?" Buh Alligator him mek answer: "No,
> Budder, nuttne nebber bodder me. Me dunno wuh you call trouble.
> Me hab plenty er bittle fuh eat. Me sleep an tek me pledjuh. Wuh
> mak you tink trouble kin come topper me?" Buh Rabbit him berry
> cunnin. Eh yent say nuttne. Eh know Buh Alligator blan [plan]
> come out de ribber an sun isself in de brown-grass fiel. Buh Rabbit,
> eh laugh overside to isself and mek plan to put trouble on Buh
> Alligator.[46]

Time, its own dimension, changes not only reality, but perceptions of
reality. It can make famous the obscure; it can make obscure the famous. And so it was with Harry Stillwell Edwards, at one time one of
the nation's leading journalists, a writer-editor whose career briefly
paralleled—some even say exceeded—that of Joel Chandler Harris. Both
were writers and editors; both lived in, and wrote about Georgia and the
South; and both achieved their literary fame by writing about and reproducing the language of Blacks. When Edwards died at the age of
eighty-three in 1938, *The New York Times* gave him a major obituary;
other newspapers and a nation mourned the loss. Yet, today he is virtually forgotten, his name not even appearing in the major journalism
histories; he was a man whose contributions to American journalism
and society were praised—then ignored and neglected.

An 1877 graduate of the Mercer University School of Law, Edwards turned to journalism and became assistant editor, then editor of the *Macon* (Georgia) *Telegraph* from 1881 to 1887, followed by a year as a staff member of the *Macon Evening News* and *Sunday Times.* Active in politics, he was postmaster of Macon from 1900 to 1913, and in 1904 seconded the nomination of Theodore Roosevelt for the presidency. But he was, throughout his professional life, a journalist—an observer and recorder of life and its people.

More than two dozen of Edwards's short stories were first published in *Century,* one of the nation's leading magazines, which frequently published the articles and stories of Thomas Wentworth Higginson, Mark Twain, and Joel Chandler Harris. "Two Runaways," which first appeared in the July 1886 issue of *Century,* is a brief scene in the life of Isam, slave of Major Crawford Worthington. At the same time every year, about the first of July, Isam ran away, only to return shortly thereafter. The mystery of Isam's escapes worried the Major for, in his mind, it was the only thing about the Black he couldn't understand. And so, when Isam left on this particular July day, the Major went along with him. After learning why Isam left every year, the two men found themselves faced by an angry buck; as the Major came to the rescue, Isam, instead of helping the Major fight the deer, scrambled to safety, explaining that "hit's better fur one ter die'n two. Hit's a long sight better."[47] Finally, the Major, by now exhausted, learned how to enlist Isam's help—offering him land and freedom had not worked, but invoking hoodoo did; and all three—the Major, Isam, and the deer—frightened by Isam's blood-curdling attack, fled. Edwards ends the tale with a message about freedom—that whether slave or master, freedom comes only briefly: "They tell it in Middle Georgia that every year thereafter, until the war cloud broke over the land, whenever the catalpa worm crept upon the leaf, two runaways fled from Woodhaven and dwelt in the swamps, 'loos' en free."[48]

"Two Runaways" later became the lead story in an 1889 anthology, which became one of the nation's best sellers during the latter part of the century. Both Major Worthington and Isam later appeared in several other short stories, each one a study of human reaction and interaction. Many of the tales woven by Edwards were later collected in a series of anthologies which were enthusiastically received and critically acclaimed.

Sons and Fathers, an original novel published in 1896, was awarded the $10,000 first prize in a worldwide literary contest sponsored by *The*

Chicago Record; and more than one million copies of *Aeneas Afri-canus,* the story of a slave as told through fictional letters, were sold since its first publication in 1919.

The dialects spoken by the Blacks in Edwards's stories are, for the most part, internally consistent and reflective of the general rules of speech for both the region and time period. In an article published in the June 1906 issue of *Century,* Edwards explained why there were few faults in his representation of Black English:

> The safest way to write dialect is to write some particular person's dialect after indicating the environment. If this is impossible, don't write in dialect, for it will illustrate nothing. In the stories I have written, every person who speaks, speaks after the fashion of some real person selected for that purpose.[49]

Edwards also illustrated how regional differences affect Black speech, by citing examples of an up-country Negro, a low-country Negro, and a rice-plantation (Island) Negro counting ducks:

> *Up-country Negro:* Hyah one; hyah nuther; hyah nuther on top er de other; hyah nuther wid es foot tied togedder.
> *Low-country Negro:* Dey wan; dey ner'r, dey ner'r top er ter'r; dey ner'r wid 'e foot tie' terge'er.
> *Rice-plantation (Island) Negro:* Yarry wan; yarry narrer; yarry nar-rer 'pan tap er tarrer; yarry narrer widdy futt tie' tergarrer.[50]

Edwards, like most of the other dialect writers of the time, had his biases about the nature of the Black language:

> The common error of people who write upon this subject is to con-sider "dialect" as a language in itself, and not as the abuse of a language; their efforts to establish a standard are based upon this assumption, and they forget that the "negroes," so called, do not constitute a race, but are the descendants of many races. Their speech cannot be described as a "dialect"; "dialects" is better, and the mere statement removes many difficulties. There can be no rule laid down for correct mispronunciation. The English language has a standard pronunciation, yet the educated people of different sec-tions do not agree, in daily use, upon any standard. Is it not absurd, then, to demand that the mispronunciations of the ignorant shall be consistent? . . .
>   The muscles and vocal organs of the negro are always relaxed, his facial muscles lazy and immobile, and his tongue action is in

speech reduced to a minimum. He has no incentive to speak accurately; the result is, he never pronounces a consonant he can avoid, and has an especial objection to *th* and *r,* one of which requires the tip of the tongue against the upper front teeth, the other its elevation to within a fraction of the palatal arch. So, for *this* and *that* he gives us, to be exact, *'tdis'* and *'tdat,'* and for *war,* "wah" ("Befo' de wah"). But the phonetic rule is entirely suspended by the negro's mood and by his emphasis; for he knows how to pronounce the common, everyday words about as well as most people about him, and can succeed by a distinct and well calculated effort.[51]

Nevertheless, although Edwards, like his contemporaries, did not have the linguistic knowledge to analyze Black English, he did have the journalistic knowledge and ability to reproduce that language graphically and to recognize regional differences. For that reason, his articles and short stories are reasonably accurate and important indicators of Black speech at one time during the nation's history.

One of the better recorders of Black folklore was Mrs. A.M.H. Christensen. Using Black dialect, she wrote a number of animal tales for the *Springfield* (Massachusetts) *Republican,* one of the nation's leading newspapers during the late nineteenth century. Several of her tales also appeared in the popular *New York Independent. Afro-American Folk-Lore, Told Round Cabin Fires in the Sea Islands of South Carolina* (1892) was a compilation of eighteen animal tales in Gullah. The tales, as told by Christensen, show distinct African influences upon an American creole. One other fact is important—the first attempts by Christensen to record folklore and language of the Gullah Black preceded those of Harris by two years. However public acceptance did not come until after the Uncle Remus tales became popular.

Between 1894 and 1896, Emma M. Backus contributed to the *Journal of American Folk-Lore* a number of folk tales in a modified Black English. An editor's note, by William Wells Newell, explains reasons for the language modification:

In printing the tales here given, the dialect has been disregarded, so far as phonetic variations are concerned; on the other hand, the errors of grammar, abbreviations, and syncopations have been retained. The spelling has been changed to the common English form, except in the case of a very few words, so familiar as to be perfectly comprehensible. It is obviously impossible by means of the regular alphabet to reproduce negro dialect with any accuracy. A phonetic alphabet is essential for such purpose, and it is desirable that a certain number of texts in such alphabet be noted, but evidently useless to multiply such texts. The dialect being once given, any person who has made himself master of it can read the common English orthography with proper dialectic sound and inflection. The dropping of the *r,* the alteration of *th* into *d,* and similar changes, can easily be reproduced. But the attempt to indicate the manner of enunciation by the usual English signs results in confusions and contradictions innumerable, and after all the dialect is without interest, save for those previously intimate with it. An equally serious fault is that the meaning and real interest of the tale is disguised; a dialectic story is apt to be a mere piece of jargon, in which the lack of deep human interest is atoned for by a spelling which is usually mere affectation. As an individual opinion, and with reservation of the right to alter the method in any particular case, the advice may be given to collectors, to follow the expression of the reciters word for word, to observe elisions and contractions, but otherwise to use ordinary English orthography. If they are capable of indicating the peculiarities of the dialect by means of a phonetic alphabet, or even by a minute account of the manner of treating the different letters, so much the better. This counsel is intended, not to contradict but to emphasize the principle, that the utility of a record depends upon its faithfulness word for word; no attempt need be made to correct the grammar.[52]

Nevertheless, the folk tales recorded by Emma M. Backus, because of language modification, tend to read as if they were told originally in a bastardized Standard English, rather than in a Black English.

Katherine Sherwood Bonner MacDowell, who wrote under the name Sherwood Bonner, contributed two books to the collection of Black folklore and language. *Dialect Tales* was published in 1883; *Suwanee River Tales* was published the following year. Alexander Bondurant, a distinguished literary critic, had nothing but praise for her: "Her writings reveal a keen insight into character and an unusual power in character portrayal; a delicate and subtle sense of humor; a deep human sympathy, which often opens the fountain of tears; and an unusual power in describing nature in many moods.[53]

As one of her numerous insights into the human condition, Mac-

Dowell, through the language of Aunt Anniky, discusses a troublesome but common problem among Blacks:

"I has gummed it fur a good many ye'rs . . . but not wishin' ter be ongrateful ter my obligations, I owns ter havin' fine nateral teef. But dey is po' sogers: dey shirks battle. One ob dem's got a little somethin' in it as lively as a speared worm, an' I tell you when anything teches it, hot or cold, it just makes me dance!. An' anudder is in my top jaw, an' ain't got no match fur it in de bottom one; an' one is broke off nearly to de root; an' de las' two is so yaller dat I's ashamed ter show 'em in company an' so I lif's my turkey tail ter my mouf every time I laughs or speaks."[54]

The portrayal of a woman and her problems shows Sherwood Bonner's sensitivity to the American slave, a sensitivity that could only be brought out by recording the language of the slave, herself.

Lafcadio Hearn, born into poverty in 1850 on the Ionian Islands, became one of America's outstanding journalists, and one of Japan's outstanding university professors. After receiving his formal education in France and England, Hearn went to America in 1869. Three years later, at the age of twenty-two, he became a reporter for the *Cincinnati Enquirer*. During his three years on the *Enquirer* (1872–75) and two years on the *Cincinnati Commercial* (1875–77), he earned a national reputation as an outstanding feature writer, a reporter able to bring out the innermost humanity of Cincinnati's less fortunate persons. It was this concern, some say an almost morbid concern, for society's "castoffs" that was the base for Hearn's studies of Creole life and language.

Between 1878 and 1881, Hearn was associate editor of the *New Orleans Item;* between 1881 and 1887, he was on the staff of the *New Orleans Times-Democrat*. During this nine-year period, he also wrote articles about the Creole life for leading magazines, including the popular and influential *Harper's Weekly*. However, it was an 1885 book which proved to be one of the most significant studies of Creole life and language. Now extremely rare, *Gombo Zhèbes* was a compilation of 350 proverbs of six Atlantic-area Creoles; each proverb was presented in its original language, then translated by Hearn into French and English. Even more remarkable was the fact that Hearn had previously transcribed each proverb in the phonetic language, a linguistic transcription which was just beginning to prove its value in folklore study.

Throughout his career, Hearn tried to understand the integration of language and culture. In "The Scientific Value of Creole," which ap-

peared in the June 14, 1886, issue of *The New Orleans Times-Democrat,*
Hearn wrote:

> The . . . picturesque history of the old Creole life would prob-
> ably have had no worthy and durable record were not the dialect
> it had created found to possess an absolute unique value for sci-
> ence. To philologists the Creole patois offered the astonishing spec-
> tacle of a language transformed and reformed within the brief in-
> terval of a century. . . .
>
> The Negro had a great variety of masters and a great variety of
> tongues thrust upon him; yet neither Dutch, nor Spanish, nor Por-
> tuguese,—much less English,—seemed to satisfy his linguistic wants.
> He manufactured various Creole dialects from his various Latin
> masters, while he only made a botch of English and Dutch. . . .
> [T]he form of the patois is solidly fixed and sharply defined, vary-
> ing but little in colonies thousands of miles away from each other,
> and among the descendants of slaves who spoke many different dia-
> lects in Africa.[55]

For an article in *Harper's Weekly,* Hearn pointed out that "creole is
the maternal speech; it is the tongue in which the baby first learns to utter its thoughts; it is the language of family and home."[56] Thus Hearn,
a journalist, not a linguist, was able to clearly distinguish the development and nature of a pidgin and how it basically differed from a creole.
And equally important, he had pointed out that knowledge and analysis
of language was one method for the preservation of culture and history.
Hearn spent 1888 and 1889 as a foreign correspondent in Martinique
and the West Indies. Beginning in 1890, and until his death in 1904, at
the age of fifty-four, Hearn lived in Japan, first as a correspondent for
Harper's Weekly, then as a teacher of English as a foreign language.
For ten years he was professor of English literature at the prestigious
Imperial University in Tokyo. Hearn is credited as having been one of
the few persons to bring the life, language, and culture of the Japanese
people to the Western world. As he was admired by the Creoles of
Louisiana, so was he admired and deeply respected by the people of Japan. His lectures were well attended; his books about America and Japan were required reading throughout the nation. Lafcadio Hearn, the
journalist, integrated language and culture, and helped preserve the history of two diverse peoples.

About the same time Lafcadio Hearn was beginning his journalistic career in Cincinnati, George Washington Cable (1844–1925) was ending

a brief, but highly respectable career with the *New Orleans Picayune*. According to Cable, he was fired by the *Picayune* for reasons not too uncommon in newspaper journalism—"I wanted to be always writing and they wanted me to be always reporting. This didn't work well . . . and I went back to bookkeeping."[57]

It was while a corporate bookkeeper for Black and Co., a position he was to hold for ten years, until 1881, that Cable wrote several of his stories about the Louisiana Creole, many of which appeared in *Scribner's Monthly*. Interestingly, one of his better stories, "Posson Jone," was published in *Appleton's* when *Scribner's* found it too coarse. Nevertheless, Cable was *Scribner's* first major "find." In 1879, *Scribner's* published *Old Creole Days,* a collection of seven tales. Shortly after that, *Scribner's* published, also in book form, *The Grandissimes,* which had run serially in the magazine during 1878, and was extensively praised in five editorials in the *New Orleans Item* between December 26, 1879, and January 13, 1881. The reviewer was Lafcadio Hearn.

Although Hearn and the Northern media praised Cable, the South— Black, White, and Creole—despised him. According to Edward Laroque Tinker, himself an authority on Southern Creole, and a biographer of both Cable and Hearn:

> The very reasons which made Cable famous in the North made him infamous in the South. Not one of her authors had ever before dared to write of the Negro except as a loyal, humble, family retainer, or as a black-face buffoon. The Negro as a flesh-and-blood human being, as a living problem in adjustment, was so sore a subject that by tacit agreement Southern society ignored the existence of this aspect and, on pain of ostracism, permitted no one to discuss it.[58]

Tinker discusses another reason why Cable's stories of quadroons and octaroons were hated by the Southern Whites, while praised by the Northern Whites:

> [A] social order . . . doomed these near-white women to an almost inevitable life of immorality. Slavery, to be sure, had been abolished, but the war rancors remained and the treatment of enfranchised blacks was still an inflamed question between the two sections of the country; so it was quite natural for the former abolitionists to welcome enthusiastically this new attack upon one of slavery's consequences—the tragedies born of miscegenation. Deep hatreds die hard, and perhaps no book since *Uncle Tom's Cabin*

stirred up as much enthusiasm as did *Old Creole Days*. These stories were so vivid, interesting, and full of sentiment that they could stand upon their own merits; and even in England, where no such bias existed, they were immediately hailed as masterpieces.[59]

But if the Southern Whites despised Cable for making the Black and the Creole a respectable part of fiction, the Creoles hated Cable even more. According to Tinker:

> The two people most heartily hated by the Creoles of Louisiana were "bloody" O'Reilly, who, when governor, executed five of their compatriots for conspiring against Spanish rule, and George Washington Cable, who had the temerity to write of their race.
>
> The Creoles considered Cable more loathsome than a Carpetbagger; called him a renegade scalawag; and when they mentioned his name they spat. "Besides," they asked, "were there no Southern ladies and gentlemen to write about, that he had to parade quadroon women across his pages as heroines and dish up the very dregs of society?" . . .
>
> [T]hey inherited from Old World ancestors an arrogant pride so sensitive that they never forgave a mention in print, and they feared that people in other parts of the country who read his stories would get the impression that their race was not of unsullied white descent. Their sense of personal dignity was further offended because Cable made his Creole characters speak a quaint lacerated dialect. Whether or not his notation of their peculiarities of pronunciation was philologically correct is open to discussion; but that many of the Creoles of his day spoke English with a decided foreign accent and used strange literal translations of French idioms, cannot be denied. . . . [Cable] could not persuade the Creoles that he was not holding them up to ridicule and advertising them to the world as an ignorant, unlettered people.[60]

Other novels by Cable were *Madamme Delphine* (1881), *Dr. Sevier* (1885), which was first serialized in *Scribner's Monthly, Bonaventure* (1888), *The Cavalier* (1901), and *Bylow Hill* (1902). *Strong Heart* (1899) was a compilation of short stories.

By the mid-1880s, Cable began to concentrate on another form of the mass media, becoming an outstanding and highly controversial pamphleteer. The former Confederate cavalry soldier, a fierce abolitionist, turned his talents to exposing conditions in prisons, insane asylums, and the unfair political and social treatment of persons and races. He would be remembered as a master reporter about people—their lives, culture, language, and conditions.

In November 1884, George Washington Cable, "the word-painter of Creole life," and Samuel Langhorne Clemens who, under the name Mark Twain was known as "the great American humorist," began a four-month lecture tour of the United States. However, by the time the tour—one of the most successful tours in American literary history—concluded in February, the two men, who had been friends for three years, were barely on speaking terms. Together in the same hotels, at the same dinners, and on the same stage, the two found themselves under a new kind of pressure. Each had his own peculiar idiosyncracies—Cable was orderly, meticulous, and very Christian; Twain was an atheist, and of the "common folk." (After an embarrassing silence, they rekindled their friendship for more than two decades.)

The two had much in common. Both were Southerners and abolitionists who had seen the brutality of slavery and the racism that pervaded not only the South but an entire nation after the Civil War. And each turned to the mass media to point out the injustices and inequalities in society—Cable, by using journalistic fiction and pamphleteering as his genre; Twain, by using humor and biting satire. But occasionally even the sharpest edge of satire could not bring out the truth as much as a carefully worded article that laid out the facts, naked and bold.

A short article in the November 1874 issue of *The Atlantic Monthly* was a powerful indictment against slavery. Entitled "A True Story, Repeated Word for Word as I Heard It," the article focused upon Aunt Rachel, a sixty-year-old slave who is talking to her friend Samuel Langhorne Clemens, himself a fierce abolitionist prior to the Civil War.[61] Clemens had asked her if she had any trouble during her sixty years:

"Has I had any trouble? Mist. C——— I's gwyne to tell you, den I leave it to you. I was bawn down 'mongst de slaves; I knows all 'bout slavery, 'case I ben one of 'em my own se'f . . .

"Well, bymeby my ole mistis say she's broke, an' she got to sell all de niggers on de place. An' when I heah dat dey gwyne to sell us all off at action in Richmon', oh de good gracious! I know what dat mean! . . .

"Dey put chains on us an' put us on a stan' as high as dis po'ch,—twenty foot high,—an' all de people stood aroun', crowds and crowds. An' dey'd come up dah an' look at us all roun', an' squeeze our arm, an' make us git up an' walk, an' den say, 'Dis one too ole,' or 'Dis one lame,' or 'Dis one don't 'mount to much.' An dey sole my ole man, an' took him away, an' dey begin to sell my chil'en an' take *dem* away, an' I begin to cry; an' de man say, 'Shet up yo' dam blubberin',' an' hit me on de mouf wid his han'. An' when de las' one was gone but my little Henry, I grab' *him* clost up to my breas' so, an' I ris up an' says, 'You shan't take him away,' I says; 'I'll kill de man dat tetches him!' I says. But my little Henry whisper an' say, 'I gwyne to run away, an' den I work an' buy yo' freedom.' Oh, bless de chile, he always so good! But dey got him—dey got him, de men did; but I took an' tear de clo'es mos' off of 'em, an' beat 'em over de head wid my chain; and *dey* give it to *me,* too, but I didn't mine dat.

"Well, dah was my ole man gone, an' all my chil'en, all my seven chil'en—an' six of 'em I hain't set eyes on ag'in to dis day, an' dat's twenty-two year ago las' Easter."[62]

Aunt Rachel's son, Henry, finally finds his mother. It was during the war and he was a soldier for the Union, his sole purpose being to go through the South trying to find her.

Twain shows a great consistency in his writing, and because he is able to distinguish a number of hard-to-detect speech patterns (for example, *se'f*), it might be assumed that preservation of the voiced labiodental fricative [v] rather than its replacement by the voiced bilabial stop [b] (as in *over* and *of*) reflects not an error, but what Twain actually heard or honestly perceived.

Samuel Langhorne Clemens was born June 30, 1835, in Florida, Missouri. Four years later his family moved to Hannibal, Missouri, which was to form the background for many of his later stories. About eighteen, having been a printer's apprentice on his brother's newspaper, Clemens became a tramp printer, stopping during the next three years at several cities including St. Louis, New York, Philadelphia, and Keokuk, Iowa. During those three years, a number of his short humor articles appeared in newspapers. In 1856, he returned to Hannibal, to the Mississippi River, and became a riverboat pilot until the Civil War closed the river to travel. Following brief service in the Confederate Army— according to his memoirs he "resigned" after two weeks—he moved to Virginia City where he was to begin a long and distinguished journalistic career, first as a reporter, then as acting managing editor for the Virginia City *Territorial Enterprise,* then as a reporter and correspondent in California for the *San Francisco Call,* the *San Francisco Bulletin,* the *Alta Californian,* and the *Sacramento Union.*[63]

On November 18, 1865, the New York *Saturday Press* published "The Jumping Frog of Calaveras County." According to Twain, another publisher had rejected the manuscript and passed it along to Henry Clapp, editor of the *Saturday Press,* who published the article in what was to be the final issue of the newspaper. But something happened—the story of the jumping frog was reprinted in newspapers throughout the United States and England. According to Twain, "It certainly had a wide celebrity . . . but I was aware that it was the frog that was celebrated. It wasn't I. I was still an obscurity."[64] Nevertheless, the "Jumping Frog" launched Twain into a national prominence that would, within a decade, establish him as the nation's leading humor writer, surpassing the fame of his close friend Artemus Ward who had first brought the "Jumping Frog" article to the attention of the New York publishing world.

But Twain, whether he wrote humor or reported news events, often combining the two forms in the same article, was always the journalist, for he determined that the difference between being merely a writer and being a journalist was that the journalist was an observer, a person trained to see and report that which most persons overlooked. It would be his journalistic skill, honed by experiences as a tramp printer, riverboat pilot, and newspaper reporter that would establish his literary reputation. In 1876, the publication of *The Adventures of Tom Sawyer* established him as one of the nation's leading novelists.

On July 29, 1877, a copyright was issued to Twain's light tragedy *Cap'n Simon Wheeler, The Amateur Detective.* The drama, never produced, was later changed to a comic novel which was not published until 1963. Toby, an "illiterate" Black fascinated by the *sound* of language, is of interest. Since Toby can neither read nor write, he asks his master to write a letter for him. Toby has a book of "suggested" letters that someone else has written. This upsets the master:

> "Do you mean to say you're not going to dictate the letter yourself, but are going to get it out of the book?"
>
> "Dictate?" said Toby, scratching his head perplexedly; "Dic . . . Mars. Hale, please don' bust dem big words at me, I don't stan' no chance 'gin 'em. Yes, Mars. Hale, dat's a prime book; I gits de mos' o' my letters out'n dat book; dey ain't nuffin in de worl' but what dat book know 'bout it. I reckon Sol'mon writ dat book, but I don' know. But it *soun* like Sol'mon, sometimes,—so de ole nigger preacher say,—and den it know so much, and say it so beautiful.— Mars. Hale, dah's *beautiful* words in dat book—great long beautiful

words dat dey ain't *no* man kin understan'. My ole mother and my brother Jim is mons'us proud o' me on accounts o' dem letters dat I gits out'n dat book: dey ain't no mo' niggers roun' heah but me dat sends letters to anybody."[65]

Hale reads the letter and finds that it has many euphemisms meant to disguise a "Dear John" letter to a sailor. After he reads the letter aloud, Toby exclaims:

"Dat's de one, Mars. Hale, dat's de one! Don't dem words taste good in you' mouff! don't day 'mind you of suckin' a sugar-rag when you was little? and don't dey *soun'* softy and goody! Don't dey blobber-blobber-blobber along like buttermilk googlin' out'n a jug! King Sol'mon he must 'a' write dat, kase I reckon dey ain't no-body else dat kin bounce words aroun' like dat. O yes, dat's de right letter, Mars. Hale. I know'd dey warn't no mistake 'bout it."

"But here! Do you really want this letter sent to your *mother?*— and as coming from *you?*"

"Yes, dat's it, Mars. Hale. You see, fust I got Miss Milly to write out dis letter and sent it to my brother Jim an' he—"

"To your brother Jim! This same letter?"

"Yes, Mars. Hale. You see Jim he's a fiel' han'; works in de cotton fiel'; so de white chillen dey read de letter to Jim, an' lots o' other niggers was dah, f'm de plantations aroun', kase it was a Sunday; an' dey tole everybody 'bout it, an' so every Sunday sence den de niggers come dah to hear dat letter; some of 'em walks fifteen mile; an' dey all say *dey* ain't never hear so sich letter as dat befo'. Dey keeps a-comin'—de same niggers an' new ones—to hear dat letter—dey don't ever seem to git enough of it. Well you see dat make Jim mighty proud. He tote de letter 'roun' all de time, an' dad fetch him he mos' too good to speak to anybody now, less'n it's seven-hund'd-dollar niggers and sich-like high flyers. Well, you see, my ole mother she don' like to see Jim a-havin' it all to hisself so; so she ast one o' de little misses for to write and ast me to write *her* dat letter, too. An' you bet she'll be powerful glad when she git it, Mars. Hale. She's a good ole 'oman, too, dat she is!"[66]

Although there are a few "flaws" in the dialect-writing (for example, the many contractions, and a few mild inconsistencies as *an'* and *and*), the dialect is, for the most part, accurately recorded. In the words of Toby, Twain has been able to illustrate the fact that the language itself has beauty, rhythm, and tone; that the language, the very sound of the language, is important.

Twain also recorded Black speech in *The Gilded Age* (1873; written with C. D. Warner), *The American Claimant* (1892), and *Tom Sawyer Abroad* (1894). *The American Claimant* was first serialized by Mc-Clure's Syndicate, and published in England's *Idler Magazine*.

Twain's strongest portraits of Blacks were those of Nigger Jim in *The Adventures of Huckleberry Finn,* and Roxana (Roxy) in "Pudd'n-head Wilson," both of which appeared in *Century Magazine*—"Pudd'n-head Wilson," serialized in its entirety, and "Huckleberry Finn," as three excerpts from the yet unpublished book. According to literary critic Robert Rowlette, "Twain's sympathetic portraits of Jim and Roxy are tacitly assured to constitute an attack, more subtle and damaging than Mrs. Stowe's [Harriet Beecher Stowe], on the stark injustices of the slave system."[67] Twain carefully and meticulously wove together the characterization of Nigger Jim so that no one could overlook the power of life placed within the heart of Nigger Jim. This was a man so fiercely opposed to slavery and so determined to gain freedom—not only of the body but of the soul as well—that he tolerated the tricks and trials put upon him by Huck. The language of Nigger Jim reinforces his basic character. Jim's inner humanity is never brought out so well as in the scene where Huck in a canoe, and Jim on a raft, are separated in a dense fog. Jim never gives up hope of finding Huck. Later, Huck finds the raft, gets on it, and almost convinced the gullible Jim that the whole adventure has been a bad dream. Jim is hurt:

> "When I got all wore out wid work, en wid de callin' for you, en went to sleep, my heart wuz mos' broke bekaze you wuz los', en I didn't k'yer no mo' what become er me en de raf'. En when I wake up en fine you back agin', all safe en soun', de tears come, en I could a got down on my knees en kiss' you' foot, I's so thankful. En all you wuz thinkin' bout wuz how you could make a fool uv ole Jim wid a lie. Dat truck [raft] dah is *trash;* en trash is what people is dat puts dirt en de head or dae fren's en makes 'em ashamed."[68]

Not all of "Huckleberry Finn" is so serious; Twain has some fun with the church:

> "What did you do with the ten cents, Jim?" [asked Huck].
> "Well, I 'uz gwyne to spen' it, but I had a dream, en de dream tole me to give it to a nigger name' Balum—Balum's Ass dey call

him, for short; he's one er dem chuckle-heads, you know. But he's lucky, dey say, en I see I warn't lucky. De dream say let Balum inves' de ten cents en he'd make a raise for me. Well, Balum he tuck de money, en when he wuz in church he hear de preacher say dat whoever give to de po' len' to de Lord, en boun' to git his money back a hund'd times. So Balum he tuck en give de ten cents to de po', en laid low to see what wuz gwyne to come of it."

"Well, what did come of it, Jim?"

"Nuffin' never come of it. I couldn' manage to k'leck dat money no way; en Balum he couldn'. I ain' gwyne to len' no mo' money 'doubt I see de security. Boun' to git yo' money back a hund'd times, de preacher says! Ef I could git de ten *cents* back, I'd call it squah, en be glad er de chanst."[69]

Why Twain would have Jim say *cents,* which includes a word-final consonant cluster, and *inves'* or *len',* which do not have word-final consonant clusters, or why some words include a postvocalic /r/ (for example, *Lord*) and some do not (for example, *po'* and *mo'*) is only partially explained by James N. Tidwell:

[Twain] revealed the salient low colloquial, Southern, and Negro features of Jim's speech, not by a thoroughly "consistent" spelling of every word, but by what is better, an accurate one. His failure to systematize his spelling allowed him to write every word as it would sound in a given sentence, and thus he could represent in full detail the nuances of Jim's pronunciation.[70]

Twain, himself, had a few words about dialect. In an explanatory note to *The Adventures of Huckleberry Finn,* he wrote:

In this book a number of dialects are used, to wit: the Missouri negro dialect; the extremest form of the backwoods South-Western dialect; the ordinary "Pike-County" dialect; and four modified varieties of this last. The shadings have not been done in a haphazard fashion, or by guess-work; but pains-takingly, and with the trustworthy guidance and support of personal familiarity with these several forms of speech.

I make this explanation for the reason that without it many readers would suppose that all these characters were trying to talk alike and not succeeding.[71]

It has only been in recent years that "Pudd'nhead Wilson" has received its deserved recognition. The story was serialized in the December 1893, to June 1894 issues of *Century;* after only two issues had appeared, it was strongly denounced. A review in the *Southern Magazine* called it "stupid . . . malicious and misleading."[72] Other periodicals were quick to take on the attack. Twain's historical-fiction story of race problems in the country had upset and torn apart the nation. It was more than three decades after the Emancipation Proclamation was issued, and yet the Blacks were not free except in the physical sense. In those three decades, the nation had grown weary of the battles over the status of Blacks. A decade before "Pudd'nhead Wilson" was published, the United States had decided that the racial problems in the South should be decided by the South and not by the federal government. And when, later in the century, laws were enacted that established literacy tests for voting, effectively disenfranchising the Blacks, and that sanctioned segregation, there was little argument in either the North or the South. Peace had finally been attained at the expense of a race of people. But Twain, still the strong abolitionist, still fighting for the human rights of all people, would not allow this "peace" to remain. His weapon was his writing. With "Pudd'nhead Wilson," he again had forced the nation to look at its collective conscience, and if the nation did not like what it saw, it was because Twain had told the truth. Emerging from his insightful study of the human condition is the unforgettable Roxy:

> To listen to Roxy's manner of speech, a stranger would have expected her to be black but she was not. Only one sixteenth of her was black but that sixteenth did not show. . . .
>
> To all intents and purposes, Roxy was as white as anybody, but the one sixteenth of her which was black outvoted the other fifteen parts and made her a negro. She was a slave and saleable as such. Her child was thirty-one parts white, and he, too, was a slave. . . .[73]

Thus Twain was also putting doubts into the minds of those persons who believed that broad noses and thick lips were responsible for the way Blacks talked. Here, a woman with none of the features attributed to the Black, spoke Black English because she was treated as a Black, and had grown up and lived among the slaves of the plantation. James D. Hart, a literary scholar, summarizes the plot:

> On the Mississippi during the 1830's . . . lives Percy Driscoll, a prosperous slave owner. On the day that his son Tom is born, his nearly white slave Roxy gives birth to a son, Chambers, whose father is a Virginia gentleman. Since Tom's mother dies when he is only a week old, he is raised by Roxy along with Chambers, whose

twin he is in appearance. Roxy, fearful that her son may some day be sold down the river, changes the two children, and upon the death of Percy, his brother Judge Driscoll adopts Chambers believing him to be Tom.[74]

Thus, although raised by Roxy, Chambers, who was unaware of his true identity, was treated as a White; his language represented the Missouri English of his White peers, not the Black English of his mammy. Tom, the White who grew and lived as a Black, and was called Chambers, spoke a variety of Black English. And each took on the lifestyle and characteristics society demanded of them. In one scene, Roxy, destitute and old, asks her biological son, a White by society, if he will help her:

> "Marse Tom, I nussed you when you was a little baby, en I raised you all by myself tell you was 'most a young man; en now you is young en rich, en I is po' en gitt'n ole, en I come heah b'lievin dat you would he'p de ole mammy 'long down de little road dat's lef' 'twixt her en de grave. . . . Ain't you ever gwine to he'p me, Marse Tom?"
>
> "No! Now go away and don't bother me any more."[75]

After the passage of time and many hardships, Roxy has had enough:

> "I mean dis—en it's de Lord's truth. You ain't no more kin to ole Marse Driscoll den I is! *dat's* what I means!" and her eyes flamed with triumph.
>
> "Yassir, en *dat* ain't all. You's a *nigger!—bawn* a nigger en a *slave!*—en you's a nigger en a slave dis minute; en if I opens my mouf ole Marse Driscoll'll sell you down de river befo' you is two days older den what you is now!"
>
> "It's a thundering lie, you miserable old blatherskite!"
>
> "It ain't no lie, nuther. It's jes de truth, en nothin' *but* de truth, so he'p me. Yassir—you's my *son.—*"
>
> "You devil!"
>
> "En dat po' boy dat you's be'n a-kickin' en a-cuffin' today is Percy Driscoll's son en yo' *marster—*"
>
> "You beast!"
>
> "En *his* name's Tom Driscoll, en you en *yo'* name's Valet de Chambers, en you ain't *got* no fambly name, beca'se niggers don't *have* 'em!"[76]

Later, Roxy tells her real son:

"Thirty-one parts o' you is white, en on'y one part nigger, en dat po' little one part is yo' *soul*. Tain't wuth savin'; tain't wuth totin' out on a shovel en throwin in de gutter. You has disgraced yo' birth. What would you' pa think o' you? It's enough to make him turn in his grave."[77]

Roxy saw few humanitarian traits in the White, and may have subconsciously preferred to remain Black, perhaps clinging to her language as the one real part of her that was Black. But Roxy did feel the bonds of motherhood, and when Chambers, her son by birth, built up an unpayable gambling debt, she offered to help. Now freed, Roxy suggests that Chambers (still known as Tom) sell her back into slavery for a year:

"Here is de plan, en she'll win, sure. I's a nigger, en nobody ain't gwyne to doubt it dat hears me talk. I's wuth six hund'd dollahs. Take en sell me, en pay off dese gamblers."

Tom was dazed. He was not sure he had heard aright. He was dumb for a moment; then he said:

"Do you mean that you would be sold into slavery to save me?"

"Ain't you my chile? En does you know anything dat a mother won't do for her chile? Dey ain't nothin' a white mother won't do for her chile. Who made 'em so? De Lord done it. En who made de niggers? De Lord made 'em. In de inside, mothers is all de same. De good Lord he made 'em so. I's gwyne to be sole into slavery, en in year you's gwyne to buy yo' ole mammy free ag'in. I'll show you how. Dat's de plan."

Tom's hopes began to rise, and his spirits along with them. He said—

"It's lovely of you, mammy—it's just—"

"Say it ag'in! En keep on sayin' it! It's all de pay a body kin want in dis worl', en it's mo' den enough. 'Laws bless you, honey, when I's slavin' aroun', en dey 'buses me if I knows you's a-sayin' dat, 'way off yonder somers, it'll heal up all de sore places, en I kin stan' 'em . . .'

"White folks ain't partic'lar. De law kin sell me now if dey tell me to leave de State in six months en I don't go. You draw up a paper—bill o' sale—en put it 'way off yonder, down in de middle 'o Kaintuck somers, en sign some names to it, en say you'll sell me cheap 'ca'se you's hard up; you'll fine you ain't gwyne to have no trouble. You take me up de country a piece, en sell me on a farm; dem people ain't gwyne to ask no questions if I's a bargain." Tom forged a bill of sale and sold his mother to an Arkansas cotton-planter for a trifle over six hundred dollars.[78]

As Twain pointed out, although Roxy looked White, her language was Black; her biological son's language was White; her "adopted" son's language was Black. And each acted according to the prescribed rules of society; language was one of the major determinants of class. The wrath of Twain's readers could not erase the story's impact upon those who wanted to believe that blackness somehow transcended all environmental factors. The tale, reflecting Twain's contempt for many of the social mores of a White citizenry, introduced another challenge to the nation of "White supremacy."

Mark Twain had once written, "Fame is a vapor; popularity an accident; the only earthly certainty is oblivion." Sometime during the evening of Thursday, April 21, 1910, seventy-five years after he was born, Mark Twain died. In a letter of sympathy to Twain's daughter, William Dean Howells—nationally known literary critic and one of Twain's closest friends—wrote, "Death had touched his familiar image into historic grandeur." And so it was; the man who had become one of the nation's greatest writers had finally transcended the fine line from oblivion to lasting fame.

Mark Twain and Thomas Nelson Page were contemporaries. Both lived in the South. Both understood the Black and were able to accurately record the language of the Black. But whereas Twain was of the "common folk" and a fierce abolitionist, Page was of aristocratic stock and, like William Gilmore Simms, an "apologist" for the "Southern way of life." Page was born in 1853 in Oakland, a Virginia plantation that would be devastated by the war. In 1874, he received a law degree from the University of Virginia, and practiced law in Richmond until 1893. It was while a lawyer that Page began writing about the South and its people. By the time Woodrow Wilson appointed him ambassador to Italy, a post he was to hold from 1913 to 1919, Page was already one of the nation's outstanding writers, and the recipient of honorary doctorates from Washington and Lee University, Yale, Harvard, Tulane, and William and Mary. As a dialect writer Page was rarely surpassed. Although his stories of the South reflected his belief that slavery was only as evil as the plantation owner, he recorded the life of the Black with a rare compassion.

In April 1877 *Scribner's Monthly* published "Uncle Gabe's White Folks," a dialect poem written by Page. But Page's abilities as a dialect writer did not become fully apparent until April 1884, when *Century Magazine* published "Marse Chan," a short story that was soon to become a classic in American literature.

Two short stories which appeared in the popular media in 1886 added to Page's reputation as an able recorder of Black English, and a writer with few peers. "Unc' Edinburg's Drowndin'," which appeared in the January 1886 issue of *Harper's New Monthly Magazine,* included Black English. Five months later, "Meh Lady: A Story of the War" appeared in the June 1886 issue of *Century.* A footnote was directed to the reader who may have had difficulty reading the Black English:

> The dialect of the negroes of Eastern Virginia differs totally from that of the Southern negroes and in some material points from that of those located farther west.
>
> The elision is so constant that it is impossible to produce the exact sound, and in some cases it has been found necessary to subordinate the phonetic arrangement to intelligibility.
>
> The following rules may, however, aid the reader:
>
> The final consonant is rarely sounded. Adverbs, prepositions, and short words are frequently slighted, as is the possessive. The letter *r* is not usually rolled except when used as a substitute for *th,* but is pronounced *ah.*
>
> For instance, the following is a fair representation of the peculiarities cited:
>
> The sentence, "It was curious, he said, he wanted to go into the other army," would sound: "Twuz cu-yus, he say, he wan'(t) (to) 'turr ah-my."[79]

In 1888, Page and A. C. Gordon wrote *Befo 'de War; Echoes in Negro Dialect.* The book, almost as popular as *Army Life in a Black Regiment,* was a compilation of thirty-two Black folk tales, told in the original dialect. The Black language is recorded with skill and perception; the tales themselves, however, reflected the Antebellum South as viewed by Whites.

His father was Gen. Ambrosio José Gonzales, Cuban freedom fighter, exile, and later artillery commander in the Confederate army. His mother was Harriet Rutledge Elliott of an aristocratic South Carolina family. He was Ambrose Elliott Gonzales—journalist, publisher, and one of the nation's leading authorities on the language and culture of the South Carolina Gullah.

Gonzales was born in 1857 in South Carolina. In 1873, at the age of sixteen he became a telegrapher and agent for the Charleston & Savannah Railway Co. In 1881, after a couple years as a farmer, Gonzales again returned to telegraphy, this time working two jobs a day in New York City for the Western Union and Postal Telegraph companies. But in 1885, the strain finally too great, he resigned both jobs to become a traveling agent and correspondent for the *Charleston News & Courier.*

While a correspondent for the Charleston newspaper, Gonzales wrote his first dialect tales, most of them published during 1886 and 1887. The dialect tales—among them "Ain' No Time fo' Chillun," "An' Chole's Judgment," "The Question of Color," and "Sunday's Sinners" among a half-dozen others—became known as the "Kinlaw Tales," and served as the base for a more extensive series five years later.

In 1891, following a year as South Carolina's secretary of agriculture, Gonzales and his brother, N. G. Gonzales, established *The State,* a newspaper with modest beginnings but which would, within the next two decades, become one of the major newspapers in the South. Editorially, it would plead for literacy for all the South's citizens—Black and White; and almost alone it would cry out against lynching. *The State,* which fought the unpopular fights and led crusades which benefited the people of South Carolina, was hated, feared, and praised, but always respected.

In 1892, Gonzales wrote a series of fourteen "Silhouettes" for *The State,* the dialect tales appearing in the Sunday editions from February 21 to May 22. For several years dialect tales, often tinged by the acceptable stereotypes of the age, had been appearing in the nation's leading newspapers. "Silhouettes," like the stories told by Joel Chandler Harris, looked beneath the surface of human experience to record the mind of the Gullah Black and, perhaps, the mind of the South. On the surface there may have been humor, but below the surface were tragic tales of human suffering.

In "Old Wine—New Bottles," the thirteenth of the series, Gonzales told about Scipio, a former house servant, now alone on what remains of his former master's plantation, burdened by what emancipation had brought, and living in "a habitation which even when new was never weatherproof, and was now in a pitiable state of dilapidation."[80] Scipio tells about his family, each of whom had left him, and about his wife who had died a few months earlier. Then, he talks about himself:

"En' now Maussa sense de gal [his wife] gone I 'ent gots nobody fuh de nuttin' fuh me. Dese niggah w'at grow up sense freedom cum een, ent gots no mannus en' dey would 'a lemme dead een dis house ef de w'ite people didn't see me t'ru. W'en ole Missis binna lib, bress Gawd, 'e always 'member de ole niggah, but now sense him dead en' de grass duh grow ober 'e grabe out yonder ondaneet' de libe oak tree, en' all de w'ite people w'at I raise, leff de ole plantessuhn en' scatter all ober de wull', en' all kind'uh low down buckra w'at couldn't 'sociate wid we w'ite people fambly een ole time, cum fuh lib on de place, please, Gawd I ent gots nuttin' much fuh lib fuh now dese days."[81]

The Gullah, represented in both "Silhouettes" and the Kinlaw tales, reflect a syntactic and phonological West African language base. However, Gonzales never recognized this, believing, as others believed, that the language was a "deterioration" of English, mutated from an Anglo-Saxon language base. Nevertheless, his "ear for the language," and his ability to reproduce it in print established him as one of the better dialect writers of an era when dialect verse and tales were flooding the nation's literary markets.

On May 22, 1892, the final "Silhouette" appeared. With the exception of some minor dialect poetry, it would be almost three decades—another time, another cycle—before Ambrose Gonzales would again write in Gullah.

ZIM, JUDGE, AND THE NEGRO STEREOTYPE

Today, few people know about *Judge* magazine; the names of its outstanding writers and cartoonists mean little. But for more than fifty years, until the mid-1930s, *Judge* was one of the nation's leading satire magazines, a weekly magazine with a broad, well-educated audience. *Judge* editors did not hesitate to let their writers and artists deflate the pompous, and point out the absurdities in American government and business.

Often the truth was too deep, perhaps too painful, to be satirized in traditional forms. Stinging indictments could be desensitized, yet still retain their importance by being delivered in the languages of the Black; the White audiences might be touched by the edge of truth while also being entertained. Although the more discerning readers may have seen the reflections of the White society under the gross exaggeration of Black stereotypes, most readers undoubtedly failed to see beneath the surface, a problem common in satire.

For *Judge,* J. A. Waldron wrote, among many other series, "Old Chocolate's Target Practice," usually eight to twelve pithy sayings meant to have impact, yet not offend:

Men am a good deal laik monkeys—de mo' solemn da look de mo' mischuf da intend.

We er apt toe claim mo' sense dan oddah animals, but am jis' laik chickens—toe fuller any han' dat scattahs cawn.

Ef de watch dog an' de tief strike up a frien'ship, good-bye chickens.

Ef politicians was good-nachued de y'ar roun smiles wud'n count 'lection day.

W'en yo' let a beggah fill his basket he swears 'case he a'n't got a biggah one.[82]

A. T. Worden, a few years later, contributed "Uncle Gabe's Sag Saws," a series not unlike that presented by Waldron:

Eber'body's mule kicks but mine, an' he guts absen'-minded once in er while.

Trubble am de umpire in de game ob life dat keeps hollerin' "Play Ball."

De Almighty kin take an aberage ib de whole human race, but we has too take a man as we fin' him.

Mah frien's, ef yo' fink dot yo' kin sing yo'rself intoe glory [in a church] yo' betah jine an opera-company an' git special rates on de railroad.[83]

Worden also contributed the "Reverend Moakley McKoon" series, short, occasionally stereotyped sermons about the state of the country:

While I enjoy de patriotic features [of July 4] I disgust de nature of its celebration. De common cotton plush mind might come to de conclusion dat de revolution was a long orgie ob intossication, an' dat de way ter celebrate was ter get drunk early in de day an' den industriously keep drunk until de mawnin' ob de Fourth.[84]

He ended his Fourth of July sermon with what he called "The National Anthem":

"My country, bless thy stars,
Sweet land of colored cars,
    Of thee I sing.
Land where they stretch our
    throat

Each time we try to vote,
Wher'er thy flag doth float
Let freedom ring."[85]

Not all of *Judge's* satire was presented in verse, pithy sayings, sermons, and short articles. Much of it was presented in cartoons. For the first thirty years of *Judge's* existence, Eugene Zimmerman—identified by the block scrawl signature "ZIM"—was one of its major cartoonists. Zimmerman was born in Switzerland in 1862, and came to America at the age of eight. During his youth he was a chore boy and fish peddler; later, he became a sign painter. In 1883, at the age of twenty-one, he became a cartoonist for *Puck,* the country's leading humor magazine. Two years later, he and a number of other writers broke away from *Puck* to found *Judge.* It was while at *Judge* that Zimmerman became known as one of the country's keenest observers of Black language and movements. Zimmerman and F. B. Opper are credited with founding and developing the school of grotesque distortion in caricature. Although Zimmerman distorted the shape of reality and presented the Black in a comical, perhaps even pathetic light, his inner humanity and sympathy for the Black often penetrated the grotesque distortions. Not infrequently, Whites were seen as the antagonists clinging to outdated lifestyles and beliefs.

The captions of Zimmerman's 600 Black-oriented cartoons illustrate many rules that were not fully described until years later. Among the rules are consonant cluster simplification in the final position, the elision of syllables, the substitution of stops for interdental fricatives, the zero copula, the dropping of morphological endings and the substitution of verbal functors in pre-verb position, the use of the all-pervasive functor form, the absence of the postvocalic /r/, and the use of the apostrophe to replace all unstressed consonants. "Sweet talk" and hypercorrection are also common. The internal phonological and syntactic rules used by Zimmerman are consistent throughout the era, changing very little with the progression of time. Not only are many of these rules present in the speech of Blacks today, but they are also present in many of the indigenous African languages. Many of the nonverbal features within Zimmerman's cartoons also have direct parallels in West African cultures. Among these are the "giving of skin" and the "rapping stances," both identified as part of Afro-American as well as African cultures. The "high handshake," often at eye level, that is present in Zimmerman's cartoons is also a feature among many people of West Africa, as is carrying objects on the head and the use of walking sticks.

Zimmerman never went to Africa; and apparently, he never knew any Africans who weren't also American residents. His cartoons and captions had to be based upon the actions and language of the Blacks living in America at that time.

Zimmerman wasn't the only major artist to utilize the Black and his language. At one time during the 1880s, more than a dozen major artists on the staffs of some of the nation's leading circulation magazines were portraying the Black.

E. W. Kemble, a *Judge* artist, produced several series for the mass media; the titles were almost as stereotyped as the images—"Blackberries," "Pickaninnies," and "A Coon Alphabet." However, the language, though not as expert as Zimmerman's, is reasonably accurate.

For *Harper's Weekly,* Sol Eytinge drew the "Blackville" series, beginning in 1872 and continuing through most of the 1880s. The concepts of this series were later copied by numerous other artists, including Zimmerman. For Currier & Ives, Thomas Wirth drew "Darktown," a set of 100 lithographed plates, each portraying a separate image of the Black and his society and language. For *Puck,* Johann Ehrnhardt, regarded as one of cartooning's giants, drew numerous studies of Blacks.

For *Judge,* during 1899–1900, Richard Felton Outcault drew "Shakespeare in Possumville," a series of twenty drawings that reflected Black interpretations of the plot and language of William Shakespeare. Outcault later became famous as the originator of the comic strips "Hogan's Alley," "The Yellow Kid," and "Buster Brown."

Joseph Keppler, Bernhard Gillam, and James A. Wales, among many others, all contributed to the graphical representation of the American Black during the nineteenth century.

ADVERTISING THE BLACK

During the Reconstruction Cycle, as newspapers and magazines became more dominant in American life, and as the Blacks began to attain mobility and purchasing power, thousands of ads were designed to carry a Black Americana appeal—either drawings of Blacks using and selling products, or products designed for Blacks only. The language of the ads was often "bastardized" Black English. Blacks in advertising soon became a sales gimmick, a device to improve sales; they were the come-ons in ads to promote the sale of gardening or farming tools, janitorial equipment, and foods. It was an often-inbred belief among Whites that because of their antebellum experience, Blacks were the master gardeners, farmers, unskilled laborers, and cooks. If a Black said such a product was good, the White Northerner reasoned it must be so. From such thinking there emerged Aunt Jemima and Uncle Ben.

The ads that appealed to the Black population, the result of increased literacy following emancipation, often reflected White values. Ads told about, and praised, hair straighteners, peroxides, light-complexioned make-up, and special clothes for that "respectable, well-dressed look." The Black, after the brutality of slavery and segregation, wished to integrate with the White society; the ads in the daily newspapers and popular magazines, the flyers and advertising postcards, told of ways to try to look white. What the advertising did not say was that no matter how white he looked, or how white he thought, he was still black, and society would not extend him the rights of equality.

With the increase in the nation's population, advertising extended beyond the periodicals into more specialized forms. Flyers and advertising postcards carrying statements in Black English became prominent. The costs for these media were less than for other forms of advertising, and the results were quite favorable; and advertisers could increase their readership without having to compete directly against other advertising or against the news in bound form. This was personal advertising—one person handing an ad to one other person. Soon, it was a rare medicine show, well promoted by flyers and banners, that did not have a Black or an American Indian as a shill, someone who would not only testify to the value of the item for sale—whether it was a cure-all for arthritis and the gout, or a machine to make money—but who would also pass out flyers, published "proof" of the item's value.

Just as with sheet music covers and printed dialect sermons, these flyers, too, have been lost in history. Of the millions printed, only a few—now yellowed and torn, and usually secreted away in museums and attics—remain to help later generations try to understand the language and culture of an earlier, different America.

RESPONSE TO PROLIFERATION

Throughout the Reconstruction Cycle, the use of "eye dialect" increased significantly as writers searched for ways to record dialect speech. These writers knew that Blacks spoke dialects different from Standard English, but they often didn't know how to record the language to reflect this difference. The result was piecemeal hash that approximated some of the Black English syntax, some of the phonology, and the use of eye dialect to show inferiority where none existed. Few writers took the time to study the language they wrote about. The proliferation of Black dialect in the mass media—dialect that was occasionally accurate, but most often little more than butchered Standard English—upset a number of scholars and writers. James Whitcomb Riley, in an article written toward the end of the Reconstruction Cycle, pleaded:

> Let him [the writer of dialect] be schooled in dialect before he sets up as an expounder of it. . . . The real master not only knows each varying light and shade of dialect expression, but he must as minutely learn the inner characteristic of the people whose nature native tongue it is, else his product is simply a pretence—a wilful [sic] forgery, a rank abomination.
>
> . . . dialect means something more than mere rude form of speech and action—that it must, in some righteous and substantial way, convey to us a positive force of soul, truth, dignity, beauty, grace, purity, and sweetness, that can touch us to the tenderness of tears.[86]

T. C. Delow also expressed his concern about a plethora of Black English items:

> That there is good in dialect none may . . . deny; but that good is only when it chances, as rarely, to be good dialect; when it is used with just discretion and made the effect of circumstances naturally arising, not the cause and origins of the circumstances itself.[87]

The increasing frequency of Black English in the mass media of the Reconstruction Cycle raised new questions, and brought a new awareness to the public. Philologists began to ask more questions about Black English. And in other parts of the world, there were more studies probing the various pidgin and creole languages that may have had their origins in West Africa.

In America, Elizabeth Kilham, a Northern teacher in the South, made a significant contribution to the understanding of Black English with her "Sketches in Color," a four-part series which appeared in the December 1869, through March 1870, issues of the popular *Putnam's Magazine.* Although she focused on Black students and their relationship to the South's system of education, Kilham discussed the language of the Black and its relationship to reading interference, perhaps the first such recognition of this problem in print. Interestingly, she also noted that her Black students were better in reading than in most other subjects.

Another early investigator of American Black English was James A. Harrison, whose articles in the *American Journal of Philology, Modern*

Language Notes, and *Anglia*—all of them technical journals rather than popular publications—are early landmarks in describing Black English. However, Harrison's conclusions were not always as solid as his descriptions, as shown in his *Anglia* article: "It must be confessed, to the shame of the white population of the South, that they perpetuate many of these pronunciations in common with their Negro dependents; and that, in many places, if one happened to be talking to a native with one's eyes shut, it would be impossible to say whether a Negro or a white person were responding."[88]

In January 1888, in *The Popular Science Monthly,* Horatio Hale observed, incorrectly, that race and linguistic stock were synonymous. In that same issue, Theodore H. Kellogg, a physician, compared British and American English. Although he made no direct references to nonstandard or Black English, Kellogg did make a number of indirect references that reflected a widespread popular belief about Blacks and nonstandard English:

> It is the duty of all educated persons to correct provincial or unauthorized utterances of the vocal-sounds as have been here described, and to strive to preserve the purity of the mother tongue. . . .
> Finally, there is a physiological difference between Americans and Englishmen in the organs of speech due to changed climatic and of physical conditions of life. That the inherent quality of voice which characterized different nationalities is due in part to differences of telluric and meteorological influences as well as to diversity of race and language can not be doubted. . . . Vocal timbre, then, is a fundamental quality of voice distinct from syllabic accent, oral adjustments, emphasis, or inflections, and it is dependent in part on the individual's physical environment.[89]

Thus, Dr. Kellogg seemed to be at odds with himself. He said that there is such a thing as a pure language (British English) and that it must be preserved, but at the same time he indicated that race and physical factors affect language. Undoubtedly, because Dr. Kellogg was a physician, a prestigious profession even in 1888, and because his article appeared in *The Popular Science Monthly,* a prestigious magazine, many persons took his word as truth; the Black became an educational pawn. Some persons, quoting Dr. Kellogg, demanded advanced education for the Black so that the English language would not be debased by the Black speaking an impure language; another group claimed that the Black could not learn Standard English because not only was he mentally and morally inferior, but Dr. Kellogg had said that the Black had different anatomical features that caused him to speak a different, perhaps debased, language.

In the 1896 annual volume of the *Proceedings of the American Philological Association,* W. S. Scarborough quite ignorantly had claimed, "Dialects and sub-dialects, the product of ignorance and environment, are so numerous that philologists are baffled to find a starting point." In *Lippincott's Magazine,* near the end of the Reconstruction Cycle, William Cecil Elam called nonstandard English, "lingo of the wholly uneducated and socially debased white."[90]

An interesting and highly important linguistic discussion occurred in the *North American Review* and *Science,* both widely circulated magazines. The June 1888 issue of the *North American Review* published a letter to the editor, written by E. M. Day, under the heading "Philological Curiosities." Day had asked about the origin of the word *brottus,* a "bonus" given by a shopkeeper to a child or Black shopper. He observed that "a request for brottus is beneath the dignity of an adult white person." According to Day: "The origin of this word is entirely unknown to me. I suppose like *buccra* (white person), or *goober* (peanut or "ground nut" as it is commonly called in the South), it belongs to some African dialect, imported with slaves from the Dark Continent."[91]

In the September 1888 issue of *The North American Review,* S. Heydenfeldt indicated that *brottus* was present in Charleston. A. F. Chamberlain, in the July 1888 issue of *Science,* gave little further insight into *brottus,* but did discuss *buccra* and *goober.* According to Chamberlain: "The word *goober* ('peanut') is, I think, of African origin. In Haussa (a West African tongue), *guja* is 'ground nut.' . . . The origin of buccra ('white man') is not clear; but in Haussa, *buttra* means 'master.' "[92]

The word *tote* ("to carry"), like the word *brottus,* has an interesting history in the popular mass media, with the lay public and scholars choosing up sides as to whether *tote* was an Old English word or whether it had African origins. The dispute is still not settled. The word was in use in the late seventeenth century, and Noah Webster, in his 1828 dictionary, described it as "a word used in slaveholding countries; said to be introduced by the blacks."

There are numerous examples of usage during the nineteenth century.

Two writers, in separate issues of *American Notes and Queries* (February 1891), attested to the presence of *tote* in Maine, Indiana, and Kentucky, and along the Ohio and Mississippi rivers. In *Modern Languages Notes* of June 1891, W. Baskerville claimed Old English origins for the word. In the December 1893 issue of *Modern Language Notes,* J. Douglas Bruce claimed that *tote* was not an Old English word. In answer to Bruce's claims of African origins, three letters appeared in *The Nation*. The first, in the February 1, 1894, issue, indicates possible African origin. Two letters in the February 15 issue again claimed British origins. And so the controversy went; some authors claimed British origins, others claimed African. The impact of these comments, published not in academic journals but in the popular media, was felt throughout the philological community. During the remainder of the century, the market was flooded with other assumptions, guesses, and hypotheses about origins of specific lexical items.

A three-page unsigned article in "The Contributor's Club" section of *The Atlantic Monthly* (August 1891), was an attempt to duplicate some of the techniques and research of such scholars as Allen, Higginson, and Harrison. It served to bring forth the language of the Black, and at the same time perpetuate the myth of the primitive savage. The opening lines of the article set the tone:

> The negroes on our Southern plantations have apparently adopted with marvelous rapidity the customs, language, and religion of the race that brought them into slavery a mere century ago. Yet, though they seem to have accepted the forms of worship of the dominant race, one finds, on looking closely in the matter, that they cling to some very barbarous beliefs and superstitions, and oftentimes these strange fancies are wrapped about with the garb of religion.[93]

The author had asked several Blacks a number of questions about the nature of the world, then reprinted their answers in their own language. He obviously believed that the Blacks, though emancipated from slavery, were still quite barbarous, a view that most of the authors and readers undoubtedly also held. Yet, the article, when read from a twentieth-century viewpoint, makes it seem as if the intelligent ones were the Blacks, and that the ignorant or barbarous one was the questioner:

> To the interrogation, "Where does snow come from?" came the reply, "It is blowed off de tops de highest mountains."
> "What are clouds made of?"

"Made of all de smoke blowed up from de worril since de worril was made."

"Of what are stars made?"

"Dee is des balls of fire hung up in de sky."

"How long will the stars hang in the sky?"

"Dee will hang twel de Great Day of Jedgement. On dat day John will take a shinin' broom in his hand, and he will sweep de sky clean of stars; sweep de sky clean of stars like a woman sweeps a floor clean of dust. De stars will fall from his broom, and will bust wid blazes and great noise des 'fo' dee touch de earth."

"You say the moon is a lump of ice; now what will become of that at the Last Great Day?" I have sometimes asked.

"Hit will drip away in blood."

The queer recitation of ignorance continued somewhat after this manner:—

"What will become of the rocks?"

"Dee will des melt. De rocks? Dee des growed. Dee'll des agin melt away. De Ocean? Hit'll only des bile away. De Sun? Well, you know de sun is a 'oman; hit got face, hit got eyes, hit can see all you do. She sings,—she do sing all day long. As she rises she sings low, but when she gits such a distance up she sings loud! All 'cross de high sky she sings loud, but when she gits sech a distance down she sings low agin. Dat's de reason noises can't carry far in de middle of de day; de sounds air des deadened by de sun's singin'. Nobody can edzactly hear what air de words of de song she sings, but ev'ybody is deefened by her hummin', 'caze hear'in' her dee can't hear no other noise to speak of."

"What," I asked one wise in the doctrines of ignorance, "are those stars with long lights streaming from them?"

"Macomet stars. Dee come fer signs of wars. And often is de times dat us see strange lights and quare shadows all over de worril in spots. I don't know what dem be, but I does know dat de worril sometimes puts on mournin'. She puts on mournin'-close same like a widow 'oman. Is you notice dat dark shadow in de moon? Dat's a man, dat is. He put dar fer workin' on a Sunday. Dat little shadder by him is his little dog. De little dog didn't do no harm; he des follered de man. When you see a rainbow," continued my informant, "you'll des know den dat de moon is done got des behime de sun, and is lookin' over her shoulder."

I discover that there are various superstitions concerning the origin of the appearance of the rainbow. One old negro tells me that rainbows are kept in the bottom of brooks until such times as they are needed to "pen de sky."[94]

And so on it goes, line after line, column after column, as the author proudly presented all the "primitive" views of the Black, including the notion that man was once a monkey when the world was founded. The Black informant also tells the author that "dar use ter be three houses clost tog'er wherever you go, and dem three houses belong ter de Injun man, de fox, and de rabbit. De white man done drive off de Injun, done mos' drive off de fox, but Brer Rabbit, he say he gwine stay."[95] The last laugh is on the author and, perhaps, on the highly influential readership of *The Atlantic Monthly*. In Afro-American folklore, the rabbit is the wisest, most crafty of all animals. The rabbit is the Black man.

Anne Weston Whitney and John Bennett contributed more substantial studies of Black English at the turn of the century. In the August 22 and August 29, 1901, issues of *The Independent,* a popular periodical, Whitney urged an in-depth study of Black dialects and their importance socially, historically, and politically. She also presented a number of features of various Black dialects, and discussed reasons why the language of the Uncle Remus tales, though linguistically accurate for one part of the South, was not accepted in many parts of the country.

Bennett contributed one of the better descriptions of Gullah. In a two-part series for *The South Atlantic Quarterly,* he alluded to possible African linguistic structures in the suprasegmental forms. He also noted that:

a great part of [Gullah] is the quite logical wreck of once tolerant English, obsolete in pronunciation, dialectal in its usage, yet the national result of a savage and primitive people's endeavors to acquire for themselves the highly organized language of a very civilized race. Its vocabulary is for the most part English of two hundred years ago.[96]

Bennett also noted that Gullah had few abstractions, but nevertheless urged that a complete linguistic study be made of Gullah. Although later proven incorrect in some of his interpretations, Bennett's description of Gullah, and his identification of the geographical boundaries, helped create a base for later research.

Just as the *Charleston News & Courier* had provided the medium for the first dialect tales written by Ambrose Gonzales, so did it provide the base for a number of dialect sermons written by the Rev. John G. Williams. The sermons, which appeared regularly during 1895, were later collected and published in 1896, as *"De Old Plantation": Elder Coteney's Sermons*. Williams's familiarity with Gullah, his ability to record it accurately and compassionately, may be partially explained by a passage in his introduction:

> Of my attempt to reproduce the pure old Gullah of "befo de wah" in the Coteney sermons, with what success I have done it it will be for others, not me, to say. I may only say here that I was born and raised in the neighborhood of the Combahee rice plantations, that I have been familiar with the rice field negro brogue from my childhood days, that before the war and since I preached a great deal to the low-country negroes, and, to cap the climax of my qualifications for writing Gullah, I was once told by a genuine 'Gullah nigger': "Mas Williams, I decla you is de best nigger preacher dat eber did preach to nigger."
>
> It will be seen, therefore, that I have had exceptional opportunities extending over a long period of time—from slavery to freedom—of becoming familiar with the 'langrige,' as it is called in Gullah. So familiar am I with it that it has been said: "He can not only write like a nigger, but think like a nigger."[97]

Among Williams's many observations about Gullah are:

> Wherever heard, it may be a thousand miles from its native habitat, it points as directly and unmistakably to the coast region of South Carolina as did the Apostle Peter's dialect point to Galilee when the Jews charged him with being a "Galileean and they speech agreeth thereto." This rice field and sea island patois is the purest and most genuine "niggertalk" of all the negro dialects, because it has been less affected by contact with white people than any other one of the negro dialects, and for that reason is, perhaps, the most interesting and the richest as a linguistic study of them all. It is wonderful with what tenacity this Gullah English of the low-country negroes holds on to life and refuses to become a "dead language," so completely has it become a part of them and ingrained, as it were into their very nature. . . .
>
> They seem to have been scarcely affected in their low-country Gullah speech by the white people that were numerous and all

around them and the negroes native to that neighborhood, who talked so differently to themselves. . . .

Is this Gullah or low-country negro dialect, when it shall no longer be "spoke," worthy to be preserved in written form? To me it seems that it ought to be written and preserved for a good many reasons, only two or three of which I will mention now, the others further on. One of these reasons is that it ought to be preserved, as already mentioned, as a memorial of the institution of slavery; and secondly, as a memorial of the old plantation life of the low-country of South Carolina, of which the Gullah negro was so large a part; and thirdly, as a grateful memorial of those whose labor in the rice fields and in the cotton fields, under the wise direction and whole-some discipline of intelligent masters, made the low-country of South Carolina, for wealth, refinement, and education, the garden spot of the State. . . .

"Gullah" is very probably a corruption of Angola, shortened to Gola, a country of West Africa, and a part of Lower Guinea, from which a great many negroes were brought to this country in the days of the slave trade. I remember hearing the old plantation ne-groes before the war speak of one as a "Gullah nigger" and another as a "Guinea nigger." In Appleton's "New American Cyclopaedia" the Guinea negroes are described as "black and having thick lips and flat noses," and the Angola or "Gulla" negroes as having "few of the negro peculiarities of form and feature. They are brown in color." These differences between negroes in the country have been often noticed and remarked upon frequently, the explanation of which differences is that the "thick lips" and "flat noses" point to Ashantee and Dahomey as the places from which their ances-tors were brought and the "brown color" and features, more like the European in some negroes, very different from the Guineas, point to Angola or "Gulla," as the country from which their an-cestors came. So deeply fixed are race and even tribal character-istics. "Uncle Jack" was a Gulla. There is history in the word "Gullah." . . .[98]

Williams also showed an amazing grasp of linguistics, the scientific study of language which was not to become a formal discipline until many years later. Williams recognized that a study of a peoples' lan-guage can lead to a thorough understanding of their lives and cultures:

At the present time the different languages of the world with their various and numerous dialects, are being studied by linguistic scholars with greater interest and perseverance than ever before. From this comparative study of language and dialect will come practical results in the three following directions: First, ethnology, an important function of which is to trace back nations to their parent stock, will be largely a gainer from it. . . . Secondly, history will gain from linguistic studies as linguistic study will also be helped by linguistics. . . . Thirdly, linguistics . . . has also a psychological value. A language is the intellectual photograph of the nation that spoke or speaks it. . . .

Take these as samples: "Ef you ent hab hoss to ride, ride cow," that is, make the best of your circumstances. "Dat nigger," or "dat buckra eye bigger dan e belly," meaning that he wanted more than was enough. "E ent matter bout de road so long is e kah you to de right place," which expresses a great truth. Of the fact that the ignorant and illiterate negro wasn't a fool, but had inborn wit and sense, we want no stronger evidence than is furnished in his folklore, which contains a wonderful amount of shrewd sense and insight into human nature. There is no doubt that the "brer rabbit," and "brer fox," and "brer cooter," and "brer bar" stories are purely the creation of negro brain, and that a people who could make "brer rabbit," and "brer fox," and "brer cooter" say and do such smart things first had the smartness and sense themselves. These very stories show, it seems to me, that the negro has the basis of good mother wit, and that he may rise to better things.[99]

THE BLACK WRITERS

During the Reconstruction Cycle, virtually all studies of Black language were undertaken by Whites; fiction that included Black language either in narration or dialogue was, likewise, usually written by Whites. But there were exceptions.

Frances E. W. Harper, born of free parents in 1825 in Baltimore, became one of the nation's most effective abolitionist orators, often drawing overflow crowds throughout the South as well as in Maine where she was employed as a lecturer by the Antislavery Society. To help finance the cause of abolition, she contributed royalties from her writings. *Poems of Miscellaneous Subjects* (1854), written in Standard English and published in Philadelphia, became a best seller, published in more than twenty editions within the next two decades.

However, Harper's attempts to write in dialect—becoming one of the first Blacks to use the language later identified as American Black English—were far below the quality of the dialect poetry written by Whites born in the deep South and exposed to the various dialects.

Her *Sketches of Southern Life* (1872) is the story of a slave woman who saw her children sold as property before the war, then lived through that war, emancipation, the constitutional but not social right to vote, and who was finally reunited with her son. The language of Aunt Chloe, the narrator of the tales, shows an inconsistent mixing of Standard and Black English, with conventional Black English forms (such as *dat* and *dem*) being the characteristics that set Black language apart from White language. Although the language was a poor recording of American Black English, the rhythm and "feel" were definitely below average—certainly far below the high level of competence shown in Harper's poetry and novels written in Standard English—the book was eagerly purchased, for it tore at human emotion and the mother-child bond.

Harper's representation of Black English improved, though not significantly, in *Iola Leroy, or Shadows Uplifted* (1892). The Black English of the book appears to be more like the hit-and-miss dialect presented by Harriet Beecher Stowe, than like the meticulous and careful recordings of Joel Chandler Harris.

Paul Laurence Dunbar, the son of former slaves, lived only thirty-four years, dying at the height of his fame. But in that short time he became one of the nation's outstanding poets, a writer able to understand and interpret the lives and feelings of the antebellum Negro.

His first poems, written while he was in high school, were published in 1888 by the *Dayton* (Ohio) *Herald,* his hometown newspaper. Yet, following graduation from high school, when Dunbar applied for a full-time position as a reporter, he was told by the *Herald* staff editors that it was against their policy to hire Blacks. Frustrated, he realized after several weeks of job searching that no matter how well he wrote, no matter how much education he had, it was never enough to break the racial barriers. To support himself he finally took a job as an elevator operator—eleven hours a day, four dollars a week. But he continued to write, for writing poetry was where his creative genius lay. He had accepted his role as an elevator-boy only because the income helped support his writing.

Dunbar's first book, *Oak and Ivy* (1892), a collection of poems, was published by the United Brethren Publishing House of Dayton. He had subsidized its publication costs of $125, and to recover his expenses, he sold the books to customers in the building where he operated the elevator.

Oak and Ivy, which included dialect poetry, attracted a number of supporters. But it wasn't until William Dean Howells, at that time the nation's leading literary critic, praised Dunbar's second book, *Majors and Minors,* that success finally came. *Majors and Minors* (1895), was almost sold out when Howells gave it a lengthy review in the June 27, 1896, issue of *Harper's Weekly.* According to Howells:

> [Dunbar] is, so far as I know, the first man of his color to study his race objectively, to analyze it to himself, and then to represent it in art as he felt it and found it to be; to represent it humorously, yet tenderly, and above all so faithfully that we know the portrait to be undeniably like. A race which has reached this effect in any of its members can no longer be held wholly uncivilized; and intellectually Mr. Dunbar makes a stronger claim for the negro than the negro yet has done.[100]

Reserving his strongest praise for the "minors" section of the book— the dialect poetry, both Black and Southern White—Howells called them "good, very good," indicating that Dunbar's strongest abilities lay not in the poetry written in Standard English, but in his dialect poems.

The review spurred sales and recognition, and led to the publication of *Lyrics of Lowly Life* (1896), a compilation of both *Oak and Ivy* and *Majors and Minors.* The introduction to *Lyrics of Lowly Life* was written by Howells who reemphasized his strong support for both Dunbar and his poetry, thus assuring it both popular and academic audiences:

> There is a precious difference of temperament between the races which it would be a great pity ever to lose, and that this is best preserved and most charmingly suggested by Mr. Dunbar in those pieces of his where he studies the moods and traits of his race in its own accent of our English. We call such pieces dialect pieces for want of some closer phrase, but they are really not dialect so much as delightful personal attempts and failures for the written and spoken language. In nothing is his essentially refined and delicate art so well shown as in these pieces, which, I venture to say, describe the range between appetite and emotion, with certain lifts far beyond and above it, which is the range of the race. He reveals in these a finely ironical perception of the negro's limitations, with a

tenderness for them which I think so very rare as to be almost quite new.[101]

Howells, in his strong praise for the dialect poetry, however, had unintentionally caused Dunbar grief, for Dunbar wished to be identified as a poet who just happened to be Black, not as a Black poet; he wished to be remembered for his poetry written in Standard English, the language he spoke. More than two-thirds of his poetry was written in Standard English, but it was the other one-third that had captivated a nation. And, although the world regarded his dialect writing as his best work, Dunbar never regarded it as such, even admitting that he spent more time writing his Standard English poetry than his poetry in Black English; as he had pointed out in his second book, dialect poetry was the "minors" of literature.

Editors for the nation's major magazines soon began demanding Dunbar's dialect poetry—and rejecting his poetry written in Standard English. In a particularly frustrating moment, Dunbar turned to verse:

He sang of life serenely sweet,
With now and then a deeper note,
On some high peak, nigh yet remote,
He voiced the world's absorbing beat.

He sang of love, when earth was young,
And love itself was in his lays,
But ah! the world, it turned to praise,
A jingle in a broken tongue.[102]

In a letter to a friend, Dunbar, frustrated by the literary community, lashed out at his literary patron, William Dean Howells: "One critic [Howells] says a thing and the rest hasten to say the same thing, in many instances using the identical words. I see now very clearly that Mr. Howells has done me irrevocable harm in the dictum he laid down regarding my dialect verse."[103] Realizing that the world was paying little attention to what he wrote in Standard English, Dunbar came to accept his fate. To his friend James Weldon Johnson, who would himself become one of the nation's better writers, Dunbar confided, "I've got to write dialect poetry, it's the only way I can get them to listen to me."[104]

With the popularity of Dunbar's dialect verse came controversy. There were those who said that dialect verse cast Blacks in the same light as the stereotyped images in minstrelsy. Some argued that Dunbar, a free Black born in the North, was really contemptuous of the Southern Black born into slavery. But there were also those strong supporters of dialect verse who saw it not as demeaning the Black but as portraying him accurately, for language is an identifier of a culture; by understanding language, it is possible to understand the person. There were those who said that Dunbar's recording of dialect was inaccurate. But, Dunbar himself pointed out numerous times that his dialect poetry was two kinds—that of the Black, and that of the Southern White, and that each dialect had its own separate rules. It was not an uncommon mistake for his critics to confuse the two dialects. Dunbar boldly noted that he "could write it as well, if not better than anyone else I knew of."[105] But meter and beat often dictated the nature of the dialect in his poetry; Dunbar believed that it was more important to project the *nature* of the language than the actual language itself. There were those who said that even if Dunbar's recording of Black English were accurate, it was a dying language. To this criticism, Edward H. Lawson, boldly answered:

> Indeed, a recent criticism of Mr. Dunbar has deplored his writing in dialect on the ground that fifty years hence there will be no such southern Negro speech. We would assure the critic that it is not the quaintness of the dialect of Dunbar's verse that allures the reader even of today, but rather the exquisite melody and harmony of the stanzas—combinations of syllables which our poet has put together in such a way as always to form pure music. Pure music stands the test of ages! Homer's dialect is out of style in Greece, yet the Greeks read Homer, and Herodotus (as well as some Americans) and if this Negro dialect is to become a dead language, may God bless Paul Dunbar for having saved it to us in his immortal lyrics.[106]

Through his writing, Dunbar was able to capture the soul of a people in bondage, to show how language and culture were so carefully integrated in the human experience that it was impossible to present one without the other. His poetry, written after the Civil War, often reflected not the freed Black, but the antebellum Negro still trapped in slavery and longing to be free.

"An Ante-Bellum Sermon," first published in *Majors and Minors,* is a thinly disguised allegory describing the slaves' hopes for freedom. On the surface, the poem appears to be a Black preacher's sermon about Moses and the freeing of the Jews from bondage 3,000 years earlier. It takes little imagination to understand that the preacher, as portrayed by Dunbar, was also pleading for God to free the Blacks from bondage and to deliver *them* into freedom. Within the eleven verse poem/sermon, Dunbar was able, through dialect, to articulate the hopes of a race of people, as well as to present the essence of their religious beliefs.

Dunbar wrote five Civil War poems; three were written in Standard English, two were written in Black English. The most powerful of his five poems, "The Colored Soldiers," written in 1895, is a capsulized sociohistory of the Blacks' roles during the war, but was written in Standard English. The poem usually remembered was written in Black English—"W'en Dey 'Listed Colo'ed Sojers," a study of one soldier's role in a war:

Dey was talkin' in de cabin, dey was talkin' in de hall;
But I listened kin' o' keerless, not a-thinkin' 'bout it all;
An' on Sunday, too, I noticed, dey was whisp'rin' mighty much,
Stan'in' all erroun' de roadside w'en dey let us out o' chu'ch.
But I did n't think erbout it twell de middle of de week,
An' my 'Lias come to see me, an' somehow he couldn't speak.
Den I seed all in a minute whut he'd come to see me for;—
Dey had 'listed col'ed sojers, an' my 'Lias gwine to wah.

Oh, I hugged him, an' I kissed him, an' I baiged him not to go;
But he tol' me dat his conscience, hit was callin' to him so,
An, he couldn't baih to lingah w'en he had a chanst to fight
For de freedom dey had gin him an' de glory of de right.
So he kissed me, an' he lef' me, w'en I'd p'omised to be true;
An' dey put a knapsack on him, an' a coat all colo'ed blue.
So I gin him pap's ol' Bible, f'om de bottom of de draw',—
W'en dey 'listed colo'ed sojers an' my 'Lias went to wah.

But I thought of all de weary miles dat he would have to tramp,
An' I couldn't be contented w'en dey tuk him to de camp.
W'y, my hea't nigh broke wid grievin' twell I seed him on de street;
Den I felt lak I could go an' th'ow my body at his feet.
For his buttons was a-shinin', an' his face was shinin', too,
An' he looked so strong an' mighty in his coat o' sojer blue,
Dat I hollarhed, 'Step up, manny,' dough my th'oat was so' an' raw,—
W'en dey 'listed colo'ed sojers an' my 'Lias went to wah.

Ol' Mis' cried w'en mastah lef' huh, young Miss mou'ned huh brothah
    Ned,
An' I didn't know dey feelin's is de ve'y wo'ds dey said
W'en I tol' em I was so'y. Dey had done gin up dey all;
But dey only seemed mo' proudah dat dey men had heerd de call.
Bofe my mastahs went in gray suits, an' I loved de Yankee blue,
But I t'ought dat I could sorrer for de losin' of 'em too;

But I couldn't, for I didn't know de ha'f o' whut I saw,
Twell dey 'listed colo'ed sojers an' my 'Lias went to wah.

Mastah Jack come home all sickly; he was broke for life, dey said;
An' dey lef' my po' young mastah some'ers on de roadside,—dead.
W'en de women cried an' mou'ned 'em, I could feel it thoo an' thoo,
For I had a loved un fightin' in de way o' dangah, too.
Den dey tol' me dey had laid him some'rs way down souf to res',
Wid de glad dat he had fit for shinin' daih acrost his breas'.
Well, I cried, but den I reckon dat's what Gawd had called him for
W'en dey 'listed colo'ed sojers an' my 'Lias went to wah.[107]

Dunbar's poem, "The Real Question," was political insight at its best;
it was journalistic editorializing in only three verses. While the nation
was debating about "crucifying man upon a cross of gold," as William
Jennings Bryan had phrased it, Dunbar had other concerns:

Folks is talkin' 'bout de money, 'bout de silvah an' de gold;
All de time de season's changin' an' de days is gittin' cold.
An' dey's wond'rin' 'bout de metals, whethah we'll have one or two.
While de price o' coal is risin' an' dey's two months' rent dat's due.

Some folks says dat gold's de only money dat is wuff de name,
Den de othahs rise an' tell 'en dat dey ought to be ashame,
An' dat silvah is de only thing to save us f'om de powah
Of de gold-bug ragin' 'ron' an' seekin' who he may devowah.

Well, you folks kin keep on shoutin' wif' yo' gold er silvah cry,
But I tell you people hams is sceerce an' fowls is roostin' high.
An hit ain't de so't o' money dat is pesterin' my min',
But de question I want answehed 's how to get at any kin'![108]

The poem regarded by literary critics as one of, if not *the* best of
Dunbar's collection, is "When Malindy Sings." Praised in the London
Daily News following an enthusiastic reception by several of that city's
critics who heard Dunbar recite it, the poem is a narrative plea to
"Miss Lucy" to "quit dat noise" she makes when attempting to sing,
and to listen to the sweet music of Malindy who can bring "yo' teahs
a-drappin":

G'way an' quit dat noise, Miss Lucy—
    Put dat music book away;
What's de use to keep on tryin'?
    Ef you practise twell you're gray,

You cain't sta't no notes a-flyin'
   Lak de ones dat rants and rings
F'om de kitchen to de big woods
   When Malindy sings.

You ain't got de nachel o'gans
   Fu' to make de soun' come right,
You ain't got de tu'ns an' twistin's
   Fu' to make it sweet an' light.
Tell you one thing now, Miss Lucy,
   An' I'm tellin' you fu' true,
When hit comes to raal right singin',
   'Tain't no easy thing to do.

Easy 'nough fu' folks to hollah,
   Lookin' at de lines an' dots,
When dey ain't no one kin sence it,
   An' de chune comes in, in spots;
But fu' real melojous music,
   Dat jes' strikes yo' hea't and clings,
Jes' you stan' an' listen wif me
   When Malindy sings.

Ain't you nevah hyeahd Malindy?
   Blessed soul, tek up de cross!
Look hyeah, ain't you jokin', honey?
   Well, you don't know whut you los'
Y' ought to hyeah dat gal a-wa'blin',
   Robbins, la'ks, an' all dem things,
Heish dey moufs an' hides dey faces
   When Malindy sings.

Fiddlin' man jes' stop his fiddlin',
   Lay his fiddle on de she'f;
Mockin'-bird quit tryin' to whistle,
   'Cause he jes' so shamed hisse'f.
Folks a-playin' on de banjo
   Draps dey fingahs on de strings—
Bless yo' soul—fu'gits to move 'em,
   When Malindy sings.

She jes' spreads huh mouf and hollahs,
   "Come to Jesus," twell you hyeah

Sinnahs' tremblin' steps and voices,
    Timid-lak a-drawin' neah;
Den she tu'ns to "Rock of Ages,"
    Simply to de cross she clings,
An' you fin' yo' teahs a-drappin'
    When Malindy sings.

Who dat says dat humble praises
    Wif de Master nevah counts?
Heish yo' mouf, I hyeah dat music,
    Ez hit rises up an' mounts—
Floatin' by de hills an' valleys,
    Way above his buryin' sod,
Ez hit makes its way in glory
    To de very gates of God!

Oh, hit's sweetah dan de music
    Of an edicated band;
An' hit's dearah dan de battle's
    Song o' triumph in de lan'.
It seems holier dan evenin'
    When de solemn chu'ch bell rings,
Ez I sit an' ca'mly listen
    While Malindy sings.

Towsah, stop dat ba'kin', hyeah me!
    Mandy, mek dat chile keep still;
Don't you hyeah de echoes callin'
    F'om de valley to de hill?
Let me listen, I can hyeah it,
    Th'oo de bresh of angel's wings,
Sof' an' sweet, "Swing Low, Sweet Chariot,"
    Ez Malindy sings.[109]

Although better known as a poet, Dunbar also wrote song lyrics, musical shows, plays, essays, magazine articles, four novels, and several short stories. "A Family Feud," a short story published in *Folks From Dixie* (1898), includes many long passages in Black English:

"I reckon I hain't never tol' you 'bout ole Mas' an young Mas' fallin' out, has I? Hit's all over now, an' things is done change so dat I reckon eben ef ole Mas' was libin', he wouldn't keer if I tol', an' I known young Mas' Tho'nton wouldn't.

"Dey ain't nuffin' to hide 'bout it nohow, 'ca'se all quality families has de same kin' o' 'spectable fusses.

"Hit all happened 'long o' dem Jamiesons whut libed jinin' places to our people, an' whut ole Mas' ain't spoke to fu' nigh onto thutty years. Long while ago, when Mas' Tom Jamieson an' Mas' Jack Venable was bofe young mans, dey had a qua'l 'bout de young lady dey bofe was a-cou'tin', an' by-an'-by dey had a du'l an' Mas' Jamieson shot Mas' Jack in de shouldah, but Mas' Jack ma'ied de lady, so dey was eben. Mas' Jamieson ma'ied too, an' after so many years dey was bofe wid'ers, but dey ain't fu'give one another yit. When Mas' Tho'nton was big enough to run erroun', ole Mas' used to try to 'press on him dat a Venable mus'n never put his foot on de Jamieson lan'; an' many a tongue-lashin' an' sometimes wuss de han's on our place got fu' mixin' wif de Jamieson servants. But, la! young Mas' Tho'nton was wuss'n de niggers. Evah time he got a chance he was out an' gone, over lots an' fiel's an' into de Jamieson ya'd a-playin' wif little Miss Nellie, whut was Mas' Tom's little gal. I never did see two chillun so 'tached to one another. Dey used to wander erroun', han' in han', lak brother an' sister, an' dey'd cry lak dey little hea'ts 'u'd brek ef either one of dey pappys seed 'em an' pa'ted 'em. . . ."[110]

On Friday afternoon, February 9, 1906, Paul Laurence Dunbar, after more than two years of suffering, died in his home in Dayton, his body wracked by tuberculosis. Excessive alcoholism, his way of coping with the world that had thrust fame upon him yet forbade him to enter certain areas of journalism, had so weakened his body that tuberculosis was finally able to destroy him.

During his lifetime, Dunbar's dialect poetry had been wrapped in controversy. But in the March 1906 issue of *The Voice of the Negro*— a magazine directed to militant Black intellectuals, and thus not likely to praise someone who held Blacks up to ridicule—the editors called Dunbar "the greatest poet that the Negro race has yet produced," and further noted that "as a lyrical interpreter of the appetites and spiritual strivings of the older generation of Negroes, Dunbar excelled all others, and it may be said of most of his writings that they showed an artistic feeling and genuine poetic ability."[111] Three months later, George Davis Jenifer, writing in the same magazine, added his praise:

He has preserved to our literature a life and patois that are doomed to pass with the diffusion of greater light among the colored people of the South. . . .

Dunbar [presented] the Negro, not as a beast, not as a fiend, but as a gentle simple-hearted man. And the Southern white man remembers again the traditional kindliness between his fathers and the fathers of his black neighbor; while the Northerner, perplexed to find a refutation of his theories, is disposed to be more generous.

Possibly, then, when the future has witnessed the complete revival of that friendship between the races, for lack of which our common country suffers today, men may see fit to raise in our National Capital, a monument to the black poet, whose songs made two angry peoples mindful of their common brotherhood.[112]

Several public schools in the country are named after Paul Laurence Dunbar. In Dayton, his home on North Summit Street has become a museum. But in the nation's capital, there are no statues, no monuments. Until such a time, let the words of George Davis Jenifer be his monument—he "made two angry peoples mindful of their common brotherhood."

For Paul Laurence Dunbar, fame came early in his career. But for James D. Corrothers, who was to form a deep and warm friendship with Dunbar, fame was elusive, always close but never within reach. Yet, it was Corrothers—himself a Black poet-journalist—who would become the first critic to bring Dunbar's poetry to the attention of a wider public. In his autobiography, published in 1917, Corrothers wrote:

It was my good fortune and pleasure to "write up" Dunbar twice during this period of literary uncertainty, once in the *Chicago Journal,* over my name, and again in the *Chicago Times-Herald,* now the *Record-Herald.* The *Journal* sketch was nearly a column long, while the *Times-Herald* article covered almost two columns. With each write-up there was a picture of Dunbar, who acknowledged the appearance of the articles with a grateful note. Perhaps a year after this, [William Dean] Howells graciously brought Dunbar to the attention of the English-speaking world.[113]

But for the first few years of his life, Corrothers, like many Blacks, considered the use of Black dialect as derogatory. In his autobiography he recalled that he "grew up in the atmosphere of pure speech and enjoyed the advantages of superior training. I have never talked Negro dialect. . . . My speech and ways were those of the white community about me."[114] But the language of Dunbar's poetry was too real, too

eloquent, to be considered inferior. The language and thought so skillfully woven within each of the poems, each element working in relation
to the other, had caused a nation to begin to take another look at its attitudes about Black English. Searching within himself, Corrothers reflected the views which led to a new public attitude about Black English:

> I had always detected Negro dialect as smacking too much of *"nig-
> gerism"* which all intelligent coloured people detest. But, with the
> advent of Dunbar, in whose stories and poems Negro dialect at-
> tained a new dignity and beauty, my eyes were opened to the fact
> that here was splendid material which I had overlooked, and which
> all Negroes but Dunbar had allowed to go begging. With Dunbar's
> success, Negro dialect became popular in literature. I saw, after I
> had read a few of his pieces, that certain thoughts could not be ex-
> pressed so well in any other way as in dialect. But I firmly resolved
> that, if I ever wrote dialect, I should not imitate Dunbar, but form
> a style of my own.[115]

Corrothers, although recognizing that certain thoughts could only be
expressed in Black English, still had doubts about the legitimacy of the
language, and was further frustrated by editors imposing their own perceptions and standards upon the language of Blacks. Referring to a series of articles he wrote for the *Chicago Tribune* profiling many of the
city's leading Blacks, Corrothers scornfully noted that "nearly every
sentence of my work has been recast into what was then the customary
newspaper way of speaking of coloured folk. . . . Even the intelligent
coloured people were commonly made to say 'dis' and 'dat' in the average newspaper."[116]

Nevertheless, Corrothers, influenced by Dunbar, did write in Black
English. His dialect poetry began appearing regularly in the *Chicago
Record,* usually at "space rates," and always with good reader acceptance. Later, as his reputation grew, his poetry was published in *Century Magazine,* and many of the nation's leading daily newspapers, including the *New York Herald,* the *New York Journal,* the *Philadelphia
Inquirer,* and the *Philadelphia Herald.*

For the *Chicago Record,* Corrothers contributed a series of dialect
tales woven around a fictional Black poet, Sandy Jenkins, whom he
playfully claimed to have found in the levee district; Jenkins was the
founder of the Black Cat Club, scene of most of the stories. The Black
Cat Club stories were later collected into book form and published in

1902. Shortly after the turn of the century, Corrothers, who had been a boxer, boot-black, sailor, critic, and journalist, turned to the ministry, noting, "a sunburst having fallen upon me." He died in 1917 at the age of forty-eight, respected and admired.

In 1893, James Edwin Campbell, who had written several dialect poems which achieved a mild success upon their publication in several newspapers, met Paul Laurence Dunbar at the Chicago World's Fair. The two writers discussed the use of dialect in poetry, exchanged ideas—there are certain linguistic similarities in the poems of both writers—and became friends. Campbell was a good poet and understood the nuances of language, both Black and White. But like James D. Corrothers, he never achieved literary fame and has been relegated to obscurity, the bulk of his poetry lost and forgotten.

Campbell was born on September 28, 1867, in Pomeroy, Ohio—almost five years before Dunbar's birth, and 140 miles east of Dunbar's Dayton home. Campbell graduated from the Pomeroy Academy in 1884. During the next six years, he taught in Buck Ridge, Ohio; became editor of *The Pioneer,* a weekly newspaper in Charleston, West Virginia; principal of the Langston School in Point Pleasant, West Virginia; and president of the West Virginia Colored Institute, now known as West Virginia State College. For a decade, beginning in 1890, he was a reporter for the *Chicago Times-Herald,* which published many of his dialect verses. Later, he became coeditor of the *Four O'Clock Review,* a literary journal.

Campbell's dialect poetry shows a distinct awareness of the phonology of Black language, especially in vowel lengthening as in *big→beeg,* and *jig→jeeg.* However, like most of the dialect poetry of the time, the syntax is inconsistent, often reflective of a Standard English modification usually made for readability, although both the deep structure copula and deep structure possessive are present. Campbell reproduced Black speech with more accuracy than Dunbar, but Dunbar was unquestionably the better poet.

Many of Campbell's poems were collected into two volumes—*Driftings and Gleanings* (1887) and *Echoes From the Cabin and Elsewhere* (1895). In the introduction of *Echoes,* Richard Linthicum, editor of the *Chicago Sunday Times-Herald,* wrote that Campbell "has caught the true spirit of the ante-bellum Negro, and in characteristic verse has portrayed the simplicity, the philosophy and the humor of the race. In no instance has he descended to caricature, which has made valueless so many efforts in this fertile field."[117] To attempt to silence those who might think that Campbell's recording of dialect was less than accurate, Linthicum wrote:

> To the capricious critics who may be inclined to find fault with the varying dialect, the following incident will be valuable:
>
> A member of a minstrel company who desired to thoroughly master the Negro dialect associated for months with the Negroes on a Virginia plantation. When he appeared on the stage in Richmond, he made an instantaneous success. Later on, he appeared in Georgia and Alabama, and no one understood him.[118]

During the early 1960s, French literary critic Jean Wagner took a look at the poetry of Daniel Webster Davis (1862–1913) and harshly proclaimed:

> Only a few of [Davis's] poems fail to employ minstrel-style buffoonery or to take over the servility of the characters inhabiting the plantation tradition. It is, furthermore, far from clear whether Davis was completely sincere or whether he instead set out to win easy popularity from an audience whose demands were slight.[119]

Wagner was not alone in his assessment of Davis's poetry; many persons—Black and White—sensitive to what they believed, "by the spirit of the times," to be "unacceptable" poetry, passed off Davis's poems as representative of the worst parts of minstrelsy, thus relegating him to literary obscurity. Yet, by using humor, not pathos, Davis was able to show another side of the Black, a beautiful side that many Black poets were afraid to explore for fear of ostracism by their fellow Blacks. This was understandable since some Whites exploited this characteristic, thus making it difficult for almost any Black writer to use humor without fear of peer retaliation. In "Miss Liza's Banjer," Davis humorously and with subtle empathy carved out a slice of life, one which paralleled and possibly even pre-dated Paul Laurence Dunbar's narrative of "When Malindy Sings":

> Hi! Miss Liza's got er banjer;
>   Lemme see it, ef yo' please!
> Now don' dat thing look pooty,
>   A-layin' 'cross yer kneeze,
> Wid all dem lubly ribbins,
>   An' silber trimmin's roun'.
> Now, mistis, please jes' tetch it,
>   To lemme hear de soun'.

'Scuze me, mistis, but dar's sumfin'
  De matter wid dem strings;
I notis it don' zackly
  Gib de proper kinder ring;
An' den de way yo' hol' it
  Ain't lik' yo' orter do.
Now, mistis, won't yo' lemme
  Jes' try a chune fur yo'?

Now lis'n to de diffunce;
  I'se got the thing in chune,
An' de music's lik' de breezes
  Dat fills de air in June.
Fur a banjer's lik' a 'ooman—
  Ef she's chuned de proper pitch,
She'll gib yo' out de music
  Dat's sof', melojus, rich.

But when yo' fail to chune her,
  Or to strike de proper string,
Yo' kin no more git de music,
  Den mek' a kat-bird sing.
An' 'taint always de fixin's
  Dat makes a 'ooman bes',
But de kind ub wood she's made un
  Is de thing to stan' de tes'.

I s'pose yer plays yer music
  Jes' lik' yo' hab it wrote,
Or—what is dat yo' call it—
  A-playin' by de note?
Yo' kin fill yer head wid music
  Ez full ez it kin hol',
But yo' nebber gwine ter play it
  'Tell yo' gits it in yer soul.

T'ain't de proper notes dat makes yo'
  Feel lik' yo' wants to cry,
But de soul dat's in de music
  Dat lif's yo' up on high;
An' 'taint always de larnin',
  'Do' a splendid thing, I kno',

Dat lif's de low an' 'umble
   To higher things belo'.

Keep larnin', den, Miss Liza,
   An' when yo' wants ter know
Ef yo' kin play de banjer,
   Jes' kum to Uncle Joe;
Jes' fill yer head wid music,
   Ez full ez it kin hol'
But de music from de banjer
   Must fust be in de soul.[120]

In "De Niggers Got to Go," Davis used Black English poetry as his medium to probe not only an emerging problem of society, but the mind of society as well:

Dear Liza, I is bin down-town
   To Marster Charley's sto',
An' all de talk dis nigger hear
   Is, "Niggers got to go."
I 'fess it bodders my ol' head,
   An' I would lik' to kno',
What all we cullud folks is do'n',
   Dat now we'z got to go?

I hear dem say dat long ago
   To ol' Virginny's sho',
Dar kum a ship wid cullud folks,
   Sum twenty odd or mo';
Dey tells me dat dey hoed de corn,
   An' wuz good wuckers, sho',
Dey made Virginny like de rose—
   But now dey's got to go.

Dat, when ol' Ginnel Washin'ton
   Did whip dem Red-koats so,
A nigger wuz de fus' to fall
   A-fightin' ub de fo';
Dat, in de late "impleasureness"
   Dey watched at Mayster's do',
Proteckin' ub his lubin' ones,—
   But now dey's got to go.

I 'fess I lubs dis dear ol' place—
   'Twuz here we beried Jo';
An' little Liza married off,
   So menny years ago.
An' now we'z feeble, an' our lim's
   A-getting mighty slo'.
We'd hate to lebe de dear ol' place—
   But den, wez got to go.

I don't kno' much 'bout politicks,
   An' all dem things, yo' kno',
But de las' 'leckshun I jes' vote
   Ez de whi' folks tol' me to;
Dey tole me vote fur Dimikrats,
   An' 'twould be better, 'do'
Sense now dey don' de leckshun win
   Dey sez we'z got to go.

Dey sez de whi' folks mad 'long us,
   'Cause we kummin' up, yo' kno';
An' sum un us is gittin' rich,
   Wid do'-bells on de do';
An' got sum lawyers, doctors too,
   An' men like dat, fur sho'.
But den it kan't be jes' fur dis
   Dat we all got to go.

De Lord he made dis lubly lan'
   Fur white and black folks too,
An' gin each man his roe to ten'—
   Den what we gwine to do?
We 'habes ouselbes an' 'specks de laws,
   But dey's peckin mo' an mo'.
We ain't don' nuffin 't all to dem.
   Den huccum we mus' go?

Fur ebry nashun on de glob'
   Dis seems to be a hom';
Dey welkums dem wid open arms,
   No matter whar dey frum;
But we, who here wuz bred an' borhn,
   Don't seem to hab no show;

We ho'ped to mek it what it is,
   But still we'z got to go.

It pears to me, my Liza, dear,
   We'z got a right to stay,
An' not a man on dis broad urf
   Gwine dribe dis nigger 'way.
But why kan't whi' folks lef us lon',
   An' weed dar side de ro';
An' what dey all time talkin' 'bout—
   "De nigger's got to go?"

" 'Rastus," Liza sed, "trus' in God,
   He'll fix things here belo',
He don't hate us bekase we'z black—
   He made us all, yo' kno';
He lubs us, ef we'z cullud folks,
   Ef de hart is white an' pure,
An' 'cepin' de Lords sez,—'Forward, march!'
   We'z not a-gwine to go."[121]

With the exception of the eye dialect words *sez* and *wuz,* the representation of Black dialect phonology in Davis's poems is much above average—certainly better than that written by Dunbar. The syntax, like the syntax in most Black English poems, follows a Standard English pattern, the rhythm and beat being not of West Africa but of America.

Many of Davis's poems were collected and published in *Idle Moments* (1895), which served as the base for a much larger collection of poems, *'Weh Down Souf,* published two years later. In 1908, the Virginia Press published *An Industrial History of the Negro in the United States,* written by Davis and Giles B. Jackson.

Daniel Webster Davis died in 1913, a minister, a man of religion and compassion who, though experiencing discrimination, tried to understand and accept what life had to offer at the moment. Davis liked the South; he was proud of it, and proud of the accomplishments of his people. He tried to understand the racist White mind, his poetry reflecting not bitterness but understanding. Yet, as fate would have it, he found only literary obscurity.

For the Black living in the late nineteenth century, the professions of education, the ministry, and journalism were the ways *out,* the ways *up.*

If the schools were segregated, it meant that there were openings in Black schools and colleges which welcomed educated men. And if the churches were for "Whites only," as most were, then it was only necessary to find a Black church. And if the newspapers, magazines, and book publishers were not hiring Blacks, there were still opportunities to freelance and earn "space rates," or work for a Black-owned newspaper or magazine. Not infrequently, an educated Black, at different times in his life, would be a journalist, teacher, and minister.

Junius Mordecai Allen was not a teacher, minister, or journalist, though many of his dialect poems first appeared in newspapers. J. Mord Allen, as he preferred his byline to read, was a skilled boilermaker. But he was also a skilled poet, the "feel" of his poems comparing favorably with those of Dunbar. A keen observer of human nature, Allen often chose deep, penetrating satire to express his views of life. In "The Squeak of the Fiddle," published in *Rhymes, Tales and Rhymed Tales* (1906), the only collection of his writing, Allen has a husband and wife imagine what would happen if a magical potion rendered them White. The poem looks not only at a Black population struggling to enter the "great White middle-class," but at the values of that White population as well:

> En den we'll j'ine er white church
>> Ter match our white-folks clo'es.
> En I b'lieve I'll run fer office
>> Lak de other white men does.
> En dese hyeah common darkies—
>> We'll quit speakin' ter 'em all;
> We'll git 'quainted wid some white folks,
>> En ax dem in ter call.
> Now, Mandy—Mandy, honey,
>> Don't it kind o' make yer smile,
> Ter think o' dem white ladies
>> Drappin' in ter set er while,
> En us er talkin' ter 'em
>> 'Bout serciety en books,
> En "Love, yer cheeks is rosy,"
>> En "Dear, how pale yer looks"? . . .[122]

Allen's poetry—both Standard English and in Negro dialect—includes the harsh sounds seldom found consistently in the poems of other poets. The heavy use of *yer, ter, ur,* and *er,* for example, establishes a rhythm that suggests a harshness of life—language influencing interpretation of culture.

The place of Charles Waddell Chesnutt has finally become secure in American literary history. Although first recognized during the Reconstruction Cycle, lasting recognition was not achieved until the Civil Rights Cycle of American Black English, almost sixty years later when the writings of the pioneer Black writers were dusted off and reintroduced into the literature of the people.

Chesnutt's formal education never went beyond elementary school, but during his lifetime he became a stenographer, the principal of a state normal school in Fayetteville, North Carolina, and a successful lawyer, as well as an excellent writer with a strong command of both Standard and Black English.

Although Chesnutt used Black English extensively in his stories, he never fully accepted the legitimacy of the language. In a letter to Walter H. Page, of Houghton, Mifflin & Co., Chesnutt wrote:

> Speaking of dialect, it is almost a despairing task to write it. What to do with the troublesome *r* and the obvious inconsistency of leaving it out where it would be in good English, and putting it in where correct speech would leave it out, how to express such words as "here" and "hear" and "year" and "other" and "another," "either" and "neither," and so on, is a "stractin" task. The fact is, of course, that there is no such thing as a Negro dialect; that what we call by that name is the attempt to express, with such a degree of phonetic correctness as to suggest the sound, English pronounced as an ignorant old southern Negro would be supposed to speak it, and at the same time to preserve a sufficient approximation to the correct spelling to make it easy reading. I do not imagine I have got my dialect, even now, any more uniform than other writers of the same sort of matter.[123]

Like many writers of the era, Chesnutt contributed his first short stories and dialect tales to the newspapers and minor magazines. Then, in August 1887, when he was twenty-nine years old, he earned his first major publication credit when *The Atlantic Monthly* published "The Goophered Grapevine," a folklore dialect tale. Its central character is Uncle Julius McAdoo, a gardener and former slave who talks about Blacks, their folklore, and slavery; as such, the tale parallels the Uncle Remus stories. Chesnutt's use of dialect, like that of Harris, is impressive and nearly flawless.

In 1899, Houghton Mifflin & Co., one of the nation's leading book publishers, published *The Conjure Woman,* a compilation of seven of Chesnutt's dialect folk tales which had appeared in the mass media. The lead tale was "The Goophered Grapevine," and each of the other six tales were tied together by the presence of Uncle Julius McAdoo.

The success of the first book led Houghton Mifflin to request a second. However, *The Wife of His Youth, and Other Stories of the Color-Line,* although composed of tales that first appeared in leading magazines, had a different emphasis than the first book. The first book reflected Chesnutt's life in Fayetteville, North Carolina; the second reflected his life in Cleveland, which he identified as Groveland. Literary critic Ruth Miller explains the difference between the two books:

> The two books taken together represent Chesnutt's own shift from Fayetteville to Cleveland. In the second collection of stories he depicts the conflicts that beset people of color as they strive to live decently in urban society. Swamps and groves give way to streets and fine houses, witchcraft to midnight suppers, superstitious uneducated field hands and house servants to light-skinned women in brocades and gentlemen who have acquired their fortunes in professions and trades; efforts to outwit the master give way to efforts to rise in society, and finally the sense of the comic—the wistful, the amiable buffoonery of the "conjure" stories—gives way before an increasingly bitter awareness of the color barrier.[124]

The success of Chesnutt's first two books led to *The House Behind the Cedars* (1900), and *The Morrow of Tradition* (1901). In 1905, *The Colonel's Dream,* a novel, was published. It was to be his last published book. *The Colonel's Dream* was a passionate appeal for understanding between the races, an appeal for an end to inequality. It fell on deaf ears. The apparent failure of *The Colonel's Dream* to evoke social change embittered Chesnutt, for he realized that it wasn't the time to change traditions and conventions that had built up for nearly three centuries. The remaining twenty-seven years of Chesnutt's life were spent in the practice of law.

Had it been published two decades earlier, or several decades later, *The Colonel's Dream* in all probability would have achieved greater sales; it would have had an impact. But this was 1905. The Reconstruction Cycle, which began shortly after the Civil War, was already drawing to a close by 1895. By 1900, few remnants remained. Only Joel Chandler Harris, Paul Laurence Dunbar, and Charles Waddell Chesnutt, almost alone among the thousands of writers who preceded them, would extend the cycle a few more years. Their books, for the most part, would be compilations of stories and poems that appeared in the leading newspapers and magazines many years earlier.

A stillness had fallen over the Reconstruction Cycle. Irwin Russell and the Laniers were dead. Thomas Dunn English died in 1902; Lafcadio Hearn died in 1904; two years after Hearn died, Paul Laurence Dunbar would die. In 1908, Joel Chandler Harris would die; in 1910, Mark Twain. No longer was *Judge* running as many dialect verses or Black dialect cartoons as it once had. The names of Zimmerman, Kembel, Wales, Frost, Ehrnhardt, and Outcault would become nearly forgotten in American history. Dialect tales disappeared from the pages of *Century, Scribner's, Appleton's, Lippincott's,* and *Harper's.* The minstrel shows, which had held the Blacks up to ridicule through much of the nineteenth century, would continue to draw audiences through the early 1930s, but even they had lost much of their popular appeal. Black newspapers, many of which were founded and ceased publication in the 1880s and 1890s, would be buried in the sands of time, only to be resurrected in a different form in a different cycle. Studies about Black English diminished and became virtually nonexistent until shortly before World War I, when another cycle would begin. And everywhere, in all the media, and in all that people read or heard, there would be that same haunting, literary stillness that marked the end of a cycle.

4. The Negro Renaissance Cycle

On June 28, 1914, Archduke Francis Ferdinand, heir to the throne of Austro-Hungary, and his wife, while riding in a parade in Bosnia, were murdered by a Serbian fanatic. A month later, Austro-Hungary declared war on Serbia. An entanglement of alliances brought virtually all of Europe into the conflict, and World War I, the war no one wanted, was declared—abruptly and unexpectedly. On August 2, 1914, *The New York Times,* reflecting public opinion, editorialized that the war in Europe was "the least justified of all wars since man emerged from barbarism." But less than three years later, the United States was drawn into the war, the "Great American Crusade," the "War To End All Wars," a "holy war" fought from the pulpits of America by the clergy who proclaimed it to be a war against "Godless Barbarism." Americans—millions of them—had found their cause; they would go to Europe and save Britain and France from the "Godless barbaric Huns" and preserve freedom for the world. Then one day, four years and 37 million deaths after it began, the war was over; an "Armistice Day" so proclaimed it. The war was the end of an era; America had lost her innocence on the bomb-scarred fields of a continent that had absorbed the dead and rejected the living. And so the soldiers returned to their homes, to participate in parades and picnics. The world, which had gone through a generation in only four years, was once again at peace with itself.

Just as the war marked the end of one era, it also marked the beginning of another, one marked by a fierce determination to block out the memories and horror that the destruction of human life brings in its wake. For far too many years, the nation lived with a grim reality; now it wanted to live in an age of escapism, an age marked by a new morality, a new literature. As the nation began to regather itself, there began a mass migration from the farms and into the cities as the citizen-soldiers began to break free of their traditional roots to search for an elusive something *else*.

Joining in this mass migration to Northern industrial cities were the Southern Blacks, seeking to escape webs of prejudice and poverty, and enticed by jobs. The largest Black community in the world emerged in New York's Harlem. Smaller Black communities grew in Chicago, Detroit, Philadelphia, and other major cities of the North. The movement brought the Blacks into closer proximity with the Northern Whites, people who frequently knew about Blacks only through the romantic literature which pictured the Black as a happy-go-lucky being, musical by nature, often lazy, and sometimes "uppety" enough to get lynched. The North was able to accept the Black, able to proclaim all kinds of edicts about equality and racial harmony—until the Black became a potential neighbor. Then it was a different matter.

But now the Black, a more militant Black, was ready to meet the challenges of the North. Black orators and philosophers had already begun whittling away at the compromise policies of Booker T. Washington, which had helped bring them into the twentieth century, and now began listening to the voices of Marcus Garvey, Alain Locke, and W. E. B. Du Bois who would become the founder of the National Association of Colored People (NAACP). In 1919, Du Bois—who had been a disciple of Washington but who broke away during the first decade of the century—aired the sentiments of Blacks who had fought "for freedom" on foreign soil, yet who now faced prejudice at home:

> Under similar circumstances, we would fight again. But by the God of Heaven, we are cowards and jackasses if now that the war is over, we do not marshal every ounce of our brain and brawn to fight a sterner, longer, more unbending battle against the forces of hell in our land.[1]

Given a unifying voice, Blacks began to respond, openly challenging time-honored Northern traditions often more confining than many of those in the South. That summer—in Washington, D.C., Chicago, Omaha, Knoxville, and twenty-two other cities—Blacks resolved to "meet violence with violence." It was a summer to be recorded in blood as the "red summer." A few, though very few, concessions were made.

During the Civil War, less than twenty per cent of all Blacks—both free and enslaved—were literate; by the 1920s, more than eighty per cent were literate. In 1910, Du Bois founded *The Crisis,* the sociopolitical journal of the NAACP; in 1916, Carter G. Woodson, the son of former slaves, founded the *Journal of Negro History;* and in 1923, Charles S. Johnson, a respected folklorist and scholar, founded *Opportunity,* a publication of the National Urban League. These three publications, along with a handful of major Black-oriented newspapers such as the *Chicago Defender,* formed the base for the emergence of a new literature, a Black literature that would lead to the Harlem Renaissance, to the Negro Renaissance.

In a literature that often spoke with the passions of bitterness and defiance, the names of Arna Bontemps, Countee Cullen, Jessie Fauset, Langston Hughes, Zora Neale Hurston,[2] James Weldon Johnson, Nella Larsen, Claude McKay, Paul Robeson, Jean Toomer, and Walter White would be etched into history. In music, the world would be hearing a new beat, led by Marion Anderson, Louis Armstrong, Eubie Blake, Harry Burleigh, Will Marion Cook, Ford Dabney, Duke Ellington, W. C. Handy, Fletcher Henderson, Blind Lemmon Jefferson, Scott Joplin, Jelly Roll Morton, and Fats Waller. And on the stage and in films, the names Eddie ("Rochester") Anderson, Josephine Baker, Willie Best, Stepin Fetchit, Charles Gilpin, Rex Ingram, Hattie Mc-Daniels, Butterfly McQueen, Florence Mills, Richard B. Harrison, Rose McClendon, Paul Robeson, Bill ("Bojangles") Robinson, and Ethel Waters would be added to the lists of the great actors in American history. A new awareness of Black achievement in the arts, the sciences, and the humanities was slowly evolving in American cultural life. It was an awareness that allowed Black genius to develop and emerge, largely unencumbered by the bonds of provincialism and stereotypical attitudes which diminished, if ever so briefly, during the 1920s.

By the 1920s, with a new social order and a new "spirit of the times," Black writers, sensitive to stereotyped images, shunned the use of dialect. They reasoned that whether or not Black English could more effectively convey certain thoughts than Standard English, it had become too readily associated with inferiority. The public was accepting Black literature written in Standard English; there was no reason to use dialect. Yet, there were exceptions.

In 1904, the F. J. Heer Co., of Columbus, Ohio, had published *Planta-tion Echoes,* a collection of dialect poems written by Elliot Blaine Henderson, a Black poet.

Most of Henderson's other dialect poetry anthologies reflected what later came to be identified as stereotyped images of the antebellum Black—*Dis, Dat, and Tutter* (1908), *Humble Folks* (1909), *Darkey Meditations* (1910), *Jes' Plain Black Fo'ks* (1913), and *Darkey Ditties* (1915).

John Wesley Holloway, born in Georgia in 1865, began writing verse at the age of eight. He attended Clark University, and graduated in 1891 from the literature program at Fisk University. Like James D. Corrothers, Daniel Webster Davis, and numerous other Black writer-journalists, Holloway turned to education and the ministry. In 1900, he became an ordained minister, and during the next four years, served as both the pastor of the Congregational Church in Guthrie, Oklahoma, and as assistant principal of Guthrie High School. He later became pastor of Congregational churches in Newark, New Jersey; Thebes, Georgia; and Anniston, Alabama.

In 1919, *From the Desert,* a collection of seventy-five poems, was published. In the foreword, Holloway explained that the purpose of the anthology was to bring to the public's attention "as soon as possible a volume devoted . . . to devotional, moral, and religious subjects." Still, it was his dialect poetry and not the religious poems that brought him critical acclaim. The representation of Black English only "suggests" the dialect rather than reproduces it. The syntax is distinctively Standard English; the phonology could, quite conceivably, be interpreted as representing the various Southern dialects; only the subjects themselves are distinctively Black-oriented.

Sometime during 1911, Raymond Garfield Dandridge, at the age of twenty-nine, was stricken by a fever; a year later, he suffered a nervous breakdown, eventually losing the use of both legs and his right arm. But during the remaining eighteen years of his life, he wrote numerous poems—in both Standard and Black English—and became literary editor of the *Cincinnati Journal.* Many of his poems appeared first in newspapers and magazines before being collected into *Penciled Poems* (1917), and *The Poet and Other Poems* (1920). Dandridge's representation of Black dialect phonology is more accurate than Holloway's, but the syntax, as was the syntax in almost all dialect poetry, was distinctively Standard English.

After a dormancy of about a generation, dialect tales once again poured forth from the nation's mass media during the 1920s, virtually blanketing the country with a genre of literature not unlike that of the Reconstruction Cycle. Black dialect was once again popular, and writers, responding to "public-and-publisher" needs, began churning out the tales at a pace far exceeding that of the Reconstruction Cycle. It soon became almost impossible to find a newspaper or magazine that had not published at least one dialect tale, usually to the delight of its substantially White subscription list, and rarely for the amusement of its few Black readers. In the Summer 1922 issue of *The Texas Review,* Edgar P. Billups deplored this exploitation:

> [T]here has been such a popular demand for negro stories that pseudo-dialect writers, taking advantage of the demand and usurping the field, have sent forth impressions of negro character which are utterly false, and the always unsuspecting public has accepted the false for the genuine; since these false impressions have had such a widespread circulation, the public has been wrongly educated. . . . This incorrect education unless soon checked, will become both universal and permanent.[3]

An editorial in the September 1924 issue of *Opportunity,* further argued:

> The caricatures of words and ideas which are now paraded as Negro dialect do not pretend to be the simple speech of illiterate Negroes,—dialect with a natural and reasonable growth, but the incongruous effect of education on rather hopeless subjects. And as dialect may represent the character of the folk employing it, so pseudo-dialect misrepresents the folk it is alleged to depict. There are legitimate uses for Negro dialect. Its haunting mellowness opens into the very heart of the romantic old South. It is rich with the broken pathos and gentle humor of a race and a social order passing slowly but inevitably into the chambers of memory. It has a place in southern literature and it deserves to be rescued from the hands of both the ignorant and the wanton exploiters.[4]

Not all dialect tales were produced by "ignorant and wanton exploiters." There were a few writers who tried to understand not only the language but the culture of the Black people. In the September

1927 issue of *The Jewish Tribune,* Arthur M. Kaplan concluded a biographical sketch by pointing out: "There is now a preponderance of stories in the Negro dialect, Jewish dialect, Italian dialect, and childish greblings, plus everything conceivable which strikes an editor as sure-fire. So, if you want the real thing . . . you must go to the master."[5] The master that Kaplan was talking about was Octavus Roy Cohen, originator of the highly popular Florian Slappey stories.

Cohen was born in Charleston, South Carolina, in 1891, and began his professional career in 1909 as a civil engineer in Birmingham, Alabama, leaving that position the following year to become a reporter for the *Birmingham Ledger.* Returning to Charleston after a few months, he completed studies for a Bachelor of Science degree in civil engineering from Clemson College while working as a reporter for the *Charleston News and Courier.* Moving to New Jersey, he became a reporter for the *Bayonne Times,* and later the *Newark Morning Star.* In 1912, he returned to Charleston to begin the study of law in his father's office, passing the bar examination a year later. In 1915—after a year as a civil engineer, slightly more than two years as a newspaper reporter, and two years as a lawyer—Octavus Roy Cohen, the son of a journalist-lawyer, sold his first short story, "Below the Surface," and began a forty-five-year career as a professional freelance writer. During his career, he wrote more than 1,000 short stories and articles, most of them appearing in the nation's leading magazines; forty-two books, almost all of them best sellers; six plays; and thirty motion pictures, including the highly popular *The Big Gamble* (1931) and *Curtain at Eight* (1935). Although recognized as one of the nation's finest mystery and romance writers, Cohen's enduring fame rests primarily on his dialect tales, most of which were first published in the *Saturday Evening Post* during the 1920s and 1930s.

Polished Ebony (1919), his first book, was a collection of dialect tales, many of which were originally published in the newspapers for which he worked. During the 1920s and 1930s, several more collections of his dialect tales were published, each receiving a warm response from the public. Florian Slappey, the Black hero of more than 200 short stories, soon achieved a popularity that some suggested even surpassed that of his creator. As times changed, many looked back on the Florian Slappey tales as caricatures of White-stereotyped images of what Blacks were "supposed" to be like. And, to a certain extent, the characters were partially stereotypical images reflective of a more sophisticated minstrelsy. The problems and lives depicted, if not real, were to a certain extent based upon reality—not a universal reality, but a reality nonetheless. Cohen deliberately created humorous situations for his characters, but he was also a writer who attempted to understand human nature; his Black characters had the same emotions and feelings as his White characters. But his White characters were often placed into dramatic settings, whereas his Black characters were seen only in humorous situations. This was enough to justify attacks on Cohen's stories as "racist," and on Cohen himself for not understanding, and thus exploiting, the Black.

Cohen's handling of Black dialect—a literary dialect which was a combination of Standard and Black English intended to give a "flavor" of the language while not reducing reading comprehension—although inaccurate, was better than that of most of his contemporaries. There is consistent exclusion of the postvocalic /r/, and occasional elision of the unstressed word-initial syllable. There is little consistency in consonant cluster reduction in either word-initial or word-medial position; consonant clusters and nasalization in word-final position are usually dropped. A few syntactic rules—though by no means consistent—are present, including deep structure possessive, verb and subject disagreement, and the use of undifferentiated pronouns. Occasionally, other rules appear.

In 1959, at the age of sixty-seven, Octavus Roy Cohen died in Los Angeles, his home since 1935. Even two decades after the peak of his fame, he was given major obituary coverage by the nation's leading newspapers and magazines; a decade later he was forgotten.

In 1922, James Weldon Johnson—journalist, poet, educator, lawyer, and field secretary of the National Association for the Advancement of Colored People—argued that the representation of dialect in poetry was no longer sufficient to express adequately the language of the Black. He argued that Black writers need to:

> find a form that will express the racial spirit by symbols from within rather than by symbols from without, such as the mere mutilation of English spelling and pronunciation. He needs a form that is freer and larger than dialect, but which will still hold the racial flavor; a form expressing the imagery, the idioms, the peculiar turns of thought, and the distinctive humor and pathos, too, of the Negro, but which will also be capable of voicing the deepest and highest emotions and aspirations, and allow of the widest range of subjects and the widest scope of treatment.
>
> Negro dialect is at present a medium that is not capable of giving expression to the varied conditions of Negro life in America, and

much less is it capable of giving the fullest interpretation of Negro character and psychology. This is no indictment against the dialect as dialect, but against the mould of convention in which Negro dialect in the United States has been set. In time these conventions may become lost, and the colored poet in the United States may sit down to write in dialect without feeling that his first line will put the general reader in a frame of mind which demands that the poem be humorous or pathetic. In the meantime, there is no reason why these poets should not continue to do the beautiful things that can be done, and done best, in the dialect.[6]

God's Trombones (1927), a collection of seven Black sermons in verse, but written in Standard English phonology, became Johnson's definitive statement about the nature of Black English and its integration with Black culture. Almost forty-five years earlier, Joel Chandler Harris had explained his reasons for writing in dialect. In the introduction to *God's Trombones,* Johnson, a Black, elaborating on his earlier philosophy about the use of Black English in literature, presented equally valid reasons why he chose not to write in dialect:

Although the dialect is the exact instrument for voicing certain traditional phrases of Negro life, it is, and perhaps by that exactness, a quite limited instrument. Indeed, it is an instrument with but two complete stops, pathos and humor. This limitation is not due to any defect of the dialect as dialect—but to the mould of convention in which Negro dialect . . . has been set, to the fixing effects of its long association with the Negro as only a happy-go-lucky or a forlorn figure. The Afroamerican poet might in time be able to break this mould of convention and write poetry in dialect without feeling that the first line will put the reader in a frame of mind that demands that the poem be either funny or sad . . . The passing of dialect as a medium for Negro poetry will be an actual loss, for in it many beautiful things can be done; and done best . . .
[The Negro preachers] were all saturated with the sublime phraseology of the Hebrew prophets and steeped in the idioms of King James English, so when they preached . . . they spoke another language, a language far removed from traditional Negro dialect. It was really a fusion of Negro idioms with Bible English; and in this there may have been. . . . Some kinship with the innate grandiloquenc [sic] of their old African tongues. To place in the mouths of the talented old-time Negro preachers a language that is

a literary imitation of Mississippi cotton-field dialect is sheer bur-
lesque.

The Negro preacher loved the sonorous, mouth-filling, ear-filling
phrase because it gratified a highly developed sense of sound and
rhythm in himself and his hearers.[7]

Roark Bradford, agreeing that the Black language could not adequately
be reduced to graphemic shapes on a printed page, pointed out that the
American Black "has created for himself a language of beauty and
rhythm that, perhaps, is more expressive and less verbose than any language extant."[8] Bradford further reasoned that the development of an
American Black English was based on a pidginization of language, although he was probably unfamiliar with the linguistic basis of pidginization:

> Here [in America], their masters' language was harsh, inexpressive,
> unworldly jumbles of sounds that could be represented by twenty-
> six letters of the alphabet. The Negro softened it, amplified it, ab-
> breviated it, simplified it, and generally adapted it to his own sense
> of the appropriate to such an extent that even the most ignorant
> Negro can get more said with a half dozen words than the average
> United States Senator can say in a two-hour speech.[9]

Recognizing that the conventional Standard English orthography
could never fully represent Black speech, Bradford, nevertheless, chose
to write in dialect, believing that a good writer could present a "feel"
for the language which would tend to shadow linguistic inaccuracies.
However, the representation of Black English by Bradford never
equalled that presented by either Joel Chandler Harris or Ambrose
Gonzales, both of whom were far more meticulous in recording the
phonology and syntax. But, there was still much to praise. Elizabeth
Lemay, writing in the May 13, 1928, issue of the *New York World,*
noted that "these stories are enjoyable any way you take them, but they
are particularly well adapted to being read aloud, both for the effect of
the dialect, and because real humor is most pleasurable shared." And
the *Louisville Courier-Journal* noted that Bradford could "draw the
Negro he knows in single situations that reveal him with the power of
insight and a magic . . . that no one else has come near."

Roark Bradford was born in 1896 on a plantation in Tennessee,
nursed and raised by a Negro mammy. After service as an army ballis-
tics expert during World War I, he became a reporter on the *Atlanta
Georgian,* leaving two years later to become first a reporter and night

city editor, then Sunday editor of the *New Orleans Times-Picayune.* His first published fiction, a series of dialect tales for the *New York World,* was the base for his most successful book, *Ol' Man Adam an' His Chillun; Being Tales They Tell About the Time the Lord Walked the Earth Like a Natural Man* (1928). Bradford says he became interested in the Black perspectives of the Old Testament after hearing some sermons from a friend of his, a Black preacher. Each of the dialect tales, molded and recreated by Bradford, focused on one aspect of the Old Testament, as seen by a "modern-day" Black trying to understand the events of his religious history.

Among Bradford's other books are *Ol' King David an' the Philistine Boys* (1930), *John Henry* (1931), and *Kingdom Coming* (1933), all of which included significant passages of Black English.

Ol' Man Adam an' His Chillun, well received as a newspaper series, became a best seller as a book, inspiring Marc Connelly to write *The Green Pastures,* a two-act comedic adaptation. The play, with an all-Black cast, opened February 26, 1930, at the Mansfield Theatre in New York City. Reviewers were not only enthusiastic, but thoroughly excited by the stage production. In the *New York Herald Tribune,* Richard Watts, Jr., called the play "one of the loftiest achievements of the American theatre." In *Theatre Arts* magazine, John Hutchens called it "an all-enveloping emotional experience . . . [Connelly] has made *The Green Pastures* express the relationship, in simple terms, of anyone and his God." And Joseph Wood Krutch, nationally respected writer, editor, and critic, a person careful in his use of superlatives, enthusiastically announced in *The Nation* that "the thing which becomes a living whole on the stage of the Mansfield is one of the most moving creations I have ever seen in the theatre."[10]

Later that year, Marc Connelly—former newspaper reporter, freelance journalist, and George S. Kauffman's collaborator on several plays, including the highly successful *Dulcey* (1921)—was awarded the Pulitzer Prize in drama for *The Green Pastures.* So successful had his play become that the original stage company, with Richard B. Harrison as "de Lawd," gave 1,779 performances in 203 cities, every performance enthusiastically received; many Americans living in New England, the Midwest, and other regions in the North, saw and heard Blacks and Black English being spoken for the first time.

Connelly understood the nuances of language, and how language and culture were indicators of each other. However, just as a script is meant only to suggest direction for the production, the representation of Black English was meant only to indicate the importance of the dialect. Actors who understood and spoke Black English internalized Connelly's words so that the phonology represented in the script was not what was heard on the stage. Nevertheless, the script's basic syntax and language patterns were usually retained in stage production.

The Green Pastures, which as a stage play excited a nation, began its transition to cinema in 1935. Connelly adapted his playscript to a movie script; filming, under Connelly's direction, began in January 1936, and continued for six weeks. In May, Warner Brothers premiered the 93-minute movie in New York City. From throughout the nation—from critics and audience—there came superlative reviews—"sensational," "brilliant," "moving."

In 1957, *The Green Pastures* was adapted for television by Connelly, and broadcast in October by the National Broadcasting Company as a "Hallmark Hall of Fame" special. NBC officials, not wishing to offend anyone, required several script changes from the stage and screen versions. Among the changes, Babylon was no longer depicted as a New Orleans nightclub, and "de Lawd"—who was now "The Lord"—no longer smoked ten-cent "see-gars," didn't wear a derby, and now sat on a "celestial throne" rather than behind a desk in what was the office of a rural Negro lawyer. But, the boldest change was in the dialect. Believing that Black English was reflective of the uneducated Black, and reflective of stereotypical attitudes, NBC required significant script modification in dialogue. Although some of the original syntactic structures remained, most of the language was modified into a bastardization of what appeared to be Southern Standard English, with some Black lexical items and Black syntactic forms added "for flavor"; the phonology depicted was distinctively Southern White.

Roark Bradford's Black dialect sermons, which had spawned *The Green Pastures,* also spawned a literary flood of similar dialect stories; none was so competently handled as the original, and most were weak imitations in both development and representation of Black language as an integral part of Black culture. However, *Black Genesis* (1930), written by Gertrude Matthews Shelby and Samuel Gaillard Stoney, was an exception. Concentrating more on the language, Shelby and Stoney, like Bradford, took stories from the Old Testament and freely translated them into Black-oriented views of religion. In "Creation," the two authors show their awareness of language:

In de beginnin' God been jus' a-projeckin' roun' in de element. Aint been no Eart' nor no Hebben. So, for please heself, he start for mek 'em.

De fust goin'-off he mek de day an' de night, an' de Sun for glorify him by day, an' de Moon by night. Only de Moon aint specify so good—it aint shine so bright. So God stick up a whole lot o' star in de hebbens, for braughtus [good measure].

'Sides dat, he git Hebben all fixed up for him to lib in, wid a fine Big House an' a long Abenue leadin' up to it, an' pearly gate for go in, an' a whole lot o' Cherubims and Seraphims for wait on him, an' tek care o' de place.

When God git kind o' satisfy wid de sky, he turn he han' to de Eart'. He fool roun' and fool roun', till he hab a big mud pie, de kind dat chillen does mek. Den, for see how de dirt stan' by heself, he ditch it good an' draw off de water, an' he mek all dem ribber, an' creek, an' branch.[11]

BLACK ENGLISH AND AMERICAN DRAMA

As the Colonial-Revolutionary Cycle drew to a close during the last decade of the eighteenth century, drama went into a century-long decline, replaced by the rise of the novel in the Antebellum Cycle, and by the short story in the Reconstruction Cycle. However, the Negro Renaissance Cycle saw a rebirth in drama. American Black English as represented in the drama of the 1920s shows fewer African-based constructions, and a greater intermixing of Standard English and Black English forms than do most plays written during the Colonial-Revolutionary Cycle, a possible clue to the decreolization process. Yet, even with the intermixing of linguistic forms, there is still a noticeable consistency, only some of which may be attributed to writer's or printer's conventions.

Among the writers who used Black English in dialogue was Eugene O'Neill, whom most critics regarded as the playwright who led the nation into a reawakening in dramatic literature.

O'Neill earned four Pulitzer prizes in drama, and in 1936, the Nobel Prize in literature. He was born in New York City in 1888, the son of James O'Neill, a nationally recognized actor, and Ella O'Neill. Between 1906, when he left Princeton University during the middle of his freshman year, and 1913, when he wrote his first drama, O'Neill was a gold miner in Honduras, a seaman on the Atlantic routes, an assistant theater manager, and a newspaper reporter. *Beyond the Horizon,* produced in 1920 when O'Neill was thirty-two years old, was awarded the

Pulitzer Prize. Two years later, O'Neill earned his second Pulitzer Prize for *'Anna Christie'*, a revision of a 1920 drama, *Chris Christopherson*. Among the more than seventy-five plays written by O'Neill during his four-decade career are *Ah, Wilderness!* (1933), *Bound East for Cardiff* (1916), *Days Without End* (1934), *Desire Under the Elms* (1924), *The Great God Brown* (1926), *The Hairy Ape* (1922), *The Iceman Cometh* (1946), *A Long Day's Journey Into Night* (written in 1940, produced in 1956; Pulitzer Prize), *A Moon for the Misbegotten* (1947), *Mourning Becomes Electra* (1931), and *Strange Interlude* (1928; Pulitzer Prize).

Largely on the strength of his Black-oriented dramas—notably *The Dreamy Kid* (1919), *The Emperor Jones* (1920), and *All God's Chillun Got Wings* (1924)—O'Neill's reputation as a major writer was established, then enhanced. *The Dreamy Kid,* first produced in New York City by the Provincetown Players, a little-theatre group, is the story of a gun-wielding gangland leader who murders a White—"he tole folks he was gwine ter git me for a fac', and dat fo'ced my hand"—and then gives up the safety of a hide-out to be with his dying grandmother.

A year after producing *The Dreamy Kid,* the Provincetown Players produced *The Emperor Jones,* an eight-scene drama which many critics regard as the finest one-act drama in American literature, a powerful sociopsychological statement of life which can be interpreted on many levels.[12] On an island in the West Indies, Brutus Jones—former Pullman car porter, now an emperor—realizes that his reign of terror is about to end. In the first scene, he and Smithers, a White lackey, reminisce about the beginnings of the reign:

Jones. And it didn't take long from dat time to git dese fool woods' niggers right where I wanted dem. [*With pride*] From stowaway to Emperor in two years! Dat's goin' some!
Smithers. [*With curiosity*]. And I bet you got er pile o' money 'id safe someplace.
Jones. [*With satisfaction*]. I sho' has! And it's in a foreign bank where no pusson don't ever get it out but me no matter what come. You don't s'pose I was holdin' down dis Emperor job for de glory in it, did you? Sho'! De fuss and glory part of it, dat's only to turn de heads o' de low-flung, bush niggers dat's here. Dey wants de big circus show for deir money. I gives it to 'em an' I gits de money. [*With a grin.*] De long green, dat's me every time! [*Then rebukingly.*] But you ain't got no kick agin me, Smithers. I'se paid you back all you done for me many times. Ain't I pertected you and

winked at all de crooked tradin' you been doin' right out in de broad day. Sho' I has—and me makin' laws to stop it at de same time! [*He chuckles.*]

Smithers. [*Grinning*]. But, meanin' no 'arm, you been grabbin' right and left yourself, ain't you? Look at the taxes you've put on 'em! Blimey! You've squeezed 'em dry!

Jones. [*Chuckling*]. No dey ain't *all* dry yet. I'se still heah, ain't I?

Smithers. [*Smiling at his secret thought*]. They're dry right now, you'll find out. [*Changing the subject abruptly.*] And as for me breaking laws, you've broke 'em all yerself just as fast as yer made 'em.

Jones. Ain't I de Emperor? De laws don't go for him. [*Judicially.*] You heah what I tells you, Smithers. Dere's little stealin' like you does, and dere's big stealin' like I does. For de little stealin' dey gits you in jail soon or late. For de big stealin' dey makes you Emperor and puts you in de Hall o' Fame when you croaks. [*Reminiscently.*] If dey's one thing I learns in ten years on de Pullman ca's listenin' to de white quality talk, it's dat same fact. And when I gits a chance to use it I winds up Emperor in two years.[13]

Even as Brutus Jones, alone and arrogant, is planning his escape through a dense forest, he has no worries; he believes he is the match for anyone:

Smithers. Don't be so bloomin' sure of it. They'll be after you 'ot and 'eavy. Ole Lem is at the bottom o' this business an' 'e 'ates you like 'ell. 'E'd rather do for you than eat 'is dinner, 'e would!

Jones. [*Scornfully*]. Dat fool no-count nigger! Does you think I'se scared o' him? I stands him on his thick head more'n once befo' dis, and I does it again if he come in my way—[*Fiercely*]. And dis time I leave him a dead nigger fo' sho'!

Smithers. You'll 'ave to cut through the big forest—an' these blacks 'ere can sniff and follow a trail in the dark like 'ounds. You'd 'ave to 'ustle to get through that forest in twelve hours even if you knew all the bloomin' trails like a native.

Jones. [*With indignant scorn*]. Look-a-heah, white man! Does you think I'm a natural bo'n fool? Give me credit fo' havin' some sense, fo' Lawd's sake! Don't you s'pose I'se looked ahead and made sho' of all de chances? I'se gone out in dat big forest, pretendin' to hunt, so many times dat I knows it high an' low like a book. I could go through on dem trails wid my eyes shut. [*With great contempt*]. Think dese ig'nerent bush niggers dat don't got brains enuff to know deir own names even can catch Brutus Jones? Huh, I s'pects

not! Not on yo' life! Why, man, de white men went after me wid
bloodhounds where I come from an' I jes' laughs at 'em. It's a
shame to fool dese black trash around heah, dey're so easy. You
watch me, man'. I'll make dem look sick. I will. I'll be 'cross de
plain to de edge of de forest by time dark comes. Once in de woods
in de night, dey got a swell chance o' findin dis baby! Dawn tomorrow I'll be out at de oder side and on de coast whar dat French
gun boat is stayin'. She picks me up, take me to the Martinique
when she go dar, and dere I is safe wid a mighty big bankroll in my
jeans. It's easy as rollin' off a log.[14]

But as the former emperor begins his journey at night, the jungle tom-
toms begin incessantly to beat out their continuing messages of death—
rhythmic heartbeat pulses crescendoing to a frenzy. Jones is lost, but his
arrogance veils his mind, each moment building onto the previous moment to *destroy* that mind: the one white stone which covered his secret
supply of food on the trail is now many stones, and Jones, hungry, can't
find the right stone; the Formless Fears appear before him; a man whom
he had killed in a crap game appears; he sees the chain gang, and the
guard he had to kill in order to escape. The sounds of the jungle—formerly *his* jungle—work on his mind:

Oh, Lawd, Lawd! Oh, Lawd, Lawd! [*Suddenly he throws himself
on his knees and raises his clasped hands to the sky—in a voice of
agonized pleading.*] Lawd, Jesus, heah my prayer! I'se a poor sinner, a poor sinner! I knows I done wrong, I knows it! When I
cotches Jeff cheatin' wid loaded dice my anger overcomes me an'
I kills him dead! Lawd, I done wrong! When dat guard hits me wid
de whip, my anger overcomes me, and I kills him dead. Lawd, I
done wrong! An' down heah whar dese fool bush niggers raises me
up to the seat o' de mighty, I steals all I could grab. Lawd, I done
wrong! I knows it! I'se sorry! Forgive me, Lawd! Forgive dis po'
sinner! [*Then beseeching terrifiedly.*] An' keep dem away, Lawd!
Keep dem away from me! An' stop dat drum soundin' in my ears!
Dat begin to sound ha'nted, too. [*He gets to his feet, evidently
slightly reassured by his prayer—with attempted confidence.*] De
Lawd'll preserve me from dem ha'nts after dis. [*Sits down on the
stump again.*] I ain't skeered o' real men. Let dem come. But dem
odders—[*He shudders—then looks down at his feet, working his
toes inside the shoes—with a groan.*] Oh, my po' feet! Dem shoes
ain't no use no more 'ceptin' to hurt. I'se better off widout dem.
[*He unlaces them and pulls them off—holds the wrecks of the shoes*

in his hand and regards them mournfully.] You was real, A-one patin' leather, too. Look at yo' now. Emperor, you'se gittin' mighty low![15]

But there is no help. Apparitions of an auction block appear before him; his mind works against itself and conjures up a jungle ceremony with a witch doctor bidding him as a sacrifice to a giant crocodile. Frightened, Brutus Jones fires his last bullet. The crocodile vanishes, but Brutus Jones is now more alone than ever; the bullet which destroyed the crocodile was meant to destroy him—it was a silver bullet, the *final* bullet he was to use to kill himself to avoid an inglorious death at the hands of the people he once ruled. Brutus Jones became emperor by playing upon the fears and superstitions of the natives: a lead bullet did not kill him two years ago; only a silver bullet could kill him now. But in the forest, those who had been ruled were now melting silver coins. Brutus Jones is lost:

What—what is I doin'? What is—dis place? Seems like—seems like I know dat tree—an' dem stones—an' de river. I remember—seems like I been heah befo'. [*Tremblingly.*] Oh, gorry, I'se skeered in dis place! I'se skeered! Oh, Lawd, pertect dis sinner![16]

As he had lived, so had Brutus Jones died. A violent death mercifully cut short by a bullet. Once bold and glorious, vain and arrogant—the servant of White men who became the master of Blacks—Brutus Jones in his final hours once again became the slave; within him was his own destruction.

O'Neill maintained consistency of Black English representation in *All God's Chillun Got Wings* (1924), a study of Black-White racial attitudes. The play, however, was banned in many cities, primarily because it focused on the psychological consequences within a racially mixed marriage. Eugene O'Neill died in 1953 at the age of sixty-five, the nation's leading playwright.

Paul Green was born in 1894 in North Carolina, graduated from Buie's Creek Academy in 1914, received an A.B. from the University of North Carolina in 1921, and spent the following year in graduate study at Cornell University. During the next two decades, he successfully combined the careers of professor and writer, achieving separate, and enduring, recognition in each field. From 1923 to 1929, he was a professor of philosophy; from 1929 to 1944, he was a professor of dramatic arts, both positions at the University of North Carolina. Green's first plays were written shortly after World War I; during his four-decade literary career, he became one of the nation's most prolific authors, writing not only drama, for which he was primarily noted, but short stories, novels, symphonic outdoor dramas, essays, radio plays, and films—his most noted being *Cabin in the Cotton* (1932), *State Fair* (1933), *Voltaire* (1933), *Dr. Bull* (1933), *David Harum* (1934), and the adaptation of John H. Griffin's *Black Like Me* (1963).

The representation of Black English in Green's one-act drama, *In Abraham's Bosom,* produced in 1924, reveals a more creolized form of the language than that depicted in the plays of Eugene O'Neill and has more rules in common with the plays of the Colonial-Revolutionary Cycle than of the Negro Renaissance Cycle. Of the plays written during the Negro-Renaissance Cycle, the deep structure possessive, for example, if it occurs, usually occurs only in second person; in Green's drama, the deep structure possessive occurs in both second and third person. Other dramas written by Green show a less creolized representation of the language—*In Abraham's Bosom* was set in the late nineteenth century, whereas Green's other dramas were set in the early twentieth century; the representation of the language clearly shows Green's awareness of language modified by time.

In the "Author's Note" section of *The Lonesome Road* (1926), a collection of six one-act plays, Green explains that "the dialect used—with the exception of that in [*In Abraham's Bosom*]—is still current among the colored farmer folk in that section of the world. As an aid to reading, the final *d's* and *g's* have been retained."[17] *The Lonesome Road* was dedicated to Abraham McCranie, "dreamer and martyr," the tragic hero of *In Abraham's Bosom* and *Your Fiery Furnace,* two one-act plays which were the basis of the full-length *In Abraham's Bosom,* produced in 1926 and winner of the 1927 Pulitzer Prize in drama.

Abe McCranie, as molded by Paul Green, was a dreamer, a mulatto—son of a White plantation owner and a Black slave—who dreamed of education, of rising out of his poverty by rising out of his ignorance. A slave of the land at a time when slavery had been abolished more than two decades earlier:

Abe. I got to work dis problem. Been on it two days now. Cain't git it out'n my head. Ain't been able to sleep two nights. . . . How many sheep? How many sheep? . . . Answer say fifteen. Cain't make it come out fifteen, cain't, seem lak, to save me. Man must have answer wrong. Six go into fo'teen, three, no, two times and two over. [*His voice dies away as he becomes lost in his work. Presently his face begins to light up. He figures faster. Suddenly he slaps his knee.*] Dere whah I been missing it all de time. I carried two 'stid o' one. Blame fool I is. . . . I got it, folkses, I got it. Fifteen! Dat white man know whut he doing. He all time git dem answer right. [*He turns expectantly towards Lije.*] Lije, I got it. [*Lije makes no answer. He turns toward Puny again, starts to speak, but sees he is asleep.*] Bud! [*But Bud makes no answer. The heavy breathing of the sleepers falls regularly upon his ears. His face sinks into a sort of hopeless brooding.*] Yeh, sleep, sleep, sleep yo' life away. I figger foh you, foh me, foh all de black in de world to lead 'em up out'n ignorance. Dey don't listen, dey don't heah me, dey in de wilderness, don't wanta be led. Dey sleep, sleep in bondage. [*He bows his head between his knees.*] Sleep in sin.[18]

Abe thinks he's ready to start a school, to help his people. He goes to his White father, Colonel McCranie, who offers no encouragement. Finally, Abe starts a school, but is forced from it, wandering from place to place—tormented by Blacks as well as Whites. He returns home, his mind now working against itself, hoping to free Blacks through education, but unable to reach that point where education itself is the means and not the end. Then Lonnie, his cruel half-brother, the White son of Col. McCranie, tells Abe he plans to seize the farm crop Abe worked so hard on. Furious that he could not rise above his status through education; furious that his grand plans to educate a race of people has failed; furious that the White man has again and again taken advantage of him, Abraham McCranie kills Lonnie, only to be hunted and trapped in a shack:

Voices. He's in there. I hear him talking. He's done talking now, goddam him! We'll show him the law all right. He's got a gun! Shoot him like a dog.
Abe. [*Wiping his brow and again speaking in the role of the educator trying to convince his everlastingly silent hearers.*] But they'll wake, they'll wake—A crack of thunder and deep divided from deep—A light! a light, and it will be! [*Goldie still sits hunched over in her chair. Abe goes to the door at the left.*] I go speak to 'em, I go tell 'em. We got to be free, freedom of the soul and of the mind. Ignorance means sin and sin means destruction. [*Shouting.*] Freedom! freedom! [*He opens the door.*]
Voice. Hell! Look out! There he is!
Abe. And guns and killings is in vain. [*He steps out on the porch.*]

What we need is to—to— [*His words are cut short by a roar from several guns. He staggers and falls with his head in the doorway.*] and we must have—have—[19]

And so Abraham McCranie, his dreams of education destroyed, was, himself, destroyed. The representation of Black English in the final scenes shows more intermixing of Standard English forms than in the earlier scenes—Green's method of indicating language acculturation as well as the passage of time—from the late 1800s to the early 1900s.

Other dramas during the Negro Renaissance Cycle which included Black English in dialogue were written by Richard Bruce (*Sahdji, An African Ballet,* 1927), Ernest H. Culbertson, (*Rackey,* 1919), Thelma Duncan (*The Death Dance,* 1923), Dorothy and DuBose Heyward (*Porgy,* 1926; see pp. 180–184), Georgia Douglas Johnson (*Plunes,* 1927), John Matheus ('*Cruitter,* 1926), Willis Richardson (*The Flight of Natives,* 1927; *The Broken Banjo,* 1925), John W. Rogers, Jr. (*Judge Lynch,* 1923), Eualalie Spencer (*The Starter,* 1927), Jean Toomer (*Balo,* 1924), Ridgley Torrance (*The Danse Calinda,* 1919; *Granny Maumee,* 1917; *The Rider of Dreams,* 1917), Lucy White (*The Bird Child,* 1922), and Frank H. Wilson (*Sugar Cane,* 1920).

BLACK ENGLISH AND THE AMERICAN NOVEL

Just as World War I had turned America in a new direction, so had it changed the nature of American literature. In this age of the "loss of innocence," there emerged giants of literature—Sherwood Anderson, Erskine Caldwell, Theodore Dreiser, T. S. Eliot, F. Scott Fitzgerald, Robert Frost, Ben Hecht, Ernest Hemingway, Sinclair Lewis, Eugene O'Neill, Carl Sandburg, Upton Sinclair, Gertrude Stein, John Steinbeck, James Thurber, Thomas Wolfe, John van Duen, *and* William Faulkner.

Yoknapatawpha County, Mississippi, the most famous county in the world, exists only in the hearts and minds of a literary consciousness of the people. But it is real enough—or, rather, is based upon reality. Its 9,313 Blacks and 6,298 Whites each have their own stories, their own histories. And it is from the people that the county exists.

William Faulkner, creator of the county with the almost unpronounceable name, was born in New Albany, Mississippi, in 1897, the great grandson of William C. Falkner,[20] Confederate army officer and lawyer, upon whom Faulkner based his prototype of Col. John Sartoris, patriarch of one of the major families in Yoknapatawpha County.

Sartoris (1929) was the first of several novels to document the lives of the Sartoris, Compson, Benbow, McCaslin, and Snopes families of Yoknapatawpha County from the eighteenth through the early twentieth centuries. The representation of Blacks in *Sartoris* shows a more individualized treatment than in Faulkner's first two novels, *Soldier's Pay* (1926) and *Mosquitoes* (1927). With few exceptions, Faulkner treats Blacks—who comprise about sixty per cent of the county's population—just as they have been treated historically by the South, as an inconspicuous majority seldom allowed to be anything more than the servants of the ruling White families. In Faulkner's novels, the White, mostly by his own doing, is as trapped by social convention as is the Black—each has established and acceded to a historical and social role which neither can now escape. Yet Faulkner, a "rebel among Rebels," continually questions racial equality, arguing in subtle ways for an equality for all persons, Black or White.

To William Faulkner, *The Sound and the Fury* (1929) was his best novel. As he later explained, "[I have] written my guts" into it. But like most of Faulkner's early novels, there were no great expectations for it. Fewer than 2,000 copies were initially printed; it was not too long before it was out of print. It was a long, tormenting two decades before the American public began to accept it as a major work of fiction.

The Sound and the Fury is as much a story of the tragic disintegration of the old aristocratic Compson family as it is the story of the enduring strength of Dilsey, family servant to the Compsons. It is Dilsey who has helped the Compsons through many of their problems; it is her son, Luster, who cares for, with devoted attention, the thirty-three-year-old mentally retarded Benjy Compson.

The speech of Dilsey, as well as the novel's other Blacks—Luster, T. P., Frony, Beacon, and the Rev'un Shegog—is a phonological mixing of Standard and Black English; there is significant prevocalic aspiration, as in *hit* for *it,* the replacement of the *th* sounds with a *d* in word-initial position, nasalization reduction, and the raising of vowels (as in *get→git, can→kin*). Consonant cluster reduction, if present, is usually in word-final position. Although Faulkner used only a few rules to identify Black speech—and these with only moderate consistency—he was careful to differentiate Black from Southern speech, and further subdivided Black and White speech, creating four distinct dialects—the educated Southern White living in cities; the uneducated Southern White living in the hills and rural towns; the Southern Black living only in the South; and the Southern Black influenced by the speech and lifestyles of the Northern cities.

Faulkner also distinguished the use of the postvocalic /r/. In a radio interview in 1957, he explained his logic:

Q. . . . In your short story, "Wash," . . . when Wash is talking about Colonel Sutpen you spell it k-e-r-n-e-l. When the Negroes are talking you spell it C-u-n-n-e-l. Is that supposed to be *kernel* that Wash says and *cunnel* that the Negroes say? In other words, the Negroes drop the *r.*

A. That's correct . . . and what we call the red-necked white man has a hard *r.* He says *fur* for *far.* He says *far* for *fire.* The Negro don't have the *r* at all.

Q. Now if Colonel Sutpen or one of his upper-class characters were speaking, then you would just use the conventional spelling which really would be rather like Wash's pronunciation though not as hard an *"r,"* but between Wash and the Negroes—*kernel* vs. *cunnel.* . . . Thomas Nelson Page, . . . when he wants to represent an old Virginia Negro who says *can't* will spell that sometimes *c-a-r-n-t,* and I notice you have done the same thing in "Wash." When the old Negro woman is talking to Colonel Sutpen she says, "Yes, master," and you spelled it *m-a-r-s-t-e-r,* and we should interpret that *mahster* rather than *maaster,* but it isn't *mar-ster,* is it?

A. No.

Q. It's *marster* and the *ar* spelling then, since we know that you are from that part of the country and you yourself dropped the *r* after a vowel, then the *ar* can be a symbol for sound *ah.*

Q. I suppose, Mr. Faulkner, that would be the same thing as when Dilsey says *window* and you spell it *winder.* That she says *winduh* rather than *winder.*

A. That's right, there's no *r.*

Q. But the backwoodsman would say *winder.*

A. That's right . . .

Q. And then you'd have a problem because you'd have to spell it the same way if you wanted to represent dialect, wouldn't you? That would be a problem for the author to worry about there.

A. I should say, being a Mississippian, I would probably put two *r's* on it.[21]

The sermon of the Rev'un Shegog in the concluding part of *The Sound and the Fury* is an insightful look into the integration of Black language and culture. At the beginning of the sermon, the Rev'un Shegog is quiet, slow, somewhat mysterious, deliberate, speaking in

Standard English; by the end of the sermon, however, he is speaking
Black English, and has whipped the congregation into a religious frenzy:

> When the visitor rose to speak he sounded like a white man. His
> voice was level and cold. It sounded too big to have come from him
> and they listened at first through curiosity, as they would have to a
> monkey talking. They began to watch him as they would a man on
> a tight rope. They even forgot his insignificant appearance in the
> virtuosity with which he ran and poised and swooped upon the cold
> inflectionless wire of his voice so that at last when with a sort of
> swooping glide he came to rest again beside the reading desk with
> one arm resting upon it at shoulder height and his monkey body as
> reft of all motion as a mummy or an emptied vessel, the congrega-
> tion sighed as if it waked from a collective dream and moved a lit-
> tle in its seats. Behind the pulpit the choir fanned steadily. Dilsey
> whispered, "Hush, now. Dey fixin to sing in a minute."
>
> Then a voice said, "Brethren."
>
> The preacher had not moved. His arm lay yet across the desk,
> and he still held that pose while the voice died in sonorous echoes
> between the walls. It was as different as day and dark from his for-
> mer tone, with a sad, timbrous quality like an alto horn, sinking
> into their hearts and speaking there again when it had ceased in
> fading and cumulate echoes.
>
> "Brethren and sistern," it said again, . . . "I got the recollec-
> tion and the blood of the lamb!" . . .
>
> "Breddren en sistuhn! . . . I got de ricklickshun en de blood of
> de Lamb!" They did not mark just when his intonation, his pro-
> nunciation, became negroid, they just sat swaying a little in their
> seats as the voice took them into itself.
>
> "When de long, cold—Oh, I tells you, breddren, when de long,
> cold—I sees de light en I sees de word, po sinner! Dey passed away
> in Egypt, de swingin chariots; de generations passed away. . . .
>
> "I tells you, breddren, en I tells you, sistuhn, dey'll come a time.
> Po sinner saying Let me lay down wid de Lawd, lemme lay down
> my load. Den whut Jesus gwine say, O breddren? O sistuhn? Is you
> got de ricklickshun en de Blood of de Lamb? Case I aint gwine
> load down heaven!"
>
> He fumbled in his coat and took out a handkerchief and mopped
> his face. . . .
>
> "Breddren! Look at dem little chillen settin dar. Jesus wus like

dat once. He mammy suffered de glory en de pangs. Sometime maybe she helt him at de nightfall, whilst de angels singin him to sleep; maybe she look out de do' en see de Roman po-lice passin." He tramped back and forth, mopping his face. "Listen, breddren! I sees de day. Ma'y settin in de do' wid Jesus on her lap, de little Jesus. Like dem chillen dar, de little Jesus. I hears de angels singin de peaceful songs en de glory; I sees de closin eyes; sees Mary jump up, sees de sojer face: We gwine to kill! We gwine to kill yo little Jesus! I hears de weepin en de lamentation of de po mammy widout de salvation en de word of God! . . .

"I sees hit, breddren! I sees hit! Sees de blastin, blindin sight! I sees Calvary, wid de sacred trees, sees de thief en de murderer en de least of dese; I hears de boasting en de braggin: Ef you be Jesus, lif up yo tree en walk! I hears de wailin of women en de evenin lamentations. . . .

"I sees de whelmin flood roll between; I sees de darkness en de death everlastin upon de generations. Den, lo! Breddren! Yes, breddren! Whut I see? Whut I see, O sinner? I sees de resurrection en de light; sees de meek Jesus sayin Dey kilt Me dat ye shall live again; I died dat dem whut sees en believes shall never die. Breddren, O breddren! I sees de doom crack en hears de golden horns shoutin down de glory, en de arisen dead whut got de blood en de ricklickshun of de Lamb!"[22]

And so it was that Dilsey, tearful in her knowledge, had witnessed the end—the end of a family, the end of the Compsons, once aristocrats in an aristocratic land, now reduced to lives of degradation.

Light in August, published in 1932, Faulkner's seventh novel and the fifth of the Yoknapatawpha series, is a powerful indictment of social bigotry and inbred racial hatreds. For the thirty-six years of his life, Joe Christmas—so named because he was found on the doorsteps of an orphanage on Christmas night—searches for an identity, knowing only that he is the son of Milly Hines and a traveling circus man who was murdered by Milly's father in the belief that Milly's lover had "Negro blood." During Joe's life he sometimes passes as a White, sometimes lives among Blacks as a Black, often boasts that he is both Black and White, never really knowing who he is.[23]

Absalom, Absalom! (1936), like *The Sound and the Fury,* explores racial bigotry and the destruction of once-lofty ideals. Thomas Sutpen leaves his wife after learning that she had a Black ancestor, and moves to Yoknapatawpha County where he develops his plans to build an aristocratic dynasty in the antebellum South. As in most of Faulkner's stories, the seeds of destruction exist within each of the characters, who act and react as if programmed by the conventions of the society in which he lives.

In *Intruder in the Dust* (1948), his fourteenth novel, Faulkner again probed the mind of the South by weaving an intricate story about Lucas Beauchamp who is arrested for the murder of a White, faces a lynch mob, but is proven innocent by sixteen-year-old Charles Millison, nephew of the county attorney. In a long, slow process of understanding and mutual respect, the boy, brought up with Southern views and prejudices, learns to accept the old Black as an equal. Although most Blacks in Faulkner's stories speak a Black English, Beauchamp speaks Standard English with a faint trace of Black English patterns—Faulkner's linguistic clue that Lucas Beauchamp was culturally different from most of the Blacks in the county.

Many of Faulkner's novels began as short stories in the leading magazines of the 1920s and 1930s. "Wash," published in the February 1934 issue of *Harper's Magazine,* was the forerunner of *Absalom, Absalom!* And six separate short stories which appeared in the *Saturday Evening Post* became six of the seven chapters of *The Unvanquished* (1938). Several chapters of *Go Down, Moses* (1942) first appeared as short stories in *Collier's* and the *Atlantic Monthly.* "Centaur in Brass," published in the February 1932 issue of *The American Mercury,* and "Mule in the Yard," published in the August 1934 issue of *Scribner's Monthly,* became the basis of *The Town* (1957). Until the early 1950s, the short stories received wider distribution than the novels. At one time during the mid-1940s, none of Faulkner's novels was in print. And it was only with the publication of *The Portable Faulkner* (1946), written by Malcolm Cowley, that the public was made aware of Faulkner and, more important, how to read and interpret his novels.

In 1950, Faulkner received the Nobel Prize in literature, much to the surprise and dismay of many of the American literary critics who did not feel that Faulkner—newspaper reporter, screenwriter,[24] and novelist— was worthy of such an international honor. In his acceptance speech upon receiving the Nobel Prize, Faulkner briefly outlined his philosophy of life and of writing. "Man will not merely endure," said Faulkner, "he will prevail . . . because he has a soul, a spirit capable of compassion and sacrifice and endurance. It is the writer's duty to write about these things." During the remaining twelve years of his life, public acceptance of his work, coupled with the passage of time and the prestige of the Nobel Prize, elevated Faulkner—one of the most proficient observers of life—to the position of one of the world's greatest authors.

In June 1921, H. L. Mencken, nationally recognized as one of the country's leading journalists, wrote to Emily Clark—editor of the small-circulation literary magazine, *The Reviewer,* published in Virginia—to tell her about a writer "who shows great promise."

At the age of forty-one, Julia Mood Peterkin, the daughter of a physician, and wife of an aristocratic landowner, became a published writer. Her first short story, "The Merry-Go-Round," was published in the December 1921 issue of *Smart Set,* an important national magazine edited by Mencken.[25] But for the next three years, her short stories about the Gullah Blacks of South Carolina appeared regularly in *The Reviewer.*

For slightly more than a decade, until she returned to farming as a full-time profession, she was one of the most celebrated, and controversial, American writers. She had grown up and lived with Gullah Blacks, understood their language, and was able to reproduce in print the essence of that language. But it was her knowledge of the culture, her ability to look deep into the problems of the South, reflected within a Black culture, that brought about the controversy. From the South's leading newspapers and magazines came caustic reviews charging her with literary nonsense; from the pulpits came sermons of invective accusing her of trying to undermine the entire social structure of the land and people she had grown up with. The criticisms cut deeply, causing wounds that could never heal. Hunter Stagg, writing in the October 1924 issue of *The Reviewer,* pointed out that "the appearance of a story by Mrs. Peterkin in *The Reviewer* was so often followed by letters of protest or remonstrance from more or less irate readers who preferred to view life through the glass of romance, if at all."

In September 1924, shortly after the publication of *Green Thursday*—a collection of twelve stories about Gullah life which would eventually receive many favorable reviews—Peterkin sadly wrote Emily Clark, by now her friend as well as editor: "I fear my own South Carolina audience will not be sympathetic [to the book]. The *State,* the leading newspaper, edited by Mr. Gonzales, who himself has written several very charming Negro books, has been careful to ignore me so far."[26] A month later, as many of the vitriolic reviews began to penetrate, Peterkin again wrote Clark:

You, a stranger, became my invaluable friend while the very people I counted on have become my harshest critics! . . . *Time* and
the New York *Times* gave me real boosts yesterday. But the Columbia *State* has never mentioned even my name! Isn't that a remarkable thing?

The *State* . . . has been almost amusing in its attitude, yet I do
wish I might have gotten sympathy there. . . . But you see, so
many of the *State* staff write Negro stories too that I am encroach-
ing on private ground, when I undertake doing them.[27]

But although she could not remove the hurt caused by rejection, she
could understand and be philosophical about why her writings brought
such rejection in the South:

In this part of the world my book has not met with much sympathy, but that does not surprise me at all. I said things that no nice
South Carolina lady ever says, and so I must be disciplined a bit
even by my friends. See? It does not worry me at all. What I have
done has given me a lot of fun just in the doing, and that is com-
pensation enough besides the joy of having some real critics to en-
courage me to go on. The most amazing thing is that in spite of
the silence of the newspapers generally, the old lady who keeps the
Relic Room of the United Daughters of the Confederacy in the
State Capitol itself has written asking for a copy to keep there. She
says: "We feel that the children of tomorrow should know about
the Negroes of today." Queer relic it would be.[28]

In the *New York World,* Laurence Stallings called *Green Thursday*
"a great American work," and for the *Saturday Review of Literature*
praised the author for her "sympathetic and understanding of negro
psychology." For the *Raleigh* (North Carolina) *News and Observer,*
Nell Battle Lewis also pointed to Peterkin's "attitude of sympathy without condescension." An unsigned review in *The New York Times* was
equally enthusiastic:

Mrs. Peterkin of South Carolina is one of the first to write a book
unaffectedly about negroes, without conscious or unconscious be-
littling mockery in view of superior white advancement. . . .

Into the mold of the graceful form she pours the distillation of a
rich human observation of the secret life of a people who have not
yet been understood by the Whites, because the Whites have al-

ways found it easier to laugh at it than to attempt to comprehend it.[29]

At a time when most Blacks systematically rejected any fiction, especially dialect tales written by Whites about Blacks, Peterkin found that many of her strongest supporters were the Blacks themselves, W. E. B. Du Bois, writing in *The Crisis,* the official publication of the NAACP, called *Green Thursday* "a beautiful book," and praised Peterkin as a woman who "has the eye and ear to see beauty and know the truth." And in *Opportunity,* another magazine edited by and for Blacks, Charles S. Johnson praised the book for subtly pointing out that Blacks "are neither crapshooters nor hilarious clowns, but field hands,—black men, women and children faced with problems of life, love and death." On November 23, 1924, *The State* broke its three-year silence on the writings of Julia Peterkin and reprinted a notice which originally appeared in the *Boston Transcript;* on January 25, 1925, it printed a staff-written review of *Green Thursday.* So pleased was Peterkin that on March 10, she wrote to W. W. Boll, editor of *The State,* personally thanking him for some kind words he had written in an editorial.

Peterkin's short sketches—many of them collected under the heading of "Imports From Africa"—were insightful looks at the human condition. In "The Ortymobile," Peterkin, in less than three hundred words, told about traditions, the conflict with the machine age, about human personality, and how killing is a part of life:

Great Gawd, is you kill him, suh? Po T'ing, an' him a layin' so peace-ful in de fench corner. No, he ain' dead, but you done break 'e leg, an' a hoss don' nebber got ober a break leg.

I declare to Gawd! An I jus tu'n him out to pick roun' a li'l by de grass been so fresh atter de rain.

I don' b'lieve no ortymobile eber did been by here befo'. Po' ol' creeter! He ain't been know wha' it was. I wouldn' a had dis do to 'em not fo' nuttin' in de worl'. No suh! An him jes a layin' down fo' res' a li'l.

Dey ain' nuttin to do now but to kill him.

No suh, I ain' got no gun. You haffer kill him suh, I couldn' do em to sabe my life. I don' know how you gwine do em. Mebbe da nigger o' yourn could do em. He look lak he t'ink he know a lot. No suh, I ain' got no axe, suh. Mebbe if he git a solid light-'ood knot he might could knock him een de dead an' kill em, ef he know de place wha for' knock him at.

Great Gawd, who would a t'ink sich a t'ing! He done lib here to be ol' ez he is, an den a ortymobile come here to em an do em so.

I gwine walk down de road a piece. I can' stand to hear da nigger knock em. Great Gawd A'-mighty!

Seems like I can' git my finger een my years tight 'nough to keep f'om hearin'.

He ain' knock em yet, no not yet.

I can' ha'dly stan' how he gwine suffer him.

Jesus! Now he knock him! Gawd! I hear him do 'em.

No, suh, no money ain' gwine he'p me, needer him. All I wants is a hoss. No, suh, you see, jus' like you can' sen' none down here, same way I can' git none down here needer.

No, suh, I don't reckon he would a been wutt much to you, suh, but he been all I had.

Yes, suh, dat so' on he back did been pester him a good deal, by de flies worried him, but de so' ain' been do him nuttin'. He could pull a plow same as a colt.

Yes, suh, nex' spring'll do. Ef you git him here by nex' spring I'll be sati-fy.

William Pinesett, suh, yessuh, dat's my name. Brook Green pos' office, yessuh.

Good-bye, suh. I too sorry to trouble you, suh.[30]

Peterkin's earliest writing shows a more accurate representation of the language than her later stories, which appear to be more Gullah-flavored Standard English than anything else. In an introduction to an anthology of many of her short stories and sketches, literary critic Frank Durham, one of her closest friends, suggests that:

> her close recording of Gullah in these early pieces is an experiment or a kind of exercise. She seems to be teaching herself to write the dialect, to learn it so thoroughly that when she uses it in her stories and novels she can . . . give the essence of the dialect through a few basic Gullah words and the Gullah syntax and rhythms but still keep the style close enough to regular English for the comprehension of the general reader.[31]

Indeed, a friend of hers once reported that Peterkin recognized that Ambrose Gonzales was:

> the final authority on Gullah, and that [she believed to write an accurate transcription of Gullah she] would make an ass of herself.

Her negro . . . dialect is entirely incidental to what she is doing
and going to do. She is not remotely an authority on Gullah, or any
other negro dialect. She knows it.[32]

Thus, whereas the accurate representation of Gullah, as the means to
understand a people's culture, became the central element in the stories
written by Ambrose Gonzales, it became only one of several, and certainly not the most important element in the stories written by Julia
Mood Peterkin. Nevertheless, there are enough distinct Africanisms in
the dialogue to suggest that Peterkin was acutely aware of the African
syntactic origins of the Gullah language. The early sketches and short
stories are marked by frequent use of the apostrophe to indicate consonant cluster reduction, nasal replacement, and the elision of syllables.
However, orthographic representations are often inconsistent. In "The
Ortymobile," for example, are the pronouns *'em, em,* and *him,* all referring to the horse.

Phonologically, Peterkin seems to have been most aware of, and thus
most consistent in, recording the literary conventions representing Black
English. Present, with internal consistency, are the substitution of the
voiced bilabial stop [b] for the voiced labiodental fricative [v] (as in
over→ober), the substitution of the voiced alveolar stop [d] for the
voiced interdental fricative [ð] (as in *the→de* and *da*), and substitution
of the unvoiced alveolar stop [t] for the unvoiced interdental fricative
[θ] with the use of the apostrophe to show what Peterkin thought to be
elision (as in *thing→t'ing*). Less consistent, but nevertheless present,
are the replacement of the vowel glide (*like→lak*), nasal replacement
(*hearing→hearin'*), and the loss of the postvocalic /r/ with the backing
of the vowel (notably *for→fo,* and *poor→po*). Loss of the postvocalic
/r/ in word-medial position is indicated by an apostrophe. Peterkin is
moderately consistent in recording the raising of certain vowels (as in
as→ez, get→git, and *in→een*), the fronting of other vowels (most noticeably *such→sich*), and a lowering of the /ɪ/ (*if→ef*). Although she
records *he* as *'e,* it is probable that this reflects not the syntactic rule of
the undifferentiated third-person pronoun but a phonological rule representing a loss of aspiration. But in her later writing, especially in her
novels, the presence of *'e* (as in " 'e dress") shows an awareness of the
syntactic rule of the undifferentiated third-person pronoun.

Syntactically, Peterkin's early writing shows the presence, but an
inconsistent recording, of the deep structure copula, deep structure possessive, and the dropping of the inflectional plural suffix. Occasionally,
but with little consistency, other Gullah syntactic rules are present.

Throughout her writing, however, it is the syntax rather than the phonology which shows distinct African origins.

Beginning in the mid-1920s, and continuing for more than a decade, Peterkin's short stories appeared with increasing frequency in many of the nation's top-paying general circulation magazines, including the *American Mercury, Century, Good Housekeeping, Ladies Home Journal,* and the *Saturday Evening Post.*

Although her short stories brought her fame, it was her novels which brought her critical acclaim. In 1927, *Black April,* the first of her three novels, was published and received favorable reviews in both the North and South. That May, her *alma mater,* Converse College, awarded her a doctorate of letters; as Durham explains, "slowly but surely she was accepted as one of South Carolina's important figures."[33] The following year, Grosset & Dunlap published *Scarlet Sister Mary,* a penetrating study of a Gullah woman, for which Peterkin was awarded the Pulitzer Prize—becoming the first South Carolinian so honored. But the aura of controversy still remained: the county library in Gaffney, South Carolina, banned the book from its shelves; the semiweekly *Cherokee Times,* however, published it serially, to the delight of many. The representation of the Gullah language in *Scarlet Sister Mary,* however, is minimal. What is presented is as much Standard English as Southern Standard English, yet, a certain "essence" of Gullah remains, indicating its African syntactic roots.

Peterkin's last novel, *Bright Skin,* was published in 1932; *Roll, Jordan, Roll,* a collection of nonfictional articles on plantation life, many of them first published in newspapers, was published in 1934; and *A Plantation Christmas,* a best-selling twenty-five page sketch, was published in 1934. But she wrote nothing after that. In 1944, in response to a query from the librarian of the South Caroliniana Library at the University of South Carolina, Peterkin wrote, "It's been so long since I've thought about writing that I've no papers left, no manuscripts. All these somehow belong to another existence of mine."[34] For a little more than a decade of her eighty-one years, Julia Mood Peterkin was a writer, but that one decade determined how she would be remembered. She died on August 10, 1961, at her home on Lang Syne Plantation, her home since her marriage in 1903, the place which gave her the background and the opportunity to be a writer.

To her friends she was Peggy Marsh, a sweet and pleasant housewife, a woman who was enjoyable to be with, but a woman unsure of her abilities. To a world of literature, she was Margaret Mitchell, author of *Gone With the Wind*.

She was born in Atlanta in 1900, and lived the forty-eight years of her life in or near the city, the site for her only novel. She was a reporter for the *Atlanta Journal* and author of numerous short stories—none of them published—and one partially completed book about the Jazz Age. She married Berrian K. Upshaw in 1922, but divorced him two years later, and in 1925 married John Marsh who was Upshaw's best man at the wedding. Marsh, an advertising executive and former newspaper reporter, encouraged his wife to write; he helped her overcome her fear of failure and frustration, and gave her the courage to complete her epic novel about the devastation the Civil War wreaked upon the South and its people.

Macmillan scheduled the first press run for 10,000 copies, with publication in April 1936, about ten years after Mitchell began the novel. But when the Book-of-the-Month Club decided to make *Gone With the Wind* its July selection, publication was delayed while 50,000 more copies were printed. Soon, the book was being hailed by the critics as an epic of American history. Within six months of publication, more than 500,000 copies had been sold; within a year, more than a million copies. It would win almost every major award possible, including the Pulitzer Prize in 1937.

The portrayal of the Blacks in *Gone With the Wind* has been a topic of conversation since publication date. There are those who believe the portrayals reflect White Southern stereotypes; there are just as many who believe that the portrayals are accurate representations. And even among dialect scholars and linguists, the arguments continue as to whether Mitchell accurately portrayed the languages of the Blacks.

In a letter to writer Sidney Howard, Mitchell noted that her attempts to accurately portray the Black language represented, to her, "just about the toughest job in the book." And, in correspondence with Herschell Brickell, she noted that in dealing with the Southern dialects, she "sweated blood to try to make the voices sound different."[35] To Garnett Laidlaw Eskew, a writer who had complimented Mitchell and had asked about the dialect representation in her book, she replied:

I gave a great deal of thought and trouble to the dialect my Negroes spoke and over a period of years I amassed a glossary of words and pronunciations. I was very anxious for my dialect to be not only phonetically accurate but easy to read. Although I am a

Southerner, I am frequently turned against books in which Negro dialect is difficult to read because of tortured spelling and too many apostrophes. I tried to simplify the spelling of words and still keep the sound correct.[36]

But, to a nation that had grown fond of the Uncle Remus tales, and believed that the dialect represented by Joel Chandler Harris was the best and most accurate representation of Black English, Mitchell quite courteously took exception. In a letter to critic Donald Adams, who had praised her book, she wrote:

And about the dialect which you didn't think Uncle Remus would have liked. No, I don't guess he would. And I sweat blood to keep it from being like Uncle Remus. Uncle Remus is tough reading as I know from having had to read it to many children. It sounds grand but it's tough reading. So is most dialect and I, a Southerner usually refuse to read any dialect stuff that's like Uncle Remus. And so do most Southerners. I wanted it [GWTW] easily readable, accurate and phonetic. And I scoured the back country of this section routing out aged darkies who were born in slavery days. I don't know about Uncle Remus liking it but his son, Lucien Harris, took the trouble to go to my father and give me a good rave. And his daughter-in-law, Mrs. Julia Collier Harris (Mrs. Julian Harris of Chattanooga), has been most kind in her letters to me. And his grand-daughter, Mary Harris, on the Georgian here has gone to bat for me in her column so frequently and so kindly that I've been embarrassed. And a grandson of Uncle Remus has been one of my kindest press agents. Dialect is tough going, even when you've been raised on it, and I take an oath I'll never try it again. The different sections of the state have different dialects. The coast darkies speaking Geechee might just as well be speaking Sanskrit for all they mean to me. The middle Georgia darkies (around Macon) have different constructions from the North Georgia ones. And those from the older sections of the state around Washington, Ga., have some pronunciations and constructions that are practically Elizabethan. When you get into such tangles as the word "if" which in some localities is "ef" in others is "effen" and in still others is "did" (for instance, "Did I picked up a snake I'd be a fool") it is enough to drive one mad. No, I'm not a dialectitian (if there is such a word!). Latin is far easier. But I'm running on and maybe you aren't interested in dialect anyway. But if you ever get down to Charleston I wish you'd go out to

Magnolia Gardens where they give you a negro guide to show you through and listen to *their* combination of English accent and Gullah. "Get" for "gate," "race" for "rice" etc. I can never understand half they say.[37]

Although Mitchell attempted to record the language of the Blacks of the Civil War era by talking with Blacks who had lived during the war, the language had undergone a continual decreolization during the six decades between the Civil War and the beginning of Mitchell's research. Also, although Mitchell had correctly assumed that the language of Blacks who had lived during the war would have been closer to the reality of language than that spoken by Blacks born in the twentieth century, she was unable to achieve accuracy, since the elderly Blacks of 1926 were the young Blacks of 1865; and, quite logically, even if there was a correlation to the language of the middle-aged Blacks and elderly Blacks of 1865, most of whom probably retained language patterns learned in West Africa, it was not a perfect correlation. Further, any attempts by language scholars to compare Mitchell's representation of Black speech with the representation of Black English from the documents and novels of the Civil War era, is virtually impossible since Mitchell simplified the representation to facilitate readability. Nevertheless the representation of Black English in *Gone With the Wind* is reasonably consistent, the speech patterns reflective of Black speech in the Atlanta area, and even if the language representation isn't as meticulous a job as that done by Joel Chandler Harris, it does reflect Black speech—though of the 1930s, not the 1860s.

The speech of the Blacks in the novel became more important as plans for the movie developed. Mitchell, a print journalist who had spent ten years writing the book, refused to become involved in the production of the movie, believing that she had made her contribution by writing the book. Nevertheless, she did have one request of producer David O. Selznick. She noted that "so many Southern people have expressed the wish that your actors will talk in good quality natural stage voices, instead of imitation 'Southern,' leaving the atmosphere to be built up by the Negroes and other actual Southerners who may be in the cast. I believe this is the dominant public sentiment and it conforms directly with my own ideas."[38] Selznick agreed, although there were "traces" of the Southern dialects in the speech of several characters. The representation of Black speech was, in fact, Black speech; Hattie McDaniel, who would win an Academy Award for her portrayal of Mammie, and Butterfly McQueen, in her portrayal of Prissy, were Blacks.

And if their dialect at times seemed stilted, it was because their own dialects were not those of the Blacks they were portraying.[39] By the time *Gone With the Wind* premiered in Atlanta on December 15, 1939, the production had cost $4.25 million, making it the most costly film in history. But so great was its appeal that within months it regained its cost; between 1940 and 1965, it was the leading box-office film of all time, eventually grossing, in over four decades, more than $77 million. In 1976, it was shown on television for the first time; the National Broadcasting Company paid $5 million for one-time television rights; more than 100 million persons watched its television premiere—thirty-seven years after it was produced.

After writing *Gone With the Wind,* Margaret Mitchell never again wrote for publication. In 1945, John Marsh, who had encouraged his wife to recognize her talents and complete her novel, suffered a severe heart attack; his wife became a caring, devoted housewife. In 1949, Margaret Mitchell, an author who neither sought nor accepted literary fame, was dead, the victim of a car accident.

> Porgy lived in the Golden Age. Not the Golden Age of a remote and legendary past; nor yet the chimerical era treasured by every man past middle life, that never existed except in the heart of youth; but an age when men, not yet old, were boys in an ancient, beautiful city that time had forgotten before it destroyed.
>
> In this city there persisted the Golden Age of many things, and not the least among them was that of beggary. In those days the profession was one with a tradition. A man begged, presumably, because he was hungry, much as a man of more energetic temperament became a stevedore from the same cause. His plea for help produced the simple reactions of a generous impulse, a movement of the hand, and the gift of a coin, instead of the elaborate and terrifying process of organized philanthropy.[40]

And so began the story of Porgy, DuBose Heyward's semifictional study of a crippled Negro beggar living in Charleston's "Catfish Row."[41] Porgy was a part of the neighborhood, a neighborhood of tenements, poverty, and crime. He wanted so much to love, so much to be loved, but was resigned to a fate that "when Gawd make cripple, He mean him to be lonely." And DuBose Heyward, a White from an upper-class background, intended to tell Porgy's story—the story of Charleston's Black people and their homes, their lives, and their values. Heyward—like William Gilmore Simms, Ambrose Gonzales, and Julia Mood Peterkin—

lived in Charleston. He had seen the tenements; he had talked with the people; he understood their lives. As he developed his outline for *Porgy,* he determined to tell the story with neither pity nor exploitation. He would record, in a fictionalized journalism, the story of a people whose lives he found admirable. He portrayed the Black as others had portrayed the White—as a human being. Many other authors had taken the Negro and romanticized or propagandized him, and in the process had cast an entire race of people as heroes, villains, or fools. To Heyward, mankind could not be so easily categorized, just as a race of people could not be labeled with any degree of accuracy. Literary critic Frank Durham, who wrote one of the best critical evaluations of DuBose Heyward, cited a scene from Porgy in order to illustrate a part of its success:

> When the crippled figure rides jauntily through the Charleston streets in his goat wagon bearing the name of a fragrant toilet soap, Heyward's amusement is saved from the stereotyped by an undeniable pathos.
>
> It was this pathos verging on tragedy that distinguished *Porgy* from the other books about the Negro. Julia Peterkin's early sketches had given hints of what might be done, but Heyward was the first to give a rounded picture . . . of the Negro as a human being. . . .
>
> [L]ike most Southerners of his class, Heyward had seen the Negro on the waterfront, the Negro in relation not only to the white man but to other Negroes. And he wrote with veracity and drama of the vibrant life in Catfish Row and on the wharves when the white man was far away. From his pen came a memorable gallery of characters and episodes of a sort unknown before in fiction dealing with the Negroes. The fierce loyalties and antipathies, the joyous moments when the stevedores swashbuckled in, the tragedy, and the passion—all these formed a new picture of Negro life.[42]

The country—both North and South—praised Heyward's book. Frances Newman, in the October 18, 1925, issue of *The New York Tribune,* said that Porgy "is undoubtedly the most admirable book about Southern Negroes that I have ever read, and it is the only one I remember which substitutes beautifully rich orchestration for a line of melody." Lloyd Morris, writing in *The New York Times* of December 6, 1925, noted that the book "lifts its subjects to a level of art and yields the true national effect of tragedy." *Independent,* on December 5, 1925, remarked that Porgy is "written with tenderness and sympathy and emotional intensity." *Outlook* called it "a Negro classic," and *The New Republic* of December 23, 1925, went even further, stating that "Porgy is another book of beauty so rare and perfect that it may be called [an American] classic."

The representation of Gullah in *Porgy* is neither as meticulous as that in the Joel Chandler Harris tales, nor is it as loose as that of the latter stories of Julia Peterkin. According to Frank Durham, although Heyward spoke Gullah fluently:

> Gullah speech did not flow from his pen spontaneously. Perhaps his eagerness to get everything down on paper played its part. The manuscript shows him wavering uncertainly between what seems more or less standard literary Negro dialect and some distinctive Gullah words and locutions. . . .
>
> Heyward seemed to be seeking two goals: first, a careful phonetic transcription that would prevent unenlightened Northerners and Middle Westerners from mistakenly giving a nasal trill to sounds more closely resembling "-ush," and, second, a form employing fairly consistent and fairly standard spelling and marks of omission. As he revised, the Gullah quality was, paradoxically, both intensified and modified. The result is a Negro dialect with the suggestion of Gullah to differentiate it from the standard but with sufficient watering down of the Gullah to make it intelligible.[43]

In a scene representative of the language, Porgy—who needs to protect and be loved—has accepted Bess as his mistress. But when he finds that Bess can't stay away from her lover, Crown, murderer of Tobbins—he asks:

> "Ef dey warn't no Crown? . . . Ef dey wuz only jes' de baby an' Porgy, wut den?"
>
> The odd incandescence flared in [Bess's] face, touching it with something eternal and beautiful beyond the power of human flesh to convey. She took the child from Porgy with a hungry, enfolding gesture. Then her composure broke.
>
> "Oh, fuh Gawd sake, Porgy, don't let dat man come an' handle me! Ef yuh is willin' tuh keep me, den lemme stay. Ef he jus' don't put dem hot han' on me, I kin be good, I kin 'member, I kin be happy."
>
> She broke off abruptly, and hid her face against that of the child.
>
> Porgy patted her arm. "Yuh ain't needs tuh be 'fraid," he assured her. "Ain't yuh gots yo' man? Ain't yuh gots Porgy? Wut kin' of a nigger yuh t'inks yuh gots anyway, fuh let annuduh nig-

ger carry he 'oman? No, suh! yuh gots yo' man now; yuh gots Porgy."[44]

But Porgy didn't get Bess; Bess—her life ruled by others, by a lack of will—returned to the South:

"Where's Bess? Tell me, quick, where's Bess?" [Porgy demanded.]

[Maria] did not answer, and after a moment her ponderous face commenced to shake.

Porgy beat the side of his wagon with his fist.

"Where, where—" he began, in a voice that was suddenly shrill.

But Maria placed a steadying hand over his frantic one and held it still.

"Dem dutty dogs got she one day w'en I gone out," she said in a low, shaken voice. "She's been missin' yuh an' berry low in she min' 'cause she can't fin' out how long yuh is lock up fuh. Dat damn houn' she knock off de wharf las' summer fin' she like dat an' git she tuh tek er swalluh ob licker. Den half a dozen of de mens gang she, an' mek she drunk."

"But wuh she now?" Porgy cried. "I ain't keer ef she wuz drunk. I want she now."

Maria tried to speak, but her voice refused to do her bidding. She covered her face with her hands, and her throat worked convulsively.

Porgy clutched her wrist. "Tell me," he commanded. "Tell me, now."

"De mens all carry she away on de ribber boats," she sobbed. "Dey leabe word fuh me dat dey goin' tek she all de way tuh Sawannah, an' keep she dey. Den Serena, she tek de chile, an' say she is goin' gib um er Christian raisin'."[45]

Dorothy Heyward, DuBose Heyward's wife and a distinguished playwright, tried to convince her husband that his novel had dramatic possibilities. But he remained unconvinced, turning to another novel, *Angel,* which received mixed reviews in 1926. It was only after Dorothy Heyward completed a first draft of a drama, based upon the novel, that DuBose Heyward realized its potential. Working together, the Heywards completed the script in 1927. In New York City's American Theatre, *Porgy* had a successful run of 217 performances before going on tour, then returning for an additional 150 performances.

The representation of Gullah in the play shows a Standard English

modification, with only a few lexical items and some syntactic constructions remaining. Originally, the Heywards wrote the dialogue in Gullah,
but changed it to "Gullah-flavored English" to increase audience comprehension of the language. Although American audiences had little
difficulty understanding the modified dialogue, other English-speaking
audiences did have difficulty. Both the reviewers, as well as producer
Charles Cochran, attributed *Porgy*'s failure in London to "the difficulty
of understanding the dialogue."[46]

On October 10, 1935, at New York City's Alvin Theatre, an American audience witnessed the birth of a new musical form—an American
opera, an American *folk* opera. Its title was *Porgy and Bess;* its authors
were DuBose Heyward, George Gershwin, and Ira Gershwin. Nine
years earlier, George Gershwin had read *Porgy* and had become so enthused that he was determined to translate the story into a powerful,
majestic musical that would tower over everything that preceded it in
musical theatre. But it wasn't until 1933 that the Gershwins and Heyward could devote the time to transform the book and play into an opera. For almost two years they worked on the opera—Heyward cutting
and shaping the play into a libretto, assisted by Ira Gershwin; George
Gershwin developing the concept of an American folk opera, then writing the score, which included a number of songs that became popular
hits, including "Summertime," "A Woman Is a Sometime Thing," and
"I Got Plenty O' Nuttin." An artistic and critical triumph, *Porgy and
Bess* ran for 124 performances on Broadway, then went on a road tour,
during which the rest of the American public shared the enthusiasm of
the New York audiences.

In 1959, *Porgy and Bess* was transformed into film and became one
of the ten best films of the year. Produced by Samuel Goldwyn, directed by Otto Preminger, with a screen adaptation by N. Richard Nash,
Porgy and Bess featured in its cast Sidney Poitier as Porgy, Dorothy
Dandridge as Bess, Sammy Davis, Jr., as Sportin' Life, Brock Peters as
Crown, and Pearl Bailey as Maria. *Porgy and Bess,* said film critic Bosley Crowther, writing in the June 25, 1959, issue of *The New York
Times,* is a "stunning, exciting, moving film. . . . It bids fair to be as
much a classic on the screen as it is on the stage." On March 5, 1967,
ABC-TV ran the film to an audience estimated at over ten million
viewers.

Neither George Gershwin nor DuBose Heyward lived to see the film
or the television adaptation, or the critically acclaimed Broadway revivals
in 1942 and 1952, and the tremendously popular international tour of
1953–55, when *Porgy and Bess* was hailed as one of the greatest folk

operas in all of musical history. George Gershwin, only thirty-nine years old, died in 1937; DuBose Heyward, fifty-five years old, died in 1940. So powerful was *Porgy and Bess* that it overshadowed both the novel and the play. Soon, few remembered that there even was a novel or a play . . . few even remembered the name DuBose Heyward.

OF A MILITANT "EVERYMAN" AND A PASSIVE FOLKLORIST

In *The Big Sea,* his autobiography published in 1940, Langston Hughes looked back on the decade of the Negro Renaissance and recalled: "I was there. I had a swell time while it lasted. But I thought it wouldn't last long . . . for how could a large and enthusiastic number of people be crazy about Negroes forever?"[47] And so it was that the Negro Renaissance, a revolution in the evolutionary process of the American arts, would begin its decline after only a decade. But during that decade—which began shortly after the conclusion of World War I and ended shortly after the stock market crash—the American arts made its boldest stand against convention, bringing with it a new literature which sought out and captured the souls and emotions of a people. Seldom in the nation's history had so many writers been given the encouragement to experiment with new art forms, to try to mold a new literature. And during that decade of the Negro Renaissance, Langston Hughes was the movement's unofficial "poet laureate of Harlem."

Hughes was born in Joplin, Missouri, in 1902, and lived in four states and in Mexico before graduating in 1920 from Central High School in Cleveland. He began to write poetry while in grammar school, and in his senior year was chosen editor of the school yearbook. The following year he entered Columbia University, during which time *The Brownie's Book,* a monthly magazine sponsored by the NAACP, published seven of his poems, as well as three stories, an article, and a one-act play. That same year, *The Crisis* published "The Negro Speaks of Rivers," his first major poem, a deeply moving tribute to the historical soul of his people. From then on, his poetry appeared almost exclusively in either *The Crisis* or *Opportunity.*

Although influenced by the poetry of Paul Laurence Dunbar, Hughes chose to avoid the phonological representation of Black English—which had by the 1920s been associated with the minstrel stereotypes—and to concentrate on the syntax and other language forms. Like James Weldon Johnson, Hughes recognized that phonology was not the base of a language, but only one part—perhaps a small part. As Johnson pointed out in *The Book of American Negro Poetry:* "Hughes . . . [does] use a dialect; but it is not the dialect of the comic minstrel tradition or of the sentimental plantation tradition; it is the common, racy, living, authentic speech of the Negro in certain phases of real life."[48]

In 1926, on the recommendation of Carl Van Vechten, distinguished critic and author, Alfred A. Knopf published *The Weary Blues,* Hughes's first collection of poetry. DuBose Heyward, writing in the *New York Herald Tribune* book section, of August 1, 1926, had nothing but praise—"Always intensely subjective, passionate, and keenly sensitive to beauty and possessed of an unfaltering musical sense, Langston Hughes has given us a 'first book' that marks the opening of a career well worth watching." His second book, *Fine Clothes to the Jew* (1927), a collection of poetry of the blues, became the center of a sociological battleground. The poems were bold studies of the Negro soul, studies of protest and pride. But the White audience didn't wish to know the truth, and the Black audience didn't approve the unflattering examples laid forth. In the *Philadelphia Tribune,* a Black-oriented weekly newspaper, Eustace Gay reflected the views of many Blacks:

> It does not matter to me whether every poem in the book is true to life. Why should it be paraded before the American public by a Negro author as being typical or representative to the Negro? Bad enough to have white authors holding up our imperfections to public gaze. Our aim ought to be to present to the general public, already misinformed both by well-meaning and malicious writers, our higher aims and aspirations, and our better selves.[49]

But Hughes, facing the same problem journalists for generations had faced, could not resign himself to trying to please everyone, to writing what people *wanted* to hear at the sacrifice of what they *should* hear. His poetry of protest, pride, and reality laid open the emotions and history of a people. If it offended, it was only because reality, itself, carries in its bosom bitterness and suffering. The American public—Black and White—came to accept this, eventually giving Hughes its highest praise.

In the 1930s, Hughes turned from poetry to prose, his writing now appearing not only in *The Crisis, Opportunity, The New Republic,* and *Vanity Fair,* but also in *Esquire, The American Mercury, Scribner's* and the other leading magazines of the decade. During the decade, he expanded his literary output, writing articles, short stories, novels, and a highly successful Broadway play. For awhile, he was also a newspaper correspondent, reporting on the Spanish Civil War.

Throughout the first two decades of his career, Hughes was identified as a protest writer, fiercely proud of his heritage and his people, and not afraid to create controversy, even if it meant alienating some people. But by the 1940s, the sting of his social protest was muted, replaced by sharp satire and humor. For this new medium of social protest, now covered by veils of humor, Hughes created an Everyman— Jesse B. Semple, formerly of Virginia, now of Harlem. Streetwise and fun-loving, Semple—Simple to his friends—is a jive-talking Black, proud of his people and his heritage, searching for universal goals of security and understanding, but never succeeding.

Jesse B. Semple first appeared in the November 21, 1942, issue of the *Chicago Defender,* a Black-oriented daily newspaper, and appeared regularly in the *Defender* and other newspapers until 1965. From the Simple series came five critically acclaimed best sellers—*Simple Speaks His Mind* (1950), *Simple Takes a Wife* (1953), *Simple Stakes a Claim* (1957), *The Best of Simple* (1961), and *Simple's Uncle Sam* (1965).

Simple is at the heart of a people, able to convey great thought and penetrating wit from a barstool; he is the voice that few Whites and not many Blacks have heard. Proud of who he is, Simple tears into the heart of social problems and social convention.

With only rare exceptions—most notably in the absence of the post-vocalic /r/, nasalization reduction, and the absence of consonant clusters in word-final position—the phonology of Jesse B. Semple is largely Standard English. However, the language patterns are a mixture of Standard and Black English, showing the migration from the rural South to the industrial North. The use of alliteration, hypercorrection, and malapropism are prevalent in Simple's speech; but he is fluent with verbal language, able to spew out, with relative ease, complex rhyming patterns and serial phrasing important to the image of a streetwise Black. His narrator-friend, Boyd—a "colledged" man—may know the "right" use of the word, but Simple knows how to use words to convey thought; Simple's literacy comes from the street, from the *creation* of language, a *Black* language.

Literary critic Eugenia W. Collier capsulizes Simple's command over his readers because of his command over language:

> The typical hero speaks to us in our American language, which has the dignity and grandiosity of epic style. . . . I only know that [Simple] speaks to me in terms that I can understand and that his speech is *right*.
>
> The truths that Simple utters are Black realities. The scope of Black American ghetto life is revealed in Simple's conversations.[50]

Jesse B. Semple—wise-cracking, fun-loving, deeply concerned barroom philosopher, was the voice of the Black who had no voice; he was the soul and spirit of a race of people. And he—and his creator—were very much loved and respected.

Many of the social and literary critics have not been kind to Zora Neale Hurston. In the vernacular of the street language, she was perceived as a "white man's nigger"; a Black writer who "danced to the white man's tune." Reviewing *Dust Tracks in the Road*, Hurston's autobiography published in 1942, Arna Bontemps, like Hurston a product of the Negro Renaissance, wrote:

> Miss Hurston deals very simply with the more serious aspects of Negro life in America—she ignores them. She has done right well by herself in the kind of world she found. . . .
>
> Always in the background stood a line of substantial friends who saw in the exuberant unspoiled colored girl the kind of Negro they wanted to encourage.[51]

Harold Peece, writing in the February 1943 issue of *Tomorrow,* referred to Hurston as, "the tragedy of a gifted sensitive mind, eaten up by an egocentrism fed on the patronizing admiration of the dominant white world." Literary critic Darwin T. Turner, sifting through and selecting the facts of Hurston's life, coldly wrote:

> The Zora Neale Hurston who takes shape from her autobiography and from the accounts of those who knew her is an imaginative, somewhat shallow, quick-tempered woman, desperate for recognition and reassurance to assuage her feelings of inferiority; a blind follower of that social code which approves arrogance toward one's assumed peers and inferiors but requires total psychological commitment to a subservient posture before one's supposed superiors. It is in reference to this image that one must examine her novels, her folklore, and her view of the Southern scene.[52]

Turner further argued:

> Contradictions in the autobiography reveal that the content was prepared with concern for its appeal to readers, especially white readers. By reporting her father's frequent warnings that her impudence will cause her to forget to remain in the docile, subservient position to which Southern society assigns Afro-Americans, Miss Hurston created a self-image as a fearless and defiant fighter for

her rights. In actuality, however, even white acquaintances were astonished by her apparent indifference to her own dignity or that of other blacks. . . . The truth is that, in public pronouncements, she ignored ill-treatment from white people.

Two causes . . . suggest themselves. One, the desire to sell her books caused Miss Hurston to conceal her resentment of white Americans. Two, she genuinely enjoyed the paternalism of her white friends.

If the first hypothesis is true, Miss Hurston was a hypocrite; if the second is true, she was immature and insecure.[53]

Even Langston Hughes, a friend and coauthor of *Mulebone,* a three-act comedy, was perturbed at her apparent lack of self-esteem or racial pride. In *The Big Sea,* his own autobiography, Hughes noted:

In her youth, she was always getting scholarships and things from wealthy white people, some of whom simply paid her just to sit around and represent the Negro race for them. . . . To many of her white friends, no doubt, she was a perfect "darkie," in the nice meaning they give the term—that is, a naive, childlike, sweet, humorous, and highly colored Negro.[54]

Whether or not Zora Neale Hurston played the "White man's game," what mattered most was that others thought she did. And soon, it made little difference whether or not she was as militant as she thought she was, or as passive as some others thought—perceptions of reality, which obscure and replace reality, established her as one "type" of person; perceptions, established and molded by each person's own background and worldviews, changed reality—and a brilliant, talented writer suffered its consequences, torn by the knowledge that although she could never be part of an assimilated White society, neither was she a part of Black society. And so she wrote, becoming a master reporter of the lives and values of Black people, *her* people, so that a White population could understand, and hopefully one day, *accept.*

Perhaps because of her own world views, perhaps for other reasons, Zora Neale Hurston never achieved the recognition she deserved, or desired; she was caught somewhere in a neverland—respected by White critics because she fulfilled their expectations of what a "colored person" should be, rejected by the Black critics because she was never militant, always passive, never offending. Even the quality of her folklore research was held up to question; many, both Black and White, claimed that she wasn't "scholarly" enough. Darwin Turner—who called her first book of folklore, "an enjoyable work of competent journalism, which offers valuable insight into a class of people and a way of life"[55]— nevertheless, with some justification, chastised her for a perceived lack of thoroughness:

> Miss Hurston repeatedly identified herself as an anthropologist, but there is no evidence of the scholarly procedures which would be expected from a formally trained anthropologist or researcher in folklore. Instead of classifying and analyzing tales, she merely reported them in the chronological order and the manner in which they had been told to her. Furthermore, she failed to ask or to answer essential questions.[56]

Langston Hughes, however, disagreed:

> Miss Hurston was clever, too—a student who didn't let college give her a broad *a* and who had great scorn for all pretensions, academic or otherwise. That is why she was such a fine folklore collector, able to go among the people and never act as if she had been to school at all. Almost nobody else could stop the average Harlemite on Lenox Avenue and measure his head with a strange-looking anthropological device and not get bawled out for the attempt, except Zora, who used to stop anyone whose head looked interesting, and measure it.[57]

What apparently had upset many of the academic scholars was that Hurston, instead of taking the "accepted" approaches to folklore research, applied what she had learned in linguistics from Lorenzo Dow Turner at Howard University, and in anthropology from Franz Boas at Barnard College, and became a reporter, rather than a classifier of folklore. With the encouragement and advice of Turner and Boas, and assisted by a monthly stipend from a wealthy patron, she began a four-year field project in 1927, to collect folklore of the South.

Traveling throughout Florida and Louisiana, stopping whenever and wherever she wished, she compiled for publication a collection of more than seventy folk tales, as well as several descriptions of voodoo and hoodoo practices. Although Hurston thought it important to include the Black English spoken by her sources, her literary representation of the dialects, as presented in *Mules and Men* (1935), is not linguistically consistent or fully accurate. Although trained in linguistics, Hurston—possibly because her own internal linguistic systems either blocked or mutated sounds—did not distinguish in print many of the speech sounds associated with the various Black English dialects of Florida and Louisiana. Her recording of the syntax, Black idiom, and certain morphological features, however, shows a keener awareness than her recording of the phonology.[58]

Hurston's second book of folklore, *Tell My Horse* (1938), was a popular and well-received account of her travels in Haiti, focusing on the people and their folk beliefs. Yet, it also came under academic attack for not being "scholarly." Nevertheless, although Hurston did not classify, evaluate, or provide deep sociological insight, she did present the basic information about a people and their culture which could later be interpreted by others.

The academic scholars and literary critics, although classifying Hurston among the "minor writers," were, nevertheless, impressed with her handling of the novel as a literary form. But, even in the novel, Hurston was swamped by the maze of contradictions—some thought she was too realistic in her portrayal of Black characters, others thought she was unrealistic; some believed she was too militant, others believed she was too passive and uncaring about her own race. Nevertheless, analysis of her novels more than four decades after they were written, shows a power of expression not present in many other stories about Black familial life; her five novels were written not out of weakness, but of strength; not from passivity, but from a profound empathy with human suffering and its consequences. If she was, as others claimed, the "good Black" who remained passive amidst the fires of militancy, it was not effectively represented in her novels.

Hurston's first novel, *Jonah's Gourd Vine* (1934), is a sociopsychological drama of intrafamilial and interracial conflict. Her second novel, *Their Eyes Were Watching God* (1937), shows a greater awareness of the process and development of the novel-form, alternating humor and tragedy until it builds to its final, almost inevitable, conclusion marked by intense suffering. In *Moses, Man of the Mountain* (1939), Hurston reworked an African legend that suggested that Moses was a mulatto, the illegitimate son of Pharaoh's daughter. Combining satire, humor, and dialect, Hurston created a delightful story that drew parallels between the Jews in enslavement and the modern Black in enslavement, and in the process treated both the Jews and the Blacks with a realism seldom before reported. In her fourth novel, *Seraph on the Suwanee* (1948), Hurston cast aside the elements of humor, prevalent in her first three novels, in order to force the reader to accept the tragic pattern that defined the life of a young woman thwarted in her ambition to become a missionary, and then, after marriage, allowed her mind to work against her until it almost destroys her and those around her.

With the exception of *Seraph on the Suwanee,* her last published novel, each of Hurston's four novels includes extensive dialogue in Black English.[59] Like the later works of Julia Peterkin, the representation of the language here is not exact, but meant only to give a "feeling" of the language as it interrelates with the culture. The representation of Black English is marked by the extensive, almost overwhelming, use of metaphorical expressions, the substitution of the *d* for *th* sounds, and the seeming dominance of *ah* for *I* throughout the stories.

During the 1950s, she worked as a maid, librarian, newspaper reporter, teacher, and freelance writer—though her literary output was scanty. Never again would she conduct folklore research; never again would she write a novel. On January 28, 1960, Zora Neale Hurston—anthropologist, folklorist, journalist, and novelist—died penniless in a nursing home in Florida, a woman loved, detested, and mourned.

THE JAZZ AGE

From the streets of New Orleans and St. Louis to the honky-tonks and nightclubs of New York, America during the early twentieth century became enamoured with a new musical expression. A new *kind* of music. A *Black* music. A music with a syncopated beat spread across the musical staff in a twelve-measure sequence at 2/4 or 4/4 time. It was the Blues, Dixieland, Ragtime, Boogie—*Jazz.* Music with the beat and rhythm of West Africa and lyrical expression of America. An extension of the pre-Civil War Negro spirituals which proclaimed joy and told of suffering. As the nation entered the twentieth century and the popularity of the Negro spirituals in White America declined, the Negro Renaissance Cycle unfolded and the "Jazz Age" began; White America rediscovered these keys to the language and culture of Black America.

Shortly before World War I, Henry Edward Krehbiel, distinguished music critic for the *New York Herald,* wrote *Afro-American Folksongs: A Study in Racial and National Music* (1914). In a chapter on Black language, Krehbiel observed that although he believed Black English had its roots in British colonial speech, the music of the spirituals exhibited distinct Africanisms—in beat, meter, and pitch. He also maintained that many words had their origins in Africa, although the original meanings were either forgotten or never learned.

No one knows how or when jazz began. The word itself, however, probably originated on the West Coast of Africa where it meant "hurry up." Transformed in America through a long process of semantic change, "jazz," as both a noun and verb, was used by Black slaves in the South

to refer to sexual intercourse. By the second decade of the twentieth
century, however, the word referred to the new musical form, and by
the early 1920s, jazz had fixed its lexical stamp upon the country; the
Jazz Age of America's history was now being reported by writers caught
in the middle of an era called Jazz Journalism.

Two outstanding collections of Black folk music were published during
1925. *St. Helena Island Spirituals,* compiled by Nickolas George Julius
Ballanta-Taylor, is a collection of 100 Gullah spirituals, with a brief
introduction to the nature of the language and the music. Dorothy Scarborough's *On The Trail of the Negro Folk-Songs,* culminating several
years of extensive field work, included not only the lyrics and music of
a large number of spirituals and folk songs, but a thorough discussion
of music's integration with the lives of Blacks.

In the introduction to Lily Young Cohen's *Lost Spirituals* (1928),
publisher Walter Neale enthusiastically explained the importance of
preserving an oral folk culture, if only through a written description:

> The title of this book, *Lost Spirituals,* is intended to comprehend
> more than music and song; it is meant to embrace the soul of the
> Negro as found in its highest expression, in his daily converse and
> folklore as well as in his melodies and in his lyrics. Here the Negro
> himself is treated as a spiritual; so is his prose; so is his verse. And
> all are *Lost.* At least the social order in which all had their birth is
> gone. . . . In this and in other books, however, the Negro lives
> and will ever live.
>
> So far as the contents of this volume are concerned, all would
> have been lost . . . if Cohen had not written out her memories of
> her childhood; if she had not put into written music the songs she
> heard sung, that, never before to her knowledge, had been tran-
> scribed; if she had not retold, in type, the folk tales told to her by
> her old family servants; if she had not here set down the verse re-
> peated to her time and again by the faithful Negroes of her tender
> years.[60]

Howard Odum, one of the nation's leading sociologists and educators, contributed a number of studies on the literature of Black American folklore, including several studies of Negro spirituals and work
songs, and a trilogy of novels: *Rainbow 'Round My Shoulder: The Blue
Trail of Black Ulysses* (1928), *Wings on My Feet: Black Ulysses at War*
(1929), and *Cold Blue Moon: Black Ulysses Afar Off* (1931). Among
Odum's books that focus upon the Black folk music are *The Negro and*

His Songs (1925), and, with Guy B. Johnson, *Negro Workaday Songs* (1926).

Other major song collections were developed by Frederick J. Work (*Folk-Songs of the American Negro,* 1907), John Wesley Work (*Folk-Songs of the American Negro,* 1915), Natalie Curtis Berkin (Hampton series of *Negro Folk-Songs,* 4 vols., 1918–1919), and Newman I. White (*American Negro Folk-Songs,* 1928).

John A. Lomax, a twenty-year-old student, came to the University of Texas armed with a trunk of cowboy songs he had collected, music never before written down. Lomax learned the realities of academic life early–his English professor looked at the music sheets, called them "worthless" and "crude," and ordered Lomax to study the "more acceptable" English ballads. Lomax studied the ballads, but refused to stop studying the folk music of the American plains, and by 1906, while studying for a Master of Arts at Harvard University, found a more receptive academic community. George Lyman Kittredge and Barrett Wendell, two of the nation's most eminent literature scholars, were enthused about Lomax's folk scholarship, and arranged a fellowship to allow him to spend three years collecting additional cowboy songs. The result was the publication of three pioneer studies of the music of the American plains–*Cowboy Songs and Other Frontier Ballads* (1910; rev. eds. in 1916, 1923 and 1938), *Book of Texas* (1916, written with H. Y. Benedict), and *Songs of the Cattle Trail and Cowboy Camp* (1919).

During the 1920s, Lomax continued his ballad hunting, but expanded his focus to include the music of Black Americana. In the early 1930s, his son, Alan, interrupted his studies at the University of Texas to begin a fifteen-year collaboration, which would result in the publication of the critically acclaimed *American Ballads and Folk Songs* (1934), *Negro Folk Songs as Sung by Lead Belly* (1936), and *Our Singing Country* (1941).[61]

In *American Ballads and Folk Songs,* John Lomax explained the methodology for collecting Black folk music:

Our purpose was to find the Negro who had had the least contact with jazz, the radio, and with the white man. Both on the farms and in the lumber camps the proportion of whites to Negroes was approximately 100 to 1. In the prison farm camps, however, the conditions were practically ideal. Here the Negro prisoners were segregated, often guarded by Negro trusties, with no social or other contacts with the whites, except for occasional official relations. The convicts heard only the idiom of their own race. Many—often of greatest influence—were "lifers" who had been confined in the penitentiary, a few as long as fifty years. They still sang the songs they had brought into confinement, and these songs had been entirely in the keeping of the black man. . . . [T]he Negro's singing, under the influence of the idiom and custom of his white neighbors, is unconsciously yet surely changed by white influences. He is apt to sing as he thinks the whites wish him to sing, and, as a result, he quickly abandons the musical nuances that make his music what it is.[62]

Although the Lomaxes tried to find Blacks who were isolated from Whites, by the mid-1930s, with increased Black migration, there was obviously a greater mixing of Standard English with the various American Black English dialects than had existed when the first major studies into Black folk music were undertaken in the 1860s and 1870s. The problem in transcribing the Black speech which had undergone significant acculturation was described by John Lomax:

Consistency in printing Negro dialect and grammar was not found possible in a book which contains Negro compositions from every Southern state. When we attempted to spell the words as the Negro singer pronounces them, with the same faithfulness with which the machine recorded the tunes he sang, we soon found that in one sentence he would, for example, pronounce "the" correctly and in the next sentence call it "de," "th'," "dee" or, possibly, "deh"; "going to" becomes "goin'," "gwine," "gwinter," "gonna," "gonter," etc. The Carolina and Virginia Negro pronounces many words far differently from the Negro of Louisiana and Mississippi. In some instances . . . we retain the precise form of the word as it comes to us. Negroes of education who sang some of these songs, dropped, perhaps unconsciously, into the idiom of the song as they in turn had heard it from a person lacking formal education. We have tried, in general, to establish a norm, having in mind always the reader who is unacquainted with the Negro's distinctive and often beautifully expressive dialect. Much that we have heard, if written out precisely as it sounded, would be unintelligible to the average reader. In the Negro songs, for instance, the r ending a word and the long i are generally to be pronounced as "ah" or "uh"; final consonants are to be slurred or dropped entirely, if one is to arrive at an approximation of Negro pronunciation.[63]

Nevertheless, the Lomaxes had one advantage that Thomas Wentworth Higginson, William Francis Allen, and Joel Chandler Harris did not have—by the 1920s, the phonograph record was already an established part of American mass communications. The Lomaxes adapted a recording device, similar to the not-yet-developed tape recorder, and "froze" music onto wax cylinders and plastic discs. These cylinders and discs, soon to number more than 5,000, enabled the Library of Congress to establish a permanent collection of recordings which could be used both to verify transcriptions, and to provide for future research into the verbal features outside the parameters of traditional phonological and syntactic transcription; for the first time, as soon as linguistic science could establish methodologies for analysis of the suprasegmentals and deep structure, there would be a large body of raw data from decades before.

> "I knows de Governor will be glad to turn me over to you if you will ask him. I ain't a bad nigger. Jes' got into trouble f'om drinkin' too much co'n whisky and gin, an' de mens don't like me much because de womens like me an' my guitar pickin'. I'll drive yo' car, cook yo' meals, wash yo' clo'es, and' be yo' man as long as I live.
>
> "I'se de best nigger in de world; I'se de best car driver in de world; I'se de best cook in de world; I'se de best bed-maker in de world. I'se de best guitar picker in de world! Start my ol' twelve-string box to twangin' in any town in dese Nunited States an' de people'll come a-runnin'. I'll make you a lot of money. You needn't give me none, 'cept a few nickels to send my woman . . .
>
> "I'se a hard-wuckin' nigger, too. I always takes de lead row in de field, an' when us niggers chops a log dey gives me de butt cut, and then I gets through before dey do."[64]

His name was Huddie Ledbetter, but to a nation soon to be enamoured by his music, he was Lead Belly, the self-proclaimed "king ob de twe'f-string guittah playuhs ob de wuhl!" The time was 1933; the place, Angola (Louisiana) State Prison Farm. For the third time in his life, Lead Belly was in prison. The first time, about 1916 or 1917, no one knows for sure, he was sentenced to a chain gang for one year for attacking a woman who refused his advances. He escaped. Then on December 13, 1917, Lead Belly was booked into the New Boston, Texas, jail and charged with murder—not premeditated murder, but murder, nevertheless. In June 1918, he entered the Texas penitentiary, under the

alias of Walter Boyd, to begin a thirty-year sentence, but he served only
a little more than six and a half years. As Lead Belly later explained:

"De governor [Pat Neff] come an' he had Mrs. Neff and a whole
car of women-folks wid him . . . [D]at man sho was crazy 'bout
my singin' an' dancin'. Ev'y time I'd sing a new song or cut a few
steps he'd roll me a bran-new silver dollar 'cross the flo'. Las' song
I sung was a song I had made up askin' him to turn me loose, let
me go home to Mary. He tol' me when I was through, say 'Walter,
I'm gonna give you a pardon, but I ain't gonna give it to you now.
I'm gonna keep you down here to play for me when I come, but
when I go out of office I'm gonna turn you loose if it's de las' thing
in de worl' I ever do.'

"Sho 'nough, I didn' hear no mo' f'om him fuh nearly a year.
Dey all tole me, say 'Dat man ain' gonna tu'n you lose, ol' Walter.
He wouldn' tu'n his own mammy loose.' But I didn' lose faith.
Nawsuh. An' you know, day after Governor Pat Neff went out of
office, Cap'n Flanagan call me an' tol' me to go home."[65]

But just five years later, he was back in prison, convicted of assault
with intent to commit murder—again, an unpremeditated assault, but assault nevertheless. His sentence was ten years. And now, on a warm day
in a Louisiana prison, Huddie Ledbetter, twice convicted of assault and
once convicted of murder, was begging John and Alan Lomax to try to
secure his release. For three days, the Lomaxes were at the Angola
prison farm recording folk music; for three days, Lead Belly begged for
his release.

One year later, the Lomaxes were back at the Angola prison farm,
this time specifically to record Lead Belly's voice and guitar music. And
Lead Belly, who once sang his way out of a thirty-year prison sentence,
was only too happy to oblige—pleading between songs and during songs,
"Please, suh, help me git out . . . Boss, please, suh, help me git outa
dis place—I jes' nachully don' like it."[66] Finally, moved by Lead Belly's
pleas for freedom, John Lomax agreed to let him record, on a two-
sided disc, a musical plea to Gov. O. K. Allen. According to John
Lomax:

[Lead Belly] dropped his faithful, adhesive-taped, green, old guitar
on the ground, clapped his hands joyfully, jumped up and down,
and exclaimed:
"Thank you, boss, thank you, thank you! I knows, ef you do, de

Governor's gwine to pardon me; when he hears dem songs he'll set me free. I'se gwine to play 'Irene' for the other side, and' I knows dat'll fix him. Thank you, boss, thank you! Jesus gwine to bless you for dis."[67]

One month later, on August 1, 1934, Huddie Ledbetter, having served almost four and a half years of a ten-year sentence, was reprieved. He was fifty years old, unemployed, with little money, almost no clothes, and his woman had left him—but he was free. Six weeks later, Lead Belly was to begin a career as a full-time professional singer. John Lomax explains:

I looked up from my newspaper as I sat in a hotel lobby in Marshall, Texas, on Sunday September 16, 1934, to see a Negro man standing timidly by my chair. He had touched my shoulder to draw my attention as he stood there, his face ashen with uncertainty and fear.

In his right hand he held a battered twelve-string guitar, in his left a brown-paper sugar bag. He wore no coat; only an old hat, a blue shirt, a patched pair of overalls and rusty, yellow shoes—gifts from the Louisiana penitentiary.

"Why, hello, Lead Belly! What are you doing here?"

"I'se come to be your man, boss: to drive yo' car and wait on you. I writes you fo' letters. I sent 'em to Austin. Yo' telegram is in dis paper sack." . . .

"Lead Belly," I began, "I do need a driver and some one to help me run my recording machine. As you know, Alan is sick and unable to travel with me. First, I'd like to know if you are carrying a gun."

Lead Belly looked at his sugar sack and replied:

"No, suh, boss, but I'se got a knife."

"Let me see it."

He handed me his knife, which I opened and balanced on my hand. It had a long, narrow blade, sharpened to a razor edge.

"Lead Belly," I said, "down in Austin I have a home and a lovely lady for my wife; also a very dear daughter . . . I hope to live a long while for their sakes. If you sometime—when we are driving along a lonely road—decide that you are going to take my money and car, you need not stick this knife into me. Just tell me and I'll hand you my money, get out of the car, and let you drive on."

"Boss," he said, as if deeply moved, "boss, I don't think you oughta talk dat way to me. Boss, dis is de way I feels about you: Ef you got in a fight wid a man an' he start to shoot you, I'd jump in between an' ketch de bullet myself an' not let it tech you. Boss, please, suh, lemme go wid you; I'll keep yo' car clean an' drive jes' like you tell me. I'll wait on you day an' night. An', boss, you'll never have to tie yo' shoes again ef you'll lemme do it."

I never saw Lead Belly shed a tear, though then he apparently came near to breaking down. He moved me, too, for I realized that probably no one in the world, except his woman, felt the slightest interest in him, that he might soon be back in the penitentiary for some crime against his own people.

Fate had chosen for my companion a Negro man whose mother had been a half-breed Cherokee Indian, his father an industrious and respected farmer. He had been twice a State convict, a county jail-bird and jail-breaker, every charge against him having been for physical violence. He had killed two men of his own race. Others he had shot or carved with his knife. His own face was scarred with jagged lines from knife cuts. His last sentence had been for using his deadly knife. He still carried that knife. I was alone and unarmed. Finally, he was fond of drink.[68]

And so, John Lomax, folklorist and scholar, and Huddie Ledbetter, "de king ob de twe'f-string guitah players ob de wuhl!" began their journey together, bringing a musical folk history to the people in prisons, on farms, and in small towns throughout the South. Within six months, Lomax and Lead Belly were in New York, greeted by reporters who had heard about this very unusual musician, this ex-con who could bring laughter and tears in the same song. Like everywhere else, the New York concerts were sellouts. The fame of Lead Belly was assured. Recording contracts and numerous concerts followed. But in 1939, Lead Belly, who could charm his audience into understanding, but whose anger was uncontrolled, was again convicted of assault, this time in Manhattan. As they had for so many years, his wife Martha—who had been the calming influence in his life, the woman who had brought him so much joy and happiness—and the Lomaxes, who had brought him the fame he so desperately needed, stood beside him. When he was released from prison in 1940, he continued his career, the legend now becoming the equal of the man.

During the next nine years, Lead Belly's fame peaked, surpassing even that of his friend Blind Lemmon Jefferson, one of the nation's greatest musicians and a pioneer in the blues tradition. Many years earlier, Lead Belly and Blind Lemmon walked the streets of New Orleans, bringing a special kind of music to a city already enriched by a long music tradition. It was Blind Lemmon who had walked with Lead Belly; it was Blind Lemmon who had taught Lead Belly much about the music and traditions of the wandering minstrelsy. And now, as Lead Belly prepared for yet another concert in Paris, his own fame had surpassed that of his friend. The power of Lead Belly's music, a hard-hitting music brought forth and reverberated by all twelve guitar strings being pushed to their limits, could bring happiness, and it could bring sorrow. With his music alone, Lead Belly would wring every emotion from his audience, leaving them physically and emotionally exhausted. Maggie Baisley, who knew Lead Belly in Louisiana long before he and his music had swept through an entire nation, remembers him because she remembers his music:

> "I *wouldn't* tell you all I *could* tell you—he was so bad. As for the good things, when he began to play was no preacher could keep from movin' his foot. Huddie could beat any bird for singin'. Yes, he could play so. That was a playin' man. . . . A good player and a good devil too; women were crazy about that man. I didn't get to but two-three parties where he was round. My husband wouldn't let me. The men sure didn't like him. That Huddie, he would do anything. And I *declare* he could play. Nobody play like that. Well, he naturally could play that guitar. He could *play,* and everyone in the world jumpin'. Now I *know* that about him. And he sing just like a bird. He could naturally sing. He sing by hisself if he didn't have no guitar. Him and that guitar could sing. And the women was *bound* to move they foot. . . .
>
> "I betcha a heap of marriage was broken up cause of him. If the men wouldn't said nothin' would a been *all*. The women left they men, cause they was crazy 'bout that music. Now, cause he *was* not pretty—wasn't even good lookin', but they was crazy 'bout his music. They don't care. And he naturally could play."[69]

They remember his music, his love of women, his quickness to anger . . . and they remember his funeral.

Sometime during the 1940s, no one knows when, Lead Belly, a powerfully built man who lived up to his claims that he could outwork any man in the fields, contracted a very rare disease. Its medical name was *amyotrophic lateral sclerosis,* and it affects the muscles of the body, usually attacking persons who are healthy, physically powerful, and active in life. On December 6, 1949, Huddie Ledbetter, at the age of sixty-four, died in New York City's Bellevue Hospital, a song on his lips. The illness which had killed Lou Gehrig, one of the nation's greatest baseball players, had killed Huddie Ledbetter, one of the nation's greatest musicians. A nation, awakened by Lead Belly's music to an understanding and appreciation of Black language and culture began its mourning.

In its December 19, 1949, issue, *Time* magazine factually, almost coldly, in its detached formula-designed obituary, simply reported:

> **Died.** Huddie Ledbetter ("Lead Belly"); sixty-ish, bad-man minstrel who brought unwritten Negro folk ballads and work songs to cafe society and the concert halls of Manhattan and Paris; of a bone infection; in Manhattan. Hard-drinking, hell-raising Lead Belly, three times convicted for knife assaults and manslaughter, specialized in "sinful" folk songs of hard work and wild love rather than "spirituals," was finally tamed by success and his sponsor, the late ballad-collecting John Lomax.[70]

Death had stopped Lead Belly's life, but it couldn't still his voice or his musical influence over a nation. He had recorded more than 100 songs—songs he composed or adapted to his own unusual guitar technique, songs that spoke of a Black culture, of a black language. These songs—not the obituaries that appeared in the newspapers and magazines, and not the memories, whether harsh or fond, that people had of him, and not the files of the prison systems of three states—are his tribute, a tribute to strength and greatness.

THE LAST NARRATIVES

The first slave narrative was written about 1760 and published in Boston. The last narratives were written between 1935 and 1939, and then only because of the Depression. On October 29, 1929—"Black Tuesday"—the stock market collapsed, plunging the country into the worst depression in its history, leading to the defeat of President Herbert Hoover and the inauguration of Franklin D. Roosevelt in 1933. Roosevelt's "New Deal" created massive recovery programs, one of which was the Works Project Administration (WPA), designed to create jobs for the unemployed. From the WPA came the Federal Writers Project, a program to provide "a series of books which would give the Nation a portrait of itself." Part of that portrait was an in-depth look at slavery, the social institution which dictated America's development and economic growth for almost two centuries and which, when struck down by presidential proclamation, left deep scars in a nation's social con-

sciousness. And so, for the only time in its history, the federal government funded a program to record the words and feelings of former
slaves, none less than seventy-two years old, and most in their 80s and
90s. Between 1936 and 1938, more than 2,000 former slaves living in
seventeen states were interviewed, their impressions and feelings translated *verbatim* into the printed word, sorted, compiled, and finally filed,
in manuscript form, in the Library of Congress.[71]

Sterling A. Brown, Negro Affairs editor for the project, in an introduction to the nature of the project noted the importance of the
narratives:

> Whether the narrators relate what they actually saw and thought
> and felt, what they imagine, or what they have thought and felt
> about slavery since, now we know *why* they thought and felt as
> they did. To the white myth of slavery must be added the slaves'
> own folklore and folk-say of slavery. The patterns they reveal are
> folk and regional patterns—the patterns of field hand, house and
> body servant, and artisan; the patterns of kind and cruel master or
> mistress; the patterns of Southeast and Southwest, lowland and up-
> land, tidewater and inland, smaller and larger plantations, and ra-
> cial mixture (including Creole and Indian).[72]

Recognizing the intertwining of language and culture, the senior editorial staff of the project in a memorandum to fieldworkers, recom-
mended that:

> the stories be told in the language of the ex-slave, without exces-
> sive editorializing and "artistic" introductions on the part of the in-
> terviewers. The contrast between the directness of the ex-slave
> speech and the roundabout and at times pompous comments of the
> interviewer is frequently glaring. Care should be taken lest expres-
> sions such as the following creep in: "inflicting wounds from which
> he never fully recovered" (supposed to be spoken by an ex-slave).[73]

The interviewers would often subconsciously cast their own language
perceptions and stereotypes onto the speech of former slaves, thus imposing White standards and perceptions. The problems of language perception were critical in that very few interviewers were trained in either
linguistics or folklore; they were reporters attempting to learn about,
then record, the life experiences of former slaves. For that reason, as
well as for reasons involving readability, the senior editorial staff determined that there would be no emphasis in the narratives of a linguisti-

cally sound phonological representation of the language, but that "truth to idiom" and accurate syntactical recording be paramount. In his instructions to field workers, John Lomax pointed out:

> Simplicity in recording the dialect is to be desired in order to hold the interest and attention of the readers. It seems to me that researchers are repelled by pages sprinkled with misspellings, commas, and apostrophes. The value of exact phonetic transcription is, of course, a great one. But few artists attempt this completely. . . . Present day readers are less ready for the overstress of phonetic spelling than in the days of local color [the Reconstruction Cycle].
>   . . . I appreciate the fact that many of the writers have recorded sensitively. The writer who wrote "rat" for right is probably as accurate as the one who spelled it "raght." But in a single publication, not devoted to a study of local speech, the reader may conceivably be puzzled by different spellings of the same word. The words "whafolks," "whufolks," "whi'folks," etc., can all be heard in the South. But "whitefolks" is easier for the reader, and the word itself is suggestive of the setting and the attitudes.
>   Words that definitely have a notably different pronunciation from the usual should be recorded as heard. More important is the recording of words with a different local meaning. Most important, however, are the turns of phrase that have flavor and vividness.[74]

Editorial changes in dialect also posed a major problem, one that Lomax and Brown hoped to avoid. Many interviewers recorded the language of the former slaves as Standard English, concentrating on information, folk mores, and the syntax of language rather than on pronunciation. However, a number of editorial changes were later made by both field workers and midlevel editors to make the language appear to be Black English. Not infrequently, *I* was recast as *ah*—whether or not the former slave actually said *I* or *ah,* or any other dialectal variation. To put a stop to editorial tampering, Lomax issued a strong directive to all field workers. Among the words—many of them representative of eye dialect—expressly forbidden in the narratives were *ah* (for "I"), *bawn* ("born"), *capper* ("caper"), *com'* ("come"), *do* ("dough"), *ebry* and *ev'ry* ("every"), *hawd* ("hard"), *muh* ("my"), *nakid* ("naked"), *ole* and *ol'* ("old"), *ret* and *raght* ("right"), *snaik* ("snake"), *sowd* ("sword"), *sto'* ("store"), *teh* ("tell"), *twon't* ("twan't"), *useter* and *uset'r* ("used to"), *uv* ("of"), *waggin* ("wagon"), *whi'* ("white"), and *wuz* ("was"). Words with a postvocalic /r/ or nasalization reduction in word-final position were usually left as Standard English, because the representation could be reflective of both Black speech or Southern White speech.[75]

In the preface of *Lay My Burden Down* (1945)—a "selection and integration of excerpts and complete narratives from the Slave Narrative Collection"—B. A. Botkin, who followed Lomax as folklore editor of the project, explained why the language in the edited manuscripts appears to be more Standard English in phonological representation than in the original:

> In accordance with the same criteria of truth and readability, the original attempts at dialect-writing, successful and unsuccessful, were abandoned, except for a few characteristic and expressive variations. Although they had been instructed to put truth to idiom first, many stressing truth to pronunciation, which led them into new and worse inaccuracies. It is true that a word like "master" may have a half-dozen variants—"marster," "moster," "mastuh," "maussa," "marsa," and "massa"—but the fine distinctions of phonetic spelling (due to differences as much in the way a sound is heard or represented as in the sound itself) are for the specialist and get in the way of essential qualities of spoken language, which are qualities of style, of word choice and word order.[76]

Although the phonology of the slave narratives is not fully representative of the language and dialects spoken by former slaves, the syntax and certain lexical items are reflective of Black English. The narratives themselves—2,000 narratives recorded on more than 10,000 typescript pages—have provided one of the most valuable and enduring clues to the development and process of slavery about the time of the Civil War, and to its effects during the seven decades after freedom.

In addition to *Lay My Burden Down,* other books developed from the slave narratives were *Drums and Shadows; Survival Studies Among the Georgia Coast Negroes* (1940); *God Bless the Devil: Liars' Bench Tales* (1940); *Folk Music in America* (1940), edited by Phillips Barry; *The Negro in Virginia* (1940); and *Gumbo Ya-Ya, A Collection of Louisiana Folk Tales* (1945), edited by Lyle Saxon, Edward Dreyer, and Robert Tallant. The complete collection, with additional comments and analysis, was edited by George P. Rawick and published in nineteen volumes between 1972 and 1976 by Greenwood Press. An additional ten volumes, published in 1977, include both original and edited manuscripts, from non-Federal Writers Project programs, as well as extensive analyses of the nature of the project and dialect differences between field notes and what was edited by the Writer's Project staff. The definitive study of the Writer's Project in Virginia is Charles Perdue's *Weevils in the Cotton* (1967). Other slave narrative collections include Julius Lester's *To Be A Slave* (1968); Gilbert Osofsky's *Puttin' On Ole Massa: The Slave Narratives of Henry Bibb, William Wells Brown, and Solomon Northrup* (1969); Norman R. Yetman's *Voices From Slavery* (1970); and John Bayliss's *Black Slave Narratives* (1970).

THE EMERGENCE OF A NEW THEORY

The first significant studies of American Black English were published shortly after the Civil War. William Francis Allen, writing in the December 1865 issue of *The Nation,* presented a reasonably accurate description of many of the features of Gullah, but called the language the result of "phonetic decay." Five years later, Col. Thomas Wentworth Higginson presented additional information about American Black English in *Army Life in a Black Regiment.*

During the next three decades, as dialect verse and dialect tales poured forth from the nation's mass media, numerous persons began investigating the nature of the language, usually concluding, as did Allen, that American Black English was an end-product of the bastardization of Standard English. A few authors recognized that there may have been some African linguistic elements present in the speech of American Blacks, but their views were seldom accepted by others. According to authors, scholars, and just about anyone who ever spent more than a few moments with Blacks, American Black English originated in England, not Africa. The arguments changed little during the first three decades of the twentieth century.

During the height of the Reconstruction Cycle of American Black English, Ambrose Gonzales wrote several folk sketches which included lengthy passages in Gullah. Although he maintained a continual interest in the Gullah people and their language, it wasn't until 1918—about three decades after his sketches first appeared in the *Charleston News & Courier* and in *The State,* and as the Negro Renaissance Cycle was unfolding—that he returned to the Gullah people as subject for study. The twenty-eight sketches published in *The State* during 1918 were added to the fourteen sketches published in *The State* during 1892, to form *The Black Border; Gullah Stories of the Carolina Coast.*

In the book's foreword, Gonzales, one of the nation's leading authorities on the Gullah language, argued that the African-born slave "retained only a few words of his jungle-tongue, and even these few are by no means authenticated. . . . As the small vocabulary of the jungle atrophied through disuse and was soon forgotten, the contribution to language made by the Gullah Negro is insignificant, except through the transformation wrought upon a large body of borrowed English words.[77]

Recognizing the pidginization of American Black English, while at the same time advancing some of the concepts of what would later be formalized into the Deficit Theory, Gonzales wrote:

> Slovenly and careless of speech, these Gullahs seized upon the peasant English used by some of the early settlers and by the white servants of the Wealthier Colonists, wrapped their clumsy tongues about it as well as they could, and, enriched with certain expressive African words, it issued through their flat noses and thick lips as so workable a form of speech that it was gradually adopted by the other slaves and became in time the accepted Negro speech of the lower districts of South Carolina and Georgia. With characteristic laziness, these Gullah Negroes took short cuts to the ears of their auditors, using as few words as possible, sometimes making one gender serve for three, one tense for several, and totally disregarding singular and plural numbers.[78]

Although Gonzales's analysis of Gullah was inaccurate and showed a certain linguistic chauvinism, his description and recording of the language was reasonably accurate, providing significant insights into the people and the culture. A ten-page description of many of the features of Gullah, and a 1,700-word glossary in *The Black Border*—although containing several eye dialect words, and primarily a phonological rather than lexical glossary—is still used by linguists and others interested in Gullah language development.

In 1924, The State Company published three more of Gonzales's books—*The Captain, Stories of the Black Border; Laguerre, A Gascon of the Black Border;* and *With Aesop Along the Black Border*. The latter book was a compilation and adaptation of Gullah Bible stories.[79]

In the introduction to *Black Cameos* (1924), an excellent collection of Black folklore, including dialect tales, music, and verse, R. Emmet Kennedy discussed a number of features characteristic of Black English. He concluded that "while it may not be called a peculiar species of English, nevertheless has as many varied dialectical shadings in the southern states where it is spoken as the English language has in the rural districts of northern England."[80] Kennedy also pointed to a "poetic sensibility" in the music of the American Blacks, and an obligation of the Whites to preserve the American Black oral folklore tradition.

In *Congaree Sketches* (1927), a book similar to *Black Cameos,* E. C. L. Adams presented fifty-four sketches of Blacks living along the lower Carolina coast. According to Adams:

> The dialect is of course English shot through and influenced by the traditions and sentiments of the African slaves. Very few genuine words are distinguishable, but there is a marked influence of the African sense of melody and rhythm. This gives to every word, even if otherwise good English, a particular dialectal sound and significance.
>
> It needs to be remembered that this particular dialect, while pure Nigger, is neither the dialect of the coast nor of the Northern part of the Black border, but is absolutely distinct, and is the product of the soil, race, and environment. In other words, it is English as adapted to the needs and knowledge of these primitive people. Sometimes a word that is pronounced correctly has several dialectal meanings and several of the same words may be found in a single sentence. There is no rule.[81]

In the June 1924 issue of the *American Mercury*—a popular magazine edited by H. L. Mencken—George Phillip Krapp, a leading authority on American language, argued that there was little or no African influence upon American Black English. Like other scholars of the period, he concluded that the base of Black English—which he identified as several dialects—was British English and not a West African pidgin English. Probably influenced by Ambrose Gonzales, Krapp claimed:

> The Gullah dialect is a very much simplified form of English with cases, numbers, genders, tenses reduced to the vanishing point. . . . Very little of the dialect, perhaps none of it, is derived from sources other than English. In vocabulary, in syntax, and pronunciation, practically all of the forms of Gullah can be explained on the basis of English, and probably only a little deeper delving would be necessary to account for those characteristics that seem deep and mysterious. . . . [I]t is reasonably safe to conclude that not a single detail of Negro pronunciation or Negro syntax can be proved to have other than an English origin.[82]

Krapp's now-classic study, *The English Language in America* (1925), reinforced his earlier article about the nature of Black English. Because the absence of a postvocalic /r/ was one of the linguistic features of Black English, as well as Southern Standard English and British English, Krapp analyzed the data and determined that "the loss of the [r], both in America and in England, was a natural and early change in language which took place in popular speech unaffected by learned or standard influence." "The negroes omitted their *r*'s," said Krapp, "because they heard no *r*'s in the speech of their white superiors."[83] He concluded that when the entire nature of Black English is considered, "there is very little evidence to show that the negroes . . . have developed a special idiom of their own or are addressed in a special idiom by their white fellow-citizens."[84] Niles Newell Puckett, a leading folklorist, disagreed. In *Folk Beliefs of the Southern Negroes* (1926), Puckett, recognizing the integration of language and culture, argued that "the greater the departure of the Negro from the standard English in dialect the less the lore of the Negro is like that of the White."[85]

Reed Smith concluded that Gullah was a legitimate dialect, with a vocabulary, phonological rules, and a historical and literary background. Accepting the premise that Gullah was English-based, Smith further concluded that the Gullah people "wrap their tongues around [the English language], and reproduce it with changes in tonality, pronunciation, cadence, and grammar to suit their native phonetic tendencies and their existing needs of expression and communication."[86] Although describing the pidginization of a language, while probably not fully understanding the nature of a pidgin, Smith never conceded that Gullah was anything but English-based. Although in error on some aspects, Smith's booklet was, essentially, a brilliant presentation and analysis of the Gullah language; it was well received by scholars and the public.

Isaiah Sanders' master's thesis at the University of Chicago—*Some Phrases of Negro English* (1926)—was an important addition to the literature of Black English. His description and analysis of the language provided a sound base for later analysis of the nature of the language.

Samuel Gaillard Stoney and Gertrude Matthews Shelby, recognizing the process of language pidginization, wrote in the introduction to *Black Genesis* (1930) that the origins of Black English "are in England's great colonial expansion of the seventeenth century."[87] The two authors also discussed the nature of a few Gullah words, but never acknowledged that the language could have been a pidgin at one time.

In *A Social History of the Sea Islands* (1930), Guion Griffis Johnson determined that the Gullah Blacks spoke "a garbled English [with] imperfect words and expressions which they and their African parents and grandparents had learned from the few whites with whom they came in contact with."[88]

In 1930, Guy B. Johnson, after lengthy research on St. Helena Island, concluded:

> Gullah has been called the most African of any of our Negro dialects, yet it can be traced back in practically every detail to English dialect speech. There has long been a popular belief in this country to the effect that Southern white speech is what it is because of the Negro. This idea needs to be reversed, for both the Negro and the white man in the South speak English as they learned it from the latter's ancestors.[89]

Johnson also concluded, in a separate article, that:

> this strange dialect turns out to be little more than the peasant English of two centuries ago. . . . From this peasant speech and from the "baby talk" used by masters in addressing them, the Negroes developed that dialect, sometimes known as Gullah, which remains the characteristic feature of the culture of the Negroes of South Carolina and Georgia.[90]

However, he also recognized a possible African influence in certain suprasegmental features of Gullah, noting that the Gullah language tempo "may be due to the African mode of speaking," and that pitch is probably "a survival of the musical accents used in the languages of West Africa."[91]

A companion volume to Guion Griffis Johnson's *A Social History of the Sea Islands,* and Guy B. Johnson's *Folk Culture on St. Helena Island, South Carolina,* is T. J. Woofter's *Black Yeomanry.* One of the chapters, "Cotton and Contrabands," written by Guion Griffis Johnson, is a summary of her research into historical documentation of the island; another of the seven chapters, "St. Helena Songs and Stories," written by Guy B. Johnson, is a capsulized account of his research into folklore and folk music, again emphasizing that Gullah is a pidginized "peasant English."

Charles S. Johnson, one of the finest chroniclers of Black social life, also concluded that Black English was derived from British English. In *The Negro and American Civilization* (1930), Johnson noted that Black English was "a repository for the early seventeenth-century speech of the first English colonizers."[92] Neither *The Negro and American Civilization,* nor Johnson's brilliantly researched and written sociological study, *The Shadow of the Plantation* (1934), contained more than a couple sentences related to dialect. Nevertheless, throughout *The

Shadow of the Plantation are transcriptions of Black speech illustrating assimilation of Standard English forms in the language of former slaves and their relatives in Macon County, Georgia. For example, although the voiced interdental fricative [ð] is usually replaced by the voiced alveolar stop [d] in word-initial position (as in *dem*), the unvoiced interdental fricative [θ] is usually present in word-medial and word-final position. There are significant variations in the phonological rules; yet, from transcription of the speech, alone, it is difficult to determine what the rules are, only that there is a significant variation between Southern White English and Southern Black English. The transcription of syntax shows more consistent rules—possibly illustrating the concept that language acculturation affects surface structure more quickly than deep structure.

Charles Boyd Guest's master's thesis at Alabama Polytechnic Institute in 1932 presented a 2,000-word Black lexicon and an excellent analysis of the language, but concluding that Black and Standard English were virtually the same language, with only minor differences.

In 1935, Cleanth Brooks, although presenting a strong linguistic description of the Georgia-Alabama dialect, nevertheless argued that "[in] almost every case, the specifically negro forms turn out to be older English forms which the negro must have taken originally from the white man, and which he has retained after the white man has begun to lose them."[93]

In the August 1937 issue of *The Writer,* a trade magazine for professional freelance writers, A. Dilworth Faber presented a "Negro American Vocabulary" of about seventy words and idioms. Faber determined that "much of the urban Negro slang is of white origin."[94] A number of his definitions and lexical etymologies were later proven inaccurate. Nevertheless, his article was read, and his statements and conclusions often accepted by many of the nation's writers, a few of whom undoubtedly incorporated into their own writings Faber's identification of Black lexicon and his general conclusions about Black English.

Two doctoral dissertations, both completed in 1937, added significantly to the literature on Black English phonology. William Edward Farrison, in his dissertation at Ohio State University, presented a detailed analysis of the phonology, including several linguistically sound transcriptions of texts, concluding that because of significant similarities between Black English and dialects of the White South, Black English could not be considered distinct or separate.

T. Earl Pardoe, in his dissertation at Louisiana State University, disagreed, arguing that although British English influenced the development of American Black English, the speech of American Blacks still contained elements of West African linguistic patterns. Presenting an extensive Black English lexicon with both orthographic and phonetic transcriptions, Pardoe carefully outlined what would later become a basis of the creolist theory of Black English, arguing that American Black English combined the influence of English-speaking masters with modifications by African phonetic patterns, to create first a pidgin, then a creole. Pardoe's dissertation was largely ignored in the academic community, and it remains largely forgotten in the development of the creole theory of American Black English.

Even H. L. Mencken, the distinguished journalist, and author of one of the definitive studies of American language, was not convinced of the validity of Black English. The first two editions of *The American Language: An Inquiry Into the Development of English in the United States* (1919 and 1921), included brief mentions of African loanwords. But by the fourth edition (1936), Mencken argued:

> The Negro dialect, as we know it today, seems to have been formulated by the song-writers for minstrel shows; it did not appear in literature until the time of the Civil War; before that, as George Philip Krapp shows . . . it was a vague and artificial lingo which had little relation to the actual speech of the Southern Blacks.[95]

In two book-length supplements (1945 and 1948), Mencken—although still believing that Black English was a "created" language, not too different from many of the Southern dialects—included information about parallel research into the nature of Gullah as a creole.

During the decade of the 1930s, Mason Crum, like many academic researchers before him, went to the Sea Islands to study the language and culture of the Gullah people. The result was *Gullah: Negro Life in the Carolina Sea Islands* (1940). In the chapter on language, Crum noted that Gullah was difficult to imitate but that the language itself "is conspicuous for its short cuts. Its grammar, which is but an abbreviated and mutilated English grammar, knows no rule except to follow the line of least resistance." Crum also said that Gullah "violates all rules of logic and [its speakers] say just that which is natural and to the point." Like Ambrose Gonzales, Reed Smith, Guy B. Johnson, and numerous other researchers, Crum accepted the theory that Black English had few or no African language characteristics: "[It] is almost wholly English—peasant English of the seventeenth and eighteenth centuries, with perhaps a score of African words remaining. Very early the slaves picked up the dialect of the illiterate indentured servants of the Colonies, the "uneducated English." And, interestingly, like many other re-searchers, while arguing that there was no African influence in lexicon, phonology, and syntax, Crum also recognized a "flavor of Africa": "It may be said that, while the body of the dialect is English, its spirit is African. Certainly there is the flavor of the slave coast in its peculiar in-tonation, its pleasing inflection, and its unique tonal quality."[96]

At that time, linguistics was still an emerging and developing science. Lexicon, phonology, and grammar could be reasonably recorded; the suprasegmentals would be "something *else*," a different and unrecord-able part of language, mentioned, then discarded as a major part of the reproduction and analysis of language.

AFRICAN SURVIVALS

To understand the nature and development of a language, it is neces-sary to understand the nature and development of the culture which de-termined that language. For more than two centuries, American schol-ars clung to beliefs that there were few, if any, Africanisms—either cultural or linguistic—in Black America. In the April 1919 issue of the *Journal of Negro History,* Robert E. Park, distinguished American so-ciologist, and a former journalist, summed up the majority opinion:

My own impression is that the amount of African tradition which the Negro brought to the United States was very small. In fact, there is every reason to believe, it seems to me, that the Negro, when he landed in the United States, left behind him almost every-thing but his dark complexion and his tropical temperament. It is very difficult to find in the South today anything that can be traced directly back to Africa.[97]

In *Shadow of the Plantation,* Charles S. Johnson wrote:

The Negro of the plantation [has] a completely broken cultural heritage. . . . There had been for him no preparation for, and no organized exposure to, the dominant and approved patterns of American culture. What he knew of life was what he could learn from other slaves or from the examples set by the white planters themselves.[98]

Even as late as 1940, E. B. Reuter, writing in the *American Journal of Sociology,* could state: "In the course of capture, importation, and enslavement [the slave] lost every vestige of African culture. The native languages disappeared immediately and so completely that scarcely a word of African origin found its way into English."[99]

But had the American Black "lost every vestige of African culture" when he was forcibly taken to the United States? Not according to Melville J. Herskovits, a distinguished American cultural anthropologist, and Lorenzo Dow Turner, whose reputation as a linguist would eventually rest on his studies of the Gullah language. A few writers and scholars had suggested the possibility—some even said probability—that there were distinct Africanisms in the language and culture of the American Black, but their research was seldom strong enough on its own merits to withstand either severe scholarly criticism or the majority's collective opinion.

After several years of extensive field research in both African and New World cultures, Herskovits—professor of anthropology at Northwestern University, and director of the university's prestigious Program in African Studies—wrote *The Myth of the Negro Past* (1941). This well-documented analysis was to shock academic scholars into eventually recognizing that there were significant Africanisms in both the language and culture of the American Black. The first paragraph of the preface set the tone of the book:

> This work represents the documentation of an hypothesis, developed in the course of two decades of research. That the scientific study of the Negro and attempts to meliorate the interracial situation in the United States have been handicapped by a failure to consider adequately certain functioning aspects of Negro life has become increasingly apparent as this investigation has gone on. Problems in Negro research attacked without an assessment of historical depth, and a willingness to regard the historical past of an entire people as the equivalent of its written history, can clearly be seen to have made for confusion and error in interpretation, and misdirected judgment in evaluating practical ends.[100]

In the section on "The Contemporary Scene: Language and the Arts," Herskovits boldly attacked much of the language scholarship that had been conducted in the past:

> Most of the work concerning speech survivals has dealt with [efforts] to discover those sounds of African or European origin to be discerned in Negro dialect and the related speech of white Southerners. Grammatical structure has been given almost no attention at all, since the approach to this aspect of the problem has been

dominated by the almost axiomatic principle that "pidgin" dialects reflect the lack of ability of inferior folk to take over the more complex speech habits of "higher" cultures . . . [T]his assumption is psychologically as well as linguistically untenable.[101]

That the book ignited the fires of controversy is not surprising. In the preface to the second edition, published in 1958, Herskovits recalled:

This book, when first published, discussed and documented a position that at the time was less than congenial to the considerable number of intellectuals who accommodated their thinking to the position of an important and established group of social scientists and of students of language and literature, a position which was challenged by its conclusions. Its point of view, moreover, was unpalatable to economic determinists. It is thus not surprising that some of its reviewers questioned or criticized the method used and the interpretation drawn.[102]

Herskovits also noted that "in the lively debate that followed the publication of this book, the validity of these facts, as such, was never challenged; rather, discussion turned on questions of method and interpretation. Thus, by consensus, the facts stand; the conceptual scheme has been sharpened, but not negated."[103]

Herskovits had dared to challenge not only recognized, but also accepted research that for over a century had asserted that the African Black "lost" all his culture, if he had any, when taken out of his homeland; that the Black's language was essentially bastardized English with virtually no African linguistic structures. As the evidence mounted in the decade ahead, the attacks diminished—a nation of scholars was beginning to accept the Herskovits hypothesis that the cultures which helped determine Black life in Africa were neither lost nor destroyed in the New World as the African slaves underwent the long process of acculturation. By 1958, Herskovits could look back on the seventeen years prior to his book's publication, and proudly write:

I could not have foreseen at the time that the challenge set forth in it—a challenge to the stereotype set up, elaborated and defended by the serious student of the Negro, and held to firmly by a vast majority of lay opinion—would be so caught up in the historical currents of the immediate years ahead as to force the profound revision of views concerning the potentialities and the role of Africans and their New World descendants that has actually occurred on the world scene. . . .

The fact that this book appeared at the moment it did was a fortuitous circumstance; but it was no accident that it was conceived and written, for this was in response to a long chain of developments in both the intellectual and political spheres. That it may have made some contribution toward an understanding of human relations, on any level, and aided in bringing about a heightened awareness that the role played by cultural continuities in New World Negro life is no different from the one it plays in the lives of other peoples, is a cause for deep gratification.[104]

Although the scholars eventually began to concede that there are certain African cultural traits in American Black society, most were unwilling to accept the hypothesis that not only could there also be certain African linguistic structures present in the speech of American Blacks, but that Black English could conceivably be a legitimate dialect. The large body of the American public, including most academic scholars, believed that Black English was, at best, bastardized English—inferior, ungrammatical, substandard . . . "bad" English. And the American dialectologists, who had argued that persons who spoke dialect were speaking linguistically valid language, believed that American Black English was more English than African in origin; its similarity to Southern regional dialects was too great even to call it a separate dialect.[105]

Into this milieu came Lorenzo Dow Turner, a young linguist who would study a number of West African languages in order to better understand one American language—Gullah, the most creolized of all Black American dialects. In *Africanisms in the Gullah Dialect,* published in 1949 after more than fifteen years of field research, Turner illustrated the vast influence of African languages on the development of speech patterns of the residents of the Sea Islands off Georgia and South Carolina. Referring to persons who described Gullah as an English-based dialect, Turner argued:

Many Americans who have attempted to explain Gullah have greatly underestimated the extent of the African element in this strange dialect. Observing many characteristics that Gullah has in common with certain British dialects of the seventeenth and eighteenth centuries, they have not considered it necessary to acquaint themselves with any of the languages spoken in those sections of West Africa from which the Negroes were brought to the New

World as slaves, nor to study the speech of the Negroes in those parts of the New World where English is not spoken; but rather have they taken the position that the British dialects offer a satisfactory solution to all the problems presented by Gullah. They contend also that Gullah is partly a survival of baby-talk which the white people, during the early period of slavery, found it necessary to use in communicating with the slaves. . . . [T]hey undertook the task of interpreting Gullah, apparently, without feeling the need of acquiring some knowledge of the Negro's African linguistic background.[106]

In studying more than twenty-five African languages, Turner observed the unique distinguishing feature in phonology, syntax, morphology, and intonation as compared to his native English. In his study of Gullah, these comparisons enabled him to distinguish more fully the differing roots of the language and to conclude:

Gullah is a creolized form of English revealing survivals from many of the African languages spoken by the slaves who were brought to South Carolina and Georgia during the eighteenth century and the first half of the nineteenth. These survivals are most numerous in the vocabulary of the dialect but can be observed also in its sounds, syntax, morphology, and intonation; and there are many striking similarities between Gullah and the African languages in the methods used to form words.[107]

Stressing that phonology and syntax do not constitute the whole of a language, Turner looked at the intonation patterns and paralinguistic features, areas of linguistic analysis seldom analyzed previously. In examining the sound patterns of Gullah, Turner found distinguishing features common to many of the West African languages but not to Standard English. According to Turner:

Probably no characteristic of the Gullah Negro's speech appears so strange to one who hears this dialect for the first time as its intonation. To understand fully the intonation of Gullah one will have to turn to those West African tone languages spoken by the slaves who were being brought to South Carolina and Georgia continually until practically the beginning of the Civil War. Among these tone languages are Mende, Vai, Twi, Fante, Gã, Ewe, Yoruba, Ibo, Bini, Efik, and a few others. In the discussion that will follow, an effort has been made merely to reveal some of the more striking similarities between certain tonal patterns of Gullah and those of a few of the West African tone languages.

So far as my own observation is concerned, features of tone in Gullah are not used as primary phonemes, i.e., the tones of Gullah words do not distinguish meanings as do tones in the African tone languages. There are in Gullah, however, several intonation patterns, used in sentences, phrases and words, that are quite common in the African languages but are not used in cultivated English under similar conditions.[108]

The Gullah people were suspicious of strangers, especially White strangers; if they talked at all, it was usually to say what they believed the White persons—the *buckra*—wanted to hear, not what the Gullah felt. And it was not uncommon for the Gullah to play linguistic games at the expense of the White researcher. Because he was Black, Lorenzo Dow Turner had an advantage no other researcher had. But it was an advantage only on the surface—he still had to develop a close understanding of the Gullah mind and mores in order to secure their confidence.

Many of Turner's preliminary findings were presented as scholarly professional papers—papers which were inbred in an academic community, and could either be ignored or dismissed as products of incomplete research. But with the publication of *Africanisms in the Gullah Dialect,* the battlegrounds were established—the creolists were forced to unite behind Turner's research, whereas the dialectologists—many trained in the same linguistic school of theory as the creolists—acknowledging the strength of Turner's research, conceded only that it was confined to a very specific and isolated linguistic community and not reflective of anything more than Gullah itself. The dialectologists further pointed out that a large portion of Turner's 4,000-word glossary was personal names rather than lexical items in everyday grammar.[109]

However, as in the past, the creolists and the dialectologists—both of whom regarded Gullah as a linguistically valid language or variety of speech—were in a minority; the vast portion of the American people—academics as well as the lay public—regarded Gullah like the other Black English dialects, as inferior substandard speech. *Africanisms in the Gullah Dialect,* like *The Myth of The Negro Past,* helped substantiate a theory that there were African survivals in the language and culture of American Blacks, but neither could successfully change attitudes—and therein lies much of the problem.

Other major research into the nature of American Black English was conducted by Elizabeth Gillespie whose master's thesis at the University of Mississippi presented a strong survey based on many specific examples; and by John Henry Faulk, whose master's thesis at the University of Texas, following the folklore methodology of John A. Lomax, probed Black speech and folklore in Negro sermons; seventy-five records of Black Negro sermons, recorded by Faulk, were filed with the national archives.

THE ELECTRONIC AGE

ST. JOHN'S, N.F., Dec. 14—Guglielmo Marconi announced tonight the most wonderful scientific development of recent times. He stated that he had received electric signals across the Atlantic Ocean from his station in Cornwall, England. (*The New York Times,* December 15, 1901, p. 1)

And so a new medium was born, a medium which would revolutionize the social, economic, and philosophical history of the world. It was a medium which began by being the channel to transmit messages from ships, later from airplanes. It was a medium which would help save lives and protect property. Within two decades, when KDKA radio, Pittsburgh, became the first commercially licensed radio station to broadcast a regularly scheduled program, it became a medium of mass communications, a medium of entertainment. But, it wouldn't be the only new medium; there would be others.

Until the nineteenth century, the preservation of ideas was largely through the print media and by an oral folklore tradition. But with the dawning of a technological age, a new communications system was developing that could preserve images to reflect a reality of life.

In 1826, Joseph Nièpce, a French physicist using concepts first established by Johann Heinrich Schulze in 1727, took the world's first photograph. By the American Civil War, photographs helped record history, and by the end of the century not only had George Eastman and others perfected cameras and film that could be used by the average citizen, they had also taken Peter Mark Roget's theory of the persistence of vision and developed moving pictures—still pictures in sequence projected within a special apparatus and viewed by one person at a time. By the turn of the century, and with new developments in projection, the first "featurettes"—no longer "peep shows" but now a form of mass communications—became a popular form of entertainment.

Many of the first featurettes, none lasting more than ten minutes, were extensions of the minstrel shows. Numerous "Sambo" and "Rastus" films carried minstrelsy and the stereotyped images of Blacks onto the screen. And as in the minstrelsy, the Black-appearing buffoons were actually Whites in make-up.

In 1903, *Uncle Tom's Cabin* was filmed, but it wasn't until 1914, in the third remake of the classic antebellum story, that a Black finally appeared on the screen.[110]

A year later, D. W. Griffith, universally recognized as one of the industry's most respected and innovative pioneers, brought *Birth of a Nation* to the public. Based upon *The Clansman,* written by Thomas Dixon, *Birth of a Nation* glorified the White American society and the rise of the Ku Klux Klan, while systematically presenting Blacks in an inferior light. But still the movies did not "speak," and audience perception of Black language was similar to audience perception of the nonverbal communication patterns thrust upon the Black and Black-appearing actors in the silent movies.

All that changed in 1927 when Warner Brothers released *The Jazz Singer,* based on a play by Samson Raphaelson, and starring Al Jolson. The movie, as the first full-length "talkie," revolutionized the industry. A major character study, *The Jazz Singer* was little more than an extension of the minstrelsy of the nineteenth century, although Jolson, like Dan Emmett in the mid-nineteenth century, studied Black language and mannerisms, hoping to mix just the right ingredients of reality and perceived reality.

As the dialect stories in the nation's magazines again proliferated, so did the appearance of Blacks on the screen, most playing roles and speaking a language not unlike that created by the dialect writers.

Hallelujah!, a Metro-Goldwyn-Mayer production, and *Hearts in Dixie,* a Twentieth-Century Fox production, both produced in 1929 during the transition from "silent films" to "talkies," were the first two major feature-length motion pictures with all-Black casts. *Hallelujah!,* directed by King Vidor, became a film classic.

The view of Black life and religion that *Hallelujah!* presented brought the film both praise and controversy. A. M. Sherwood, Jr., writing in the October 16, 1929, issue of *Outlook and Independent,* called *Hallelujah!* "one of the phoniest photoplays we have ever attended. . . . Its plot is nil and its conclusion weak." Others attacked the movie for what they believed to be stereotyped portrayals of Blacks. Others countered that the movie was a major achievement in cinematography. Creighton Peet, writing for the *New York Evening Post,* called *Hallelujah!* "a truly great motion picture." And Richard Watts, Jr., writing for the *New York Herald Tribune,* called it, "one of the most distinguished and exciting moving pictures ever made." Most film scholars tend to agree with Peet and Watts, although noting that the actors tended to be cast in roles that preserved commonly held stereotyped images of the Southern Black.

Soon, the "movies" became a dominant mass medium, co-existing with radio, by now an equally potent entertainment medium.

In 1925, two modern-day minstrels began broadcasting some of their sketches over WEBH radio, owned by and located in Chicago's Edgewater Beach Hotel. The two men—a "song and chatter team" fluent in Black dialect—were not critical successes at first. Their knowledge of stage theatre—they had been directors and producers—was good, but their knowledge of this new medium known as radio, was weak. Nevertheless, within a half-year, they became one of Chicago's most famous radio teams. Before they retired from broadcast entertainment four decades later, each would have become a millionaire; as a team they were later able to command several thousand dollars for one performance. But in 1925, as radio was just becoming a mass medium, no performer was paid. The two performers received only dinners; nothing more. But for them, as for most of broadcasting's pioneers, radio was a chance for exposure to an audience of thousands, maybe even millions, a chance to reach more persons in one broadcast than they could ever reach in a lifetime on the stage.

Seven months after their first broadcast on WEBH, the two performers switched radio stations and received their first salaries for broadcasting—$25 a week each. They had been enticed by WGN, the *Chicago Tribune* radio station, to develop a broadcast comic strip based upon their Black dialect routines. The result was *Sam 'n' Henry,* one of the first continuing comedy serials in broadcast history. *Sam 'n' Henry,* the story of two indigent Blacks was portrayed not with bias or sarcasm, but with sympathy and a certain amount of pathos. For more than two years—586 five-a-week episodes—*Sam 'n' Henry* was one of the most popular serials on radio. Then in 1928, the series moved to WMAQ, the *Chicago Daily News* station. Each performer was now paid $150 per week. However, because *Sam 'n' Henry* was copyrighted by WGN, a new title—and new character names—had to be found. It wasn't until the night of their first broadcast for WMAQ that character names were determined. Going up the elevator to the studio, the two performers heard the elevator operator greet one passenger as "Famous Amos," and another, a carpenter, as "Handy Andy." The two performers looked at each other and agreed. That night—March 19, 1928—*Amos 'n' Andy,* a slightly modified *Sam 'n' Henry,* was broadcast for the first time. The performers were Freeman Gosden and Charles Correll.

Freeman Fisher Gosden—who portrayed the hard-working Amos, driver of the one-taxi, "Fresh Air Taxi Company, Incorpulated, of Harlem"—was born in Richmond, Virginia, in 1899. Gosden, like Joel Chandler Harris, had lived and worked with Blacks much of his life. As a boy, he was cared for by a Negro mammy; one of his best friends was a young Black whom Gosden later said was one of the strongest influences behind the successful development of *Amos 'n' Andy.* Within a few years, Gosden, like Harris before him, became a master at telling dialect stories; like Dan Emmett, he skillfully mastered the banjo. After a brief time as a tobacco salesman, Gosden began working for the Joe Bren Company, a traveling theatrical troupe which organized and produced local stage and minstrel shows, reviews, and carnivals for clubs, churches, lodges and other organizations throughout the country. It was while working for Joe Bren that Freeman Gosden met Charles Correll.

Charles J. Correll, who portrayed the lazy Andy, was born in Peoria, Illinois, in 1890. During the days he helped his father in the construction business; at night he was a movie house pianist. Because of his talents, he, like Gosden, was recruited by Joe Bren. By 1925, when they began broadcasting on WEBH, each was earning $100 a week from the Joe Bren Company. When they began broadcasting for WGN seven months later, at $25 each week, they left the company to become full-time broadcast entertainers.

Amos 'n' Andy, one of broadcasting's first continuing serials, also became radio's first syndicated series when the *Chicago Daily News* began distributing discs of their fifteen-minute daily programs. Within months of its premiere on WMAQ, *Amos 'n' Andy* was broadcast on more than thirty radio stations throughout the country. Within a year, the *Chicago Daily News* was publishing a daily *Amos 'n' Andy* comic strip; thousands of Americans were buying *Amos 'n' Andy* phonograph records, produced and marketed by Victor, owned by the Radio Corporation of America (RCA) which also owned the National Broadcasting Company (NBC). In 1929, Freeman Gosden and Charles Correll, by now two of the most popular—some say *the* most popular—entertainers in radio's history, signed a contract with the NBC radio network for $100,000 a year. RCA-NBC, which had earned much of its income not from advertising but from the sale of radios, reported that between

1928 and the end of 1929, sales of radio sets and parts, of all companies, increased from $650 million to $843 million, much of the increase attributed to the success of *Amos 'n' Andy*.

So popular had the serial become that between 7:00 p.m. and 7:15 p.m., Mondays through Fridays, hotels, restaurants, businesses, and movie theaters were forced to suspend or interrupt their services in order to broadcast the show. It was a commonly held belief that President Calvin Coolidge and later President Herbert Hoover refused to be interrupted while *Amos 'n' Andy* was on the air. At one point, according to network policy, only the president of the United States was allowed precedence of the airways while *Amos 'n' Andy* was being broadcast. By the time the show moved to the Columbia Broadcasting System (CBS) in 1939, more than 40 million people—about one-fourth of the nation's entire population, about one-half of all persons who had access to a radio—were regular listeners. But less than four years later, as time and the world at war changed a nation, the ratings began to drop. Campbell's Soup, the show's sponsor, had begged Gosden and Correll to drop the daily fifteen-minute programs and, in line with other radio shows, broadcast one thirty-minute program weekly. The two stars turned down the pleas. The ratings fell. On February 19, 1943, *Amos 'n' Andy,* once the nation's highest-rated radio show, now sixtieth in popularity, was cancelled in its fifteenth year.

Eight months later, however, it was back on the air, now a half-hour show broadcast once a week by the NBC radio network and sponsored by Rinso. The format had changed—no longer did each episode lead into the next one; each program was now a complete entity with a separate and distinct storyline. For the first time there was a studio audience and an orchestra; and the broadcasts originated not in New York but in Hollywood where more guest stars were available. Against the strongest competition it ever faced, *Amos 'n' Andy* began a dramatic rise in the ratings, eventually again becoming one of the most popular shows on the air.

During the early days of the show's popularity, Amos and Andy were the two major characters. But as the show matured, other roles were developed and expanded. As the role of George Stevens—the "Kingfish"—portrayed by Gosden, developed, the role of Amos, also portrayed by Gosden, diminished.[111] Within a few years, many of the storylines centered on attempts by the Kingfish—the shrewd, crafty, intelligent con man—to get out of his own financial predicaments by putting "the sting" on the naive Andy. The problems and predicaments associated with money was always part of the storyline, for just as the country found its problems created or solved by the absence or presence of money, so did the characters of the radio drama.

The rules of language varied as the characters varied. Sapphire and Henry van Porter, for instance, spoke virtually Standard English. Other characters spoke a mixture of Standard and Black English; all had come from the South; all were now living in the North, in Harlem. Nevertheless, a few rules remained fairly consistent. Gosden and Correll usually dropped the postvocalic /r/ in the speech of most of their characters; when it was included, it was usually in word-medial position and muted. Occasionally, when one of the characters, notably the King-fish, was emphasizing a point, the postvocalic /r/, usually in word-final position, was included. In most characters' speech, there is a consistent substitution of the voiced alveolar stop [d] for the voiced interdental fricative [ð], as in *dere, dat's,* and *dese.* However, there is little substitution of the unvoiced alveolar stop [t] for the unvoiced interdental fricative [θ]. Nasal replacement (as in *huntin'*) is consistent, but consonant cluster reduction is inconsistent. In the speech of most of the major characters are numerous examples of the elision or loss of the unstressed word-initial syllable, as in the Kingfish's almost-idiomatic expression, "I gonna 's'plain dat to you." Consonant inversion, as in the use of *aks* for *ask* is also frequent, but not consistent. Syntactically, there is occasional, though by no means consistent, use of both the deep structure copula and deep structure possessive; there is almost no use of the invariant *be.* The substitution of *done* as a verbal functor in preverb position, as in "I done go now" is frequent.

Freeman Gosden and Charles Correll had made the public aware of a Black language that few persons in the North had previously heard. In the South, Blacks and Whites, though segregated by law, were nevertheless forced to coexist—to talk with each other. In the North, there were no laws of segregation; it wasn't necessary—there were fewer Blacks. It was possible for a White to be born, grow up, and die without ever seeing a Black. *Amos 'n' Andy* changed some of that; it brought language, the medium for understanding a people and a culture, to almost every home in the country. The extensive use of malapropism by the star characters—"Recordin' to my figgers in de book," "I'ze regusted," and "Is you mulsifyin' or revidin'?"—may have been humorous to a White American audience which, through ignorance, may have believed that the English spoken by Blacks was a substandard or inferior language. But it was still a part of the Blacks' Afro-American heritage. It was a pidginization of language; it was taking the rules of an African language experience, an experience passed by oral tradition from generation to generation, and trying to adapt them to an American language. Soon, there was even a "backwash" effect, as Americans, fascinated by the hypercorrection, by the "sweet talk," by the distinctly African syntactic and phonological language characteristics, began to imitate, then adopt the language of the characters in the series. "I'ze regusted" became a part of the White American language, certainly a more effective language emotion than, "I am terribly upset at this very moment." The general public was also using "check and double check," "Hold de phone," "Sho, sho!" and many other Afro-American idiomatic expressions, some of which became stereotypes, as modified by the Amos and Andy characters.

Beginning in 1951, *Amos 'n' Andy* was adapted for television and broadcast on the Columbia Broadcasting System (CBS), against the vigorous objections of the NAACP. But even the NAACP's censure was not enough to keep *Amos 'n' Andy* from being ranked one of the top ten shows that season.

Sensitive to a more reasonable portrayal of the Black, the leading actors—Tim Moore (the Kingfish), Spencer Williams (Andy), Alvin Childress (Amos), and Earnestine Wade (Sapphire)—changed a number of character traits from the radio show which had, by the mid-1950s, passed from the realm of "reasonable portrayal" to "stereotyped portrayal." Among the major changes was in the representation of dialect.

Gosden and Correll understood and spoke one variety of American Black English; it was a variety less decreolized than most similar dialects spoken in the deep South by Blacks who had not been exposed to Standard English instruction, and which contained a mixture of African language traits and minstrel dialect for humor. For the radio show, much of the humor was predicated by the use of the language. However, the leading actors for the television series spoke dialects which were more Standard than Black English, and the representation of dialect was a very sensitive subject. Freeman Gosden, who was a story consultant for the television series, tried to get the actors to speak the same dialect he and Charles Correll spoke on the radio show; the actors refused. As Spencer Williams pointed out in 1961:

> We couldn't get together on this use of dialect. He wanted me to say "dis here and dat dere" and I just wasn't going to do it. He said he "ought to know how Amos 'n' Andy should talk," but I told him Negroes didn't want to see Negroes on TV talking that way. Then I told him I ought to know how Negroes talk. After all, I've been one all my life. He never came back on the set.[112]

After two seasons of production, CBS finally yielded to pressure from the NAACP and other public groups, although never officially acknowledging it, and suspended production. However, the series still retained its popularity, which, surprisingly, included a significant Black population. It remained in network syndication for a decade, finally being removed from the air in 1964—again because of pressures placed upon the network.

Amos 'n' Andy on radio during the 1920s and 1930s seemed to belong, to be a part of America; *Amos 'n' Andy* on television during another era was a show doomed to controversy. It was a different time, and different circumstances. There was a new movement in the country—perhaps even a revolution—for Black rights. As the nation entered the "nuclear age," a race of people was mounting a campaign that would change the nature of the country, to force an entire population to look within itself at its own hatreds and injustices. *Amos 'n' Andy,* whether intending to perpetuate stereotypes or not, was the first hurdle . . . the first victim.

5. The Civil Rights Cycle

On Thursday evening, December 1, 1955, Mrs. Rosa Parks, a forty-two-year-old seamstress, was arrested and jailed by Montgomery, Alabama, police on charges of violating section 11, chapter 6 of the Montgomery City Ordinance which gave bus drivers police powers in determining seating arrangements according to race. Mrs. Park's offense was that she was Black.

Just prior to her arrest, she and twenty-one other Blacks—sitting at the back of the bus—and fourteen Whites—sitting at the front of the thirty-six-passenger bus—were told by the bus driver that he was stopping at the Empire Theatre to pick up some White passengers. To make room for the White passengers, he ordered Mrs. Parks and several other Blacks to vacate their seats and move further to the rear of the bus, an order which would have forced several of them to stand in order to "equalize the seating." Mrs. Parks refused to move. She was tired; tired of sitting or standing at the rear of the bus; tired of having to leave her seat once she sat down; tired of conditions, situations, and attitudes that claimed, "Well, that's the way things are."

There were other Blacks who were also tired, and now they were going to do something about it. Within forty-eight hours, mimeographed flyers calling for Blacks to boycott the city's buses for one day saturated Montgomery. On Monday, December 5, the day Mrs. Parks was fined $14 for not obeying the lawful orders of a bus driver, the boycott began; more than ninety per cent of the city's Blacks refused to ride the buses; they walked, formed car pools, or rode in taxis. The Black-owned taxi companies that day charged only ten cents a ride from 4:00 to 9:00 a.m. and from 3:00 to 11:00 p.m. So successful was the one-day boycott that the Blacks voted to continue it. The Civil Rights era in America's history—which had been gestating for several decades, occasionally with violence—came alive with the strength of unity.

At first, the Blacks of Montgomery weren't even asking that the city's buses be desegregated. All they asked for was that seating be on a "first come/first served" basis—Blacks would continue to sit in the rear, and Whites would continue to sit in the front; when all the seats were filled, the next passenger—whether Black or White—would stand. But, this was too much for the bus company to accept. The boycott continued.

On January 9, slightly more than a month after the boycott began, the bus company was forced to raise its fares. For the low-income Whites, who were now most of the bus line's passengers, the fare increase was monumental.

On January 10, as had been ordered in November, seating on interstate public transportation was integrated. But still the bus boycott in Montgomery continued.

On January 31, the house of the Rev. Dr. Martin Luther King, Jr., one of the boycott's leaders, was bombed by "person or persons unknown." The boycott continued.

On February 21, 1956, the grand jury issued 105 indictments against ninety persons for instigating an unlawful boycott. The indictment proclaimed, piously and boldly, "We are committed to segregation by custom and by law; we intend to maintain it." Among those arrested were Dr. King, the Rev. Ralph Abernathy, and twenty-two other Black ministers. The boycott continued. But by now it was no longer just a problem faced by a few Blacks in one Southern city; it was a problem beginning to gnaw on the conscience of a nation. The South retaliated, forming White citizen councils determined to fight integration with "all lawful means." In one of his most heated statements, Sen. James Eastland of Mississippi, who saw what was happening to time-honored traditions, argued, "The Negro race is an inferior race. . . . We will maintain control over our elections and . . . will protect and maintain white supremacy throughout eternity." On March 12, 1956, the Senate of the United States was presented a manifesto, signed by eighty-two representatives and nineteen senators, that urged the legislative branch of government to use "all lawful means" to reverse the Supreme Court decision of 1954 that had struck down the separate but equal laws.

In November, U.S. Attorney General Herbert Brownell, Jr., called in the U.S. attorneys from the thirty-four federal districts which had not repealed the Jim Crow laws, and ordered them to enforce compliance with the Supreme Court rulings on integration. On November 14, the

Blacks of Montgomery, meeting in their churches, voted to end the boycott as soon as the Supreme Court sent its rulings on integration back to the district courts for implementation and enforcement.

On December 20, more than a year after the boycott began, U.S. marshals presented federal orders prohibiting segregation on buses. The Blacks of Montgomery had won the nation's first major test of civil rights legislation. On December 21, the Blacks again began riding the buses.

But not all traditions were to fall. On December 2, 1955, the day after Mrs. Parks was arrested in Montgomery, Georgia's Governor, Marvin Griffin, committed what *Time* magazine would call a "pinhead act," and asked the state's board of regents to forbid any athletic team from the University of Georgia or the Georgia Institute of Technology—the state's two public universities—from playing against any team or in any stadium that was integrated. His target was Georgia Tech, which was scheduled to play the University of Pittsburgh on January 2, 1956, in the Sugar Bowl in Baton Rouge. Pitt's offense? It had a Black reserve fullback. Gov. Griffin, voicing the views of many, argued:

> The South stands at Armageddon. The battle is joined. We cannot make the slightest concession to the enemy in this dark or lamentable hour of struggle. There is no more difference in compromising the integrity of race on the playing field than in doing so in the classrooms. One break in the dike and the relentless seas will rush in and destroy us.[1]

That evening, 2,000 Georgia Tech students stormed through the streets of Atlanta, pushed their way past startled police, marched onto the state capitol, then to the governor's mansion to protest the governor's actions. Within the next two days, some of the state's leading journalists also spoke out against Griffin.

On December 5, the day the bus boycott began in Montgomery, the Georgia Board of Regents gave Georgia Tech its approval to play in the Sugar Bowl. But it was a hollow victory. The regents, although issuing a policy that athletic teams from Georgia Tech and the University of Georgia must "respect the laws, customs, and traditions of the host state" in games outside Georgia, also ordered that neither university "in the future" would be allowed to schedule home games with teams that were integrated; segregated seating in Georgia would also be maintained.

On February 3, 1956, Authurine Lucy, under federal orders, became the first Black to register at the University of Alabama. Riots, instigated by White students and residents of the area, forced the university to suspend Ms. Lucy, an action that was later rescinded.

In addition to the thirteenth, fourteenth, fifteenth, and nineteenth amendments to the Constitution, the Congress passed a "Voting Rights Act" in 1957. It proved to be ineffective.

Little Rock, Arkansas, in 1957, became the next battleground. Federal marshals were called in to protect Black children attempting to attend federally ordered integrated schools. The first major sit-ins, initiated by the Student Nonviolent Coordinating Committee (SNCC), began on February 1, 1960, in Greensboro, North Carolina. During the turbulent decade of the 60s, there would be many more sit-ins, as well as "wade-ins" and limited boycotts, all directed against the time-honored traditions of segregation.

In April and May 1963, dogs and firehoses were turned against Black protesters in Birmingham, Alabama; more than 2,400 were arrested. Barely one month later, civil rights leader Medgar Evers was shot and killed in his home in Jackson, Mississippi. On September 15, 1963, four Black girls were killed in a bomb explosion in Birmingham. On June 20, 1964, three civil rights workers—two Jews and one Black—were murdered on a lonely road in Mississippi. Soon, the cities of Selma and Bogulusa took their place with Montgomery and Birmingham as symbols of resistance.

Lyndon Johnson, one of three senators who did not sign the "Southern Manifesto" of 1956, was now president. With a strong determination, he pushed through Congress the massive Civil Rights Act of 1964, which made segregation in public facilities illegal. Within two years, more than half the eligible Blacks in the South were registered to vote. But the fight continued. The 1960s would not be a peaceful decade. In the hot summer of 1964, Harlem erupted into riots; later, Rochester, New York; Camden, New Jersey; and Philadelphia became battlegrounds. And then Watts. At first it was only some hot and rebellious militant Blacks in a Black section of Los Angeles protesting the arrest of a reckless driver. But when it ended four days later on August 15, 1965, thirty-four persons lay dead, more than 1,000 injured, 4,000 arrested. And Watts, home of most of the city's Blacks, lay in ruin—more than $40 million damage, according to the best estimates.

The civil rights era, like the Reconstruction and Negro Renaissance eras before it, forced Blacks and Whites to reassess their lives and their values. It forced them to reflect upon what they believed, to better understand what they were trying to accomplish. It was from this awareness that there came a new literature—a Black literature. It was a deep, searching literature that told not about the horrors of a physical slavery, but the pain of a mental and social slavery.

Paul Laurence Dunbar had once said that he was forced to write in dialect because it was the only way he could get people in a White society to listen to what he had to say. But the dialect of his poetry was much more than words and phrases upon paper, for it reflected the culture and beliefs of a people.

But now in a different era, the new militancy, supported by a collective White guilt, tried to bury not only the stereotyped images of the Black and Black language, as presented by myriad writers with little knowledge of Blacks and even less of their language, but also the actual Black English spoken by the Antebellum and Reconstruction Blacks. For some, the Black English creole was an embarrassment.

In one of the great social ironies, the Uncle Remus stories—reflecting an integral part of Black folklore, and written in near-linguistic precision by one of the nation's leading journalists—fell into disrepute. By the time the best-selling *Uncle Remus Stories*—published in 1946 by Western Publishing Co. for Walt Disney Productions, which had just released *Song of the South*—had reached its thirty-seventh printing in 1975, the American public had already given it a mark of shame; many branded it racist.[2] The thirty-seventh printing became the last. According to Delores Draper, editor for Western:

> We have not received any favorable comments about this title in the last few years. . . . We have received . . . unfavorable response these past few years criticizing the dialect and its improper use of the English language. We've explained to these readers that the correctness or incorrectness of the way a particular language is used depends on the customs of the area from which it comes.[3]

Although the new militant writers could not accept the creolized Black English, neither could they accept the White Standard English. The new militancy could not destroy; it needed to build, to establish an identity completely different from the White. Now they cried out for a new Black literature, using a new Black language reflecting Black worldviews and Black culture. It was to be a new literature, forged by a different language to emphasize a culture that never was White; that never could be White. It was Black. Distinctively Black. Far different from the language of the Antebellum and Reconstruction Negro. It identified the people who spoke it as Black; a clue to their language and culture.

But this time, in this new era of social concern, the writers who chose to write in a form of Black English, whether or not they understood the linguistic rules and concepts, were not bowing to the needs and beliefs of a White audience, for they had chosen to use language to shock that audience, an audience that largely believed that Standard English was not only the proper English, but the *only* proper English. The new language now served to attack White mores, customs, and culture. It served to establish an identity that told even the most passive or most racist—White and Black—that there was a difference. Whites and Uncle Toms spoke Standard White English, and some Blacks spoke "uneducated" linguistic remnants of nineteenth-century language; "real" Blacks spoke "something *else*." It was a language that often appeared to have the same syntax as Standard English, but it was not Standard English. The lexicon was different; the rhythm and prose were different; the semantic deep structure was Black, or what many Blacks may have consciously or subconsciously perceived to be Black. It was English spoken by Blacks, but not necessarily a Black English.

The foundation of this new Black literature, a literature of protest, was laid not during the Civil Rights Cycle, but more than three decades earlier, in a time caught between two world wars. Richard Wright, who had grown up in poverty and was one of thousands employed by the Federal Writers Project—a massive antidepression program funded by the federal government—took the experiences and emotions of his thirty years and channeled his bitterness into the printed word.

In *Lawd Today,* written in 1936 but not published until 1963, in an era of renewed Black pride, Wright probed the mind of Jake Jackson, a Black postal clerk working in Chicago. For the framework of the novel, Wright selected one day—February 12, 1936—divided the book into three sections—"Commonplace," "Squirrel Cage," and "Rat's Alley," each encompassing about eight hours—and proceeded to peel away layer after layer of man's mind until the reader is emotionally drained.

Lawd Today is a different novel, an experimental novel. Wright follows the conventional grammatical rules for fiction and exposition only when it suits his purpose, and breaks those rules—carefully, deliberately, . . . BOLDLY, . . . *HARSHLY* . . . when those rules no longer apply, . . . when those rules can no longer express thought. Modifying Standard English syntax, Wright squeezes from Standard English orthography something that, although it can never adequately express a four-dimensional world, nevertheless goes beyond the traditional two-dimensional world of print. In some places, Wright is the master reporter, the careful observer of human life, recording that life as Heywood Broun or Theodore Dreiser might have recorded it. In other places, Wright forces the printed language to indicate the unknown psychology, much as Henry James attempted in his poetic-journalistic stream-of-consciousness style. Integrating Black language thought processes with Standard English phonology and orthography, Wright carried the representation of Black English into another direction, one which, although never popular, was nevertheless another good attempt to represent *all* of language on a very uncompromising, very unyielding, almost unchangeable two-dimensional page.

In one section of *Lawd Today* Wright introduces a snake charmer:

LAdees'n' Gen'meeeeeeens: Ah'm's the SNAKE MAN! Ah wuz BO'N 'bout FORTEEEEY YEars erGO on the banks of the FAMous NILE in the great COUNtreeeeey of AFRIKer, yo' COUNtreeeeey 'n' mah COUNtreeeey—in tha' LAN' where, in the YEars gone by, yo' FATHER 'n' mah FATHER ruled suPREME! In mah FATHER'S day the PRINCES 'n' CROWNED heads of YOURpe came t' his feets astin' fer ADVICE, astin' t' be tol' things they couldn't TELL themselves, astin' t' have things DONE they couldn't do themselves. THE CROWNED heads of YOURpe respected mah FATHER—he wuz the WISE man of the NILE! Mah FRIENDS, Ah'm's mah FATHER'S son, not only in FLESH, but in SPERIT! FER TWENTEEEEEEEY YEars Ah set at mah FATHER'S feets 'n' soppedup the WISDOM OF his GREAT MIN'! T'DAY, Ah'm's here t' give YUH the beneFIT of mah FATHER's GREAT WISDOM! Ah'm's here t' TELL yuh the SECRET of GOOD 'n' the SECRET of EVIL! Ah'm's here t' TELL yuh the SECRET of LIFE 'n' the SECRET of DEATH! . . . Be still, Patsy, be still! . . .

He paused and stroked the rattler's scaly body.

"Say, he's from Africa!"

"Yeah, he knows a lot of secrets!"

"He sure must know something to charm that snake that way!"

"You telling me?"

". . . But 'fo' Ah goes inter that, mah FRIENDS, Ah wanna give yuh some INDIcation of mah SINGULar POWERS! Yuh see HERE in mah han's is TWO steel rings MADE in the FAR OFF COUNtreeeeey of JApan. Mah FRIENDS, these rings is made of SOLID STEEL, 'n' if there's anybody in this DISTINGUISHED AUDIENce, be he MALE or FEMALE, who thinks he kin BEN' or BREAK these rings he has a chance t' try 'n' win FIVE DOL-LARS in COL' CASH! ANYbody wanna try? Who? Who? WHO? DON'T BE SCARED, FOLKS! STEP right up 'n' try! Now, WHO wanna try? WHO? Yuh, Mister? Yes, suh! Here yuh is! TRY wid all yo' MIGHT 'n' STRENGTH! PULL HARD, Mister, PULL HARD! Why, whut's the MATTER, Mister? Can't yuh BEN' or BREAK these LITTLE rings? NAW? Sho' 'nough? Haa! Haa! Give 'em here! Waal, who else wanna try?"[4]

In 1938, Harper & Bros. published Wright's *Uncle Tom's Children,* a bold, powerful collection of short stories dominated by the themes of violence and mob rule directed against Blacks.

Also in 1940, Harper & Bros. brought out Wright's *Native Son,* a powerful story about a young Black who had grown up in a rat-infested one-room apartment in Chicago, and was now trapped by events that would ultimately lead to his execution for murder. Often compared fa-vorably to Theodore Dreiser's *An American Tragedy* (1925), *Native Son* achieved a popular and critical acclaim, a recognition never before achieved by a novel written by a Black. In 1945, Wright's autobiogra-phy *Black Boy,* was published. He was thirty-seven years old. Fifteen years and several books later, Richard Wright, at the age of fifty-two, was dead.

In literature, a number of great and lasting works often have opening lines that are remembered long after the details of the plot fade from memory or become jumbled in their reconstruction. In 1952, another opening line was added—"I am an invisible man." The author was Ralph Ellison; the book, *Invisible Man.* After briefly discussing what invisi-bility wasn't, Ellison explained what it was:

That invisibility to which I refer occurs because of a peculiar dis-position of the eyes of those with whom I come in contact. A mat-ter of the construction of their *inner* eyes, those eyes with which they look through their physical eyes upon reality. I am not com-plaining, nor am I protesting either. It is sometimes advantageous to be unseen, although it is most often rather wearing on the nerves. Then too, you're constantly being bumped against by those with poor vision. Or again, you often doubt if you really exist. You wonder whether you aren't simply a phantom in other people's minds. Say, a figure in a nightmare which the sleeper tries with all his strength to destroy. It's when you feel like this that, out of resentment, you begin to bump people back. And, let me confess, you feel that way most of the time. You ache with the need to convince yourself that you do exist in the real world, that you're a part of all the sound and anguish, and you strike out with your fists, you curse and you swear to make them recognize you. And, alas, it's seldom successful.[5]

Invisible Man was a new novel, angry and bitter. It tore at the hatreds and injustices of the world, using symbolism to ask, but never answer, the question of life. It bared the soul of one Black as he was transformed from a youth accepting the social values of the South, into a man forced to totally reject society after being involved in a race riot in Harlem. The critics reluctantly praised it, but compared it to the works of Richard Wright, often saying that although Ellison was a good writer, Wright was the best of the Black writers. Those who tried to ignore the novel, claiming, among other reasons, that it distorted life, soon found they were facing an impossible task. The novel was there, in the marketplace; it could not be ignored. Soon, critics began favorably comparing it to William Faulkner's *Light in August*. In 1953, Ellison received, for *Invisible Man,* the National Book Award for the outstanding work of fiction. A Book Week poll in 1966, rated *Invisible Man* as the most significant work of fiction between 1945 and 1965.

In 1953, the name of James Baldwin was added to the list of Black protest writers. His first novel, *Go Tell It on the Mountain,* grabbed the reader and forced him to experience the language and religion of a small Black congregation in Harlem in order to better understand the sufferings of a race of people. So carefully and so powerfully had Baldwin woven his story that when fourteen-year-old John Grimes is able to break free of the domination of his stepfather, an angry but eloquent storefront preacher, the presence of God—a god seen through Black eyes, a god mentioned only by reference—seems to dominate and encompass not only the fictional John Grimes but the reader as well.

In "This Morning, This Evening, So Soon"—a short story first published in *The Atlantic Monthly,* and later included in *Going to Meet the*

Man (1965), a collection of eight short stories—Baldwin recognized the role that language plays in the culture of a people:

> Harriet has been teaching Louisa French and Swedish expressions, and Louisa has been teaching Harriet some of the saltier expressions of the black South. Whenever one of them is not playing straight man to the other's accent, they become involved in long speculations as to how a language reveals the history and the attitudes of a people. They discovered that all the European languages contain a phrase equivalent to "to work like a nigger." ("Of course," says Louisa, "they've had black men working for them for a long time.") "Language is experience and language is power," says Louisa, after regretting that she does not know any of the African dialects. "That's what I keep trying to tell those dicty [sic] bastards down South. They get their own experience into the language, we'll have a great language. But, no, they all want to talk like white folks." Then she leans forward, grasping Harriet by the knee. "I tell them, honey, white folks ain't saying *nothing*. Not a thing are they saying—and *some* of them knows it, they *need* what you got, the whole world needs it." Then she leans back, in disgust. "If you think they listen to me? Indeed they do not. They just go right on, trying to talk like white folks."[6]

Like the militant writers, Langston Hughes was determined that America would see for itself the injustices with which it enveloped the Black. But unlike LeRoi Jones, H. Rap Brown, Eldridge Cleaver, or any of dozens of other militant writers, Hughes was not a bitter person, nor did he believe that advocating Black nationalism or Black separatism would eliminate or assuage the most basic problems which both Black and White faced. As the "poet laureate of Harlem," Hughes had been a part of the 1920s Negro Renaissance. He had been a protest writer without peer; a writer whose pride in his own heritage and race had brought with it a new beauty, and new awareness. And only a writer at peace with himself could have produced the genius of Jesse B. Semple.

In 1965, Langston Hughes wrote his final Jesse B. Semple column. In the twenty-three years since Semple made his first appearance in the *Chicago Defender,* the times had changed, largely as Semple had wished, but never as much as he had hoped. After generations of indifference, a nation's collective conscience had been awakened to the Black concerns which Semple had first spoken about. The public could no longer read in the newspapers about the nation's most famous barroom philosopher, but they would instinctively know that Langston Hughes and Jesse B.

Semple had somehow been a guiding force behind the new Civil Rights movement.

During the turbulence of the 1960s, the writings of Wright, Ellison, Baldwin, as well as Claude McKay, H. Rap Brown, and Eldridge Cleaver, all appeared on the best-sellers lists. Soon, the writings of Paul Laurence Dunbar and Charles Waddell Chesnutt, Arna Bontemps and Zora Neale Hurston would be dusted off by a new generation. The new militant writers, their sarcasm dripping with invective, would call their predecessors "Uncle Toms." To build their own case for militancy, the militant had to destroy, to become more militant than militant, more Black than Black. It was only when the public began to take a hard look at the Black dialect writers of the late nineteenth and early twentieth centuries that some truths emerged—for their time, Dunbar and Chesnutt were militant. If their militancy in 1900 was not the militancy of 1970, it was because seventy years can change not only time, but perceptions of time as well. It was not too long before even Richard Wright and Ralph Ellison were called "Uncle Toms."

The language of LeRoi Jones is the language of hatred forged by bitterness and militant Blackness. But when the "hype," pomposity, and hyperbole are peeled away, a language emerges that is reflective of one part of Black society. In his essay, "Expressive Language," Jones says that "speech is the effective form of a culture. . . . Words' meanings but also the rhythm and syntax that frame and propel their concatenation, seek their culture as the final reference for what they are describing of the world."[7] By using elements of many American languages, Jones could destroy and violate what others called "rules" in order to add another dimension to the written language, a dimension that told about part of a culture.

Reviewing *Dutchman,* one of the finest one-act plays in contemporary American literature, critic Ronald Bryden called it "a posturing, inflammatory, deliberately dishonest work, destructive for the malicious excitement of destruction." But Bryden also noted that "such is the talent of its [*Dutchman's*] writing that, after it, it's difficult even to remember what the first play [by another author] had to say."[8]

Jones was born in 1934 and grew up with the largely White 1950s beat generation of Greenwich Village. He was a Black writer at the beginnings of the civil rights movement who could provide a collective White guilt. When publishers recognized what the White public wanted, they began publishing Jones's poetry and drama, essays and fiction.

Jones had once said that he writes not for Whites, but for Blacks. But he needed the White society. He had been created by it, and pampered by it. It was that White society he had attacked that first recognized him as a good writer; it was that society which published his writing; it was that society which bought his writing.

But when Jones's attacks became so vicious—he argued that all Blacks in America must destroy all Whites before there could be any equality—the White society of guilt-ridden persons who believed they could be defined as "liberal," whether they were or not, began to desert him, just as he had deserted them. LeRoi Jones, who now called himself Imamu A. Baraka, was no longer any "fun." And, more important, the civil rights movements had gone in other directions; he was no longer relevant.

LeRoi Jones separated the Black, propagandized him, threw it at a receptive audience, and collected the profits. He successfully incited fear, hatred, and distrust. But his games with White patrons did little to tell the reader about the Black experience; Blacks who were proud of their distinctively African past and hopeful of the future. Both Jones and his publishers could use the mass media to play upon deeply felt, often subconscious guilt feelings of a nation; publishers could claim to present a "new voice" to the public—while also collecting profits and distributing royalties from their psychologically induced "guilt number."

The language of Claude Brown, like that of LeRoi Jones, is a language of militancy. But unlike Jones, who used the art of rhetorical passion to inflame racial hatreds and moral indignation, Brown chose the art of subtle manipulation, combining the skills of the reporter and writer to document a slice of life, letting the words lie before the reader as though a bomb with inches left of a long fuse.

Manchild in the Promised Land, Brown's best-selling 1965 autobiography, tells of gangs and drugs and racial inequality, but it also tells about the maturing of a boy caught in an age of conflict and torment. R. F. Kugler, writing in the August 1965 issue of the *Library Journal,* said that if Brown's book is widely read, "it will spur presidential efforts to rid America of the ghetto and injustices." And although the ghettos and injustices remained almost impenetrable against a massive anti-poverty campaign, *Contemporary Authors,* reflecting upon the socio-literary history of the book, could argue that *Manchild in the Promised Land* "became a harbinger of hope to the civil rights movement as it drew increasing interest and concern to the plight of urban blacks."

But the language of the text led to controversy. Kugler correctly predicted that "the language will shock some." And Romulus Linney, writing in the August 22, 1965, issue of the *New York Times Book Review,* trying to explain the nature of the language, pointed out that the book was "written with a brutal and unvarnished honesty in the plain talk of the people, in language that is fierce, uproarious, obscene and tender, but always sensible and direct."

Although certain words offended, many were offended by the presentation of the syntax—most of the dialogue was written in a decreolized Black English, language that reflected the people of Harlem. The phonology was for the most part not too unlike Standard English, but the syntax—"bad" and "substandard" grammar according to some—reflected an African-language base. The absence of the Standard English copula and of possessives are two of Brown's major clues that not only did the people of the urban Black communities have their own culture, but they also had their own language.

BLACK DRAMA

As the nation found a new awareness during the Civil Rights Cycle, drama written by and about Blacks began once again to take its place beside the fiction and poetry. One of the first dramas written by Blacks during the Negro Renaissance-Civil Rights intercycle was *St. Louis Woman*—adapted for stage by Arna Bontemps and Countee Cullen from their novel, *God Sends Sunday,* and produced on Broadway in 1946. Other Broadway productions written by Blacks included *Take a Giant Step* (1953), by Louis Peterson; *In Splendid Error* (1954), by William Branch; *Trouble in Mind* (1955), by Alice Childress; and *Simply Heavenly* (1957), by Langston Hughes.

On March 11, 1959, in Broadway's Ethel Barrymore Theater, a new drama premiered, one that told about a Black family living on Chicago's South Side, a family trying not merely to live, but to survive. The play was *A Raisin in the Sun;* the author, Lorraine Hansberry, whose life would be cut short at the age of thirty-four. But *Raisin,* produced on Broadway, then by numerous theatrical companies throughout the country, would become one of the nation's outstanding dramas.

Purlie Victorious, written by actor/playwright Ossie Davis, and first produced on Broadway on September 28, 1961, is a broad social satire, deep and probing, of Black-White relations in the South. It is a cross-section of people—Black and White—and only incidentally a look at Black religion. As the play opens, the Rev. Purlie Victorious Judson has returned home to Georgia to find that bullwhip-wielding Ol' Cap'n Stonewall Jackson Cotchipee, who owns most of the land as well as a $500 lien against the Black church, is plotting a "take-over."

Purlie Victorious, with actors Ossie Davis, Ruby Dee, Godfrey Cambridge, and Sorrell Booke, was favorably reviewed, closing after 261 performances. In 1963, it was adapted for the screen under the title, *Gone Are the Days,* but did not become successful until the title of the play was restored to the film. In March 1970, *Purlie Victorious* became *Purlie,* a musical comedy regarded by theatre critics as one of the better musicals in the history of Broadway. Cleavon Little, who had taken the role of Purlie, was voted best actor on Broadway for the 1970–71 season.

CHILDREN'S LITERATURE

In mass communications, it is often difficult to present the public with a balance of what it wants and what it needs. It is even more difficult and complicated because what the public *actually* wants and needs can be quite different from what editors and publishers *think* the public wants and needs. It is no different in Black literature.

For almost a decade, beginning shortly after World War II ended, Lorenz Graham tried to sell *South Town.* His novel for children was about the life of one young Black in the South who dreamed of becoming a doctor, then returning home to help his people. It was a novel that showed life as it was—with its frustrations and hatreds, its hopes and sacrifices. But publishers weren't interested in the reality of the masses. Instead, they were mainly interested in stereotypes that portrayed the Black in a "traditional" role as the passive, comical, trickster Negro; or stereotypes that showed the "modern" Black as a militant, determined to fight back and crush—even at his own expense, even at the expense of his society—what he thought were the causes of his own social predicament. David Williams, Graham's young protagonist, was neither passive nor militant. He was a young Black, like millions of other young Blacks, caught in a web of prejudice, bigotry, and poverty, but with hopes and dreams, fears and frustrations and, occasionally, bitterness and hatred. It was not a picture or theme that was accepted in the 1950s. The result was that publishers almost systematically rejected the book. Finally, near the end of the decade, the Follett Publishing Co. took a chance; *South Town* was published in 1958. At first, distributors wouldn't carry it; librarians wouldn't buy it; the public wouldn't read it. To promote the lagging sales, Graham went from school to school, reading passages from the book, perhaps selling a few copies. Then, as if a mythical gatekeeper had proclaimed, "This is now an acceptable book," sales began to increase. Soon, libraries began ordering *South Town;* the public began reading it; distributors, who had once scorned it, now eagerly requested copies for distribution. *South Town,* a "different" kind of book, was reprinted nine times in hardcover before it was published in paperback. By 1980, it had reached the eleventh paperback printing, with more than 300,000 copies sold.

North Town (1965) and *Whose Town?* (1969) followed; *Return to South Town* (1976) completed the series. None of the books contained identifiable passages of Black English. However, the four South Town books are important linguistically for the same reason that James Weldon Johnson's *God's Trombones,* written in Standard English, became significant. Lorenz Graham does not recognize American Black English as a linguistically valid language. He had grown up in New Orleans and says that the dialect spoken by Blacks is virtually the same dialect as that spoken by Whites. Thus, the reader is undoubtedly influenced to believe that Blacks speak just like Whites; and educated Blacks speak Standard English or Southern Standard English, or whatever the dialect of that particular geographical location is; uneducated Blacks, like uneducated Whites, speak a broken, bastardized English, a substandard or ungrammatical English. Graham does not accept the theoretical arguments that Black English is a separate language, dialect, or variety of speech, or that it had once gone through a process of creolization in America. However, Graham, one of the nation's most brilliant writers, knows and understands the pidginization of language in West Africa, and many of his African tales are written in a form of a West African Pidgin English, a language that could have served as a base for American Black English at one time.

For four years, between 1924 and 1928, Graham was a teacher in Liberia. It was from this experience that, two decades later, he wrote his first books. *Tales of Momolu* (1946) written in Standard English, but with some dialogue in West African Pidgin English, is the story of a young West African Black and his father.

How God Fix Jonah (1946) is a collection of twenty-one Bible stories, in verse, retold in a variety of West African (Liberian) Pidgin English. In the foreword to the book, W. E. Burghardt Du Bois, Graham's brother-in-law, pointed out that:

These little poems are bits of literature which now and then bring us insight into the working of the minds of men. The stories . . . are told here in the words and thought patterns of a modern African boy who does not use the conventional words and phrases which by long usage often obscure the meaning of these tales in the minds of Europeans and Americans. . . .

Climate, the slave trade and the Industrial Revolution have made the preservation of African literature dependent more on tradition and folklore than the written record. These modern bits of poetry rescued from passing oblivion remind us of what Africa has thought and done in the long past.[9]

In a four-page introduction, Graham briefly acquainted his readers with some of the language conventions in West Africa, and explained why, although he retained the Liberian-English syntax, he converted the phonology to Standard English:

Little attempt has been made to break the spelling into phonetic representation of the African's pronunciation. "The" may be read conventionally or as "de." The sound of R after the vowel may be used or omitted. The idiom, the word pictures, the beauty of the simple thought will be the same.[10]

How God Fix Jonah enjoyed only modest sales and was out of print when the Thomas Y. Crowell Co. selected several of the tales and decided to make each one into a separate picture book. From this decision came *Every Man Heart Lay Down* (1970), *David He No Fear* (1971), *God Wash the World and Start Again* (1971), *A Road Down by the Sea* (1971), and *Hongry Catch the Foolish Boy* (1973).

In 1966, Crowell published *I, Momolu,* a 227-page sequel to *Tales of Momolu.* Like the earlier book, the narration was in Standard English, but many of the phrases in dialogue were in West African Pidgin English. In 1975, the third Momolu book was published—*Song of the Boat,* a short tale presented in picture book format similar to the tales from *How God Fix Jonah.* The phonology and orthography of the picture book stories are Standard English; the syntax and lexicon, though inconsistent in some places, are distinctively a modified West African Pidgin English:

Flumbo walk about in Bonga Town.
He say How-Do to everybody,
But him heart no lay down, cause he no got boat.
Alligator did break him canoe.

All the people know Flumbo and they like him.
Flumbo be strong. He be strong past them other men.

He strong and he good.
The people like him plenty.

When Flumbo go for waterside,
Plenty people say to him,
"Oh, this time you no got canoe;
So now you go in my canoe;
Make it my canoe be same way for your own canoe."

Flumbo say "No!" and he laugh.
Flumbo say, "If Flumbo take other man canoe,
By and by alligator going break him,
Same way alligator did break my own."
Flumbo laugh for him mouth.
But Flumbo no laugh for him heart.[11]

Another series of children's books that tested the intricacies of public opinion were those of John Steptoe. In 1969, *Stevie,* a picture book for elementary schoolchildren, was published by Harper & Row. *Uptown* (1970) and *Train Ride* (1971) followed. *My Special Best Words* (1974) and *Marcia* (1976), published by Viking, were written for adolescent audiences.

According to Steptoe, he became a writer because there was a "great and disastrous need for books that Black children could honestly relate to. . . . I was amazed to find that no one had successfully written a book in the dialogue which Black children spoke."[12] However, Steptoe's books were written more in Standard English than in Black English; significant inconsistencies of language in the books show a "cleansing" of the language to achieve better readership. The representation of Black English in *Marcia,* for example, is inconsistent; Steptoe relied primarily upon the inclusion of the invariant *be* and the dropping of the word-final *-g,* as in *beginnin,* for his rules.[13]

In 1971, the Thomas Y. Crowell Co., publishers of the Lorenz Graham tales in a West African Pidgin English, published *His Own Where,* a children's novel written by June Jordan. *His Own Where* soon became recognized as the first major children's novel to be written in Black English. The representation of the language, however, is extremely inconsistent. Only a handful of rules are included—notably, the deep structure copula, deep structure possessive, and the replacement of Standard English tense markers with Black English tense markers. But even these rules are used inconsistently. In one section, for example, Jordon wrote,

"The police demanded to talk to Angela mother" (p. 31), showing both the presence of Standard English copula ("to talk"), and the absence of a Standard English possessive ("Angela mother"). In another section, Jordan wrote, "A short man, Buddy's father . . ." (p. 14), showing the presence of a Standard English possessive case. Throughout the book there is no systematic representation of the possessive. Possessives might be represented in Standard English in one place (as in "his dream"), and in a form of Black English in another (as in "they legs"). In one section, Angela says, "Buddy, this no place to stop," showing both the deep structure copula ("this no place") and the presence of a surface structure copula ("to stop"), a remote possibility. The phonology is Standard English.

Although critically acclaimed by librarians and teachers, Jordan's second book in Black English, *Dry Victories* (1972), shows no improvement in the representation of Black English. Although *be* often replaces *am, are,* and *is* to indicate Black speech ("If they be really parallels"), Jordan also has her characters of the story use Standard English contractions of the copula, such as *I'm* and *it's.* There is no linguistic consistency in plurals; syntactic rules are often inconsistent. Phonologically, the same character says *min'* and *mind*—consonant cluster reduction occurs in some places, is disregarded in others; nasal replacement is inconsistent.

Nevertheless, because of the success of the fiction of John Steptoe and June Jordan, publishers began searching for Black writers to write in the "Black idiom." Soon, several children's books, written in a rough approximation of Black English, were on the market.

AND ALL THAT JAZZ

Many people, both Black and White, perceive Black English not as a system of rules of syntax and phonology, but merely as a lexicon. It is the words and phrases and idioms that many incorrectly believe is what Black English *really* is. And so, to make their characters "sound Black," writers will insert, at appropriate places, Black lexicon. To many, Black language is "Jazz."

As jazz developed and enveloped the musical world, its language— some called it slang, others called it argot, but all knew it as "jive"— began to fascinate those who were not a part of that world. Soon there appeared numerous studies—both academic and popular—to explain not only the nature and history of jazz, but its language as well. Some authors merely took a few words and briefly translated them; others offered in-depth explanations of the role of the language and the etymology of many of the words.

One of the first and most comprehensive studies of jazz language was *Dan Burley's Original Handbook of Harlem Jive* (1944). The book contained many of the dialogues in jive-talk first published in Burley's column, "Back Door Stuff," in the Black-owned *New York Amsterdam News*.[14] In the introduction to the book, linguist Earl Conrad explained the possible development and nature of the language and culture of jazz:

> Jive is one more contribution of Negro America to the United States. White America perpetrated a new and foreign language on the Africans it enslaved. Slowly, over the generations, Negro America, living by and large in its own segregated world, with its own thoughts, found its own way of expression, found its own way of handling English, as it had to find its own way in handling many other aspects of a white, hostile world. Jive is one of the end-results. In its present form it may be transitory, subject to note change. . . . Jive may go way back, deep into the bowels of the Negro-American experience, back into the revolutionary times when it was necessary for the Negro to speak, sing and even think in a kind of code.[15]

Burley extended Conrad's explanation, defining jazz as "language in motion," and noting:

> It supplies the answer to the hunger for the unusual, the exotic and the picturesque in speech. It is a medium of escape, a safety valve for people pressed against the wall for centuries, deprived of the advantages of complete social, economic, moral and intellectual freedom. It is an inarticulate protest of a people given half a loaf of bread and then dared to eat it; a people continually fooled and bewildered by the mirage of a better and fuller life. Jive is a defense mechanism, a method of deriving pleasure from something the uninitiated cannot understand. It is the same means of escape that brought into being the spirituals as sung by the American slaves; the blues songs of protest that bubble in the breasts of black men and women believed by their fellow white countrymen to have been born to be menials, to be wards of a nation, even though they are tagged with a whimsical designation as belonging to the body politic. Jive provides a medium of expression universal in its appeal. Its terms have quality, sturdiness, rhythm and descriptive impact. It is language made vivid, vital and dynamic.[16]

In addition to the dialogues in jazz, and the description and analysis of jazz, Burley's book included jive-talk parodies, poems, and a basic glossary.

In 1945, Lou Shelly edited *Hepcats Jive Talk Dictionary*. But, it wasn't until two decades later, when the Civil Rights era had brought with it a reawakening of the contributions of Black entertainers, that the next major jazz dictionary appeared. For the December 1957 issue of *American Speech,* an academic journal, Robert S. Gold had written "The Vernacular of the Jazz World," an article which attracted significant attention in both the jazz and linguistic worlds. That article became the base for Gold's *A Jazz Lexicon* (1964). Using the research techniques of historical lexicography, Gold combined traditional and contemporary cultural definitions of jazz words and phrases. For each entry, he included its first known recorded use, its semantic and accepted meanings, and a brief etymology. In a sixteen-page introduction, Gold explained that:

> The language of the jazz world is neither the language of the jazz musician nor the language of the Negro people, but a fusing of the two. It is the language spoken by jazz musicians and appreciators, giving to and receiving from the Negro people new words and phrases. It is a language that would be only partly comprehensible to Negroes not interested in jazz, or to white musicians who play 'Mickey Mouse' (i.e., popular music). And it is a language which has always told a great deal about the lives and attitudes of its speakers.[17]

In his conclusion, apparently directed to those who equated the jazz slang lexicon with the language itself, Gold wrote that "vocabulary is not the whole of communication; nuance, inflection, gesture, and innuendo will immediately betray the speaker whose intimacy with the vocabulary does not extend to the culture itself."[18] Gold followed up *A Jazz Lexicon* with *Jazz Talk* (1975), a 322-page jazz glossary.

Clarence Major's short, but definitive text, *A Dictionary of Afro-American Slang,* was published in 1970. Major's premise was that Black English slang and colloquialisms stemmed from the Blacks' rejection of White lifestyles and social patterns, and argued that White slang is largely Black in origin. Major's book received national exposure when it was favorably reviewed by H. D. Quigg of United Press International,

thus allowing readers of even the smallest newspapers in the most remote areas of the country to be aware not only of the dictionary but of
Major's basic hypotheses as well.

A 1,000-word glossary of Black terms and phrases, compiled by Hermese
Roberts, principal of a Chicago elementary school, was published as a
pamphlet in 1971. The pamphlet, which had an initial distribution of
10,000 copies, had an added benefit—According to Ms. Roberts, "We
got extra copies, sold them for 10 cents each, and used the money to buy
shoes for the youngsters who needed them to get to school." Mention in
the Chicago newspapers about the glossary spurred sales and, according
to Roberts, allowed her students to "stand a little taller and smile a little brighter when they talk about it."[19] An article in *The Washington
Post* of January 2, 1972, increased exposure to another half-million
readers; over two million more readers were made aware of the glossary
a few months later when *Newsweek* briefly reviewed it. In 1972, the
glossary was published as an appendix to the *Living Webster Encyclopedic Dictionary of the English Language,* making it available in a more
permanent form to language scholars as well as the general public.

Some of the earliest articles about Black slang appeared in *The New
York Times*. Gilbert Millstein's article in the April 30, 1961, *Times* discussed humor in Black language. Slightly more than a month later, *The
New York Times Magazine* published, "If You Think It's Groovy To
Rap, You're Shucking." Written by Mike Jahn, the article focused upon
the White use of "hip" terms and phrases, but included a brief mention
of the "hip black subculture." In the May 20, 1962, issue of *The New
York Times Magazine,* William Melvin Kelly discussed Black slang. Included in that article was a glossary of about fifty words. Slightly more
than two years later, in the August 23, 1964, issue, Junius Griffin discussed the uses of slang in Harlem, pointing out that Black language is,
in itself, a part of the Black identity. *The Times* published its next major
article about Black English slang on December 25, 1966. Using a narrative format to describe an actual incident, John M. Brewer discussed
the "hidden language" of Blacks. With numerous illustrations and examples, Brewer carefully explained many of the features, including lexicon, that distinguish Black English.

  In the October 26, 1967, issue of *The Washington Post,* Nicholas
Von Hoffman took a writer's look at the Haight-Ashbury section of San
Francisco, and concluded that the language of the White drug culture
was, in essence, largely derived from the Black ghetto.

A 21-question Black slang quiz for "Honkies," developed by social worker Adrian Dove, appeared in *The Post,* and was later reprinted by several newspapers throughout the country. According to Dove, "A score of 11 or less classifies you as an intellectual failure—a ghetto drop-out. It means, in the argot of the middle class social workers, that you are 'culturally deprived.' "[20] Later that year, Dove wrote, for *The New York Times,* "Soul Story," a strongly worded plea for the elimination of racial language bias in job testing. A 25-word glossary was included in the article.

The April 1968 issue of *Esquire,* a general interest magazine with a circulation of more than one million, featured Claude Brown's "The Language of Soul," an overview of Black language. Brown touched upon both the connotative and denotative meanings of many of the words attributed to Black slang. Part of his conclusion was that Black English is distinguishable by phonological rules, stress, and intonation.

Several articles appeared in the *Milwaukee Journal.* The first of these articles was written by Kenneth Walker, a nineteen-year-old Black journalism student at Eau Claire University. In an article appearing in 1969, Walker discussed features and aspects of the Black lexicon. A glossary of forty-six items was included.

The *Milwaukee Journal* also featured a periodic column, "Write On," in which Black staff journalists expressed personal viewpoints and opinions. In the 500,000-circulation Sunday edition of November 1, 1970, Edward H. Blackwell focused upon a two-word phrase used by Blacks, and appropriated by Whites, meaning "having sexual relations with one's mother." Blackwell traced the sociological and psychological importance of this two-word phrase, noting that it had changed semantic connotations and had become a vital part of the Black vocabulary. In his conclusion, Blackwell emphasized that "the Black dialect and its words and expressions are as legitimate as a Brooklyn or Southern accent."[21]

In the September 17, 1972, issue of the *Milwaukee Journal,* Jay Anderson challenged his White readers to a 24-question test of Black vocabulary items. In his introductory statements, Anderson pointed out that:

Inner city residents have a language that differs greatly from outside areas. It has nothing to do with literacy. . . . For inner city pupils it's an everyday thing, not a once in a while use to appear hip or in.

Inner city pupils are forced to learn the language of [White] educators while educators owe no such responsibility—a one way street that adds to the pupils' frustrations.[22]

Two books published in 1972 added further information about the nature of Black English lexicon. David Claerbant's *Black Jargon in White America* concentrated on a teaching program to introduce Black jargon to White students. Mary Anne Gross's *Ah, Man, You Found Me Again* includes an informal collection of urban Black dialect.

For a Sunday newspaper feature syndicate, Jerry Leblanc interviewed linguist Edith A. Folb who discussed the use of Black jargon in an urban setting. The article, which included a 30-word glossary, was published in the October 7, 1973, issue of *The Cleveland Plain-Dealer,* as well as in several other newspapers.

Sandra Haggerty, a Black journalist for *The Los Angeles Times,* wrote several columns in the early 1970s which focused on Black language. In two of her columns, she discussed the shift of semantic meaning of phrases which are identical in surface structure in both standard and Black English. Another column focused upon the role of humor in Black language. However, in another column, she briefly reviewed The Dozens, the Black verbal insult game, and argued that "times have changed, but not obviously enough. Hopefully one day the dozens will be phased out and relegated to history."[23]

Sandra Haggerty was reflecting the views of many Blacks who successfully made the transition into middle- and upper-class American culture and felt embarrassed by the verbal traditions of Africa. Some Blacks might have preferred to believe that a Black subculture did not exist. This embarrassment was heightened by the work of American folklorists who legitimized those traditions by observing, explaining, and analyzing the uniquely Afro-American worldviews and verbal traditions.

THE MODERN FOLKLORIST

The folklorist, with traditions embedded in American literary history, used the techniques of the journalist to observe, explain, and analyze the uniquely Afro-American culture of the American Black. It was the folklorist who was able to synthesize many diverse bits of data to present accurate reflections of the integration of language and culture in Black American society. During the Antebellum Cycle, it was James Fenimore Cooper who understood and wrote about the American plainsman as well as the Blacks' role in a developing nation. During the Reconstruction Cycle, it was Thomas Wentworth Higginson, William Francis Allen,

George Washington Cable, Lafcadio Hearn, Joel Chandler Harris, Mark Twain, Charles Waddell Chesnutt and many others who brought the meaning of the Black verbal traditions to a White American audience. In the Negro Renaissance Cycle, it was Ambrose Gonzales, Howard Odum, J. Frank Dobie, Alan and John Lomax, Zora Neale Hurston, B. A. Botkin, and Melville Herskovits. During the Civil Rights Cycle, it was Richard M. Dorson, John Mason Brewer, and Roger D. Abrahams who brought new insight into Black folklore studies.

Because of their accurate transcriptions and careful research, the folklore studies of John Mason Brewer are valuable to an understanding of Black life and language. In explaining the nature of American Black folklore, Brewer drew upon a knowledge of the sociohistory of the American slave in order to explain the interrelationships of language and culture:

> The folk literature of the American Negro has a rich inheritance from its African background. Without this major cultural ingredient there would be no Negro folklore as distinct from that of other regional folk literatures of the New World. Probably no people have been so completely the bearers of tradition as the African slave-immigrants. They brought with them no material possessions to aid in preserving the arts and customs of their homeland. Yet though empty-handed perforce, they carried in their minds and hearts a treasure of complex musical forms, dramatic speech, and imaginative stories, which they perpetuated through the vital art of self-expression. Wherever the slaves were ultimately placed, they established an enclave of African culture that flourished in spite of environmental disadvantages. As a result, the original treasure has diffused and grown, for the enrichment of themselves and of others.[24]

In *American Negro Folklore* (1968), Brewer compiled a number of types of folklore, much of it presented in Black dialect reflecting an African language base. Included were a few animal tales from Uncle Remus, the "How Come?" and "Why?" tales, tales of folk figures, ghost stories and superstitions, religious tales, sermons and prayers, spirituals, folk blues and ballads, proverbs, rhymes, riddles, game songs, and toasts, and street cries. The recording of the language is reasonably accurate, often paralleling many of the linguistic-literary conventions of Joel Chandler Harris and other folklorists noted for their accurate transcriptions. Among the many books Brewer has written are *Negrito, Negro Dialect Poems of the Southwest* (1933); *The Word in the Brazos:*

Negro Preacher Tales From the Brazos Bottoms of Texas (1953); *Aunt Dicy Tales* (1956); *Snuff-Dipping Tales of the Texas Negro* (1956); *Dog Ghosts and Other Texas Folk Tales* (1958); *Worser Days and Better Times* (1965); and *The Folk-Lore of the North Carolina Negro* (1965).

The first major study of The Dozens—the Black verbal insult game against which Sandra Haggerty had editorialized—was conducted by John Dollard, and published in November 1939, as the lead article in the premiere issue of *American Imago,* a journal of psychoanalysis edited by Sigmund Freud. It was in this article that Dollard explained the nature and function of The Dozens in Black society. But it wasn't until more than two decades later that the next major analysis of The Dozens and Black verbal games was conducted. The researcher was Roger D. Abrahams, a young graduate student in folklore at the University of Pennsylvania. His informants were the Black residents of a small section—"Camingerly"—of South Philadelphia. His research became the basis for a doctoral dissertation which was later published by Folklore Associates as *Deep Down in the Jungle* (1964), a book which quickly had a major impact upon the study of Black English in America.

Every folklorist, each in his own way, understands why folklore is important, and each tries to explain the *why* of recording folklore. In *Deep Down in the Jungle,* Abrahams added his view:

> One of the major cultural differences between the white middle class and ghettoized Afro-Americans is that the latter have preserved an oral-aural world view while the former have invested their creative energies and imaginations heavily in books, in the typographic-chirographic world. As we know from many recent works on media, this difference is of much greater importance than simply illustrating the ability or inability to read. In point of fact, there wasn't one Camingerly resident who could not read, but reading simply did not enter their lives very often.
>
> Many ethnocentric judgments about blacks stem from the white man's inability to understand or appreciate the creative aspects of living in an oral atmosphere.[25]

In *Positively Black* (1970), a sequel to the first edition of *Deep Down in the Jungle,* Abrahams not only refined some of his thinking about the nature of Black English, but took a few pokes at the nation's educational system as well:

One of the statements most often repeated by white elementary teachers about "them"—their Negro charges—is that they have no verbal resources, and, because of this, no language ability. This is commonly followed by one of two rationalizing statements: either "these poor children have never been taught to speak correctly" or "they couldn't have developed verbal skills since they come from families with so many children that there isn't any time for communication with parents." ("Why some of them don't even know who their fathers are!") Both these statements are ethnocentric in the extreme, even if they are well-meaning.

In regard to the supposed substandard language of lower-class Negroes, schooled investigators are just beginning to recognize that Negro speech is not a dialect of English at all but rather part of a language system unto itself which differs from "standard" English in everything but vocabulary. . . . Rather than viewing the various types of Negro speech as different dialectal corruptions of English, it is more meaningful to view them as one creole language, whole unto itself, which has been progressively gravitating toward the regional English dialects with which it has come in contact.[26]

Abrahams's introductory comments to both *Positively Black* and *Deep Down in the Jungle* provide significant insight into the nature of folklore research and analysis, as well as a major sociomethodological problem confronting the researcher. In *Positively Black,* Abrahams argued that:

[On] looking at the history of the black problem and the ways in which scholars' data and conclusions have been presented and used, it becomes obvious that the academic generally has been just as unconscious of his motives and just as caught up in the tides of public sentiment as the politician or the man-on-the-street. He has thereby often exhibited the same patterns of thought, rested his arguments on the same unexamined assumptions, and been unconsciously drawn to the same stereotyped traits as those with less knowledge about blacks. (And I do not exclude myself from the burden of these remarks.)

Unfortunately, such a school investigator is not just another human being, he is one who is regarded as an expert in the field and who is consulted in discussions on the subject. He therefore cannot afford to resign responsibility for his arguments or even his data. The mask of objectivity must be understood for what it is—in the main, just a mask, a pose assumed by the writer-observer to make informed argument more persuasive.

In most cases, the social scientist's failure to recognize that he is unconsciously falling into these habits of mind makes little difference, for who listens to him but other members of his discipline? But in matters concerning blacks in America, his work, though usually in diluted form, is used to affect public attitudes and sometimes even governmental policy.[27]

Abrahams's introduction to the second edition of *Deep Down in the Jungle* presented his serious concerns about human fallibility and explained why a second edition became necessary:

> Since the publication of *Deep Down* . . . in 1964, I have been hoping for the chance of this second say. I sensed from the beginning of the writing that I was not capturing the spirit of my experiences and the essentials of my observations and this was unwillingly playing into the hands of racists. It wasn't until the era of black militancy (which began a year after its writing), however, that I was able to see how my *ex post facto* judgments had been conditioned by my reading of the scholarship on black life rather than by the life style I had observed and experienced. . . .
>
> My black neighbors were telling me about a way of life that calls for a constant consideration of the importance of the "me" element, and it was this very perspective that in my zeal to appear to be a scholar I eliminated from the first recounting of the experience. I eliminated myself from the proceedings, neglecting to build into the account the tremendous importance placed upon friendships, and rivalries, loves and animosities, all of which I was part of. . . . Gone from the account were the cultural gaffes I committed by which I learned so much. Missing were the experiences where taking my ethnocentric conceptions of trust and friendship into an encounter, I found to my dismay and disappointment that my values were not shared. All this crucial interpersonal data was hidden behind the curtain of objective description. . . .
>
> Objectivity in a field situation is only an ideal toward which we strive; but focus of interest will always be determined, at least in part, by personal problems.[28]

Roger Abrahams, the sensitive folklorist/scholar had finally come to understand the problems facing any reporter who attempts to observe and analyze society and its people. Just as the journalist is influenced by what he is reporting, so is the folklorist, the anthropologist, and the ethnolinguist. Almost a decade after his dissertation was accepted at the University of Pennsylvania, Roger Abrahams recognized the limitations of folklore research and, more important, recognized that the interpretation and analysis of the integration of language and culture within the Black community could be meaningful only in relation to one's self. The insertion of the "me" in his second edition gave an added dimension to his research, and offered additional clues about the people of "Camingerly" and their use of language. Abrahams, who had become one of the nation's leading folklorists, had reinterpreted his earlier scholarship to make it meaningful not only to academic scholars, but to all persons; in the process, he made it more reflective of reality.

Abrahams further refined his thinking about Black speech in *Talking Black* (1977), a series of essays that focused "specifically on the systems of communication that operate within and between various social segments of Afro-American communities in the United States."[29]

During the early 1950s, Herbert L. Foster, a veteran of World War II who earned his college degree on the GI Bill, learned about battles that no army ever had to fight. His first assignment was to teach a New York "inner-city" class comprised of what some would call "incorrigibles," and what others would call "socially disadvantaged." According to Foster, "I was the sixth substitute for this class since the regular teacher resigned a few weeks ago."[30]

During the next few years he developed an ability to make discipline an integral part of the classroom so that an atmosphere could be created for study, and he developed a knowledge and competence in the Black language so that communication could be established with his students. According to Foster:

Our schools . . . are highly developed verbal institutions where language consisting of Standard English verbal symbols is the main instrument of communication. Teacher-student and student-teacher communication depends upon the students' ability to understand what each is saying to the other. . . . The black disadvantaged child's jive lexicon may be the only language he possesses. He may not have any additional stock of vocabulary words from which to choose. Therefore, at certain times and under certain conditions, it is possible that neither the child nor his teacher possesses a vocabulary that is compatible with the other's.[31]

From Foster's experiences in the classroom came the *Jive Lexicon Analogy Test, Series I* and the *Jive Lexicon Analogies Test, IIA*. Instead of Standard English words—"White" words—Foster used Black English—"Black" words. That was the only difference; the test was constructed along the same lines as the analogies test section of the Graduate Records Examination (GRE) and the Millers Analogies Test, both which are used for admission to graduate study in the United States. The results were almost predictable. According to Foster, "On my first version of the test . . . with a white population of 322 and a black population of 90, blacks scored higher and race was significant at the > .0001 level."[32]

Foster's 1969 dissertation at Columbia University, *Dialect-Lexicon and Listening Comprehension,* discussed geographical differences and how a knowledge of Black language could aid teachers. During the next five years, he combined the scholarly aspects of the dissertation with the practical aspects of his teaching years to write *Ribbin', Jivin', and Playin' the Dozens,* a book—perhaps even a survival guide—for inner-city teachers. Spicing the book with several "realities," anecdotes illustrating the integration of language and education in the classroom, Foster points out that a lack of knowledge of Black English lexicon, syntax, semantics, and the nonverbal and paralinguistic features of the language, often leads to significant problems in teaching. As one example, he noted that the word "trim" has different meanings in Black English ("a sexual act") and in Standard English, and the lack of that knowledge caused severe classroom disruption when a teacher tried to explain to her English class the meaning of the poetic term "trimeter."

Nevertheless, Foster's research and observations, although considered significant, met with hostility or indifference by many teachers and administrators who, in the 1970s, refused to believe that Black English was anything more than "substandard."

A NEW MEDIUM

The mass media are not stable elements in any nation's history; time, the economy, and the process of socialization not only changes the media, but views of the media as well. As America entered mid-century, the media again faced a change, one destined to dominate the publishing industry for most of the remainder of the twentieth century. At one time, magazines were published "for everyone." Each magazine had something for everyone; each could be read by everyone. But during the middle of the twentieth century as publishers were faced with severe postage and newsprint increases, a larger, better-paid labor force, and circulations rising into the millions, they again raised their advertising rates. As the circulations increased, advertisers found that the rates were too high to continue justifying a "shotgun approach" to reaching the public; they wanted a "rifle," something that could pinpoint a target to achieve a better return on their investments. The former giants of the industry—*Liberty, Colliers, Life, Look, The Saturday Evening Post,* and many others—crumbled . . . dinosaurs of journalism. In their place, specialized magazines arose; publishers with less to invest could select a focus, start a "small magazine" and secure the necessary advertising.

As the nature of the media changed, academic scholars found fewer outlets for their writing. Newspapers and magazines no longer published scholarly articles, works of fiction, essays, or poetry. But the "publish or perish" doctrine in American education, whether real or just perceived as such, remained to plague academics—to "sort out" those whom administrators regarded as "scholars," not by their teaching, but by their "academic" writing. To fill the void that the newspapers and magazines had left came the academic journals—specialized magazines with circulations occasionally approaching 50,000, but usually much below 5,000, often only in the hundreds—limited publications to serve limited needs. By the 1960s, there would be hundreds of academic journals covering almost every facet of scholarship. The "small magazines"—their focus on fiction, poetry, and essays, their contributors usually university professors or students—would become a major force in American publishing.

The economics of publishing that had forced a new concept and direction in magazine publishing also forced a new direction in book publishing. Large trade publishers who attempted to "cover the field" soon found that the smaller publishers who concentrated only on certain markets were able to secure a better return on their investment. Publishing for specialized audiences, now that the nation, itself, was no longer as homogenized as it was at its birth, gave scholars additional outlets; it was now profitable for publishers, incorporating new technology, to publish books that might have sales of only 1,500–2,000 instead of 4,000–5,000.

THE EMERGENCE OF A NEW THEORY

In 1957, the Mouton publishing company of The Hague, The Netherlands, a specialist in language books, published a 118-page highly technical, almost unreadable book that outlined a new theory of linguistics.

For several years, the book was largely ignored, just as the manuscript had previously been ignored or rejected by several publishers. Then, as linguists became intrigued by its new approach, the book's sales began to increase. Soon it became one of the most widely read books in the field; the theory it propounded would become dominant in the analysis of language. The book was titled *Syntactic Structures*. The author, Noam Chomsky.

Syntactic Structures outlined a theoretical concept of language which argued that utterances can be traced to the generating thought through a deep structure. The deep structure, said Chomsky, is never generated on the surface, but determines all surface utterances. Phonology, there-fore, is irrelevant to the study of deep structure because it is added at the end of the process; the utterance itself is merely the end-product. The theory, now known as transformational grammar, delineated rela-tionships between similar sentences containing the same meaning to a common origin which, by means of various transformations, could gen-erate the sentences which the Structuralists had previously listed as separate sentences. Several apparently different sentences could, there-fore, have the same theoretical deep structure; conversely, the same sentence, spoken at different times or by different persons, could have different deep structures. For example, "A detective saw her," and, "She was seen by a detective," as well as all possible variations, could have the same deep structure; however, "He sick," spoken by two different persons, could have two different deep structures. Chomsky's theory argued that the deep structure cannot be measured empirically; the Structuralists argued that since deep structure could not be measured empirically, it was impossible to determine its existence—"You cannot measure a man's mind," they argued. Since the human mind could not be sorted out in an empirical study, Chomsky's theory could be tested only through application—could it adequately describe a language? Dur-ing the next few years, Chomsky modified some parts of his theory, and answered some of the concerns expressed by other linguists. The result was *Aspects of the Theory of Syntax,* published in 1965 by the MIT Press.

The theory of transformational grammar allowed linguists to take a fresh look at language, to see new ways of better understanding and analyzing the nature of language. For many years, scholars could only hypothesize that there was a creole substratum in American Black En-glish. Now with the development of the transformational grammar the-ory, some could actually begin to test their hypotheses.

The pioneering studies into the many West African pidgins and creoles by Paul Christophersen, David Dalby, David DeCamp, J. L. Dillard, Robert A. Hall, Ian Hancock, Gilbert D. Schneider, and William Stewart among others, had led American linguists to recognize that there were distinct surface structure similarities, especially in phonology and syntax, between American Black English and the Black languages of the West coast of Africa.[33] But the American dialectologists, who were among the first to argue for the linguistic validity of all dialects, had, through extensive field work, shown phonological similarities between Black speech and the various dialects of Southern White speech. Black English, they argued, varied only as the geography varied. The basis of both Black English and Southern Standard English was in Elizabethan English; if Black English was different, it was different because of a decay, or transformation, in Elizabethan English in America, not because it was a different dialect or language.

The creolists—whether they were structuralists working with surface structure, or transformationalists working with deep structure—now had the methodological ammunition to argue for the existence of the creole substratum in American Black English. With the development of the transformational grammar theory, the creolists could accept that there were structural and surface similarities between American Black English and many of the Southern dialects. However, they could also point out that not only were there significant surface similarities between American Black English and the West African languages, but also that American Black English, when analyzed according to the methodology of transformational grammar, showed probable common origins with many of the West African languages; American Black English, therefore, not only had a creole substratum but was often structurally closer to the West African languages, probably a West African Pidgin English, than to any of the Southern dialects.

A CREOLE BASE

One of the major linguistic analyses of the Civil Rights Cycle, using modern theoretical methodologies to analyze the nature of American Black English, was conducted by George N. Putnam and Edna M. O'Hern and published as a monograph supplement to the October-December 1955, issue of *Language*. The study, conducted in a small section of Washington, D.C., concluded that the "most striking" difference between Standard and Black English is in phonology. As part of their studies into phonology, Putnam and O'Hern also analyzed segmental phonemes and the suprasegmentals, especially length, stress, and intonation. However, they did not discuss juncture because, in their opinion, there was no adequate linguistic base for such analysis. Also discussed were morphology, syntax, and lexicon. Included were twelve short transcriptions.

Many of the pioneering studies into the nature of American Black English were written by William A. Stewart, who used historical data to point to a creole substratum in the language. His two seminal articles—"Sociolinguistic Factors in the History of American Negro Dialects" (1967) and "Continuity and Change in American Negro Dialects" (1968)—have been reprinted numerous times in several texts. Stewart later turned his attention to reading programs, teaming with Joan Baratz to develop bidialectal readers and reading programs in Washington, D.C.

In its July 19, 1969, edition, the prestigious *Times* of London published a major article about Black English. Written by David Dalby, a distinguished language scholar, the article was soon reprinted by several American newspapers. Dalby's insightful article discussed the historical bases of American Black English, as well as origins for many of the words and phrases currently in popular use in Black as well as standard English. Dalby's research indicated that Wolof was possibly the most common language understood by American Black slaves. Dalby concluded:

> It would be rash to suggest that all American items discussed here can be derived with certainty from Wolof. On the other hand, the frequency of those resemblances is unlikely to be the result of chance and points to the contribution of at least one African language to American (and hence British) vocabulary.[34]

Gilbert D. Schneider, who had written the definitive grammar of West African Pidgin English, agreed that Wolof might have been one of the languages which contributed to the development of American Black English, but that the historical process probably arose when Wolof and many other languages contributed to the development of West African Pidgin English which, in turn, provided the African language base for American Black English. Schneider's research into West African Pidgin English of the Cameroons, which he labeled *Wes-Kos,* led to further research—by Walter Milton Brasch, J. L. Dillard, David Dwyer, Ian Hancock, David M. Smith, William A. Stewart, and Colston Westbrook, among many others—into the historical-linguistic nature of American Black English. Westbrook, using Schneider's linguistic studies of Wes-Kos as a base, conducted additional field research in Cameroon, concluding that there are significant African parallel structures in intonation (including pitch, stress, and juncture) between American Black English and many of the West African languages to warrant further study. Westbrook also concluded that "synchronic dialectology might show connections with African languages, possibly at syntactic and semantic levels."[35]

Ian Hancock also contributed significantly to an understanding of American Black English, writing several articles about the nature of the language. His primary focus was on the languages of West Africa, notably in Sierra Leone (Krio) and Liberia (Liberian Pidgin English). In the early nineteenth century, the country of Liberia was forged out of the West Coast of Africa to serve as a homeland for American Blacks who had either been freed or who had escaped from slavery. The languages of the Liberian region, which had contributed to a West African pidgin language, and later to a creolization stage in American Black English, now produced a "backwash"; the languages of many African regions, mixed with various American dialects to create a number of American creoles, now returned to the Liberian region to influence further language development. By extensive analysis of contemporary Sierra Leone Krio and Liberian Pidgin English, Hancock has been able to shed new light on possible linguistic development of American Black English.

Another major linguistic analysis of American Black English was conducted by William Labov in New York City. According to Labov's research—formally presented in *The Social Stratification of English in New York City* (1966), published by the Center for Applied Linguistics—not only could sound change be observed directly, but language *feelings* could be monitored. Two years later, Columbia University published a two-volume set, *A Study of the Non-Standard English of Negro and Puerto Rican Speakers in New York City,* written by Labov, Paul Cohen, Clarence Robins, and John Lewis, and based upon extensive field work in New York. The study became the first major research to use transformation grammar to probe into the presence of a creole substratum in American Black English. Volume 1 is a phonological and grammatical analysis of both structural and functional differences between the Black English of central Harlem and what was identified as Standard English. Volume 2 focuses on the use of language in a Black community. Both the 1966 and 1968 books served not only as major resource texts in graduate programs in linguistics, but as bases for further research into the nature of the language. Numerous academic articles were developed from the field work research in New York City, and four of those articles served as the building blocks for Labov's *Language in the Inner City: Studies in the Black English Vernacular* (1972). Using sociometric and statistical analysis to understand the integration of language and culture, Labov focused on the language of the street gangs, correlating linguistic structures with social factors relating to the vernacular of the culture.

About the same time Labov and his research team were conducting field studies in New York City, Roger W. Shuy, Walter A. Wolfram, and William K. Riley were studying urban Black speech in Detroit. *Linguistic Correlates of Social Stratification in Detroit Speech* (1967), the final report of the year-long study, indicated that there was a distinct linguistic pattern among the 700 respondents in Detroit, to show that Black English was a separate variety of speech. A year later, the Center for Applied Linguistics published *Field Techniques in an Urban Language Study,* written by Shuy, Wolfram, and Riley, which outlined the methodology of the Detroit study, and included detailed discussions about procedures, field worker orientation, and field work design and evaluation. The book soon became a required text in many graduate courses in sociolinguistics, and served as a primary text for subsequent field work research into the nature of Black English.

Ralph W. Fasold also looked into the urban Black speech in Detroit, the research concluding with publication in 1968 by the Center for Applied Linguistics of *A Sociolinguistic Study of the Pronunciation of Three Vowels in Detroit Speech*. Fasold and Wolfram later teamed up to write a mildly technical presentation of many of the features of Black English, an article that has been widely reprinted.

In 1969, the Center for Applied Linguistics published Wolfram's *A Sociolinguistic Description of Detroit Negro Speech,* which concluded that there was a high correlation of phonological and grammatical variables with the social variables of sex, age, racial isolation, and style in the speech of Detroit's Black English speakers. Wolfram later refined and extended the field techniques of the Detroit study to analyze linguistic assimilation among Puerto Ricans in New York City.

In the late 1960s and early- and mid-1970s, linguists on the staff of the Southwest Regional Laboratory for Educational Research and Development conducted extensive research into Black English speech patterns in Los Angeles. Robert Berdan, Stanley Legum, Carol Pfaff, Gene Tinnie, and Michael Nicholas, working both independently and in small groups, wrote several monographs detailing their research, some of which led to a preliminary hypothesis that Black English may have rules which differ very little throughout the country.

Not all research has concluded that Black English was separate and distinct from Standard English. Using rigorous methodology, Lee A. Pederson and Juanita Williamson conducted separate studies in the mid- and late-1960s. Pederson's study of speech in Chicago, and Williamson's study of Memphis led them to conclude that, at least in those cities, there was little difference in the phonology between the White and Black populations.

But phonology is just one aspect to language, and has had very narrow limits. Creolists and other linguists have been looking at other elements of language to try to understand the nature and historical development of Black English.

During the past three decades, as better methodologies for language analysis developed, a number of researchers have pointed to "special" surface structure verbal features of Black English in its relationships to West African languages, especially West African Pidgin English. Elaine Tarone, among others, noted that words in Standard English which appear to be missing in Black English are often replaced by intonation; Kenneth Johnson described the falsetto and subfalsetto registers as distinct phonological features in the Black language; and Roger Abrahams, Gilbert Schneider, Thomas Kochman, Ernie Smith, and Colston Westbrook, among others, have all described certain paralinguistic and metalinguistic features of Black English that are similar to features in West African Pidgin English and several Bantu languages that are not duplicated in Standard English.

THE PAPER EXPLOSION

Lured by academic, foundation, and federal grants, as well as greater opportunities to see their research published (and tenure "secured") many academic scholars, during the late 1960s, began to investigate all facets of Black life. Investigating Blacks—"minorities," "the culturally disadvantaged," "the culturally deprived," "the culturally underprivileged," "the socially disadvantaged," "the socially deprived," "the socially underprivileged," or whatever the "buzz words" at the Department of Health, Education, and Welfare were that particular month—became profitable. Investigating Blacks led to grants and publication credits, and publication credits led to merit increases, tenure, and promotion. It was inevitable that many scholars, whether or not they understood the concepts of linguistics, quickly realized that investigating Black English could also be profitable. Soon, the careful linguistic studies of Black English and American dialects that appeared in such scholarly publications as *American Speech, The Florida FL Reporter, The Journal of American Folk Lore, Language, Language Sciences, Lingua, Linguistics, Publication of the American Dialect Society,* and others, were blunted by a plethora of articles appearing in almost every conceivable type of magazine or journal. There were hundreds of publications and hundreds of "writer/researchers" who were quick to fill the printed page with ill-conceived or poorly written studies. Even the legitimate researchers were not immune from "milking" some of their studies to gain additional academic credits. Articles soon duplicated other articles; opinions, when separated into classifications, began to sound remarkably alike. Soon, term papers, theses, and dissertations flooded the market. Some added significantly to the knowledge of Black English; many, however, accomplished little more than securing another degree—often an Ed.D. or a Ph.D.—for their authors.[36]

The research linguists who had gone into the field to study and analyze contemporary Black English, its usage and effects, had inadvertently opened a Pandora's box. The systematic linguistic study of American Black English (as accomplished by Roger D. Abrahams, Frank Anshen, Beryl Bailey, Joan C. Baratz, Robert Berdan, Walter Milton Brasch, Robbins Burling, Bernice Cullinan, A. L. Davis, Lawrence Davis, J. L. Dillard, Ralph Fasold, Irwin Feigenbaum, Joan Fickett, Kenneth Goodman, Ian Hancock, Charles G. Hurst, Jr., Kenneth Johnson, Thomas Kochman, Mary Ritchie Key, William Labov, Stanley Legum, Marvin D. Loflin, Philip Luelsdorf, Claudia Mitchell-Kernan, William K. Riley, Roger W. Shuy, James Sledd, Ernie Smith, Riley Smith, William A. Stewart, Elaine Tarone, Lorenzo Dow Turner, Colston Westbrook, Juanita Williamson, and Walter A. Wolfram, among others) was now being politicized by persons with only a fleeting knowledge of linguistics, and virtually no knowledge of sociolinguistics. Black English once again passed from a scientific study of a complex problem into an emotional battleground waged by invective, slander, and diatribe. Everyone had an idea; everyone had an opinion. Black English was now more controversial than ever. The linguists and dialectologists, academic scholars who had studied and tried to understand the nature of language, never knew where the attacks, or the support, would come from—whether from Blacks or Whites, liberals, conservatives, radicals, or reactionaries; all could justify their respective logic by attaching themselves to one of the major theories. A militant Black and a racist Klansman could easily spout forth the same arguments in support of or in opposition to any of the theories. It was now the educators, English teachers, psychologists, and large numbers of sociologists and other social and behavioral scientists who provided the major opposition to the linguistic concepts of language. "There *is* a standard English," they would tell their colleagues and students, "and that standard English is the *correct* English; all others are substandard, inferior, or grammatically incorrect. To help the child, we must force him to learn standard English." Although the dialectologists and creolists disagreed on many of the concepts of Black English, they were united in their opposition to such thinking.

In 1965, Raven I. McDavid, Jr., one of the nation's leading dialectologists, and a scholar who vigorously argued for the social acceptance of all dialects, wrote "Sense and Nonsense About American Dialects." The article—published in the May 1966 issue of *PMLA,* the official journal of the Modern Language Association and republished several times—almost immediately became the center of controversy. Many scholars and teachers, still clinging to the beliefs that dialects were somehow inherently "inferior," argued that the only nonsense that existed was the article itself; others, recognizing the intrinsic values of language, argued that not only was the article a sensible analysis of the linguistic situation, but also that it clarified many complex issues.

A year later, the National Council of Teachers of English (NCTE) published *Discovering American Dialects,* a 68-page monograph written by Roger W. Shuy, which further explored the nature of dialects and extended McDavid's call for the social acceptance of dialects in American society. Then in 1969, William Labov added to the debate, writing "The Logic of Nonstandard English," a sharply worded forty-four page article, which tore into the deficit arguments of Basil Bernstein, arguing that extensive linguistic analysis has shown there is a *logic* as well as a systematic set of rules in nonstandard language, especially Black English. In 1970, the NCTE published Labov's *The Study of Nonstandard English,* a revision of an earlier monograph published by the Center for Applied Linguistics.

But still the battles raged, battles fought through the academic journals and in the classrooms. Argument brought counterargument; "conclusive proof" of one theory brought "conclusive proof" of another theory. It was not long before the controversy spilled into the mass media.

A three-column headline in the September 9, 1967, issue of the *San Diego Union* boldly proclaimed "Rafferty Slaps Any Use of Dialects in

Schools." The kicker head—a smaller headline usually placed over the major headline—quoted the controversial California Superintendent of Public Instruction: "Only 1 Correct Grammar." Max Rafferty, writing an opinion column for statewide distribution, had declared that "The Negro . . . has the right to demand that the schools tell his children there is only one correct grammar. One right way to spell. One right way to conjugate verbs."[37]

What triggered Rafferty's comments was an article that appeared in the fourteen million circulation newspaper supplement, *Parade*. Written by Lloyd Shearer, the article quoted Kenneth S. Johnson, a language specialist, and Charles G. Hurst, Jr., chairman of the Department of Speech at Howard University. According to Hurst:

> The current system of teaching English has got to be thrown out, and thrown out now. The Negro students have lost faith in it. I also think many of the teachers have. It's the older teachers, however, and the department heads, set in their ways, who refuse to budge. It shakes up some of the basic tenets which have guided their instructional philosophy all these years. . . .
>
> They simply have got to stop dealing in rights and wrongs. They've got to accept the dialect the student brings with him and respect it because it represents his own culture.[38]

Rafferty's counterargument was just as strong:

> If everybody at home [speaks Black English], everybody at home is speaking bad English. And the sooner the schools point this out, the better. . . .
>
> Schools are not to put "seals of approval" on the status quo brought to them by the kids from home. . . . It is the educator's job to deal in rights and wrongs—that because a child counts on his fingers and toes at home doesn't make it right.[39]

Rafferty's comments, made to a general public, but read and understood by California's teachers, undoubtedly influenced many to accept the eradicationist arguments and to make special efforts to assure that their students acquired that "one correct grammar."

But not all educators agreed with Rafferty. One of the outstanding articles pertaining to dialect in the classroom was written by Herbert Kohl for the *New York Review* of November 17, 1966. Kohl, who taught in a Harlem school, discussed his techniques of helping Blacks achieve dialect pride through creative writing. His book, *36 Children*

(1967), focused the nation's attention upon problems that White teachers encountered in Black ghetto schools, problems often caused by academic and administrative ignorance. The book included an expansion of his *New York Review* article on language arts programs for Black English speakers.

Kohl taught in an urban ghetto school. Pat Conroy—also White, but born and raised in the South—taught in a rural district. His 1972 book, *The Water Is Wide,* is an autobiographical account of the year he spent as a teacher on one of the South Carolina Sea Islands. Conroy's book, like Kohl's, is also a powerful indictment against alleged inferior and inadequate educational policies affecting the Gullah-speaking Blacks of Yamacraw Island. Identifying his experiences with the Gullah language, Conroy noted:

> When the kids were conversing normally, there was not a tinker's chance in hell that I could understand them. . . . I could not decipher the ordinary conversation of any of the children in the class. They spoke like machine guns. . . . I could not grasp the syntax, nor could I follow any logical sentence pattern, nor could I participate in their discussions by placing together words I did catch accidentally. . . . To make matters even more serious, none of them could understand me.[40]

In addition to recording brief conversations, Conroy included occasional mention of Gullah naming practices.

Normally, such a book, even with good promotion, might have sales of only a few thousand. But the times were right for such a book; *The Water Is Wide* proved to be an exception, a best seller. Shortly before it was published, a crisply edited version appeared as a major feature in *Life* magazine. By the time the book was published, more than seven million *Life* subscribers, and a potential readership in excess of ten million, had been exposed to the June 2, 1972, issue. A few months later, the book was published in paperback. In 1974, it was released as a feature motion picture, *Conrack,* adapted for the screen by Irving Ravetch and Harriet Frank, Jr., and directed by Martin Ritt. The movie featured Gullah-speaking children of Yamacraw Island, their actions and speech patterns virtually unmodified by dialogue coaches.

Kohl and Conroy, although naive about language and linguistics when they entered the teaching profession, nevertheless soon accepted a premise that for education to be effective, the language of the child—whether Harlem Black English or Gullah—could not be destroyed.

A brief news feature in the February 18, 1966, issue of *Time* reported about second-language teaching programs in several urban school systems. Three years later, *Time* published an article that focused on verbal and nonverbal Black language. The staff-written article discussed the sociolinguistic basis of Black English, and reviewed Black dialect readers being developed under the direction of William A. Stewart. Neither article advanced an opinion as to the legitimacy of the language. During the 1970s, several teachers, psychologists, and language specialists created dialect readers, each reader an attempt to get Black English-speaking students to learn to read by first learning to read texts in Black English. Several linguists—including Joan Baratz, Bernice Cullinan, Ralph W. Fasold, Irwin Feigenbaum, and William A. Stewart—conducted research into the effectiveness of the dialect readers. Although there is some evidence that dialect readers may have helped some students learn to read, there are as yet no conclusive studies. However, there is evidence that the use of the methodology of second language acquisition has aided Black English-speaking students to learn Standard English. One of the more successful proposals was outlined in 1973 by Carroll E. Reed in the *TESOL Quarterly*. And one of the most successful programs was developed at Brooklyn College.

Franz Fanon's popular book, *Black Skin, White Masks* (1967), includes a chapter on "The Negro and His Language." Fanon presented a well-reasoned discussion of what Black English is and is not, and how it is interpreted, accepted, or rejected by Blacks as well as Whites.

In the June 11, 1967, issue of *The Washington Post,* a newspaper which at that time served a city with a population that was about seventy per cent Black, Peggy Thomson described "Washington's Second Language." Her article, appearing in the widely read *Potomac* magazine section, discussed many of the arguments and controversies surrounding Black English study in Washington, D.C. Her focus was on the Urban Language Study Program, funded by the Ford Foundation, and conducted by the Center for Applied Linguistics (CAL). The program itself concentrated on twenty-five of the city's eighty-two inner-city schools. Thomson also interviewed and quoted, at length, William S. Carroll, J. L. Dillard, Irwin Feigenbaum, and William A. Stewart. For most readers of *The Washington Post,* it was not only the first time they had heard of these distinguished language scholars, but it was also the first time they knew there was formal study of the variety of speech identified as Black English.

The December 22, 1968, issue of the *Post* again attacked the controversy head-on. Under a full-page banner headline that asked, "Negro

Dialect: Should the Schools Fight It?", staff writer Herbert H. Denton discussed the programs of the Center for Applied Linguistics and its opposition to certain teaching practices within the school system of the nation's capital. Denton pointed out that the center, which was spearheading the fight against the deficit and eradicationist arguments of Black English, opposed the district's English education programs, ". . . not only because of its failure to come to grips with the dialect, but because they consider it unnecessary. To teach standard English, they say, a program should be derived that focuses on grammar and structure of sentences. Tedious drills to get students to speak the King's English pronunciation is unnecessary, they argue."[41]

Other cities were also having their problems with the emergence of the newer linguistic theories about the nature of Black English. In Philadelphia, one-third of whose population in 1969 was Black, a seemingly innocent memorandum distributed on July 31, 1969, created a fusilade of protests. Gail M. Donovan, an administrative assistant to the superintendent of schools, had sent a memo to senior administrators that outlined the contents of an anthology-textbook that discussed Black English and dialects as being "intrinsically sound." The book—*Teaching Black Children To Read,* edited by Joan C. Baratz and Roger W. Shuy, and published by the Center for Applied Linguistics—included articles written by Baratz, Ralph Fasold, Kenneth Goodman, William Labov, Raven I. McDavid, Jr., Roger W. Shuy, William A. Stewart, and Walt Wolfram, all of them respected scholars in the field of language. On August 11, 1969, the *Philadelphia Daily News* headlined an article, "Order to OK 'Black English' in Schools Comes Under Fire." However, Donovan's memo had not even suggested that Black English was a legitimate and separate language, or that it was "OK"; it had only suggested that administrators might wish to read the arguments presented in the textbook.

The Evening Bulletin the following day, in its first article about the controversy, explained that the memo "is for the information of staff members and does not represent the views of either Shedd [Dr. Mark R. Shedd, superintendent of schools] or the school board." The article, written by John T. Gillespie, briefly outlined some of the major arguments presented in the textbook. However, the four-column headline— "Nichols Raps Memo Approving 'Black English' "—had again given the impression that teaching Black English as a legitimate variety of speech had somehow been approved. The Rev. Henry H. Nichols, a Black minister and vice-president of the Board of Education, reflected a general opinion shared by the board as well as most of the district's educators when he presented arguments supporting the deficit theory of Black English and successfully urged that future memos include disclaimers that such memos do not represent policy of the Board of Education or the superintendent of schools.

On August 13, the *Daily News,* in an editorial headlined "One for the Wastebasket," argued that the Rev. Nichols was "quite right in scorning a memorandum advocating acceptance of 'Black English.' " The editorial further asked: "How can educators expect ghetto youngsters to compete in higher education and in career opportunities while saddled with a crippling handicap represented by poor command of the language? This is an area where compromise is capitulation."[42]

On August 15, four days after the *Daily News* brought the controversy to the public, three senior school district administrators issued a strongly worded position paper establishing a policy that, as far as educators in the district should be concerned, Black English is neither a linguistically distinct dialect nor a language. The controversy simmered briefly, then died out.

The *Philadelphia Inquirer* had become involved in the controversy only indirectly. Three months earlier, it had run an eight-column banner feature which quoted Joseph C. Hall, a reading specialist at Cheyney State College. According to Hall, Blacks who speak a nonstandard dialect or Ghetto English, should be taught reading in that dialect before being taught to read in Standard English. The *Inquirer* didn't involve itself in, or report on, the later controversy.

In November 1970, a number of newspapers—including the *Philadelphia Inquirer, Atlanta Constitution,* and *Los Angeles Times*—published a brief news-interview with Marvin Loflin, who argued for the educational acceptance of the linguistic validity of Black English.

One of the better overviews of the controversies surrounding Black English appeared in the November 28, 1970, issue of *The New Republic,* a magazine with a circulation of about 140,000. While taking essentially an antieradicationist position, Olivia Mellan objectively underscored the dispute between eradicationism and bidialectism. A number of leading language scholars and educators were interviewed and quoted. Mellan's article generated two published letters to the editor. John Pairman Brown, in the January 16, 1971, issue, suggested that a program of urban dialect enrichment for suburban Whites be established; Thomas R. Lopez, Jr., discussed reasons for bidialectal training in the schools.

The National Association for the Advancement of Colored People (NAACP) officially entered the controversy in 1971, when it argued through *The Crisis,* its official magazine, that "the so-called 'Black English' is basically the same slovenly English as spoken by the South's undereducated poor White population," and then called a Black English training program at Brooklyn College "a cruel hoax." The editorial further urged that "Black parents throughout this nation should rise up in unanimous condemnation of this insidious conspiracy to cripple their children permanently. . . . Let the Black voice of protest resound thunderously throughout the land."[43] *The Crisis,* however, had completely misinterpreted the purpose of the Brooklyn College program; it was not to teach Black English, but to teach Black English speakers the nature of Black English in order to understand Standard English.

An article in the May 9, 1971, issue of *The New York Times* briefly explained a reading and speech program under the direction of Bernice Cullinan at New York University. A week later, the *Times* placed a seven-column banner—"Use of Black English To Help Children Fit in at School Is Debated Here"—over staff writer C. Gerald Fraser's explanatory article about the controversy surrounding Black English. Fraser, who interviewed linguists J. L. Dillard and William Labov for much of his source material, also included in the article some of the distinguishing rules of Black English. The articles in both *The Crisis* and *The New York Times* triggered an unusually high reader response about Black English programs. In a letter to the editor, Thomas W. Patrick, a Black physician, argued that "to teach a Black child Black English is equivalent to leading him down the back road, at an early age, to illiteracy, frustration, failure, and despair."[44] The letter was first printed in the July 17, 1971, issue of the *Times,* then reprinted in the August issue of *The Crisis.* In another of the many letters received by the *Times,* Beatrice Petrella, a teacher in a ghetto junior high school, used eradicationist arguments to oppose any attempt to teach Black children about Black English. In reply, J. L. Dillard argued that linguists don't make up the language, they only describe it.

Bayard Rustin, nationally syndicated columnist and civil rights leader, also voiced his opposition to the linguistic validity of Black English. In an article appearing in the Black-oriented *New York Amsterdam News* and several other newspapers, Rustin argued:

> In keeping with the mood of the times, the updating of old racial myths has taken the form of cults of one sort or another. There is always some "new" angle to the race problem, or some new gimmick that people latch onto in the hope of finding a short-cut solution. But easy answers always indulge in racial mythology because

they must—if they are to be easy answers—obscure the depth of the race problem. Today's cultists are the natural descendants of the procreators of all our racial stereotypes.

One of the new cults is "Black English." . . .

No doubt the motives of some of these new "black linguistics experts" are sincere. They want to see black children learn, but do they want to prepare them for life outside the ghetto? Do they want to see them become first-class citizens? "Black English," after all, has nothing to do with blackness but derives from the conditions of lower-class life in the South (poor Southern whites also speak "Black English"). Reinforcing this consequence of poverty will only perpetuate poverty since it will prevent black children from mastering the means of communication in an advanced technological society with a highly educated population.

I am sure there are some black proponents of "Black English" who feel that we must retain our racial distinctiveness and avoid the self-negating process of assimilation. But this is really a false issue. Immigrants who were much more foreign to American culture than Negroes realized when they arrived in America that in order to succeed they had to master certain skills, and they did so while retaining their ethnic distinctiveness.[45]

Rustin concluded his article by agreeing with the editorial in *The Crisis* that the "cult" of legitimizing Black English must be destroyed.

Rustin's article was later reprinted in the August 1 issue of *The New York Times* as paid advertising. Each Sunday, the *Times* published, as paid advertising, an opinion column written by, or for, Albert Shanker, at that time president of the 65,000-member United Federation of Teachers (UFT), the New York City local of the 275,000-member American Federation of Teachers (AFT) which he would later head. (He would later become vice-president of the AFL-CIO.) For the August 1 issue, Rustin was the guest columnist.

Whether Rustin's opinions influenced or changed any previously held attitudes among the city's elementary and secondary school teachers can only be conjecture. However, it would be foolish to believe that the UFT financed the publication of views contrary to its own policies or those of its leadership. Thus, the Rustin column took on added significance.

In the November 19, 1971, issue of *Commonweal,* Dorothy Z. Seymour outlined many of the distinguishing features of Black English which she identified as a separate language rather than "ungrammatical"

English or a separate variety of speech. Her article generated two published letters to the editor. C. Gilbert Romero agreed with Ms. Seymour on accepting Black English as a separate, viable language. Roland Laird disagreed. According to Laird, "After generations of subjugation, humiliation, and victimization, do Blacks have to depend for their dignity and identification on exotic or quaint speech?"[46] One month later, in a separate feature article in *Commonweal,* William W. West discussed social and economic advantages of Blacks being bidialectal, indicating that he believed schools should assist Blacks in learning both dialects.

In the October 19, 1971, issue of *The New York Times,* poet W. H. Auden claimed that "as a poet—not as a citizen—there is only one political duty, and that is to defend one's language from corruption. And that is particularly serious now. It's being so quickly corrupted. When it's corrupted, people lose faith in what they hear, and this leads to violence."[47]

Douglas Bush, retired professor of American Literature at Harvard University, agreed with Auden. In a major essay, first published in the Spring 1972 issue of *The American Scholar,* then reprinted under the headline, "Does Anybody Here Speak English?" in the *Washington* (D.C.) *Sunday Star,* Bush editorialized that:

> While an aroused public applauds the exposure of civic corruption and environmental pollution, neither the public at large nor officialdom has any concern with the corruption and pollution of language except to contribute to it. And this kind of corruption is quite as disastrous as any other, if not more so, partly because common violation of traditional usage is an ugly debasement of our great heritage, partly because sloppy English is a symptom and agent of sloppy thinking and feeling and of sloppy communication and confusion. . . .
>
> Language must be protected not only by poets but by the saving remnant of people who care.[48]

Both Auden and Bush were accurate in a few of their observations about language, but the impressions created were that there was *one* correct grammar and that it must be protected.

T. J. Sellers, special assistant in the New York City school system, and a former editor of the *New York Amsterdam News,* in an opinion-feature published in *The New York Times,* argued that "it is a cruel hoax for teachers and poets or editors or 'leaders' to make children feel that a romantic excursion into distorted grammar will help them with this overwhelming task [to learn English.]"[49]

Slightly more than two weeks later, the *Washington Post,* in its June 25 issue, gave major feature play to an edited version of Dorothy Z. Seymour's *Commonweal* article.

William Labov, who had contributed much of the important linguistic research into the nature of Black English, and who, by mid-1972, had already written more than two dozen articles for scholarly and academic publications, turned to the mass media to reach a broader audience. In a strongly worded article which appeared in *The Atlantic Monthly,* a magazine which at that time had a circulation of about 340,000, Labov lashed out against the deficit theory, charging:

> These notions are based upon the work of educational psychologists who know very little about language and even less about Black children. The concept of verbal deprivation has no basis in social reality. . . . The myth of verbal deprivation is particularly dangerous because it diverts the attention from real defects of our educational system to imaginary defects of the child.[50]

After presenting a scholarly discussion of the linguistic finds of his study of Black speech in New York City, Labov again attacked the deficit theory:

> Linguists are in an excellent position to demonstrate the fallacies of the verbal-deprivation theory. All linguists agree that nonstandard dialects are highly structured systems; they do not see these dialects as accumulations of errors caused by the failure of their speakers to master standard English. When linguists hear black children saying "He crazy" or "Her my friend" they do not hear a "primitive language." Nor do they believe that the speech of working-class people is merely a form of emotional expression, incapable of relating logical thought. Linguists, therefore condemn with a single voice Bereiter's view that the vernacular can be disregarded.
>
> There is no reason to believe that any nonstandard vernacular is in itself an obstacle to learning. The chief problem is ignorance of language on the part of all concerned. Our job as linguists is to remedy this ignorance: Others want to reinforce it and justify it. Teachers are now being told to ignore the language of black children as unworthy of attention and useless for learning. They are being taught to hear every natural utterance of the child as evidence of his mental inferiority. As linguists we are unanimous in

condemning this view as bad observation, bad theory, and bad practice.

That educational psychology should be strongly influenced by a theory so false to the facts of language is unfortunate; but that children should be the victims of this ignorance is intolerable. If linguists can contribute some of their valuable knowledge and energy toward exposing the fallacies of the verbal-deprivation theory, we will have done a great deal to justify the support that society has given to basic research in our field.[51]

Walter Mercer, a Black professor of education at the Florida A & M University, disagreed with Labov. Writing for *The Floridian,* the Sunday magazine supplement of the *St. Petersburg Times,* Mercer conceded that Black English "is a systematic linguistic pattern with its own rules and vocabulary," but argued:

Regardless of the "genuineness" of the dialect, regardless of how remarkably it may add flavor and soul to a poem or song or novel, regardless of the solidarity it may lend to a political rally, I say it is illogical, nonsensical, and harmful to teach an innocent black child that it's quite all right to say "I done gone to school." I've also noticed that the black advocates of teaching black dialect all can use impeccable standard English. . . .

I maintain that teachers who teach only the black dialect are doing black children a disservice, even an injustice. They are *not* building on positive grounds, no matter what the National Council of Teachers of English says. They are building on the sands of condescension, for they reject the idea that the black child has enough brains and abilities to master the dominant speech of his native country. Teachers must demand that black students discard their substandard dialect as a step in the process of discarding substandard citizenship. . . .

Black dialect is not sanctioned by society as an acceptable dialect, and it's unrealistic to imagine it could ever become a prestige dialect. That judgment by society may not be wise or fair, but blacks must realize that they will have to read and speak as fluently a socially acceptable dialect—standard English—if they are to have any hope of upward social mobility.[52]

J. Mitchell Morse, professor of English at Temple University, carried an emotional argument even further. In *The Irrelevant English Teacher,* a much-praised book published in 1972, Morse lashed out against English teachers for not understanding the concepts of English, for not understanding their students, and for not being responsive to the needs of communication in society. However, Morse also argued that "[Black English] is demoralized language, an idiom of fettered minds, the shuffling speech of slavery. It served its bad purposes well. It can not serve the purposes of free men and women. Those who would perpetuate it are romanticists clinging to corruption."[53]

Strictly Speaking (1974), Edwin Newman's best-selling commentary on American speech patterns, focusing upon pompous and pretentious language, does not include a discussion about Black English. But Kenneth Johnson, distinguished professor of psychology at the City University of New York, felt a need to editorialize. For the back jacket of the book, Johnson, in reviewing the book, noted that "those of us who recoil at attempts to make some educational virtue out of 'black English' . . . now have a civilized advocate and defender in Edwin Newman."

Most of the nation's educators, clinging to the "deficit theory," were unwilling to accept the linguistic concepts of Black English, arguing that Standard English—"correct" English—must be the medium of communication for any transmission of knowledge.

The Black churches, however, had long before realized that the medium of communication must be in the language of the people. Possibly because of this belief, it was the Black church and not the school system that had been a focus for Black life. Throughout the history of the country—whether during the Revolution or during the civil rights movement—the Black church served as a vital force in the lives of Blacks. It was not merely a place to pray, but a place to *be*. It was a place to meet people, to help people, to cope with life's demands.

Before the Civil War, the church served as an important communication link between slavery and freedom. Following the Civil War, it accepted a more difficult duty—to give direction to a movement for full equality. The Black churches had given hope where there was none. If the White society did not accept the Blacks' cultural values, the Black church did. If "The Man" did not understand their speech, God did.

Because language is an integral part of identity, Black preachers realized the importance of not only understanding, but also speaking, the language of their congregation—no matter what the dialect. Preachers who knew, and used, Black English in their churches acquired a following—they *understood* their congregation. Black preachers who spoke

Standard English found that they could not communicate with their Black congregations; Standard English was "the White Man's talk."

In *Black Preaching* (1970), one of the better studies of the Black preacher in contemporary times, Henry M. Mitchell recognized the extent of the problem:

> No language is improper among its own users. . . . [Missionaries] take great care to learn the communication system of the people among whom they are to work. However, in America, a diabolical combination of racism, class, snobbery, and naiveté has caused Blacks as well as Whites to assume consciously or unconsciously, that there is a single proper American English, and that the language spoken by most Black people is a crude distortion of it. In religious circles, standard White middle-class English is assumed to be the only vehicle for the preaching of the gospel and the praising of the Lord in public. The results have been rather disastrous for the church of the Black masses, because the vast majority of Black-culture churches have found it difficult to understand or relate to trained Black clergymen preaching White to them. Consequently, those trained Blacks who are also fluent in Black English— the language of their people—are conspicuously effective and in great demand.[54]

Mitchell also pointed out that many of the Black theological seminaries now have courses in Black English to help the Standard English speaker communicate with his congregation.

Comedian Flip Wilson's portrayal of a street-wise "sweet-talking" Black minister, based upon reality, yet without the gross distortions prevalent during the era of minstrelsy, gave the White American audiences not only moments of humor, but insights into the role, and language, of the Black minister. Wilson's minister was heard first in nightclubs, then on records and television, the mass media providing the forum for millions of people to be entertained, yet be the recipients of passive information. Other Black comedians using the mass media to present images of Black characters speaking variations of Black English, are Redd Foxx, Scatman Crothers, and Richard Pryor.

Nevertheless, the controversy continued—educators and psychologists for the most part claiming that whether or not Black English is a language, it represents a deficiency in cognitive abilities; dialectologists arguing that a person's dialect or language does not represent a deficiency, but that most of the rules that distinguish Black English also distinguish the dialects of the American South; and the creolists who contended that although some surface structures of Black English may appear to be similar to various Southern dialects, the deep structure, the syntax of the language, has its own identifying rules that once were the base for a creolized language.

The mass media by the early 1970s were flooded by charges and countercharges, by unsubstantiated opinions posing as facts and, occasionally, by well-reasoned research into the nature of Black English. But as the controversy continued, the creolist position, as developed under the direction of William A. Stewart, began to evolve, gaining a following not only among academic scholars but among the public as well. In August 1972, J. L. Dillard's long-awaited book, *Black English: Its History and Usage in the United States,* was published by Random House and "pushed" not as an academic book, but as a trade book intended for the general public. Almost as soon as the book was published, reviews appeared in *Time, Newsweek, The New York Times, The Nation, Book World,* and other major national publications. For the first time, a book about Black English written for the general public was receiving national attention, and the reaction was generally favorable. The book quickly climbed into the best-sellers charts; the time was right.

In its review of August 7, *Time* not only reviewed Dillard's book, but discussed the controversial Black dialect readers. Charles Michener, reviewing the book a week later for *Newsweek* readers, pointed out that "Dillard writes in a laborious, take-nothing-for-granted style that makes for heavy going." But he also noted that it is a worthwhile book, and that Dillard "marshalls an impressive case."[55]

J. L. Dillard, a professor of linguistics and a student of William A. Stewart, had, indeed, marshalled "an impressive case" for the creolist position of Black English, but it was a case that opened wounds, created unto itself more controversy, and led a number of linguistics scholars, many of whom were creolists, to feel that Dillard was too forceful with some of his statements and careless with some of his facts. Nevertheless, academic reviews, some appearing several years after publication of *Black English,* found more to praise than to criticize.

To justify the development of the creolist position, Dillard was forced to attempt to destroy the other two major theories. He opened his attack by pointing a number of barbs at dialect geographers. On his first page, he claimed:

American linguistics has failed to provide accurate information about Black English because of the myopic nature of most historical work on American English. Dialectologists . . . have concerned themselves almost exclusively with patterns of migration from the British Isles and with what they think of as the spread of British regional features throughout the United States.[56]

Dillard's attack on H. L. Mencken was blunt—"Mencken always seemed somewhat confused as to whether he was dealing with something real or with something invented by literary men." Dillard also pointed his barbs at Raven I. McDavid, Jr., who, with Hans Kurath, probably did more to research American dialect and successfully promote the linguistic acceptance of dialect than almost anyone else. The attack was brutal: "The 1963 *Abridgement* of Mencken's work by dialect geographer Raven I. McDavid, Jr. (the chief distinction of which is the addition of summaries of geography-oriented research in brackets throughout the text) carries research on Negro dialect to an all-time low."[57]

Dillard then picked apart Mencken's voluminous work, *The American Language,* by arguing that Mencken had overlooked specific items, charging that:

> The reason for the lack of study in the area of Black English seems to be that the theory of exclusively British origins is seriously challenged by the pidgin/creole theory. Members of the geography-oriented Establishment must have been aware of the possibility of a challenge from that theory for quite some time and have constructed defenses against it.[58]

Dillard's deepest enmity and wrath, however, was reserved for the educators. In this respect, both the dialect geographers and the creolists are often in agreement. According to Dillard:

> Many are the teachers who derive a kind of compensation for their limitations from the belief that they are superior to their students in their "better" grammar. Such teachers are frequently unwilling to entertain the idea that the grammar of their students is not worse but only different. . . .
>
> Misunderstanding of the grammatical patterns of the disadvantaged Negro's speech frequently leads to the conclusion that he has no grammar, a completely untenable position from the point of view of any linguist. . . .
>
> Although most teachers would need to acquire some linguistic

sophistication and some knowledge of Negro nonstandard English before they would be capable of evaluating really good papers in Black English, the use of a student's native dialect could easily result in an upgrading rather than lowering of standards.[59]

To justify his interpretation of the creolist position, Dillard brought together a scattering of data and drew broad, sweeping conclusions, prompting literary critic Christopher Lehmann-Haupt, writing in *The New York Times,* to point out that "the evidence here is scanty, but Mr. Dillard makes the most of it. . . . [H]is logic seems overwhelming."[60]

Dillard's book—although it must be read with the understanding that it does not present definitive answers as the author might like to claim—is comprehensive, including a brief discussion of the historical bases of Black English, the linguistic structure of the language, comparisons and contrasts between Black and Southern English, the nature of pidgin languages in America, and the positions of the American educational communities regarding the nature of Black English. Dillard also included a guide to the pronunciation of Black English and a brief bibliography. Because *Black English* filled a void and is something that the average person could read and understand, it became valuable. Because it was the first such book placed in the public market, and because it has been legitimized through the media itself, *Black English* was looked to by much of the public as a definitive text. This obviously has proven to be frustrating to those opposed to many of the concepts formulated or refined by the creolists. Dillard followed up on his "popular" book with two "academic" books—*Perspectives on Black English* (1975), (an anthology of major writings of other scholars), and *Black Names* (1976), both published by Mouton, a Dutch-owned publisher specializing in linguistics.

Dillard's *Lexicon of Black English* (1977), published by the Seabury Press, is an extension and reiteration of his earlier arguments about the nature of Black English, but with a focus on the nature and development of the lexicon of the language. In the introduction, Dillard explained the reason for the book: "This book attempts to justify the production of such a dictionary [of Black English] on the grounds that there are enough differences between that language variety . . . and ordinary American 'Standard' English."[61]

Although the book does present rather lengthy essays about certain aspects of Black language, it is not conclusive that a separate dictionary is needed, especially since almost all words now used in American Black

English are the same as in American Standard English, with the difference being not the lexicon but the use. More appropriately, a book detailing the nature of American Black English, focusing upon deep structure differences to American Standard English, as well as upon *use* of the language in context, is called for.

In Dillard's sweeping hyperbolic effort to justify the creolist position, he again boldly attacked several researchers, including James Sledd, one of his more vociferous opponents. And in a separate article appearing in the journal *American Speech,* Dillard used personal invective and minimal logic to justify the creolist position, thus furthering the division between the traditional dialect geographers and the creolists, and also alienating many creolists.

Nevertheless, Dillard's "shock tactics" brought a new vitality to Black English research and the public's understanding of a very complex sociolinguistic problem and forced the public to recognize that there is a creolist position, just as valid as any other, and that there is a strong possibility this position offers a major explanation of the nature of American Black English.

Less than a year after Dillard's first book was published, *English in Black and White* (1973), written by Robbins Burling, was published. Burling's study of the nature of Black English, and public perceptions of the language, was careful and thorough. In the final two chapters—after posing the questions, "What should we do about it?" and "Can we help children toward literacy?"—Burling presented the foundation for a program that would help teachers help students who speak nonstandard dialect. However, Burling's book was a text, written for, and read by, a specific academic audience. It was a major contribution to Black English understanding, but it was Dillard's book that pushed public awareness of Black English to a new peak. Within months of the publication of Dillard's book, the mass media were printing articles about Black English.

The December 3, 1972, issue of the (Tucson) *Arizona Daily Star* published a half-page banner spread—"Black English: Check It Out, Man." Staff writer Alex Dreshler discussed some of the features that distinguish Black English from Standard English, but the focus of the article was on Augusta R. Narcisse, a high school teacher who taught a Black dialects course for one year.

The Dayton (Ohio) *Daily News,* located in a city in which forty-five per cent of the residents are Black, published a major feature to point out that Black English and Standard English are two separate, legitimate languages. Writing for the February 12, 1973, issue, staff writer Dennis Polite discussed the Model Cities program, which "is trying to bridge the gap that separates the two languages by sponsoring minority workshops in schools in the component's target area." Gertrude Hutter, a workshop leader, discussed "standards" and part of the philosophy behind the Model Cities program:

> Let's not say raise the standard but change the standard. [Black English and standard English] are equal. . . .
>
> The educational system does not tolerate variety in language. It is a myth that there is a correct way to speak.
>
> The correct way is so the people to whom you are talking will understand you—if you know their language.[62]

On July 1, 1973, *The Washington Post* again published another major feature which discussed the controversies surrounding the study of American Black English. Written by Joel Dreyfuss—who had interviewed and quoted the views of J. L. Dillard, Nick Aaron Ford, June Jordan, William A. Stewart, and Walter A. Wolfram—the article briefly traced the major research being done in Black English. Referring to lexicon to show a deeper structure, June Jordan is quoted as saying:

> White people read our language all the time. They use "baby" to refer to a woman, but they can't use the word "mama." The experience, the history of white women is so utterly different. On the other hand, a black man will hardly ever call a black woman "darling." Those little things show a vast difference between our peoples.[63]

Walter A. Wolfram argued: "I think that language can interfere with the learning process, but there are other factors. The way the school system is set up, it forces the child to make a choice. Either he aligns with school values or with values outside of school."[64]

Extending Wolfram's argument, William A. Stewart noted that every year the New York City reading scores drop, causing administrators and educators to "agonize over what the reasons may be." But, Stewart also pointed out:

> They never touch the issue of language differences because it's too hot. They find the issue of school failure easier to deal with. . . .
>
> There is a real gut fear involved. People are frightened by the idea that kids not only may look different but may be different. There is nothing in our national rhetoric [sic] which allows for such differences.[65]

Nick Aaron Ford, professor of English at Morgan State College, agreed with Stewart and Wolfram that there must be greater tolerance in the school systems, but argued that "there is no reason to jump to conclusions that because they [the students] are not doing well now, if you give them Black English they will do better."[66] Ford also pointed to a very real sociolinguistic problem—in his view, Black students, teachers, and parents generally do not accept Black English as a "proper" language. During the next few years, newspaper syndicates and both major wire services transmitted articles—occasionally opinion presented as fact—about Black English. Susan Houston, a psycholinguist, presented her views to the public in an article appearing in the March 1973 issue of *Psychology Today*. Then, a few months later, in an interview with a reporter from United Press International (UPI), she claimed, based upon her research, that Black English was phonological, not syntactic, thus showing her apparent lack of understanding of current research. Riley B. Smith, who has conducted significant research into Black English phonology, responded to Houston's comments which UPI had treated as fact. In an article appearing in the spring-summer 1974 issue of *American Speech*. Smith discussed the historical development of Black English, then argued that Houston's "analysis is probably seriously flawed, and there are few valuable data that can be called new."

Part of the problem with the media stories about Black English is a problem with human psychology. Although reporters are trained to be a little bit cynical, and to investigate and verify all facts, they, like most people, are often in awe of the very subjects they are interviewing. When the subject of Black English became a popular subject, editors assigned reporters to report it. Many reporters looked for and found an academic scholar who was working in the field of Black English. The reporter spent some time with the professor, or a couple of professors, then strung together quotes with narrative to create a feature article about Black English. Some articles were written very well; some weren't. But there was no investigation of the claims made by the professor, and the statements about Black English became "expert opinion" when sanctified by appearing in the mass media.

THE ANN ARBOR DECISION

For almost three centuries, the question of the "legitimacy" of American Black English was one of emotion, racism, pedagogy, philology, and linguistics. Then, on July 28, 1977, it became a legal question when attorneys for Michigan Legal Services of Detroit filed suit in U.S. District

Court for the Eastern District of Michigan, on behalf of eleven Black children who lived in the Green Road Housing Development project of Ann Arbor and attended, or were scheduled to attend, the Martin Luther King, Jr., Elementary School. The Green Road project was a "scatter" project—a federally funded housing program for low-income families, usually from minority races and cultures, established in middle- and upper-middle-class neighborhoods to give economic and racial balance. About eighty per cent of the students at the school were White; about thirteen per cent were Black; the remaining seven per cent were Asian or Hispanic. Three of the twenty faculty members were Black.

The attorneys based their suit upon Section 1706 of Title 20 of the U.S. Code, which permitted individuals to bring civil suit against school districts and other agencies which denied "equal educational opportunity."

Five of the six complaints against the district were dismissed, but the sixth—that the district discriminated against speakers of Black English by not providing them with special programs to assist them to learn Standard English—went to trial in June 1979 after several delays and preliminary motions.

The basic issues, as outlined by District Judge Charles W. Joiner, were "whether the children have a language barrier . . . whether, if they have a language barrier, that barrier impedes their participation in the instructional program offered by the defendant . . . whether, if the defendant Board has not taken 'appropriate action' this failure denies equal educational opportunity to plaintiffs 'on account of race.' "[67] The school board, represented by John H. Weaver and John Dudley, tried to prove that although the students may have spoken a language or dialect other than Standard English, that it was not a barrier to effective learning, and that if the students encountered any difficulties in class, they were caused by social, cultural, or economic factors, and not the direct responsibility of the school district.

The plaintiffs, represented by Gabe Kaimowitz and Ken Lewis, responded by arguing that Black English was a system of formalized language rules, that the dialect or language impeded educational progress, and that the teachers failed to take that dialect/language into account when teaching the essentials of reading. Expert witnesses called were Richard W. Bailey, J. L. Dillard, David F. Fader, Kenneth Haskins, William Labov, Gary Simpkins, and Geneva Smitherman, all of whom testified that Black English was a language system different from Standard English.

On July 12, 1979, Judge Joiner ruled:

The language of "black English" has been shown to be a distinct, definable version of English, different from standard English of the school and the general world of communications. It has definable language patterns, syntax, grammar and history.

In some communities and among some people in this country, it is the customary mode of oral, informal communication.

A significant number of blacks in the United States use or have used some version of "black English" in oral communications. Many of them incorporate one or more aspects of "black English" in their more formal talk.

"Black English" is not a language used by the mainstream of society—black or white. It is not an acceptable method of communication in the educational world, in the commercial community, in the community of arts and sciences, or among professionals. It is largely a system that is used in casual and informal communication among the poor and lesser educated.

The instruction in standard English of children who use "black English" at home by insensitive teachers who treat the children's language system as inferior can cause a barrier to learning to read and use standard English. The language is not as discriminating in its use of sounds as is standard English and much of its grammar is simpler. There are fewer reading models in the life of a child who uses "black English."[68]

Referring to pedagogical issues, the Judge continued:

The research evidence supports the theory that the linguistics of reading can be hurt by teachers who reject students because of the "mistakes" or "errors" made in oral speech by "black English" speaking children, who are learning standard English. This comes about because "black English" is commonly thought of as an inferior method of speech and those who use this system may be thought of as "dumb" or "inferior."[69]

Looking at the overall actions of the teachers and the school system, Judge Joiner had only praise: "There is no evidence in this case that any instructional program has been withheld from any plaintiff on account of his or her race . . ."[70] [the teachers] act in a responsible and rational manner to try to help the children[71] . . . and there is no evidence that any of the teachers have in any way intentionally caused psychological barriers to learning."[72] But, he also pointed out:

The evidence suggests clearly that no matter how well-intentioned the teachers are, they are not likely to be successful in overcoming the language barrier caused by their failure to take into account the home language system unless they are helped . . . to recognize the existence of the language system used by the children in their home community and to use that knowledge as a way of helping the children to learn to read standard English.[73]

The judge then ordered the school board to present an acceptable program to acquaint all teachers with the principles of Black English and with concepts of teaching that take into account a student's home language. To implement the judge's ruling, the Ann Arbor school district established a comprehensive twenty-hour instructional program. The first three sessions were conducted in October, November, and December 1979, by Thomas Pietras, the district's language arts coordinator; two more sessions were conducted in January 1980, by Roger Shuy and William S. Hall. It was estimated that the cost to initially implement the judge's decision was about $42,000. The cost of the trial, paid for through tax monies, was estimated at more than $210,000.

Had it not been for the nation's newspapers and magazines, the ruling and impact would have been significantly diminished. The mass media, because of a traditional "hard news" orientation, are especially cognizant of issues that become "official"—that are entered into public record; the courts, police, and governmental agencies provide sources for much of the news that fills their pages. When suit was filed in U.S. District Court, it sparked the media's interest. During the latter half of the 1970s, very few articles about Black English appeared in the media; the civil rights era was almost over, and the media were looking into other popular issues. But a *court case*—well, that was different.[74]

The first articles about the case appeared in the *Ann Arbor News* shortly after the suit was filed. During the next three years, Katherine Hulik and Katherine Green would each write more than twenty articles about the case and the trial; the *News* would publish more than sixty articles and features, run more than thirty letters to the editor, and present six editorials. Many of the articles written by Hulik and Green would be placed on the wires of the Associated Press; and both the AP and United Press International would have their own reporters cover the trial. Both the *Detroit News* and the *Detroit Free Press*—most of the *Free Press* articles were written by Donna Britt—published more than fifty articles between them. Soon, articles began appearing in the nation's leading newspapers and magazines. *The New York Times* and *The Washington Post* each published four articles, and articles appeared in the *Gary* (Ind.) *Post-Tribune, Cleveland Plain-Dealer, Kansas City Star, Chicago Tribune, Saturday Review, Time,* and *U.S. News and World Report.* Metropolitan and suburban newspapers soon began running one or two, sometimes even three, articles about the trial, most of them sent out by one of the two major wire services. Some newspapers even localized the stories or developed their own editorials based upon information presented by the wire services. Three of the better articles about the case were written by Jerry Colburn, a doctoral student in comparative literature at the University of California, and published in the *New Orleans Times-Picayune* between April and July 1979. The first article was based on an interview with J. L. Dillard; the other two articles focused upon the nature of the issues that were brought to trial. Nationally syndicated columnists quickly picked up the pace. Soon, columns by Roy Wilkins, Carl Rowan, and William Raspberry appeared in the nation's media. And for the July 29, 1979, issue of *The New York Times,* James Baldwin asked, "If Black English isn't a language, then tell me what is?" A month earlier, the *Times,* following editorial arguments presented by other newspapers, editorialized that Black English be recognized as a dialect, and that teachers should be made more aware of the nature of Black English, that teachers should make "special efforts" to teach the "needy" children.[75]

But there was significant opposition to the judicial opinion as numerous magazines and newspapers published articles, editorials, and letters opposed to acknowledging Black English as its own language system, not inferior or substandard to any other language system.

The strongest academic opposition to the ruling came from Benjamin H. Alexander, a Black and president of Chicago State University. In September 1979, Alexander, addressing the Fellows of the American Council on Education, argued that Judge Joiner's decision, "which calls for implicit recognition of Black English, is nothing more than blatant plantation mentality. I cannot support it. This ruling is criminal, a travesty of justice, because it implies that Blacks are still on the plantation—despite the passage of over 100 years—that Blacks are basically inferior and must be treated differently." Because the decision did not establish precedent, many of the nation's school districts chose to ignore the problem, calling the solution proposed by the decision "unworkable"; and large numbers of teachers still consider Black English to be substandard.

The decision gave a legal status to Black English, but also created more controversy. The court had ruled that Black English, a language system, was not a language but a dialect of English; it ruled that Black English probably had a creole base; that Black English, although not "inferior" or "substandard," was not acceptable in American society, especially in the educational area; that Black English speakers have a linguistic barrier to learning to read Standard English; that Black English was spoken primarily by lower-income Blacks. At the same time that the court pointed out the legitimacy of the nature of Black English, it also created a stronger foundation for eradicationist arguments.

THE PRESENT AND THE FUTURE

The study of American Black English remains as controversial as ever. Although attempts to wipe out Black English have failed, attempts to give Black English a universal acceptance have also failed. The eradicationists and the bidialectals after more than three decades of challenge and counterchallenge, much of it fought with invective, are still at a stand-off. The deficit theorists, seeking to "correct" Black English through the rote memorization of "proper" speech, have been unable to convince the dialect geographers and creolists that Black English represents a cognitive deficiency; the dialect geographers and creolists have been unable to convince the deficit theorists of the linguistic legitimacy of the dialect. Dialect geographers can't convince the creolists that Black English, being similar to certain Southern dialects, should not be considered a separate language; the creolists, noting the historical similarities between American Black English and pidgins and creoles in other parts of the world, have been unable to convince some dialect geographers that Black English is a consistent linguistic system with a marked creole substratum with roots in West Africa rather than in the American South. And the proponents of the Ebonics theory have outlined what they believe to be a valid explanation for the origin and genesis of American Black English (identified as Ebonics), an explanation that rejects arguments for a creole substrata, and focuses upon the distinct possibility that Ebonics is a linguistic continuum of Hamito-Semitic and Bantu language families.

So the research continues, often webbed by opinion and emotion, with adherents of each group hoping to find that one piece of evidence to prove its case, that one bit of data that could substantiate a theory. During the latter part of the 1970s, as scholars began finding and selecting evidence to test their theories, new ideas emerged from a small but growing number of researchers who carefully examined historical and descriptive data, and combined it with the results of better field methodologies and recording techniques to present a unified theory of American Black English; a theory growing out of existing theories, but separated from them by a newer synthesis of data, a complex theory to explain a complex phenomenon. It thus seeks to mold a new concept about language, one which combines the separate theories into one theory divided by time—reflective of educational, social, economic, and political pressures—into various stages. The unified theory, developed by Walter M. Brasch, argues that there is no "absolute truth" in language, for reality is determined only by *perceptions* of reality; time, its own fourth dimension which controls and determines all other dimensions, changes both reality and perceptions of reality. The theory also argues that all historical development manifests uniform cycles, each cycle representing various genres and conditions. The unified theory argues that it is important and necessary to understand the historical development and perceptions of Black English, for only in this way can the present be understood.

As the nation passed its Bicentennial and approached the 1980s, signs of declining interest in Black English became apparent. The civil rights unrest of the 1960s had spawned massive socioeconomic programs which were usually advocated, then studied, by the nation's social and behavioral scientists. In academic circles, spurred by financial aid and publication credits, it became fashionable, even "trendy," to study Black poverty and to cast opinions about Black language. But soon the grants ran out and academic journals reached their saturation point with articles about Black English. The researchers looked elsewhere, their interest in Black English waning as financial aid and publication opportunities diminished, or because they had done what they intended to do, what they *could* do, in the study of Black English, and were pressed to meet new challenges in new areas. Even the Center for Applied Linguistics, which had provided a base for research into Black English, now turned its resources and focus onto other areas. The Civil Rights Cycle of American Black English, a cycle in which the linguistics and sociopolitical studies into Black English paralleled civil unrest in the nation, began to fade as the nation entered the decade of the 1980s—a different nation with different concerns. By the end of the decade, the cycle will have been brought to its conclusion. Time, relative to all dimension, has brought the study of American Black English to five separate and distinct peaks; time will bring it to its fifth conclusion. More important, time will create a newer dominant genre and the sixth cycle of American Black English.

Appendix

General Language Observations

These "observations" are based upon analysis of the printed literature, and are not meant to be universal rules of Black English. Nor should it be assumed that American Black English speech is consistent with, or correlates highly to written language in all instances.[1] In addition, these observations reflect "translation" from Standard English to American Black English, and not American Black English on its own. Thus, for example, when we speak of a consonant cluster reduction (for example, "desk," a CVCC formation becomes in American Black English "des'," a CVC formation), we refer only to differences between the Standard and the American Black English, as seen in translation. Obviously, native speakers of American Black English, as well as all Bantu languages and Black English creoles, do not consider that their languages reflect a "reduction," "absence," or "loss," of anything, and might even assume that it is Standard American English that adds consonants to the language.

GRAMMAR

1. *Deep Structure (zero) Copula.* American Black English does not signal a copula in surface structure; the copula, however, is present in deep structure. A typical deep structure copula sentence might be, "He hoein'," meaning "He is hoeing at this very moment." When used in the mass media, the absence of the copula (known as zero copula) is often meant, whether subconsciously or not, to indicate a verbal inferiority or substandard English. In reality, it means no such thing. Some of the problems in understanding the deep structure copula are due to a lack

of a broader linguistic knowledge in such areas as stress, pitch, the suprasegmental length, vocal qualifiers, and numerous nonverbal paralinguistic features. These features, which are nearly impossible to record accurately, can often indicate the presence of a copula in surface structure. Thus, what is believed to be the absence of a copula, based on apparent graphemic evidence, may in fact be a copula which exists in the spoken, but not the written language. Often, in the mass media, a surface structure copula is inserted by a writer whose language system dictates the presence of a copula, even if no such copula exists in the speech of the informant.

2. *Deep Structure (zero) Possessive.* All languages have a possessive case. The deep structure possessive, like the deep structure copula, is not present in the written surface structure of American Black English, but does have an African-language deep structure. Thus, the American Black English speaker might say, "It be Jack hoe," or "It be you hoe." The meaning is conveyed by the speaker and understood by the Black English-speaking listener and, thus, does not in any way represent a cognitive deficiency or lack of "proper" grammar.

3. *Invariant "Be."* The verb "to be" has caused some confusion to the Standard English speaker and to persons attempting to describe American Black English. The *am, is,* and *are* reflexes of the "to be" conjugation are not realized in Black English, just as they are not realized in West African Pidgin English, in that each has its own syntactic structure. What is realized is the verb *be.* Some linguists call this the invariant *be.* Thus, the Standard English speaker would conjugate the verb "to be" in the present tense as "I am," "you are," "he is," "we are," "you are," and "they are." The American Black English speaker says, "I be," "you be," "He be," "we be," "you (all) be," and "they be." However, the exact meaning of *be* is not a literal gloss of the words *am, are,* or *is.* "He be good" does not translate as "He is good." In Black English, the sentence, "He be wo'kin' " (invariant *be*) has a different meaning than "he wo'kin' " (deep structure copula). "He wo'kin' " indicates that, at this present moment, that person is working. The sentence, "He be wo'kin' " means that the person has a job and that this job continues over a longer period of time, but it does not mean that the person is working at this very moment. The presence of the invariant *be* in the mass media may or may not reflect the fact that the writer does not know the reason for its presence; usually, the writer doesn't understand the rule.

4. *Absence of English Verb Inflections and the Substitution of Verbal Functors in Pre-Verb Position.* Unless a situational context is avail-

able, it is difficult to gloss or translate, without lengthy discourse, American Black English functor forms *done* and *been* in pre-verb position. The mass media, throughout the various cycles, have given us numerous examples of these functor forms in pre-verb position, as in the examples, "He done go fo' fahm," "He been go fo' fahm," "He done been go fo' fahm," and "He been done go fo' fahm." Each sentence has a different meaning that can not be translated literally into Standard English. It is doubtful that the mass media writers, themselves, were aware of the finer distinctions, and they may have been writing sentences of which they did not know the true meaning.

5. *Pronominal Cross-Reference Marker.* The American student who dares to say, "My bruddah he no go fo' wo'k" ("My brother is not going to work") is admonished for speaking "bad" English. Here, the use of the pronominal cross-reference marker, which has its roots in many West African languages, is acceptable and logical American Black English. The word *he* does not belong to the noun phrase, as believed by English "purists," but is part of the verb phrase. The pronominal cross-reference marker, surprisingly, is also common in Middle and Elizabethan English, as in the Biblical passage, "Thy rod and thy staff, they comfort me." The word *they* is the cross-reference marker. However, we cannot simply say that in this case Middle English influenced West African languages which in turn influenced American Black English. What undoubtedly happened was a mutual, though separate, development in both Middle English and West African Pidgin English (based upon a number of West African languages).

6. *The Nominative Pronoun.* It is not too uncommon in the mass media to find such phrases as "wid he hoe" (literally, "with his hoe") and "it be good fo' we" (literally, "it is good for us"). The use of the nominative case in such instances does not reflect substandard English or a lack of cognitive abilities, since meaning is understood and conveyed.

7. *Existential "It."* The existential *it,* in the American mass media, as it does in West African Pidgin English (*dey*), serves a major function, as exemplified in the sentence, "It a boy name Jack" (literally, "There is a boy named Jack"). Although the surface structure might suggest that the word *it* replaces the words "there is," the deep structure implies a far greater meaning which may only be approximated by the sentence, "There is, right now in this place at this very moment in time, a boy. That boy is named Jack. Jack is the boy." Less frequently, the existential *it* serves as a replacement of the word *there* in surface structure, as in the question, "Is it two cow in yo' ba'n?" ("Are there two

cows in your barn?"). Nevertheless, the existential *it* is noted infrequently in the mass media.

8. *Number Inflection.* The dropping of the inflectional plural suffix is a feature of Black English, as in the examples, "He fifteen year old" and, "He hab two dog." Because the number, itself (*fifteen, two*), carries the plural, to say, "He is fifteen years old," or "He has two dogs" would be redundant. In Standard English, the rule applies to collective plurals, such as "I shot two moose" or "I caught two fish." Black English speakers many times make *mooses* the plural of *moose, fishes* the plural of *fish.* It is also not uncommon to find the words *childrens, foots,* or *womens* in the lexicon of American Black English, this being the result of hypercorrection. Number inflection in Black English is also closely related to consonant cluster reduction. Orthographically, words ending in *-s, -p, -t,* or *-k* as part of consonant clusters in Standard English will be dropped and *-es* added. *Desk* in Standard English becomes *des'* in Black English; the plural becomes *desses. Test* becomes *tes';* the plural then, by regular rules, becomes *tesses.*

9. *Undifferentiated Third-Person Pronouns* ["he," "she"]. It is quite common in the mass media to find such sentences as, "Dat woman he no good" (literally, "That woman is not good"). In West African Pidgin English, the third-person marker becomes a third-person substitute marker as well as a cross-reference marker. Neither distinguishes sex identity, just as in Standard English the plural markers in surface structure do not differentiate sex identity. Black English and Pidgin English use the pronoun factor form /i/ (pronounced as the vowel in *beet*), as in the sentence, "Dat woman i no good." Standard English speakers, as others, tend to transfer and substitute linguistic forms and sounds, as perceived within their own language system. The Black English speaker may have said *i,* but the Standard English speaker heard the word *he,* because in Standard English the word *i* would be ungrammatical. Thus, in the mass media, the undifferentiated word *i* is transferred to the differentiated word *he* because of similarity of sound. Occasionally, an adept writer will record *e* in the speech of his Blacks.

10. *Absence of the Third-Person Singular Present Tense Marker* [-*s*]. American Black English, following its own grammar structure, does not possess the third-person singular present tense marker [-*s*], as present in Standard English. Thus, "he walk," not "he walks" is acceptable Black English grammar. "He walk," a feature also present in West African Pidgin English, does not represent substandard language or cognitive deficiency.

11. *Absence of the Indefinite Articles.* In contemporary studies, the

articles *a* and *an* seldom appear in the speech of young Blacks or those who have not had a Standard English education. They do appear, especially the *a,* in the speech of Blacks who have come in contact with Standard English. Indefinite articles are not present in the surface structure of West African Pidgin English, nor in many languages. In the mass media, a diachronic study shows that indefinite articles are occasionally present in the speech of Blacks. The appearance of these indefinite articles are often attempts by the author, whether subconscious or not, to Anglicize the written language; the writer adds an *a* or *an,* either because he believes he heard these words in the speech of the Black or because he believes that they should be there. Either way, the appearance of *a* or *an,* especially *an* in texts, is often the result of a writer superimposing his own language system upon another.

12. *Negation.* Perhaps the myth most difficult to destroy is the belief, certainly among many teachers, that double-negative construction is "bad" English. Equally offensive is the purists' inexcusable attempts at logic by stating that two negatives really make a positive. Thus, they attempt to explain to the Black child that the sentence "I ain't got no dog" really means that the child really does have a dog. Multiple negation, not only in American Black English grammar, but also in a number of West African languages, often implies emphasis. And woe to the child who dares to tell his teacher, "Ah ain gonna gib nuffin to nobody *neba!*" Interestingly, Standard English also has double negation, as in the sentence, "It is not impossible," but language purists tend to overlook the fact that *not* and *im-* are negatives, believing that "It is not impossible" and "It is possible" have two different semantic meanings. The same is true in American Black English; multiple negation serves to emphasize a change in meaning.

13. *Semantic Inversion.* A Black "dude" who is considered to be "bad" (more specifically, "baad") by those "on the street," has a lot to be proud of. However, "bad/baad" has neither the connotations given to it by Whites—urban or otherwise—nor the opposite of the White word "good." A true semantic inversion would equate "bad/baad" in Black English with "good" in Standard English. In most instances, semantic inversion refers to a lexical item that does not have the same meaning in Black English as it does in Standard English, and although closer to the opposite meaning, is not quite completely opposite, and may, in fact, be on different levels.

PHONOLOGY

14. *Substitution of the Alveolar Stops* ([*d*] *and* [*t*]) *for the Interdental Fricatives* [ð] *and* [θ]). In American English, the digraph *th* has two pronunciations. The *th* in such words as *the, them,* and *that* is phonetically represented by a [ð]. The *th* sound in *cloth, think,* and *fifth* is represented by a [θ]. One of the characteristic features of Black speech in the mass media is the replacement in word-initial position of [ð], the voiced *th* sound, by a [d], as in the words *de* ("the"), *dem* ("them"), and *dat* ("that"). The voiceless *th* sound [θ] is replaced by a [t], as in the word *clot'* ("cloth"), *tink* ("think"), and *t'ank* ("thank"). Many languages of the world, including the West African languages, do not have interdental *th* sounds. It is logical for a speaker of a language that does not include the interdental sounds in its inventory to substitute [d], [t], [z], or [s]. This does not mean that West African languages or American Black English are deficient in phonology, for each language has a common core of sounds unique to its own system. English utilizes sounds that African languages do not utilize; African languages have sounds that English does not have. Neither language is deficient. This phonological feature is not confined to the Black languages, however, since some contemporary New Yorkers substitute /d/ for /ð/; and Germans, when learning English, substitute /t/ or /s/ for /θ/.

15. *Substitution of the Labiodental Fricatives* (*v* and *f*) *for Interdental Fricatives* ([ð] and [θ]). This rule occurs in word-medial or word-final position. A common example in the mass media is *nuffin* for "nothing." "Both" becomes *bofe,* "mouth" becomes *mouf,* and "with," which is often written *wid,* can also become *wif,* depending upon phonological context, notably progressive and regressive assimilation.

16. *Substitution of the Voiced Bilabial Stop* ([*b*]) *for the Voiced Labiodental Fricative* ([*v*]). The use of the words *bery* or *berry* ("very"), *ebry* or *ebery* ("every"), *gib* ("give"), *hab* ("have"), *hebby* ("heavy"), and *neber* or *nebber* ("never") are major indicators of Black speech in the mass media. The same rule is present in West African Pidgin English.

17. *Consonant Cluster Reduction.* In Black English, as well as West African languages, there are no consonant clusters consisting of a fricative plus a stop in word-initial position. Thus, in Standard English words which have a fricative ([s]) plus a stop ([p or [t]), the fricative is usually dropped, as in the words *peke* or *peak* ("speak"), *poon* ("spoon"), and *tan* ("stand"). Consonant clusters in word-final position are rare in both Black English and West African languages. "Best," for example,

becomes *bes';* "desk" becomes *des';* "plant" becomes *plan'.* In informal English speech, it is common for the final consonant cluster to be simplified if the immediately succeeding word begins with a consonant; for example, "East Side" becomes "Eas' Side." But if the succeeding word begins with a vowel, the consonant cluster of the preceding word is not reduced; for example, it would be "cold applesauce" not "col' applesauce"; in Black English "col' applesauce" would often be elicited.

18. *Nasal Replacement.* The digraph of the bound form *-ing,* phonetically represented as one sound ([ŋ]), is a velar nasal. Standard English words which contain the velar nasal are replaced in Black English by the alveolar nasal ([n]). Orthographically, in the mass media *-ing* is replaced by *-in'.* Thus, "running" becomes *runnin',* "shouting" becomes *shoutin',* and "shooting" becomes *shootin'.* However, "singing" does not become *sin'in'* but, rather, *singin',* because medial nasalization is not affected if it would change the meaning of the word, or if it belongs to a stressed free form.

19. *Absence of the Postvocalic [r].* This feature is characteristic not only of West African languages and American Black English, but of several regional American dialects as well, and is a major indicator in the mass media of Black English. In word-initial position, the [r] is always pronounced in one-syllable words. In word-medial position, the [r] is dropped and the preceding vowel is lengthened, as in the examples *ba'n* or *bahn* ("barn"), *haht* ("heart"), and *sahtin* ("certain"). Occasionally, the vowel is replaced by a schwa [ə] as in *buhd* ("bird"). In word-final position, the [r] is replaced by the schwa [ə], and the preceding vowel is lengthened, as in the examples *dolla, dolluh,* or *dohllah* ("dollar"), *Massa* or *Maussa* ("master"), and *sistuh* ("sister"). Occasionally, the [r] is dropped and the final vowel undergoes change; for example, "sure" would be written as *sho',* and meant to be pronounced as *show.* The loss of the postvocalic [r] often eliminates a consonant cluster, as in *bahn* ("barn") and *fahm* ("farm").

20. *Absence of the Postvocalic [l].* This rule is more limited than that of the loss of the postvocalic [r]. It generally applies in word-final position and in final consonant clusters as in *steuh* ("steal"), *he'p* ("help"), and *se'f* ("self"). The postvocalic [l] is often lost in many Standard English words, such as *folk, talk,* and *walk.*

21. *Replacement of the Vowel Glide.* The vowel glide is a complex articulatory phenomenon which implies motion from one position to another. Black English substitutes a relatively steady vowel for the English diphthongs. These vowels replace the Standard English glides by clipping and, many times, lengthening the vowel. A simple description

of this rule is represented by the shift in pronunciation of the word *time* (pronounced *taim* in Standard English) to *tahm* (present in Black English as well as a number of regional varieties of American English). The attempt to distinguish this feature is often represented in the media by the use of *ah* (for example, *faht* for "fight") or by an apostrophe (for example, *fa't* for "fight").

22. *Devoicing of the [b], [d], and [g] to [p], [t], and [k].* The voiced sounds [b], [d] and [g] in word-final position are usually not present in the sound system of American Black English, and occur only rarely in literature. When these sounds do occur, they are usually devoiced. In American Black English, final voiced stops are voiceless, just as in West African Pidgin English. Thus, *tub* would be pronounced *tup, road* would be pronounced *roat,* and *pig* would be pronounced *pik;* each voiced stop of Standard English matched by a corresponding voiceless one (b→p, d→t, g→k). This rule is often overlooked in the mass media, and when words are spelled with voiceless stops in word-final position instead of the expected Standard English voiced equivalent, it may be assumed that the writer had a good ear for Black dialect.

23. *Elision or Loss of Unstressed Word-Initial Syllable.* The most common application of this rule is the loss of the unstressed schwa [ə] in word-initial position, as in *'bout* ("about"), *'gree* ("agree"), *'low* ("allow"), and *'pon* ("upon"). Frequently, more than the syllabic vowel drops. The unstressed word-initial syllables, themselves, may be lost, as in *'bacco* ("tobacco"), *'cept* ("accept" or "except," depending upon the semantic field), *'flec* ("reflect"), and *'member* ("remember").

24. *Elision of Syllables and Reconstruction.* A number of rules often work together in elision of syllables and reconstruction of words. It is doubtful that many, if any, of the dialect-writers of the mass media were even fully aware of the reasons for the elision. *Gemmen* is a reconstruction of the word "gentleman." At least three separate rules work on the word "gentleman," the rules acting to assimilate a Standard English compound word into a new word in line with rules of Black English. In the word "gentleman," the syllabic *l* is dropped; the *t* is dropped to avoid a consonant cluster; and a process known as internal sandhi dictates that the remaining word *geneman* become *gemman.*

25. *Consonant Inversion.* When present in the mass media, consonant inversion is often used for comical effect to mock the Black or attempt to show his verbal deficiency. Examples are *ax* ("ask") and *perten'* ("pretend"). However, these forms are common in Black English speech.

26. *Hypercorrection.* American Black English has its own rules of phonology and grammar. Standard English has its own rules. However, the Black English speaker in American society has been so pressured into believing that Standard English is what is "good and proper" that he often tends to overcorrect in attempts to speak Standard English, thus integrating two languages or codes into one. In the mass media, hypercorrection often is presented for comical effect in order to epitomize the "verbal incompetence" of the Black. Thus, the Black might say *fishes* or *childrens,* or, perhaps "Ah goes" and "We done went" in attempts to regularize the Standard English.

27. *Sweet Talk.* In every language there is an endless variety of lexical items that can be generated from the rules of that language. No language, however, can contain all possible words and combinations. In "sweet talk," a Pan-African language feature, new forms are often created to fit a particular setting or situation. The rhythm, harmony of sound or phonotactic balancing, and the adding of morphological endings to unlikely bases or roots are all part of the embellishment of the language. "Sweet talk" is often a completely misunderstood stylistic verbal feature by those not familiar with such phenomena. When the American Black English speaker tells his audience, at the start of a folktale, "Ah jus now go bring you jol'fication, hap'fication, an' mo'tification 'bout dese tale 'bout de 'gata an' de rabbit," a meaning is conveyed to the audience that could not be conveyed by the use of lexical, phonological, or syntactic items already in existence within the language. "Sweet talk" also serves to establish a verbal superiority; the master of language is a master of man. And for some strange reason, the "illiterate" African or American Black can often function more literately in the language system of the "literate" White than can the "literate" White who has learned that his language contains a finite limit of possibilities and that deviation is "bad" English. In the mass media, unfortunately, the use of "sweet talk" is limited, and when it is used, though with exceptions in the Uncle Remus stories, it is used for comical effect, meant to show the ignorance of the Black.

28. *Eye Dialect.* Changing the spelling of words, without changing the sound, in order to characterize a speaker is known as "eye dialect." For example, "was" is often spelled *wuz,* although both are pronounced the same. The use of eye dialect, a nonlinguistic use of language by the writer, is prevalent in the mass media.

Notes

INTRODUCTION

1. The outstanding linguistic analyses of West African Pidgin English were done by Dr. Gilbert D. Schneider who, with Charles Kraft, coined the language name Wes-Kos (pidgin for "West Coast") to agree with the name *Swahili,* the trade language of the East Coast of Africa (the name, in Arabic, means "East Coast"). Schneider's many analyses of West African Pidgin English serve as an important base for comparative analysis with American Black English, and are part of the data used to justify the creolist theory of American Black English. See Gilbert D. Schneider, *West African Pidgin-English* (Athens, Ohio: Center for International Studies, 1966).

2. John C. Merrill and Ralph L. Lowenstein, *Media, Messages, and Men: New Perspectives in Communication* (New York: David McKay Co., 1971), chap. 2.

3. The concept of the *mass* was first presented formally by sociologist-journalist Robert E. Park in 1904, then revised by Herbert Blumer in 1946. The definition presented here is based upon the studies of Park and Blumer, but differs slightly in that it assumes that there are loose individual ties between members, the ties being, perhaps, no more than the fact that both exist within the same basic culture, and are bound by certain historical and cultural patterns; that members may, in fact, know each other, but that it is on the basis of numerous small, individual groups, rather than a collective whole; and that leadership may exist, but that it is an informal leadership created by the mass and developed from it.

4. There is no *one* Black English; rather, it is a generic term encompassing many dialects—everything from the English spoken by Blacks in Jamaica to the English spoken by Blacks in Harlem. In this book, American Black English and Black English are used interchangeably except where there might be confusion, in which case *American Black English* refers to region; *Black English* is the generic term.

5. Roger D. Abrahams, *Talking Black* (Rowley, Mass.: Newbury House Publishers, 1977), p. 13.
6. William Smith, *A New Voyage to Guinea* (London: J. Nourse, 1744), p. 28.
7. A pidgin language is a second language spoken primarily for trade among persons of many different ethnic and linguistic backgrounds. When a pidgin language becomes the first language of a group of people, it is said to have been creolized and is referred to as a creole.
8. Raven I. McDavid, Jr., addendum to his "Relationship of the Speech of American Negroes to the Speech of Whites"; and Virginia Glenn McDavid, in *Black-White Speech Relationships,* ed. Walt Wolfram and Nona H. Clarke (Washington, D.C.: Center for Applied Linguistics, 1971), pp. 38–39.
9. Mervyn Alleyne, "Linguistic Continuity in the Caribbean," in *Topics in Afro-American Studies,* ed. Henry J. Richards (New York: Black Academy Press, 1971), p. 126.
10. Ernie A. Smith, *The Historical Development of Ebonics,* Seminar Paper Series, no. 38 (Department of Linguistics, California State University at Fullerton, 1977), p. 6.
11. Smith, *op. cit.,* pp. 6–7. Other major position papers by Smith outlining the nature of Ebonics are *A Case for Bilingual and Bicultural Education for United States Slave Descendants of African Origin* (1977); *A Diagnostic Instrument for Assessing the Phonological Competence and Performance of the Inner City Afro-American Child* (1978); *Ebonics and Mental Retardation* (1978); and *The Retention of the Phonological, Phonemic, and Morphophonemic Features of Africa in Afro-American Ebonics.*

CHAPTER I. THE COLONIAL-REVOLUTIONARY CYCLE

1. See Gilbert D. Schneider, *West African Pidgin-English: An Historical Overview* (Athens, Ohio: Center for International Studies, 1966), pp. 9–11. Although there is evidence that the term "Black English" was used during the Colonial-Revolutionary Cycle to describe the language of a large number of Blacks, other terms, such as "Colored English," "Negro English," and "broken English" were also used.
2. Samuel G. Drake, *The Witchcraft Delusion in New England, exhibited by Dr. Cotton Mather in the "Wonders of the Invisible World" and by Mr. Robert Calef in his "More Wonders of the Invisible World"* (Roxbury, Mass.: W. Elliot Woodward, 1866), pp. 290, 271.
3. The first major crusade in journalism history occurred when James Franklin, publisher of *The New-England Courant,* and an opponent of smallpox inoculation, attacked Cotton Mather, who supported the inoculation program. Evidence indicates that Mather's support of smallpox inoculation was based upon his knowledge of the procedure told to him by slaves in the colonies who knew about it from West Africa.
4. Cotton Mather, *Angel of Bethesda,* unpublished medical treatise, American Antiquarian Society archives.
5. There are two major linguistic rules that suggest "by 'nd by" was really *baimbai*. First, because consonant clusters in word-final position are rare in most West African languages, the voiced alveolar stop [d] would have been

deleted in the word *'nd*, leaving only the alveolar nasal [n]. It is possible that, because of his own linguistic sound system, Mather perceived a [d] to exist, in that an *-nd* cluster is common in standard English. Second, the process of regressive assimilation occurs. The alveolar nasal [n], identified as being at a specific point of articulation, would have to remain a nasal sound. The bilabial [b] of the immediately succeeding sound (the second "by") would determine that the preceding point of articulation would also be a bilabial. Thus it would appear that a bilabial nasal [m] would occur in such environments. This, in fact, is exactly what happens. "By 'nd by" was, thus, originally *baimbai*.

6. Blacks, operating within their own world views and with deep-structure rules already firmly embedded, may also "incorrectly" perceive Standard English words and phrases, adapting the Standard English to Black English rules. Also, it is possible that Standard English speakers may be able to record accurately varieties of Black English without understanding the semantic importance.

7. G. L. Campbell, "Itinerant Observations in America," *London Magazine,* Vol. 15 (July 1746), p. 330.

8. J. F. D. Smyth, *A Tour in the United States of America,* Vol. 1 (Dublin: Price, Moncrieffe, 1784), pp. 78–79; *Ibid.,* p. 38.

9. Smyth, *op. cit.,* Vol. 1, p. 121.

10. Rev. Hugh Jones, *The Present State of Virginia* (London, 1724), p. 75.

11. John Leland, *The Virginia Chronicle* (Fredericksburg, Va.: T. Green, 1790), p. 13.

12. Benjamin Franklin, "Information to Those Who Would Remove to America," in *Some Information Respecting America,* ed. Thomas Cooper, 2d ed., (London: J. Johnson, 1795), pp. 230–31.

13. The pioneering efforts to identify newspaper advertising which included references to slave speech were made by Allen Walker Read. See Read's articles, "Eighteenth-Century Slaves as Advertised by their Masters," *Journal of Negro History,* Vol. 1, no. 2 (April 1916), pp. 163–216; and "The Speech of Negroes in Colonial America," *Journal of Negro History,* Vol. 24, no. 3 (July 1939), pp. 247–58.

14. Richard Walser, "Negro Dialect in Eighteenth Century Drama," *American Speech,* Vol. 30, no. 4 (December 1955), p. 169.

15. Announcement, *Pennsylvania Gazette,* April 16, 1767, p. 3.

16. Walser, *op. cit.,* p. 270.

17. [Andrew Barton, pseud.] *The Disappointment; Or, The Force of Credulity* (New York: William Goddard, 1767), p. 53.

18. Inconsistency itself does not necessarily negate the quality of transcription or reproduction of the spoken language. Bilingual speakers often change languages within one sentence, and occasionally apply the rules of one language to another. Linguists refer to this as "diglossia." However, in the representation of Black English in the mass media, inconsistencies in the written language usually reflect inaccurate transcription or recording rather than diglossia.

19. If the word *alewments* is written to be pronounced *aloohments,* then it would be Sweet Talk. If, however, it was written to be pronounced *aluhments,* then

it would be a reflective of the rule describing the omission of a postvocalic [r]. Taken in context of the complete phrase, however, it would appear that it was meant to be Sweet Talk.

20. Robert Munford, "The Candidates; Or, the Humoris of a Virginia Election" in *A Collection of Plays and Poems by the late Col. Robert Munford* (Petersburg, Va.: William Prentiss, 1798), pp. 13, 16.

21. *The Trial of Atticus Before Justice Beau, For a Rape* (Boston: Isaiah Thomas, 1771), p. 22.

22. John Leacock, *The Fall of British Tyranny; Or, American Liberty Triumphant* (Philadelphia: John Gill and Powers and Willis, 1776), pp. 46–47.

23. [Samuel Low], *The Politician Out-Witted* (New York: W. Ross, 1789), p. 55.

24. *Occurrences of the Times; Or, A Transaction of Four Days* (Boston: n.p., 1789), p. 7.

25. *Occurrences of the Times, op. cit.,* p. 12.

26. J. Robinson, *The Yorker's Strategem; Or, Banana's Wedding* (New York: T. & J. Swords, 1792), pp. 9, 17.

27. John Murdock, *The Triumph of Love; Or, Happy Reconciliation* (Philadelphia: R. Folwell, 1795), pp. 51–52.

28. Murdock, *op. cit.,* p. 53.

29. Arthur Hobson Quinn, *A History of the American Drama; From the Beginning to the Civil War* (New York: Harper & Bros., 1923), pp. 125–26.

30. [John Murdock], *The Politicians; Or, A State of Things* (Philadelphia: n.p., 1798), p. 1.

31. [Murdock], *The Politicians, op. cit.,* pp. 19–20.

32. [Murdock], *The Politicians, op. cit.,* pp. 30–31.

33. H. H. Brackenridge, *Modern Chivalry; Containing the Adventures of Captain John Farrago, and Teague Oregon, His Servant,* pt. 1 (Philadelphia: John M'Culloch, 1792), p. 291.

34. Walser, *op. cit.,* p. 47.

35. Modern West African Pidgin English, however, contains no Dutch substratum.

36. Tabitha Tenney, *Female Quixoticism; Exhibited in the Romantic Opinions and Extravagent Adventures of Dorcasina Sheldon,* Vol. 2 (Boston: I. Thomas and E. T. Andrews, 1801), p. 81.

37. Tenney, *op. cit.,* Vol. 2, p. 109.

38. Untitled speech of W. B. Hodgson, presented at a meeting of the Ethnological Society of New York, October 13, 1857; published by the society, p. 5.

CHAPTER 2. THE ANTEBELLUM CYCLE

1. Charles William Janson, *Stranger in America* (London: J. Cundee, 1807), p. 380.

2. J. L. Beach, *Jonathan Postfree; Or, The Honest Yankee* (New York: David Longworth, 1807), p. 1.

3. Henry Bolingbroke, *A Voyage to Demarary* (London: R. Phillips, 1807), p. 341.

4. Tremaine McDowell, "The Negro in the Southern Novel to 1850," *Journal of English and Germanic Philology,* Vol. 25 (October 1926), p. 457.

5. Samuel Clemens, however, disagreed. Writing in the prestigious *North American Review,* Clemens classified "nineteen rules governing literary art in the domain of romantic fiction," then systematically argued that, in *The Deerslayer,* Cooper violated eighteen of the rules. He further noted that "Cooper's word-sense was singularly dull. When a person has a poor ear for music he will flat and sharp right along without knowing it. He keeps near the tune. When a person has a poor ear for words, the result is a literary flatting and sharping; you perceive what he is intending to say, but you also perceive that he doesn't *say* it. This is Cooper. He was not a word-musician. His ear was satisfied with the approximate word."

6. James Fenimore Cooper, *Satanstoe; Or, The Littlepage Manuscripts* (New York: Burgess & Stringer, 1846), p. 158.

7. James Fenimore Cooper, *Redskins; Or, Indians and Injins* (New York: Burgess & Stringer, 1846), p. 148.

8. Anne Newport Royall, *The Tennessean,* privately printed (New Haven, 1827), p. 127.

9. Edward William Sidney, *The Partisan Leader; A Tale of the Future,* Vol. 2 (Washington, D.C.: J. Caxton [D. Green], 1856 [1836]), p. 22.

10. Sidney, *op. cit.,* p. 100.

11. William Alexander Caruthers, *The Knights of the Horse-Shoe* (Wetumpka, Ala.: Charles Yancey, 1845), pp. 61, 62, 82.

12. Herman Melville, *Moby-Dick; Or, The Whale* (New York: Harper & Bros., 1851), p. 118.

13. Melville, *op. cit.,* p. 328.

14. *Ibid.*

15. Melville, *op. cit.,* p. 330.

16. Edgar Allan Poe, "The Gold-Bug," *Philadelphia Dollar Newspaper,* June 21, 1843, p. 1.

17. Poe, *op. cit.,* June 21, 1843, p. 1.

18. Poe, *op. cit.,* June 28, 1843, p. 1.

19. *Ibid.*

20. J. Allen Morris, "The Stories of William Gilmore Simms," *American Literature,* Vol. 14 (March 1942), pp. 35, 30.

21. Raven I. McDavid, Jr., "The Dialects of American English," in *The Structure of American English,* ed. W. Nelson Francis (New York: Ronald Press, 1958), p. 542.

22. William Gilmore Simms, "The Lazy Crow," in *The Wigwam and the Cabin* (New York: Wiley and Putnam, 1882), p. 346.

23. *Ibid.*

24. Simms, "The Lazy Crow," *op. cit.,* p. 347.

25. In plantation economy and sociology, a driver is a Black in charge of a group of other Black slaves. Although a slave himself, the driver functions in the hierarchy between the Black slave and the White overseer who, in turn, reports to the owner.

26. William Gilmore Simms, "The Loves of the Driver," *The Magnolia,* Vol. 3 (July 1841), p. 318.

27. Simms, "The Loves of the Driver," *op. cit.* (May 1841), p. 227.

28. Excellent field work has been done by Roger D. Abrahams of American

306 Black English and the Mass Media

Black Sounding in the mid-twentieth century. See especially *Deep Down in the Jungle* (1964), *Positively Black* (1970), and *Talking Black* (1977).

29. William Gilmore Simms, *Guy Rivers; A Tale of Georgia* (New York: J. W. Lovell, 1885), p. 494.

30. William Gilmore Simms, *The Yemassee* (New York: Harper & Bros., 1835), p. 392.

31. William Gilmore Simms, *The Partisan; A Romance of the Revolution* (New York: J. W. Lovell, 1885), pp. 349, 427.

32. William Gilmore Simms, *The Sword and the Distaff* (New York: Lippincott, Grambo, 1853), p. 70.

33. Simms, *The Sword and the Distaff, op. cit.,* pp. 75, 196, 353, 450, 365.

34. William Gilmore Simms, *Eutaw* (New York: J. S. Redfield, 1856), pp. 108, 307, 379.

35. Elizabeth McClellan Fleming, *William Gilmore Simms's Portrayal of the Negro,* Master's thesis, Duke University, 1965, p. 77.

36. Caroline Howard Gilmore, *Recollections of a Southern Matron* (New York: Harper & Bros., 1828), p. 40.

37. Gilmore, *op. cit.,* pp. 15, 48, 80, 94, 95, 105.

38. Gilmore, *op. cit.,* pp. 18, 33.

39. Joseph Holt Ingraham, *The Southwest by a Yankee,* Vol. 2 (New York: Harper & Bros., 1835), pp. 17–18.

40. Ingraham, *op. cit.,* Vol. 2, p. 56.

41. Ingraham, *op. cit.,* Vol. 2, p. 248.

42. John Holt Ingraham, *Lafitte, the Pirate of the Gulf,* 2d ed. (New York: Pollard and Mass, 1889), p. 110.

43. Frances Anne Kemble, *The Journal of a Residence on a Georgian Plantation* (New York: Harper & Bros., 1863), pp. 210–11.

44. Kemble, *op. cit.,* pp. 238–39.

45. An excellent account of this class dichotomy by language is presented in George Bernard Shaw's *Pygmalion,* later developed into the musical *My Fair Lady,* by Alan Jay Lerner and Frederick Loewe.

46. Charles Lyell, *A Second Visit to the United States of America,* Vol. 2 (London: J. Murray, 1849), p. 80.

47. Lyell, *op. cit.,* Vol. 2, p. 15.

48. Lyell, *op. cit.,* Vol. 1, p. 263.

49. Africans, as well as many tribes of American Indians and numerous other ethnic groups, often name their children after the day, month, or season of birth, or after events taking place prior to or at birth—certainly just as original and descriptive a technique of naming children as naming children after other persons or after saints. Ironically, some of the more common names of twentieth-century American women are April, May, and June.

50. Charles Colcok Jones, *Religious Instruction of the Negroes* (Savannah, Ga.: Thomas Purse, 1842), pp. 17, 18.

51. James Redpath, *The Roving Editor; Or, Talks With Slaves in the Southern States* (New York: A. B. Burdick, 1859), pp. 117, 63, 30.

52. Redpath, *op. cit.,* p. 80.

53. Dan Emmett, "Foa Whoebber Sez 'Taint So, Am a Fool in He Heart, an

Got No Edguficashum," unpublished manuscript, in collection of Ohio Historical Society.

54. Mattie Griffith, *The Autobiography of a Female Slave* (New York: J. S. Redfield, 1857), p. 53.

55. Griffith, *op. cit.*, pp. 55–56.

56. Tremaine McDowell, "The Use of Negro Dialect by Harriet Beecher Stowe," *American Speech*, Vol. 6 (June 1931), p. 324.

57. Harriet Beecher Stowe, "The Minister's Wooing," *Atlantic Monthly*, Vol. 3 (April 1859), p. 512.

58. Stowe, "The Minister's Wooing," *op. cit.*, p. 513.

59. McDowell, *op. cit.*, p. 326.

CHAPTER 3. THE RECONSTRUCTION CYCLE

1. During the Civil War, a number of teachers and missionaries on the Sea Islands kept diaries which included their observations about the language and culture of the Gullah people. Most of these diaries, written in longhand and never published, have disappeared. However, one diary was published in 1906 under the title, *From A New England Woman's Diary in Dixie in 1865*. The author, Mary Ames, made a number of references to Black dialect.

2. Marcel [William Francis Allen], "The Negro Dialect," *The Nation*, Vol. 1 (December 14, 1865), p. 744.

3. *Ibid.*

4. Marcel, *op. cit.*, pp. 744–45.

5. Marcel, *op. cit.*, p. 744.

6. *Ibid.* What Allen did not realize is that the lengthening of the vowel, which may have been a European sound, was also a distinct Africanism.

7. *Ibid.*

8. William Francis Allen, Charles Pickard Ware, Lucy McKim Garrison, *Slave Songs of the United States* (New York: A. Simpson, 1867), p. iii.

9. Allen, Ware, Garrison, *op. cit.*, p. xxix.

10. Allen, Ware, Garrison, *op. cit.*, p. xvii.

11. Thomas Wentworth Higginson, *Army Life in a Black Regiment* (Boston: Fields & Osgood, 1870), p. 196.

12. Higginson, *op. cit.*, p. 23.

13. Higginson, *op. cit.*, p. 151.

14. Higginson, *op. cit.*, p. 173.

15. Higginson, *op. cit.*, p. 201.

16. Higginson, *op. cit.*, p. 200.

17. Frederick Douglass, *Narrative of the Life of Frederick Douglass, an American Slave, Written by Himself* (1845; reprint ed., New York: Signet, 1968), p. 31.

18. Thomas P. Fenner, Frederick G. Rathbun, Bessie Cleaveland, *Cabin and Plantation Songs*, 3d ed. (New York: G. P. Putnam's Sons, 1901), p. iv.

19. *Ibid.*

20. Dan Emmett, "Negro Sermon," *New York Clipper*, August 9, 1873, p. 3.

21. Thomas Dunn English, "Caesar Rowan," *Scribner's Monthly*, Vol. 2 (July

1871), p. 300; "Leonard Grimleigh's Shadow," *Lippincott's Magazine*, Vol. 8 (September 1871), pp. 256–59.

22. Thomas Dunn English, "Momma Phoebe," *Scribner's Monthly* (O.S.), Vol. 3 (November 1871), pp. 62–63.

23. Quoted in Aubrey Harrison Starke, *Sidney Lanier: A Biographical and Critical Study* (Chapel Hill: University of North Carolina Press, 1933), p. 185.

24. Irwin Russell, "Uncle Cap Interviewed," *Scribner's Monthly*, Vol. 11 (January 1876), p. 455.

25. Irwin Russell, "Uncle Caleb," in *Christmas Night in the Quarters and Other Poems*, ed. Maurice Garland Fuller (New York: Century, 1917), pp. 171–74.

26. Irwin Russell, "Christmas Night in the Quarters," *Scribner's Monthly*, Vol. 15 (January 1878), p. 446.

27. Joel Chandler Harris, "Introduction," *Christmas Night in the Quarters and Other Poems*, ed. Maurice Garland Fuller (New York: Century, 1917), p. x.

28. "Revival Song," published in the January 18, 1877, issue, is believed to be the first dialect poem Harris wrote for the *Constitution*.

29. Julia Collier Harris, *The Life and Letters of Joel Chandler Harris* (Boston: Houghton Mifflin and Co., 1918), p. 143.

30. During the 1960s and 1970s, when almost anything written by Whites which included Black English, especially nineteenth-century folklore, was denigrated, the Uncle Remus tales were often treated by many scholars, as well as the uneducated lay public, on a continuum ranging from "inaccurate" at best to "blatantly racist" at worst. Harris, however, was keenly aware of the racist stereotypes ascribed to the Black, and on numerous occasions spoke out against the stereotypes associated with the minstrelsy. In *Lexicon of Black English* (1977), J. L. Dillard suggests that "some of the academic suspicion of Harris is because the academics have seen Harris only through the Disney versions" (p. 177).

31. Joel Chandler Harris, "Why The Alligator's Back Is Rough," *Century Illustrated Magazine*, Vol. 26 (August 1883), pp. 614–15.

32. Joel Chandler Harris, *Nights With Uncle Remus* (Boston: J. R. Osgood & Co., 1883), pp. xxxii–xxxiv.

33. Joel Chandler Harris, letter to the editor, *New York Evening Post*, May 19, 1880.

34. Joel Chandler Harris, *Uncle Remus, His Songs and Sayings; The Folklore of the Plantation* (New York: D. Appleton & Co., 1881), pp. 3–4.

35. Joel Chandler Harris, *Uncle Remus . . . , op. cit.*, p. 11.

36. Harris, *Nights With Uncle Remus, op. cit.*, p. xxxii.

37. Joel Chandler Harris, *Uncle Remus and His Friends: Old Plantation Stories, Songs, and Ballads, with Sketches of Negro Character* (Boston: Houghton Mifflin and Co., 1892), pp. viii–ix.

38. Sidney Lanier, "The New South," *Scribner's Monthly*, Vol. 20 (October 1880), p. 847.

39. C. Alphonso Smith, "Dialect Writers," in *Cambridge History of American Literature*, Vol. 2 (New York: G. P. Putnam's Sons, 1918), p. 349.

40. J. P. Fruit, "Uncle Remus in Phonetic Spelling," *Dialect Notes*, Vol. 1 (1896), p. 192.

41. C. Alphonso Smith, *op. cit.,* Vol. 2, pp. 355–56.

42. Stella Brewer Brooks, *Joel Chandler Harris, Folklorist* (Athens, Ga.: University of Georgia Press, 1950), p. 111.

43. Sumner Ives, "Dialect Differentiation in the Stories of Joel Chandler Harris," *American Literature,* Vol. 27 (March 1955), p. 91.

44. Gilbert D. Schneider, *The Uncle Remus Dialect and Its Value to the Serious Scholar* (paper presented at the Linguistics Colloquium on Black English, Athens, Ohio, February 20, 1973).

45. Joel Chandler Harris, *Uncle Remus Stories,* adaptation by Marion Palmer (Racine, Wisc.: Western, 1946), p. 7.

46. Charles Colcock Jones, Jr., *Negro Myths From the Georgia Coast, Written in the Vernacular* (Boston: Houghton Mifflin, 1888), p. 1.

47. Harry Stillwell Edwards, "Two Runaways," *Century,* Vol. 10 (July 1886), p. 386.

48. *Ibid.*

49. Harry Stillwell Edwards, "The Negro and the South," *Century Illustrated Magazine,* Vol. 50 (June 1906), pp. 212–15.

50. *Ibid.*

51. *Ibid.*

52. W. W. N., editor's note to "Animal Tales from North Carolina," by Emma Backus, *Journal of American Folk-Lore,* Vol. 11 (October–December 1898), pp. 291–92.

53. Alexander Bondurant, "Sherwood Bonner," in *Library of Southern Literature,* ed. Anderson Alderman and Joel Chandler Harris (New Orleans: Martin and Hoyt, 1907), p. 445.

54. Sherwood Bonner, *Dialect Tales* (New York: Harper & Bros., 1883), p. 93.

55. Lafcadio Hearn, "The Scientific Value of Creole," *New Orleans Times-Democrat,* July 14, 1886.

56. Lafcadio Hearn, "The Creole Patois," *Harper's Weekly,* Vol. 19 (January 10, 1885), p. 27.

57. Robert F. Spiller, Willard Thorp, Thomas H. Johnson, and Henry Seidel Canby, eds., *Literary History of the United States* (New York: Macmillan, 1955), pp. 855–56.

58. Edward Laroque Tinker, "Cable and the Creoles," *American Literature,* Vol. 5 (January 1934), p. 318.

59. *Ibid.*

60. Tinker, *op. cit.,* pp. 310, 318–19.

61. Although most persons equate Twain with Clemens, they were two distinct personalities. In private life, it was always Samuel Langhorne Clemens; in public life, especially writing, it was Mark Twain.

62. Mark Twain, "A True Story, Repeated Word for Word as I Heard It," *The Atlantic Monthly,* Vol. 34 (November 1874), pp. 591–92.

63. In 1863, at the age of twenty-seven, Samuel L. Clemens signed the name "Mark Twain" to an article in the *Territorial Enterprise.* At first, the name Mark Twain was signed only to humor articles; later, it was signed to all writing. "Mark Twain" is a riverboat phrase ordering the measurement of two fathoms of water, generally the lowest allowable limit of riverboats. It

is estimated that Twain wrote more than 2,000 articles while a newspaper reporter.

64. Samuel Langhorne Clemens, *The Autobiography of Mark Twain,* ed. Charles Neider (New York: Harper & Bros., 1959), p. 152.

65. Mark Twain, *Simon Wheeler, Detective* (New York: New York Public Library, 1963), p. 49.

66. Twain, *Simon Wheeler, Detective, op. cit.,* pp. 50–51.

67. Robert Rowlette, *Twain's Pudd'nhead Wilson: The Development and the Design* (Bowling Green, Ohio: Bowling Green University Popular Press, 1971), p. 1.

68. Mark Twain, *The Adventures of Huckleberry Finn* (*Tom Sawyer's Comrade*) (New York: Charles L. Webster, 1885), p. 121.

69. Mark Twain, "Jim's Investments, and King Sollermun," *Century,* Vol. 23 (January 1885), p. 457.

70. James Nathan Tidwell, "Mark Twain's Representation of Negro Speech," *American Speech,* Vol. 17 (October 1942), p. 176.

71. Twain, *Huckleberry Finn, op. cit.,* p. 8.

72. See "In Re 'Pudd'nhead Wilson'," by Martha McCullock Williams, *Southern Magazine,* Vol. 2 (February 1894), pp. 99–102.

73. Mark Twain, "Pudd'nhead Wilson," *Century,* Vol. 47 (December 1893), p. 236.

74. James D. Hart, *The Oxford Companion to American Literature,* 4th ed. (New York: Oxford University Press, 1964), p. 683.

75. Twain, "Pudd'nhead Wilson," *Century,* Vol. 47 (January 1894), p. 399.

76. Twain, "Pudd'nhead Wilson," *Century,* Vol. 47 (February 1894), p. 549.

77. Twain, "Pudd'nhead Wilson," *Century,* Vol. 47 (March 1894), p. 779.

78. Twain, "Pudd'nhead Wilson," *Century,* Vol. 47 (April 1894), pp. 820–21.

79. Thomas Nelson Page, "Meh Lady: A Story of the War," *Century,* Vol. 32 (June 1886), p. 187.

80. Ambrose E. Gonzales, "Old Wine—New Bottles," *The State* (Charlestown, S.C.), May 15, 1892, p. 5.

81. *Ibid.*

82. J. A. Waldron, "Old Chocolate's Target Practice," *Judge,* Vol. 11 (March 12, 1887), p. 5; *Ibid.;* J. A. Waldron, "Old Chocolate's Target Practice," *Judge,* Vol. 10 (July 31, 1886), p. 5; *Ibid.;* J. A. Waldron, "Old Chocolate's Target Practice," *Judge,* Vol. 11 (February 12, 1887), p. 5.

83. A. T. Worden, "Uncle Gabe's Sage Saws," *Judge,* Vol. 31 (July 25, 1896), p. 50; *Ibid.;* A. T. Worden, "Uncle Gabe's Sage Saws," *Judge,* Vol. 30 (May 16, 1896), p. 335.

84. A. T. Worden, "Reverend Moakley McKoon," *Judge,* Vol. 31 (July 11, 1896), p. 28.

85. *Ibid.*

86. James Whitcomb Riley, "Dialect," *Forum,* Vol. 14 (December 1893), p. 466.

87. T. C. Delow, "The Day of Dialect," *Lippincott's Magazine,* Vol. 60 (November 1897), pp. 679–83.

88. James A. Harrison, "Negro-English," *Anglia,* Vol. 7 (1884), p. 232.

89. Theodore H. Kellogg, "English Phonology," *Popular Science Monthly,* Vol. 32 (January 1888), pp. 340–51, 387.

90. W. S. Scarborough, "Notes on the Function of Modern Languages in Africa," *Proceedings of the American Philosophical Association,* Vol. 27 (1896), pp. xlvi–xlvii; William Cecil Elam, "Lingo In Literature," *Lippincott's Magazine,* Vol. 55 (February 1895), pp. 286–88.

91. E. M. Day, "Philological Curiosities," *North American Review,* Vol. 146 (June 1888), p. 709.

92. A. F. Chamberlain, "Negro Dialect," *Science,* Vol. 12 (July 13, 1888), p. 23.

93. "Certain Beliefs and Superstitions of the Negro," *Atlantic Monthly,* Vol. 68 (August 1891), p. 286.

94. *Ibid.*

95. "Certain Beliefs . . ." *op. cit.,* p. 287.

96. John Bennett, "Gullah: A Negro Patois," *South Atlantic Quarterly,* Vol. 7 (1908), p. 338.

97. John G. Williams, *"De Ole Plantation": Elder Coteney's Sermons* (Charleston, S.C.: Walker, Evans and Cogswell, 1895), p. vi.

98. Williams, *op. cit.,* pp. v, xi.

99. Williams, *op. cit.,* pp. vi, ix.

100. W. D. Howells, "Life and Letters," *Harper's Weekly,* Vol. 40 (June 27, 1896), p. 630.

101. W. D. Howells, introduction to *Lyrics of Lowly Life,* by Paul Laurence Dunbar (New York: Dodd, Mead & Co., 1899), pp. xvii–xviii.

102. Paul Laurence Dunbar, "The Poet," *Lyrics of Love and Laughter* (New York: Dodd, Mead & Co., 1903), p. 82.

103. Letters from Paul Laurence Dunbar to "W. C.," March 15, 1897, in *The Crisis,* Vol. 20 (June 1920), p. 73.

104. James Weldon Johnson, introduction to *The Book of American Negro Poetry* (New York: Harcourt, Brace & World, 1931), pp. 35–36.

105. Addison Gayle, *Oak and Ivy: A Biography of Paul Laurence Dunbar* (Garden City, N.J.: Doubleday, 1971), p. 38.

106. Edward H. Lawson, "Paul Laurence Dunbar," *Alexander's Magazine,* Vol. 1 (March 1906), p. 49.

107. Paul Laurence Dunbar, "W'en Dey 'Listed Colo'ed Sojers," *Candle-Lightin' Time* (New York: Dodd, Mead & Co., 1901), pp. 81–89.

108. Paul Laurence Dunbar, "The Real Question," *Lyrics of the Hearthside* (New York: Dodd, Mead & Co., 1899), pp. 143–44.

109. Paul Laurence Dunbar, "When Malindy Sings," *Majors and Minors* (Toledo, Ohio: Hadley & Hadley, 1895), pp. 138–40.

110. Paul Laurence Dunbar, "A Family Feud," *Folks from Dixie* (New York: Dodd, Mead & Co., 1898), pp. 138–39.

111. "Paul Laurence Dunbar," *The Voice of the Negro,* Vol. 3 (March 1906), p. 173.

112. George Davis Jenifer, "The Services of Dunbar," *Voice of the Negro,* Vol. 3 (June 1906), pp. 408–9.

113. James D. Corothers, *In Spite of the Handicap* (New York: George H. Doran & Co., 1916), p. 125.

114. Corrothers, *op. cit.,* p. 20.

115. Corrothers, *op. cit.,* p. 127.

116. Corrothers, *op. cit.,* pp. 84, 82.

117. Richard Linthicum, "Introduction," *Echoes from the Cabin and Elsewhere,* by James Campbell (Chicago: Donohue & Henneberry, 1895), pp. 9–10.
118. *Ibid.*
119. Jean Wagner, *Black Poets of the United States,* trans. Kenneth Douglas (Urbana: University of Illinois Press, 1973), p. 138.
120. Daniel Webster Davis, "Miss Liza's Banjer," *'Weh Down Souf* (Cleveland: Helman-Taylor Co., 1897), pp. 103–5.
121. Daniel Webster Davis, "De Nigger's Got to Go," *'Weh Down Souf, op. cit.,* pp. 48–52.
122. J. Mord Allen, "The Squeak of the Fiddle," *Rhymes, Tales and Rhymed Tales* (Topeka: Crane & Co., 1906), pp. 62–63.
123. Letter from Charles Waddell Chesnutt to Walter H. Page, May 20, 1898, recorded in Helen M. Chesnutt, *Charles Waddell Chesnutt, Pioneer of the Color Line* (Chapel Hill: University of North Carolina Press, 1952), pp. 94–95.
124. Ruth Miller, *Blackamerican Literature* (Beverly Hills: Glencoe Press, 1971), pp. 160–61.

CHAPTER 4. THE NEGRO RENAISSANCE CYCLE

1. W. E. B. Du Bois, "Opinion," *The Crisis,* Vol. 18 (May 1919), p. 14.
2. Although Hurston was not a "protest writer," her writings were part of the Harlem Renaissance and showed elements of protest. See pp. 309–15.
3. Edgar P. Billups, "Some Principles for the Representation of Negro Dialect in Fiction," *Texas Review,* Vol. 8 (Summer 1922), pp. 122–23.
4. "Negro Dialect," *Opportunity,* Vol. 2 (September 1924), p. 259.
5. Arthur M. Kaplan, "A Master of Negro Dialect," *Jewish Tribune,* September 23, 1927, p. 61.
6. James Weldon Johnson, *The Book of American Negro Poetry* (New York: Harcourt, Brace and Co., 1922), p. xli.
7. James Weldon Johnson, *God's Trombones; Seven Negro Sermons in Verse* (New York: Viking Press, 1927), pp. 7–9.
8. Roark Bradford, *Ol' Man Adam an' His Chillun; Being Tales They Tell About the Time the Lord Walked the Earth Like a Natural Man* (New York: Harper & Bros., 1928), pp. xiii–xiv.
9. Bradford, *op. cit.,* p. xiv.
10. The play was censored in London, but published by the *London Evening Standard.*
11. Samuel Gaillard Stoney and Gertrude Matthews Shelby, *Black Genesis* (New York: Macmillan, 1930), p. 9.
12. Charles Gilpin and Paul Robeson, two of America's finest actors during the Negro Renaissance, each portrayed the Emperor Jones.
13. Eugene O'Neill, "The Emperor Jones," *Theatre Arts,* Vol. 5 (January 1921), p. 33.
14. O'Neill, *op. cit.,* pp. 37–38.
15. O'Neill, *op. cit.,* p. 52.
16. O'Neill, *op. cit.,* p. 55.

17. Paul Green, *The Lonesome Road* (New York: Robert M. McBride & Co., 1926), p. xx.

18. Paul Green, "In Abraham's Bosom," *The Lonesome Road, op. cit.,* pp. 18–19.

19. Paul Green, "Your Fiery Furnace," *The Lonesome Road, op. cit.,* p. 216.

20. The family name is Falkner.

21. Frederick L. Gwynn and Joseph L. Blottner, eds., "William Faulkner on Dialect," *University of Virginia Magazine,* Vol. 2 (1958), pp. 10–11.

22. William Faulkner, *The Sound and the Fury* (New York: Random House, 1946), pp. 309–13.

23. There is a thread of similarity between Joe Christmas's problem in *Light in August,* and Roxy's problems in Mark Twain's "Pudd'nhead Wilson."

24. Faulkner was a reporter in New Orleans in 1924 and 1925; he wrote the screenplays for *The Road to Glory* (1936), *Slave Ship* (1937), *To Have or Have Not* (1944), and *The Big Sleep* (1946). In addition, during the 1930s, he contributed dialogue and revisions for several screenplays.

25. Although *The Reviewer* was dated October 1928, it was probably issued after *The Smart Set,* which was dated December 1928.

26. Quoted in Emily Clark, *Innocence Abroad* (New York: Alfred A. Knopf, 1931), p. 223.

27. Quoted in *Innocence Abroad,* written by Emily Clark, *op. cit.,* p. 224.

28. *Ibid.*

29. "Again a Serious Study of Negroes in Fiction: Green Thursday," *The New York Times,* September 28, 1924, sec. 3, p. 8.

30. Julia M. Peterkin, "Imports From Africa—The Ortymobile," *The Reviewer,* Vol. 2 (January 1922), pp. 199–200.

31. Frank Durham, ed., *Collected Short Stories of Julia Peterkin* (Columbia, S.C.: University of South Carolina Press, 1970), p. 6.

32. John Marshall to Yates Snowden, March 11, 1925, South Caroliniana Library.

33. Durham, *Collected Stories of Julia Peterkin, op. cit.,* p. 43.

34. Julia Peterkin to Margaret Meriwether, June 13, 1944. South Caroliniana Library.

35. Margaret Mitchell to Sidney Howard, November 21, 1936, library archives, University of Georgia, and included in *Margaret Mitchell's 'Gone With the Wind' Letters, 1936–1949,* ed. Richard Harwell (New York: Macmillan, 1976), p. 93; Margaret Mitchell to Herschell Brickell, October 9, 1936, library archives, University of Georgia, and included in Harwell, *op. cit.,* p. 75.

36. Margaret Mitchell to Garnett Laidlaw Eskew, July 17, 1939, library archives, University of Georgia, and included in Harwell, *op. cit.,* p. 244.

37. Margaret Mitchell to Donald Adams, July 9, 1936, library archives, University of Georgia, and included in Harwell, *op. cit.,* pp. 32–33.

38. Margaret Mitchell to David O. Selznick, January 30, 1939, library archives, University of Georgia, and included in Harwell, *op. cit.,* p. 244.

39. The speech of both Ms. McDaniel and Ms. McQueen are excellent sources for a study of Black screen speech of the late 1930s.

40. DuBose Heyward, *Porgy* (New York: George H. Doran & Co., 1925), p. 11–12.

41. *Porgy* is a local regionalism for "Soup." William Gilmore Simms previously used the name in several of his novels written during the Antebellum Cycle of American Black English, although it is doubtful that Heyward was aware of this.

42. Frank Durham, *DuBose Heyward: The Man Who Wrote Porgy* (Columbia, S.C.: University of South Carolina Press, 1954), p. 69.

43. Durham, *DuBose Heyward: The Man Who Wrote Porgy, op. cit.*, p. 59.

44. Heyward, *op. cit.*, p. 65.

45. Heyward, *op. cit.*, pp. 194–95.

46. Durham, *DuBose Heyward, op. cit.*, p. 114.

47. Langston Hughes, *The Big Sea* (New York: Alfred A. Knopf, 1940), p. 228.

48. James Weldon Johnson, *Book of American Negro Poetry*, 2d ed. (New York: Harcourt, Brace & Co., 1931), p. 4.

49. Eustace Gay, "Facts and Fancies," *The Philadelphia Tribune*, February 5, 1927, p. 16.

50. Eugenia W. Collier, "A Pain in His Soul: Simple as Epic Hero," in *Langston Hughes: Black Genesis; A Critical Review*, ed. Therman B. O'Daniel (New York: William Morrow & Co., 1971), pp. 127–28.

51. Arna Bontemps, review of *Dust Tracks in the Road*, in *New York Herald Tribune*, Vol. 19 (November 22, 1942), p. 3, Book Review.

52. Darwin T. Turner, *In a Minor Chord: Three Afro-American Writers and Their Search For Identity* (Carbondale and Edwardsville, Ill.: Southern Illinois University Press, 1971), p. 98.

53. Turner, *op. cit.*, p. 91.

54. Hughes, *The Big Sea, op. cit.*, p. 239. [Also in the *Saturday Review of Literature*, Vol. 22 (June 22, 1940), p. 14.]

55. Turner, *op. cit.*, p. 117.

56. *Ibid.*

57. Hughes, *The Big Sea, op. cit.*, p. 239.

58. At the time Hurston began writing in the late 1920s, her own speech patterns were beginning to undergo a process of change. In an article appearing in the July 1960, issue of the *Yale University Library Gazette* (p. 17), novelist Fannie Hurst, for whom Hurston worked as a secretary during the late 1920s, recalled that Hurston had a dialect "as deep as the deep South." However, Hurston's physician, Dr. Clem Benton of Fort Pierce, Florida, in 1975, recalled that she "really had perfect expressions. Her English was beautiful!"

59. In *Seraph on the Suwanee*, the primary dialects were Southern Standard English and a lower-class Southern Standard English.

60. Walter Neale, introduction to Lily Young Cohen, *Lost Spirituals* (New York: W. Neale, 1928), p. ix.

61. Alan Lomax eventually graduated from the University of Texas, *summa cum laude*, and undertook graduate work at Harvard University.

62. John A. Lomax and Alan Lomax, *American Ballads and Folk Songs* (New York: Macmillan, 1934), p. xxx.

63. John A. Lomax and Alan Lomax, *op. cit.*, p. xxxiii.

64. Quoted in John Lomax and Alan Lomax, *Negro Folk Songs as Sung by Lead Belly* (New York: Macmillan, 1936), p. 31.

65. Quoted in *Negro Folk Songs as Sung by Lead Belly, op. cit.,* pp. 21–22.

66. Quoted in *Negro Folk Songs as Sung by Lead Belly, op. cit.,* pp. 31–32.

67. John A. Lomax in *Negro Folk Songs as Sung by Lead Belly, op. cit.,* p. 33.

68. John A. Lomax in *Negro Folk Songs as Sung by Lead Belly, op. cit.,* pp. 29–30, 35.

69. Quoted in John Mason Brewer, *American Negro Folklore* (Chicago: Quadrangle Books, 1968), pp. 43, 44.

70. "Milestones," *Time,* Vol. 54 (December 19, 1949), p. 71.

71. The entire project was under the direction of Henry P. Alsberg. Sterling A. Brown was director for the Negro Affairs section; John A. Lomax, and later B. A. Botkin, were folklore editors.

72. Sterling A. Brown, *Slave Narratives,* Works Project Administration/Federal Writer's Project, memorandum included in Library of Congress microfilm edition, Vol. 1, p. vi.

73. The memorandum, included in the Library of Congress archives, was unsigned, but possibly written by John A. Lomax.

74. Memorandum in *Slave Narratives, op. cit.,* Vol. 1, pp. xxvii, xxix.

75. Memorandum in *Slave Narratives, op. cit.,* Vol. 1, p. xxx.

76. B. A. Botkin, *Lay My Burden Down* (Chicago: University of Chicago Press, 1945), pp. vii–viii.

77. Ambrose Gonzales, *The Black Border* (Columbia, S.C.: The State Co., 1922), pp. 17–18.

78. Ambrose Gonzales, *op. cit.,* p. 10.

79. Gonzales wrote his books after being partially paralyzed by a stroke. He never recovered full use of his speech, and died in 1926.

80. R. Emmet Kennedy, *Black Cameos* (New York: A. & C. Boni, 1924), p. xiii.

81. Edward C. L. Adams, *Congaree Sketches* (Chapel Hill: University of North Carolina Press, 1927), p. vii.

82. George Philip Krapp, "The English of the Negro," *American Mercury,* Vol. 2 (June 1924), p. 193.

83. George Philip Krapp, *The English Language in America,* Vol. 2 (New York: Century, 1925), p. 227.

84. Krapp, *op. cit.,* Vol. 1, p. 162.

85. Niles Newell Puckett, *Folk Beliefs of the Southern Negroes* (Durham: University of North Carolina Press, 1926), p. 21.

86. Reed Smith, *Gullah* (Columbia, S.C.: Bureau of Publications of the University of South Carolina, 1926), p. 22.

87. Stoney and Shelby, *op. cit.,* p. x.

88. Guion Griffis Johnson, *A Social History of the Sea Islands; With Special Reference to St. Helena Island, South Carolina* (Chapel Hill: University of North Carolina Press, 1930), p. 127.

89. Guy B. Johnson, *Folk Culture on St. Helena Island, South Carolina* (Chapel Hill: University of North Carolina Press, 1930), p. 6.

90. Guy B. Johnson, "St. Helena Songs and Stories," in T. J. Woofter, *Life On St. Helena Island* (New York: H. Holt, 1930), p. 53.

91. Guy B. Johnson, "St. Helena Songs and Stories," *op. cit.,* p. 53.

92. Charles S. Johnson, *The Negro in American Civilization* (New York: Henry Holt, 1930), p. 132.

93. Cleanth Brooks, *The Relationship of the Alabama-Georgia Dialect to the Provincial Dialects of Britain* (Baton Rouge: Louisiana State University Press, 1935), p. 64.

94. A. Dilworth Faber, "Negro American Vocabulary," *Writer,* Vol. 50, no. 8 (August 1937), p. 239.

95. H. L. Mencken, *The American Language; An Inquiry into the Development of English in the United States,* 4th ed. (New York: Alfred A. Knopf, 1936), pp. 71–72.

96. Mason Crum, *Gullah: Negro Life in the Carolina Sea Islands* (Durham, N.C.: Duke University Press, 1940), pp. 102, 111.

97. Robert E. Park, "The Conflict and Fusion of Cultures with Special Reference to the Negro," *Journal of Negro History,* Vol. 4 (April 1919), p. 119.

98. Charles S. Johnson, *Shadow of the Plantation* (Chicago: University of Chicago Press, 1930), p. 3.

99. E. B. Reuter, book review, "The Negro Family in the United States," by E. Franklin Frazier, *American Journal of Sociology,* Vol. 45 (March 1940), p. 799.

100. Melville J. Herskovits, *The Myth of the Negro Past* (New York: Harper & Bros., 1941), p. xiii.

101. Melville J. Herskovits, *op. cit.,* p. 276.

102. Melville J. Herskovits, *The Myth of the Negro Past,* 2d ed. (Boston: Beacon Press, 1958), p. xxviii.

103. Herskovits, *The Myth of the Negro Past,* 2d ed., *op. cit.,* p. xvi.

104. Melville J. Herskovits, *The Myth of the Negro Past,* 2d ed., *op. cit.,* pp. xv–xvi.

105. During that time, Hans Kurath and others were working on development of the *Linguistic Atlas of the United States.* The theoretical methodology of the atlas was that of dialect geography. Thus, it did not include any special notation of Black speech as different from White speech.

106. Lorenzo Dow Turner, *Africanisms in the Gullah Dialect* (Chicago: University of Chicago Press, 1949), pp. 5, 11.

107. Lorenzo Dow Turner, *op. cit.,* p. v.

108. Lorenzo Dow Turner, *op. cit.,* p. 249.

109. One of the most thorough reviews of Turner's work was made by Raven I. McDavid, Jr., and published in *Language* (April–June 1950), pp. 323–33.

110. For an excellent description of the development of Black films, consult Peter Noble, *The Negro in Films* (Port Washington, N.Y.: Kennikat Press, 1949).

111. Huey Long, known as the "Kingfish," took his name from the *Amos 'n' Andy* character.

112. Quoted in Edward T. Clayton, "The Tragedy of Amos and Andy," *Ebony,* Vol. 16 (October 1961), p. 68.

CHAPTER 5. THE CIVIL RIGHTS CYCLE

1. Quoted in "Armageddon To Go," *Time,* Vol. 66 (December 12, 1955), p. 24.

2. Interestingly, much of the criticism came from Whites who had merely per-

ceived what they thought Blacks would have said had they said it. Few Whites understood the nature of Black English, or the nature of language.

3. Letter from Delores Draper, editor, Western Publishing Co. (Racine, Wisconsin), May 27, 1980.

4. Richard Wright, *Lawd Today* (New York: Walker & Co., 1963), pp. 84–85.

5. Ralph Ellison, *Invisible Man* (New York: Random House, 1952), p. 3.

6. James Baldwin, "This Morning, This Evening, So Soon," *The Atlantic Monthly,* Vol. 206 (September 1960), pp. 36–37.

7. LeRoi Jones, "Expressive Language," *Kulchur,* Vol. 3, no. 12 (Winter 1963), pp. 77, 79.

8. Ronald Bryden, "LeRoi Jones," *Contemporary Authors,* Vols. 21–22 (1969), p. 279.

9. W. E. Burghardt Du Bois, foreword, *How God Fix Jonah,* by Lorenz Graham (New York: Reynal & Hitchock, 1946), p. ix.

10. Graham, *How God Fix Jonah, op. cit.,* p. xiv.

11. Lorenz Graham, *Song of the Boat* (New York: Thomas Y. Crowell, 1975).

12. "John Steptoe," *Contemporary Authors,* Vols. 49–52 (1974), p. 522.

13. Although it is possible that the inconsistencies reflect cultural and linguistic assimilation, the probabilities of such, reflected in the representation of Black English in these instances, are remote.

14. Burley, a leading journalist, was also managing editor of the *New York Amsterdam News.*

15. Earl Conrad, introduction, *Dan Burley's Original Handbook of Harlem Jive,* by Dan Burley, published by the author (New York, 1944), pp. 5–6.

16. Dan Burley, *Dan Burley's Original Handbook of Harlem Jive, op. cit.,* p. 11.

17. Robert S. Gold, *A Jazz Lexicon* (New York: Alfred A. Knopf Co., 1964), pp. xvii–xviii.

18. Gold, *op. cit.,* p. xxvi.

19. Mary Jane Bezark, "Pull Your Coattails To This: Webster Has A Black Glossary," *The Washington* [D.C.] *Post,* January 2, 1972, p. F–6.

20. Adrian Dove, "Attention Honkies: Are You Deprived?" The *Washington* (D.C.) *Post,* February 15, 1968, p. A–24.

21. Edward H. Blackwell, "2 Little Words Can Mean A Lot," *Milwaukee Journal,* November 1, 1970, p. 1, Accent section.

22. Jay Anderson, "How Can You Do In Street Talk," *Milwaukee Journal,* September 17, 1972, p. 1, Accent section.

23. Sandra Haggerty, "Doin' The Dozens A Poor Game," distributed by the Los Angeles Times Syndicate, January 1973.

24. J. Mason Brewer, *American Negro Folklore* (Chicago: Quadrangle Books, 1968), p. ix.

25. Roger D. Abrahams, introduction, *Deep Down in the Jungle: Negro Narrative Folklore from the Streets of Philadelphia* (Hatboro, Pa.: Folklore Associates, 1964).

26. Roger D. Abrahams, *Positively Black* (Englewood Cliffs, N.J.: Prentice-Hall, 1970), pp. 15–16.

27. Roger D. Abrahams, *Positively Black, op. cit.,* p. 4.

28. Roger D. Abrahams, *Deep Down in the Jungle: Negro Narratives from the*

Street of Philadelphia, rev. ed. (Chicago: Aldine Publishing Co., 1970), pp. 1–3.

29. Roger D. Abrahams, *Talking Black* (Rowley, Mass.: Newbury House, 1977), p. ix.

30. Herbert L. Foster, *Ribbin', Jivin', and Playin' the Dozens* (Cambridge, Mass.: Balinger Publishers, 1974), p. 8.

31. Foster, *op. cit.,* pp. 117, 125.

32. Foster, *op. cit.,* p. 121.

33. Although many of the creolists were structuralists, their field work has proven invaluable for deep-structure analysis. However, a major need in the field is still a definitive study, utilizing deep structure arguments, to determine the presence of a creole substratum.

34. David Dalby, "Americanisms That Once May Have Been Africanisms," *The Times* [of London], July 19, 1969, p. 9.

35. Colston Westbrook, *The Dual Linguistic Heritage of Afro-Americans,* Master's thesis, University of California at Berkeley, 1974, pp. 61–62. One of the strongest analyses of intonation patterns in American Black English, in isolated analysis, was conducted by Joan C. Fickett as part of a doctoral dissertation in 1970. Her study, "Aspects of Morphemics, Syntax, and Semology in Inner-City Dialect (Merican)" was later published by Meadowood Publishers in 1970, and the Department of Anthropology of Southern Illinois University in 1974.

36. One of the by-products of this massive academic explosion has been the publication of more than three dozen "readers" in Black English and closely related fields; there is significant overlapping of contents.

37. Max Rafferty, "Rafferty Slaps Any Use of Dialects in Schools: 'Only 1 Correct Grammar,' " *San Diego Union,* September 10, 1967, p. A–28.

38. Lloyd Shearer, "Americans Who Can't Speak Their Own Language," *Parade,* June 11, 1967, p. 4.

39. Rafferty, *op. cit.,* p. A–28.

40. Pat Conroy, *The Water Is Wide* (Boston: Houghton Mifflin, 1972), pp. 39–40. [Also appeared in *Life* magazine of June 2, 1972.]

41. Herbert H. Denton, "Negro Dialect: Should the Schools Fight It?" *The Washington* (D.C.) *Post,* December 22, 1968, pp. C1–C2.

42. Editorial, *Philadelphia Daily News,* August 13, 1969, p. 5.

43. "Black Nonsense," *The Crisis,* Vol. 78 (April–May 1971), p. 78.

44. Thomas W. Patrick, M.D., "Black English; Road to Failure," *The New York Times,* July 7, 1971, p. 51.

45. Bayard Rustin, "Won't They Ever Learn?" *New York Amsterdam News,* May 29, 1971, p. 14; also in *The New York Times,* August 1, 1971, sect. 4, p. 7.

46. Roland Laird, Letter to the Editor, *Commonweal,* Vol. 95 (January 14, 1972), p. 359.

47. Bernard Weinraub, "Auden: A Difference in Memories," in *The New York Times,* October 19, 1971, p. 52.

48. Douglas Bush, "Does Anybody Here Speak English?" *Washington* (D.C.) *Evening Star,* March 19, 1972, pp. B–3, B–4.

49. T. J. Sellers, "English Not Dialect," *The New York Times,* June 9, 1972, p. 37.
50. William Labov, "Academic Ignorance and Black Intelligence," *The Atlantic Monthly,* Vol. 239 (June 1972), p. 59.
51. Labov, *op. cit.,* p. 67.
52. Walter Mercer, "When School Children Talk Black . . . At the Teacher," *Floridian* magazine of the *St. Petersburg* (Fla.) *Times,* Nov. 5, 1972, p. 12.
53. J. Mitchell Morse, *The Irrelevant English Teacher* (Philadelphia: Temple University Press, 1972), p. 89. [Chapter 7, "The Shuffling Speech of Black Slavery: Black English," appeared in *College English* (March 1973), an academic journal.]
54. Henry M. Mitchell, *Black Preaching* (Philadelphia: J. B. Lippincott, 1970), p. 149.
55. Charles Michener, "Talking Black," *Newsweek,* Vol. 80 (August 14, 1972), p. 81.
56. J. L. Dillard, *Black English: Its History and Usage in the United States* (New York: Random House, 1972), p. 3.
57. Dillard, *op. cit.,* p. 7.
58. Dillard, *op. cit.,* pp. 9–10.
59. Dillard, *op. cit., passim.*
60. Christopher Lehmann-Haupt, review of J. L. Dillard's *Black English, The New York Times,* August 29, 1972, p. 31.
61. J. L. Dillard, *Lexicon of Black English* (New York: Seabury Press, 1977), p. ix.
62. Dennis Polite, "Black Standard English Be 2 Kinds," *Dayton* (Ohio) *Daily News,* February 12, 1973, p. 30.
63. Joel Dreyfuss, "Black English: Who's to Say," *Washington* (D.C.) *Post,* July 1, 1973, p. L–7.
64. *Ibid.*
65. *Ibid.*
66. *Ibid.*
67. Charles W. Joiner, legal opinion, *Martin Luther King Jr., Elementary School Children, et al.* v. *Ann Arbor School District Board,* United States District Court for the Eastern District of Michigan; published in *Federal Supplement,* West Publishers, vol. 473 (1979), pp. 1374–75.
68. Joiner, *op. cit.,* p. 1378.
69. Joiner, *op. cit.,* p. 1377.
70. Joiner, *op. cit.,* p. 1380.
71. Joiner, *op. cit.,* p. 1382.
72. *Ibid.*
73. Joiner, *op. cit.,* p. 1383.
74. An excellent bibliography of articles about the court case was prepared by Dr. Richard W. Bailey, professor of English at the University of Michigan.
75. See *The New York Times* of June 18, 1979.

GENERAL LANGUAGE OBSERVATIONS

1. Two of the better lists of features of Black English speech in contemporary urban settings were prepared by Ralph W. Fasold and Walt Wolfram ("Some Linguistic Features of Negro Dialects," in *Teaching Standard English in the Inner City,* ed. Fasold and Roger W. Shuy [Center for Applied Linguistics, 1970]); and Robbins Burling (*English in Black and White* [Holt, Rinehart, and Winston, 1973] pp. 29–46, 48–74). Unlike the list presented here, which concentrates upon the written language and literary perceptions of the speech, the lists of Fasold and Wolfram, and Burling, are based upon linguistic field research of the spoken language.

Selected List of Works Cited

Abrahams, Roger D. *Deep Down in the Jungle: Negro Narrative Folklore From the Streets of Philadelphia*. Aldine Publishing Co. Copyright 1963, 1970 by Roger D. Abrahams.

Abrahams, Roger D. *Deep Down in the Jungle: Negro Narrative Folklore From the Streets of Philadelphia*. Folklore Associates. Copyright 1964 by Roger D. Abrahams.

Abrahams, Roger D. *Positively Black*. Prentice-Hall. Copyright 1970 by Roger D. Abrahams.

Abrahams, Roger D. *Talking Black*. Newbury House. Copyright 1977 by Roger D. Abrahams.

Adams, Edward C. L. *Congaree Sketches: Scenes From Negro Life in the Swamps of the Congaree and Tales by Tad and Scip of Heaven and Hell with Other Miscellany*. The University of North Carolina Press. Copyright 1927 by University of North Carolina Press.

Anderson, Jay. "How Can You Do In Street Talk?" *Milwaukee Journal* (September 17, 1972). Copyright 1972 by the Milwaukee Journal.

"Armageddon to Go." *Time* (December 12, 1955). Copyright 1955 by Time, Inc. Reprinted by permission from *Time,* The Weekly Newsmagazine; copyright Time Inc.

Baldwin, James. "This Morning, This Evening, So Soon." *Atlantic Monthly* (September 1960). Copyright 1960 by James Baldwin. Reprinted by permission of Edward J. Acton, Inc.

Bayliss, John F., ed. *Black Slave Narratives*. Collier Books. Copyright 1970. Reprinted by permission of Macmillan Publishing Co.

Bezark, Mary Jane. "Pull Your Coattails to This: Webster Has a Black Glossary." *Washington Post* (January 2, 1972). Copyright 1972 by the Washington Post Co.

"Black Nonsense." *The Crisis* (April–May 1971). Copyright 1971 by Crisis Publishing Co., Inc.

Blackwell, Edward H. "2 Little Words Can Mean a Lot." *Milwaukee Journal* (November 1, 1970). Copyright 1970 by the Milwaukee Journal.

Botkin, B. A., *Lay My Burden Down*. The University of Chicago Press. Copyright 1945 by the University of Chicago Press.

Bradford, Roark. *Ol' Man Adam an' His Chillun; Being Tales They Tell About the Time When the Lord Walked the Earth Like a Natural Man.* Harper & Bros. Copyright 1928 by Harper & Bros. Reprinted by permission of Harper & Row.

Brewer, John Mason. *American Negro Folklore.* Quadrangle Books. Copyright 1968 by Quadrangle Books.

Brooks, Cleanth. *The Relationship of the Alabama-Georgia Dialect to the Provincial Dialects of Great Britain.* Louisiana State University Press. Copyright 1935 by Louisiana State University Press.

Brooks, Stella Brewer. *Joel Chandler Harris, Folklorist.* The University of Georgia Press. Copyright 1950 by the University of Georgia Press.

Burley, Dan. *Dan Burley's Original Handbook of Harlem Jive.* Introduction by Earl Conrad. Published by Dan Burley. Copyright 1944 by Dan Burley.

Bush, Douglas. "Does Anybody Here Speak English?" *Washington Evening Star* (March 19, 1972). Copyright 1972.

Chesnutt, Helen M. *Charles Waddell Chesnutt: Pioneer of the Color Line.* The University of North Carolina Press. Copyright 1952 by University of North Carolina Press.

Clayton, Edward T. "The Tragedy of Amos n' Andy." *Ebony* (October 1961). Copyright 1961 by Johnson Publishing Co., Inc. Reprinted by permission of *Ebony* magazine.

Clemens, Samuel Langhorne. *The Autobiography of Mark Twain.* Edited by Charles Neider. 1959 edition. Harper & Row, Publishers, Inc. Copyright 1917, 1940, 1958, 1959 by the Mark Twain Co. Copyright 1959 by Charles Neider. Reprinted by permission of Harper & Row, Publishers, Inc.

Collier, Eugenia W. "A Pain in His Soul: Simple as an Epic Hero." In *Langston Hughes: Black Geneses: A Critical Review.* Edited by Therman B. O'Daniel. William Morrow & Co. Copyright 1971 by William Morrow & Co.

Conroy, Pat. *The Water Is Wide.* Houghton Mifflin Co. Copyright 1972 by Houghton Mifflin Co.

Crum, Mason. *Gullah: Negro Life in the Carolina Sea Islands.* Duke University Press. Copyright 1940 by Duke University Press.

Dalby, David. "Americanisms That Once May Have Been Africanisms." *The Times* (London) (July 19, 1969). Copyright 1969 by Times Newspapers, Ltd.

Denton, Herbert H. "Negro Dialect: Should the Schools Fight It?" *Washington Post* (December 22, 1968). Copyright 1968 by the Washington Post Co.

Dillard, J. L. *Black English: Its History and Usage in the United States.* Random House. Copyright 1972 by Random House, Inc.

Dove, Adrian. "Attention Honkies: Are You Deprived?" *Washington Post* (February 15, 1968). Copyright 1968 by the Washington Post Co.

Dreyfuss, Joel. "Black English: Whose to Say." *Washington Post* (July 1, 1973). Copyright 1973 by the Washington Post Co.

DuBois, W. E. B. "Opinion." *The Crisis* (May 1919). Copyright 1919 by Crisis Publishing Co., Inc.

Dunbar, Paul Laurence. "Letters to W.C." *The Crisis* (June 1920). Copyright 1920 by Crisis Publishing Co.

Durham, Frank. *Collected Short Stories of Julia Mood Peterkin.* The University of South Carolina Press. Copyright 1970 by University of South Carolina Press.

Durham, Frank. *DuBose Heyward: The Man Who Wrote Porgy.* The University of South Carolina Press. Copyright 1954 by University of South Carolina Press.

Editorial. *Philadelphia Daily News* (August 13, 1969). Copyright 1969 by Philadelphia Daily News.

Ellison, Ralph. *Invisible Man.* Random House. Copyright 1952 by Random House, Inc.

Faber, A. Dilworth. "Negro American Vocabulary." *The Writer* (August 1937). Copyright 1937 by The Writer, Inc.

Faulkner, William. *The Sound and the Fury*. Random House. Copyright 1929 by William Faulkner. Reprinted by permission of Random House.

Foster, Herbert L. *Ribbin', Jivin', and Playin' the Dozens*. Balinger Publishers. Copyright 1976 by Herbert L. Foster.

Gayle, Addison, Jr. *Oak and Ivy: A Biography of Paul Laurence Dunbar*. Doubleday & Co., Inc. Copyright 1971 by Addison Gayle, Jr. Reprinted by permission of Doubleday & Co., Inc.

Gold, Robert S. *A Jazz Lexicon*. Alfred A. Knopf and Co. Copyright 1964 by Robert S. Gold.

Gonzales, Ambrose. *The Black Border*. The State Co. Copyright 1922 by Ambrose Gonzales, The State Co.

Graham, Lorenz, *How God Fix Jonah*. Foreword by W. E. B. DuBois. Reynal & Hitchcock. Copyright 1946.

Graham, Lorenz. *Song of the Boat*. Thomas Y. Crowell Co., Inc. Copyright 1975 by Lorenz Graham. Reprinted by permission of Thomas Y. Crowell and Co., Inc.

Green, Paul. *Lonesome Road*. Robert M. McBride Co. Copyright 1926, 1954 by Paul Green.

Haggerty, Sandra. "Doin' the Dozens: A Poor Game." Distributed by the Los Angeles Times Syndicate. Copyright 1973 by Los Angeles Times Co. Reprinted by permission.

Harris, Joel Chandler. "Introduction." *Christmas Night in the Quarters and Other Poems*. Edited by Maurice Garland Fuller. Century. Copyright 1917 by Century Publishing Co.

Harris, Joel Chandler. *Uncle Remus Stories*. Adaptation by Marion Palmer. Western Publishers. Copyright 1946 by Walt Disney Productions.

Harris, Julia Collier. *The Life and Letters of Joel Chandler Harris*. Houghton Mifflin Co. Copyright 1918 by Houghton Mifflin Co., Inc.

Herskovits, Melville J. *The Myth of the Negro Past*. Beacon Press. Second edition. Copyright 1958 by Melville J. Herskovits. (First edition, copyright 1941 by Harper & Bros., Publishers.)

Heyward, DuBose. *Porgy*. George H. Doran & Co. Copyright 1925, 1934 by DuBose Heyward.

Hughes, Langston. *The Best of Simple*. Hill & Wang. Copyright 1961 by Langston Hughes, Hill & Wang. Reprinted by permission of Farrar, Straus & Giroux, Inc.

Hughes, Langston. *The Big Sea*. Farrar, Straus & Giroux, Inc. Copyright 1940 by Langston Hughes. Reprinted by permission of Farrar, Straus & Giroux, Inc.

Hughes, Langston. *Simple Takes a Wife*. Simon & Schuster. Copyright 1953 by Langston Hughes. Reprinted by permission of Harold Ober Associates.

Ives, Sumner. "Dialect Differentiation in the Stories of Joel Chandler Harris." *American Literature* (March 1955). Copyright 1955 by Duke University Press.

Johnson, Charles S. *The Negro in American Civilization*. Henry Holt & Co. Copyright 1930 by Henry Holt & Co. Reprinted by permission of Holt, Rinehart, and Winston, Inc.

Johnson, Charles S. *Shadow of the Plantation*. The University of Chicago Press. Copyright 1930 by University of Chicago Press.

Johnson, Guion Griffis. *A Social History of the Sea Islands, With Special Reference to St. Helena Island, South Carolina*. The University of North Carolina Press. Copyright 1930 by University of North Carolina Press.

Johnson, Guy B. *Folk Culture on St. Helena Island, South Carolina*. The University of North Carolina Press. Copyright 1930 by University of North Carolina Press.

Johnson, Guy B. "St. Helena Songs and Stories." In *Black Yeomanry: Life on St. Helena Island*. T. J. Woofter. Henry Holt & Co. Copyright 1930, 1958 by T. J. Woofter. Reprinted by permission of Holt, Rinehart, and Winston, Publishers, Inc.

Johnson, James Weldon. *The Book of American Negro Poetry*. Harcourt, Brace & World. Copyright 1931 by Harcourt, Brace & World. Reprinted by permission of Harcourt Brace Jovanovich, Inc.

Johnson, James Weldon. *God's Trombones: Seven Negro Sermons in Verse*. The Viking Press. Copyright 1927 by Viking Press. Reprinted by permission of Viking Penguin.

Jones, LeRoi. "Expressive Language." *Kulchur* (1963). Copyright 1963 by LeRoi Jones.

"LeRoi Jones." *Contemporary Authors* (1969). Copyright 1969 by Gale Research Co., Inc.

Kennedy, R. Emmet. *Black Cameos*. A & C Boni. Copyright 1924 by A & C Boni. Reprinted by Arno Press.

Krapp, George Philip. *The English Language in America*. Century. Copyright 1925 by the Modern Language Association of America. Copyright 1952 by Elizabeth Krapp.

Krapp, George Philip. "The English of the Negro." *American Mercury* (June 1924). Copyright 1924 by the American Mercury.

Labov, William. "Academic Ignorance and Black Intelligence." *Atlantic Monthly* (June 1972). Copyright 1972 by Atlantic Monthly. Reprinted by permission of William Labov.

Laird, Roland. Letter to the Editor. *Commonweal* (January 14, 1972). Copyright 1972 by Commonweal.

Lehmann-Haupt, Christopher. "Review of J. L. Dillard's Black English." *New York Times* (August 29, 1972). Copyright 1972 by The New York Times Co. Reprinted by permission.

Lomax, John A., and Alan Lomax. *American Ballads and Folklore*. Macmillan. Copyright 1934 by Macmillan. Reprinted by permission of Alan Lomax.

Lomax, John, and Alan Lomax. *Negro Folksongs as Sung by Lead Belly*. Macmillan. Copyright 1936 by John Lomax and Alan Lomax.

McDavid, Raven I., Jr. "The Dialects of American English." In *The Structure of American English*. Edited by W. Nelson Francis. The Ronald Press. Copyright 1958 by The Ronald Press Co., New York.

McDavid, Raven I., Jr. and Virginia Glenn McDavid. "Relationship of the Speech of American Negroes to the Speech of Whites." In *Black-White Speech Relationships*. Edited by Walter A. Wolfram and Nona H. Clarke. Published by the Center for Applied Linguistics. Copyright 1971 by the Center for Applied Linguistics.

McDowell, Tremaine. "The Negro in the Southern Novel to 1850." *Journal of English and Germanic Philology* (October 1926). Copyright 1926 by the University of Illinois Press.

McDowell, Tremaine. "The Use of Negro Dialect by Harriet Beecher Stowe." *American Speech* (June 1931). Copyright 1931 by the American Dialect Society.

Mencken, H. L. *The American Language: An Inquiry Into the Development of English in the United States*. Alfred A. Knopf, Inc. Copyright 1919, 1921, 1923, 1926 by Alfred A. Knopf, Inc.

Mercer, Walter. "When School Children Talk Black . . . At the Teacher." *Floridian,* magazine of *St. Petersburg Times* (November 5, 1972). Copyright 1972 by the St. Petersburg Times.

Michener, Charles. "Talking Black." *Newsweek* (August 14, 1972). Copyright 1972 by Newsweek, Inc.

"Milestones." *Time* (December 19, 1949). Reprinted by permission from *Time,* The Weekly Newsmagazine; Copyright 1949 by Time, Inc.

Miller, Ruth. *Blackamerican Literature.* Glencoe Press. Copyright 1971 by Ruth Miller.

Mitchell, Henry M. *Black Preaching.* J. B. Lippincott Co., Inc. Copyright 1970 by J. B. Lippincott Co., Inc.

Mitchell, Margaret. *'Gone With the Wind' Letters.* Macmillan. Copyright 1978 by Stephens Mitchell and Richard B. Harwell.

Morris, J. Allen. "The Stories of William Gilmore Simms." *American Literature* (March 1942). Copyright 1942 by Duke University Press.

Morse, J. Mitchell. *The Irrelevant English Teacher.* Temple University Press. Copyright 1972 by Temple University Press.

O'Neill, Eugene. "The Emperor Jones." *Theatre Arts* (January 1921). Copyright 1921 by Eugene O'Neill. Reprinted by permission of MCA Publishing, Inc.

Park, Robert E. "The Conflict and Fusion of Cultures With Special Reference to the Negro." *Journal of Negro History* (April 1919). Copyright 1919 by the Association for the Study of Afro-American Life and History, Inc.

Patrick, Thomas W. "Black English: Road to Failure." *The New York Times* (July 7, 1971). Copyright 1971 by The New York Times Co. Reprinted by permission.

Polite, Dennis. "Black Standard English Be 2 Kind." *Dayton Daily News* (February 12, 1973). Copyright 1973 by the Dayton Daily News.

Puckett, Niles Newell. *Folk Beliefs of the Southern Negro.* The University of North Carolina Press. Copyright 1926 by University of North Carolina Press.

Quinn, Arthur Hobson. *A History of the American Drama: From the Beginning to the Civil War.* Harper & Bros. Copyright 1923 by Harper & Bros. Reprinted by permission of Harper & Row.

Rafferty, Max. "Rafferty Slaps Any Use of Dialects in Schools: 'Only 1 Correct Grammar.' " *The San Diego Union.* Copyright 1967 by the Los Angeles Times Syndicate. Reprinted by permission.

Reuter, E. B. Review of *The Negro Family in the United States,* by E. Franklin Frazier. *American Journal of Sociology* (March 1940). Copyright 1940 by the University of Chicago Press.

Rowlette, Robert. *Twain's Pudd'nhead Wilson: The Development and the Design.* The Bowling Green University Popular Press. Copyright 1971 by Bowling Green University Popular Press.

Rustin, Bayard. "Won't They Ever Learn?" *New York Amsterdam News* (May 29, 1971). Copyright 1971 by *New York Amsterdam News.* Reprinted by permission.

Schneider, Gilbert D. "The Uncle Remus Dialect and Its Value to the Serious Scholar." Paper presented at the Linguistics Colloquium on Black English (February 20, 1973). Copyright 1973 by Gilbert D. Schneider.

Sellers, T. J. "English Not Dialect." *New York Times* (June 9, 1972). Copyright 1972 by The New York Times Co. Reprinted by permission.

Shearer, Lloyd. "Americans Who Can't Speak Their Own Language." *Parade* (June 11, 1967). Copyright 1967 by Parade.

Smith, C. Alphonso. "Dialect Writers" in *Cambridge History of American Literature.* G. P. Putnam's Sons. Copyright 1918 by G. P. Putnam's Sons.

Smith, Reed. *Gullah*. The University of South Carolina Press. Copyright 1926 by Bureau of Publications, University of South Carolina.

Spiller, Robert F., Willard Thorp, Thomas K. Johnson, and Henry Seidel Canby, eds. *Literary History of the United States*. Macmillan. Copyright 1955 by Macmillan Publishing Co., Inc.

Starke, Aubrey Harrison. *Sidney Lanier: A Biographical and Critical Study*. The University of North Carolina Press. Copyright 1933 by University of North Carolina Press.

"John Steptoe." *Contemporary Authors* (1974). Copyright 1974 by Gale Research Co., Inc.

Stoney, Samuel Gaillard, and Gertrude Mathews Shelby. *Black Genesis*. Macmillan. Copyright 1930 by Macmillan Publishing Co., Inc.

Tidwell, James Nathan. "Mark Twain's Representation of Negro Speech." *American Speech* (October 1942). Copyright 1942 by the American Dialect Society.

Tinker, Edward Laroque. "Cable and the Creoles." *American Literature* (January 1934). Copyright 1934 by Duke University Press.

Turner, Darwin T. *In a Minor Chord: Three Afro-American Writers and Their Search for Identity*. Southern Illinois University Press. Copyright 1971 by Southern Illinois University Press.

Turner, Lorenzo Dow. *Africanisms in the Gullah Dialect*. The University of Chicago Press. Copyright 1949 by University of Chicago Press.

Twain, Mark. *Simon Wheeler, Detective*. The New York Public Library. Copyright 1963 by the Trustees under the will of Clara Clemens Samoussoud.

Wagner, Jean. *Black Poets of the United States*. Translated by Kenneth Douglas. The University of Illinois Press. Copyright 1973 by University of Illinois Press.

Walser, Richard. "Negro Dialect in Eighteenth Century Drama." *American Speech* (December 1955). Copyright 1955 by The University of Alabama Press.

Weinraub, Bernard. "Auden: A Difference in Memories." *New York Times* (October 19, 1971). Copyright 1971 by The New York Times Co. Reprinted by permission.

Wright, Richard. *Lawd Today*. Walker & Co. Copyright 1963 by Walker and Co.

Index

AP, 285
Abernathy, Ralph, 228
Abolition, 24, 68
Abrahams, Roger D., xxv, 250, 251–
   252, 262, 263, 305 n
Absalom, Absalom! (Faulkner), 169–
   170
Acababe (Brasch), ix, x
Adams, Donald, 178
Adams, E. C. L., 207
Adventures of Huckleberry Finn, The
   (Twain), 103–104
Adventures of Tom Sawyer, The
   (Twain), 101
Advertising, xi, 6–8, 114–115
Aeneas Africanus (Edwards), 92
Africanisms in the Gullah Dialect
   (Turner), 215–217
Afro-American Folk-Lore (Christen-
   sen), 93
Afro-American Folksongs (Krehbiel),
   192
Ah, Man, You Found Me Again
   (Gross), 249
Ah, Wilderness! (O'Neill), 159
"Ain' No Time fo' Chillum" (Gon-
   zales), 110
Alexander, Benjamin H., 286
All God's Chillun Got Wings (O'Neill),
   159, 162
Allen, Junius Mordecai, 142–143
Allen, O. K., 197
Allen, William Francis, xii, 61–64, 68,
   119, 196, 205, 249, 307 n
Alleyne, Mervyn, xxvii
Alsberg, Henry, 315 n
Alta Californian, 100

American Ballads and Folksongs
   (J. Lomax, A. Lomax), 195
American Black English. *See* Black
   English
American Claimant, The (Twain), 103
American Dialect Society, ix, x
American Imago, 251
American Journal of Philology, 116
American Journal of Sociology, 212–
   213
American Language, The (Mencken),
   211, 277
American Mercury, 170, 176, 186, 207
American Negro Folklore (Brewer),
   250
American Negro Folk-Songs (White),
   194
American Notes and Queries, 119
American Speech, 263, 280, 282
American Tragedy, An (Dreiser), 234
American Weekly Mercury, The, 6, 7
Ames, Mary, 307 n
Amos 'n' Andy, 220–225, 316 n
"An' Chloe's Judgment" (Gonzales),
   110
Anderson, Eddie ("Rochester"), 149
Anderson, Jay, 248–249
Anderson, Marion, 149
Anderson, Sherwood, 165
Angel (Heyward), 183
Anglia, 117
Angola, 123
Angola State Prison Farm, 196
Ann Arbor Decision, 282–287
Ann Arbor News, 285
'Anna Christie' (O'Neill), 159
Anshen, Frank, 263

Antebellum Cycle of Black
 English. *See* Black English Cycles—
 Antebellum
"Ante-Bellum Sermon, An" (Dunbar),
 128–129
Appleton's (magazine), xii, 61, 97,
 145, 149
Arena, The, 79
Arizona Daily Star, 280
Armstrong, Louis, 149
Army Life in a Black Regiment (Hig-
 ginson), 65–66, 109, 205
Ashantee, 123
"Aspects of Morphemics, Syntax, and
 Semology in Inner-City Dialect
 (Merican) (Fickett), 318 n
Aspects of the Theory of Syntax
 (Chomsky), 257
Associated Press (AP), 285
Atlanta Constitution, The, 79–80, 84,
 86, 269, 273, 308 n
Atlanta Georgian, 155
Atlantic Monthly, The, 56, 61, 99, 119,
 121, 143, 170, 235
Auden, W. H., 272
Aunt Dicy Tales (Brewer), 251
*Aunt Phillis's Cabin; Or, So Life as it
 Is* (Eastman), 55
Autobiography of a Female Slave, The
 (Griffith), 52–54

Backus, Emma M., 93–94
Bailey, Beryl, 263
Bailey, Pearl, 184
Bailey, Richard W., viii, 283, 319
Baker, Josephine, 149
Baldwin, James, xiv, 235–236, 237
Ballanta-Taylor, Nickolas George
 Julius, 193
Balo (Toomer), 165
Bantu, xxx, 262, 287
Baraka, Imamu, 238
 See also Jones, LeRoi
Baratz, Joan, 238, 259, 263, 267
Barnum, P. T., 47
Barry, Phillips, 204
Barton, Andrew, 9
Bayliss, John, 205
Bayonne Times, 152
Beach, L., 25
Befo' de War: Echoes in Negro Dialect
 (Gordon, Page), 109
"Below the Surface" (Cohen), 152
"Ben Bolt" (English), 75
Bennett, James Gordon, 24
Bennett, John, 121
Benton, Clem, 314 n
Berdan, Robert, 261–262, 263

Berkin, Natalie Curtis, 194
Best, Willie, 149
Best of Simple, The (Hughes), 187
Beyond the Horizon (O'Neill), 158–
 159
Bibb, Henry, 205
Bidialectal readers, 259, 267, 270, 277
Bidialectal Theory. *See* Black English—
 theories, Bidialectal; Dialect readers
Big Gamble, The (Cohen), 152
Big Sea, The (Hughes), 185, 189
Billups, Edgar P., 151
Bini, 216
Bird Child, The (White), 165
Birmingham Ledger, 152
Birth of a Nation, 219
Black American churches, 44, 67–68,
 229, 250–251, 275, 276
Black American folklore, 78–93, 110–
 111, 188–192, 193, 207, 209, 217–
 218, 249–251, 305 n–306 n; Civil
 Rights Cycle, 249–254; Dozens, 249,
 251, 255, 305 n; Negro Renaissance
 Cycle, 189–192, 207; Reconstruction
 Cycle, 79–94, 110–111
Black American music: Antebellum
 Cycle, 46–50, 67–68; Negro Renais-
 sance Cycle, 192–201, 204; Civil
 Rights Cycle, 244–246; Reconstruc-
 tion Cycle, 66–69
Black April (Peterkin), 176
Black Border (Gonzales), 205–206
Black Boy (Wright), 234
Black Cameos (Kennedy), 206, 207
Black Cat Club, 135–136
Black English
—defined, 301 n
—geographical studies: Ann Arbor,
 282–287; Chicago, 262; Dayton, 280–
 281; Detroit, 261; Los Angeles, 261;
 Memphis, 262; New York, 260;
 Washington, D.C., 267
—Gullah, xviii, 11, 36, 62–64, 68, 80,
 83, 93, 109, 110, 119, 121, 122, 123,
 174, 175, 176, 182, 205–217 passim,
 266
—jive, 245–249
—legal cases: Ann Arbor Decision,
 282–287
—lexicons, 118–119, 255, 279, 302–
 303 n, 306 n, 308 n; slang, 245–249,
 279–282
—linguistic rules, 291–299; alveolar
 stops, 296; bilabial stops, 296; consonant clusters, 296–297; consonant
 inversion, 298; deep structure copula,
 291–292; deep structure possessive,
 292; devoicing, 298; elision, 298; eye
 dialect, 17, 103, 115, 141, 199, 203;

existential *it,* 293–294; fricatives, 296; hypercorrection, 299; indefinite articles, 294–295; interdental fricatives, 296; invariant *be,* 292; labiodental fricatives, 296; markers, 294; nasal replacement, 297; negation, 295; nominative pronoun, 293; number inflection, 294; possessives, 292; postvocalic [l], [r], 297; pronominal cross-reference marker, 293; pronouns, 293–294; semantic inversion, 295; stops, 296; sweet talk, 42, 299; third-person pronoun, 294; verb inflections, absence of, 292–293; verbal functors, 292–293; voiced bilabial stops, 296; voiced labiodental fricatives, 296; vowel glide, 297–298; word-initial syllable, elision of, 298; zero copula, 291–292; zero possessive, 292
—pedagogy, 254–255, 265–276; dialect readers, 259, 267, 277, 280–286
—theories, xv–xvi, xxii–xxix, 287–288; Antieradicationist, 269; Bidialectal, 259, 267–269, 272, 287–288; Creolist, xvii, xxv–xxvi, 83, 95, 98, 116, 210–211, 231, 241, 257–262, 264–280 passim, 287–288, 318 n; Cycle, x–xv, xvii, xix–xx, xxix, 287–288; Deficit, xv, xxii–xxv, 206–212, 241, 262–265, 267–276, 278–279, 287–288; Dialect geography, xxv–xxvi, 209–210, 241, 258, 262, 264, 276–278, 280, 287–288; Ebonics, xxvii–xxviii, 287–288, 302 n; eradicationist, 115–118, 267–275, 278–279, 281, 286, 287–288; "thick lips," xxiv; Unified, 278–279
"Black English: Check It Out, Man" (Dreshler), 280
Black English Cycles
—Antebellum, 23; first intercycle, 24–25; mass media, 23–24; minstrelsy, 46–50; novel, xii, 25–31, 54–58; observations, 41–46; short story, 31–41; slave narratives, x, xii, xx–xxi, 50–54, 59, 69, 158, 249; travelers' commentaries, xii
—Civil Rights, x, xiv, xviii, xxi, xxviii, 143, 227–288; changes in mass media, 255–256; children's literature, 239–240; controversy, 262–282; drama, 237, 239–240; folklore, 249–254; historical background, 227–230, 287; jazz, 244–246; linguistic studies, major, 257–265, 277–280, 283–287; mass media, changes in, 255–256; Montgomery, Ala., bus boycott, 227–229; music, 244–246; "new" literature, 231–240; novels, 239–240; pedagogy, 254–255, 265–276, 280–287; slang, 246–249, 279–282; transformational grammar, 256–257; Unified Theory of, defined, 287–288
—Colonial-Revolutionary, x–xi, xviii, xix, xx, 1–21, 158, 163; drama, xi, 8–17; early references, 3–8; intercycle, first, 24–25; novels, 17–20; travelers' commentaries, xi, 4–6
—Negro Renaissance, x, xiii–xiv, xx, xxi, 147–227, 250; dialect sermons and tales, 150–158; drama, xiii, 158–165; film, xiv, 218–220; folklore, 189–192, 207; Harlem Renaissance, xiii, 149 ff; jazz, 192 ff; music, 192–201; novel, xiii, 165–192; philological/linguistic studies, xiii, 207–218; radio, 218, 220–225
—Reconstruction, x, xii, xiii, xviii–xxi, 59–145, 151, 159, 205, 231, 249; advertising, 6–8, 114–115; Black writers, 124–145; dialect sermons, 69–70; fiction, 70–110, 124–125, 143–145; folklore, 79–94, 110–111; Harris, Joel Chandler, 79–90; historical background, 24, 59–61, 65, 231; music, 66–69; philological discussions, 61–66, 115–124; poetry, 71–78, 124–142; stereotyped humor, 111–114
—Sixth Cycle, xxix, 288
Black English: Its History and Usage in the United States (Dillard), 277–279
Black Genesis (Shelby, Stoney), 157–158, 208
Black Jargon in America (Claerbant), 249
Black Names (Dillard), 279
Black Preaching (Mitchell), 276
Black religion. *See* Black American churches
"Black Saxons, The" (Child), 30
Black Skin, White Masks (Fanon), 267
Black Slave Narratives (Bayliss), 205
Black Yeomanry (Woofter), 209
"Blackberries" (Kemble), 114
"Blackville" series (Eytinge), 114
Blackwell, Edward H., 248
Blake, Eubie, xiii, 149
Blumer, Herbert, 301n
Boaz, Franz, 190
Bolingbroke, Henry, 25
Bonaventure (Cable), 98
Bondurant, Alexander, 94
Bonner, Sherwood, 94–95
Bontemps, Arna, xiii, 149, 188, 237, 239
Book of American Negro Poetry, The (J. W. Johnson), 185

Book of Texas, The (J. Lomax), 194
Booke, Sorrell, 24
Boston News-Letter, 2
Boston Transcript, 173
Botkin, B. A., 204, 250, 315 n
Bound East for Cardiff (O'Neill), 159
Boyd, Walter, 197; *See also* Ledbetter, Huddie
Brackenridge, H. H., 18–19, 29
Bradford, Roark, xiii, 155–156, 157
Brasch, Helen Haskin, v, viii
Brasch, Milton, v, viii
Brasch, Walter Milton, viii, ix–x, 259, 263, 288
Bren Co., Joe, 221
Brewer, John Mason, 247, 250–251
Brickell, Herschell, 177
"Bride of the Battle, The" (Simms), 39
Bright Skin (Peterkin), 176
Britt, Donna, 285
Broadway Journal, 31–32
Broken Banjo, The (Richardson), 165
Brooklyn College, 270
Brooks, Cleanth, 210
Brooks, Stella Brewer, 87
brottus, 118
Broun, Heywood, 233
Brower, Frank, 47
Brown, Claude, xiv, 238–299, 248
Brown, H. Rap, 236, 237
Brown, John, 50
Brown, John Pairman, 269
Brown, Sterling, 202–203
Brown, William Hill, 18
Brown, William Wells, 51, 205
Brownell, Herbert, Jr., 228
Browney, Martha Griffith, 52–54
Brownie's Book, The, 185
Bruce, J. Douglas, 119
Bruce, Richard, 165
Bryant's Minstrels, 48
Bryden, Ronald, 237
Burleigh, Harry, 149
Burley, Dan, 245, 317 n
Burling, Robbins, 263, 280, 320 n
Bus boycott (Montgomery, Ala.), 227–229
Bush, Douglas, 272
"Buster Brown" (Outcault), 114
Bylow Hill (Cable), 98

CBS, 222–225
Cabin in the Cotton (Green), 162
Cabin and Plantation Songs (Fenner, et al.), 68–69
Cable, George Washington, 96–99, 250
Caldwell, Erskine, 165
Calhoun, John C., 50

Cambridge, Godfrey, 240
Camden, N.J., riots, 230
Campbell, G. L., 4
Campbell, James Edwin, 136–137
Campbell, John, 2
The Candidates (Munford), 9–10
Cap'n Simon Wheeler, The Amateur Detective (Twain), 101–102
Captain, The; Stories of the Black Border (Gonzales), 206
Carroll, William S., 267
Caruthers, William Alexander, 30
Cameroon, 259. *See also* West African Pidgin English
Cavalier, The (Cable), 98
"Centaur in Brass" (Faulkner), 170
Center for Applied Linguistics (CAL), 260, 261, 264, 267, 268, 288
Century Illustrated Monthly Magazine, xii, 61, 80, 91, 92, 103, 109, 145, 149, 173, 176
Chamberlain, A. F., 118
Charleston News & Courier, 110, 122, 152, 205
Chesnutt, Charles Waddell, xii, xiv, 142–144, 237, 250, 312 n
Chicago Daily News, 220, 226
Chicago Defender, 149, 187, 236
Chicago Journal, 134
Chicago Record, 92
Chicago Record-Herald, 134, 135
Chicago Times-Herald, 134, 136
Chicago Tribune, 135, 200, 286
Child, Lydia Maria, 30
Children's literature, 240–244
Childress, Alice, 239
Childress, Alvin, 224
Chomsky, Noam, 256–257
Christensen, Mrs. A. M. H., 93
Christian Examiner, The, 51
"Christmas-Night in the Quarters" (Russell), 77–78
Christopherson, Chris (O'Neill), 159
Christopherson, Paul, 258
Churches, Black. *See* Black American churches
Cincinnati Commercial, 95
Cincinnati Enquirer, 95
Cincinnati Journal, 150
City Gazette and Daily Advertiser, 8
Civil Rights Act of 1964, 230
Civil Rights Cycle of Black English. *See* Black English Cycles–Civil Rights; Mass Media–Civil Rights Cycle
Civil War. *See* United States History, Civil War
Claerbant, David, 249
Clansman, The (Dixon), 219

Clapp, Henry, 100
Clark, Emily, 171
Clark, Nona H., 302 n
Classical Dictionary of the Vulgar Tongue, The (Grose), 6
Classified advertising, xi, 6–8
Cleaveland, Bessie, 68
Cleaver, Eldridge, 236, 237
Clemens, Samuel, xii, xviii, 50, 91, 99–108, 145, 250, 305 n, 309 n
Cleveland Plain-Dealer, 249, 286
Cochran, Charles, 184
Cohen, Lily Young, 193
Cohen, Octavus Roy, xiii–xiv, 151–153
Cohen, Paul, 260
Colburn, Jerry, 286
Cold Blue Moon: Black Ulysses Afar Off (Odum), 193
Collier, Eugenia W., 187
Collier's (magazine), 170, 256
Colonel's Dream, The (Chesnutt), 144
Colonial-Revolutionary Cycle of Black English. *See* Black English Cycles—Colonial-Revolutionary; Mass Media—Colonial-Revolutionary Cycle
"Colored Soldiers, The" (Dunbar), 129
Columbia Broadcasting System (CBS), 222–225
Columbia University, 255, 260
Commonweal, 271–272, 273
Comprehensive Annotated Bibliography of American Black English, A (Brasch), ix, x
Congaree Sketches (Adams), 207
"Conjure Woman, The" (Chesnutt), 144
Connelly, Marc, xiii, 156–157
Conrack, 266
Conrad, Earl, 245
Conroy, Pat, 266
"Continuity and Change in American Negro Dialects" (Stewart), 259
Converse College, 176
Cook, Will Marion, 149
Coolidge, Calvin, 222
"Coon Alphabet, A" (Kemble), 114
Cooper, James Fenimore, xii, 25–28, 32, 57, 249, 305 n
Correll, Charles, 220–225
Corrothers, James D., 134–136, 150
Cosmopolitan, 61
Countryman, The, 79
Cowboy Songs and Other Frontier Ballads (J. Lomax), 194
Cowley, Malcolm, 170
Creole, xxvi, 83, 95–96, 98, 116, 302 n. *See also* Black English—theories, Creolist; Hearn, Lafcadio; Tinker, Edward Laroque

Crisis, The, 149, 173, 185, 186, 269, 270, 271
Crothers, Scatman, 276
Crowell Co., Thomas Y., 242, 243
Crowther, Bosley, 184
Crucible, The (Miller), 3
'Cruitter (Matheus), 165
Crum, Mason, 211–212
Culbertson, Ernest H., 165
Cullen, Countee, xiii, xiv, 149, 239
Cullinan, Bernice, 263, 267, 270
Currier & Ives, 114
Curtain at Eight (Cohen), 152
Cycle theory. *See* Black English Cycles; Black English—theories, Cycle

D. Appleton & Co., 84
Dabney, Ford, 149
Daddy Jack, 80, 83, 89–90. *See also* Harris, Joel Chandler
Dahomey, 123
Daily News (London), 130
Dalby, David, 258, 259
Dan Burley's Original Handbook of Harlem Jive, 245
Dandridge, Dorothy, 184
Dandridge, Raymond Garfield, 150–151
Danse Calinda, The (Torrance), 165
Darkey Ditties (Henderson), 150
Darkey Meditations (Henderson), 150
"Darktown" (Wirth), 114
David Harum (Green), 162
David He No Fear (Graham), 242
Davidson, James Wood, 86
Davis, A. L., 263
Davis, Daniel Webster, 137–141, 150
David, Lawrence, 263
Davis, Ossie, 239–240
Davis, Sammy, Jr., 184
Day, Benjamin H., 24
Day, E. M., 118
Days Without End (O'Neill), 159
Dayton Daily News, 280
Dayton Herald, 125
Death Dance, The (Duncan), 165
DeCamp, David, 258
Dee, Ruby, 240
Deep Down in the Jungle (Abrahams), 251–254
Deerslayer, The (Cooper), 26, 205 n
Deficit Theory. *See* Black English—theories, Deficit
Defoe, Daniel, 17–18
Delow, T. C., 116
"De Niggers Got to Go" (Davis), 139–141
"De Old Plantation; Elder Coteney's Sermons" (Williams), 122–124

Denton, Herbert H., 268
Desire Under the Elms (O'Neill), 159
Detroit Free Press, 285
Detroit, linguistic study, 261
Detroit News, 285
Dialect geography theory. *See* Black English—theories, Dialect geography
Dialect-Lexicon and Listening Comprehension (Foster), 255
Dialect Notes, 86, 87
Dialect poetry: Negro Renaissance Cycle, 150–151, 154–155; Reconstruction Cycle, 71–78, 108–109, 125–155
Dialect readers, 259, 267, 270, 277
Dialect sermons: Civil Rights Cycle, 250–251; Negro Renaissance Cycle, 154–158; Reconstruction Cycle, 69–70
Dialect tales: Antebellum Cycle, 25–41; Negro Renaissance Cycle, 151–152, 155–156; Reconstruction Cycle, 70–110, 124–125, 143–145
Dictionary of Afro-American Slang (Major), 246–247
Diglossia, 303 n
Dillard, J. L., 258, 259, 263, 267, 270, 277–280, 281, 283, 308 n
Disappointment, The (Barton), 9
Dis, Tat, and Tutter (Henderson), 150
Discovering American Dialects (Shuy), 264
Disney, Walt, 89, 231
"Dixie" (Emmett), 47–48
Dixon, Thomas, 219
Dobie, J. Frank, 250
Dr. Bull (Green), 162
Dr. Sevier (Cable), 98
Dog Ghosts and Other Texas Folk Tales (Brewer), 251
Dohn, Norman H., vii
Dollard, John, 251
Donovan, Gail M., 268
Dorson, Richard M., 250
Douglass, Frederick, 51–52, 67
Dove, Adrian, 248
Dozens, 249, 251, 255, 305 n. *See also* Abrahams, Roger D.; Dollard, John; Foster, Herbert; Haggarty, Sandra
Drake, Samuel G., 3
Drama: Civil Rights Cycle, xiii, 237, 239–240; Colonial-Revolutionary Cycle, xi, 8–17; Negro Renaissance Cycle, xii, 156–157, 158–165, 184–185
Draper, Delores, 231
Dreamy Kid, The (O'Neill), 159
Dred; A Tale of the Great Dismal Swamp (Stowe), 56

Dreiser, Theodore, 165, 233–234
Dreshler, Alex, 280
Dreyer, Edward, 204
Dreyfuss, Joel, 281
Driftings and Gleanings (Campbell), 136
Dry Victories (Jordan), 244
DuBois, W. E. B., xiii, 148, 149, 173, 241–242
Dudley, John, 283–287
Dulcey (Connelly, Kauffman), 156
Dunbar, Paul Laurence, xii, xiv, 125–134, 135, 136, 137, 141, 144, 145, 185, 231, 237
Duncan, Thelma, 165
Durham, Frank, 174, 181, 182
Dust Tracks in the Road (Hurston), 188
Dutchman (Jones), 237
Dwyer, David, 259

Eastland, James, 228
Eastman, George, 218
Eastman, Mary, 55
Eau Claire University, 248
Ebonics theory. *See* Black English—theories, Ebonics
Echoes From the Cabin and Elsewhere (Campbell), 136
Edwards, Harry Stilwell, 90–93
Efik, 216
Ehrnhardt, Johann, 114, 145
Elam, William Cecil, 118
Eliot, T. S., 165
Ellington, Duke, 149
Elliott, Harriet Rutledge, 109
Ellison, Ralph, xiv, 234–235, 237
Emmett, Daniel Decatur, 47–48, 70, 219, 221
Emperor Jones, The (O'Neill), 159–162
English, Thomas Dunn, 71–75, 145
English in Black and White (Burling), 280
English, Elizabethan, xxv. *See also* Black English—theories, Dialect geography
English Language in America, The (Krapp), 207–208
EPS (Elite-Popular-Specialized) Theory, xx–xxi
Eradicationist Theory. *See* Black English—theories, Deficit; and Black English—theories, Eradicationist
Eskew, Garnett Laidlaw, 177
Esquire, 186, 248
Ethnological Society of New York, 20
Evers, Medgar, 230

Every Man Heart Lay Down
  (Graham), 242
Everybody's (magazine), 61
Ewe, 216
Eye dialect. *See* Black English—
  linguistic rules, eye dialect
Eytinge, Sol, 114

Faber, A. Dilworth, 210
Fact and Fiction (Child), 30
Fader, David F., 283
Fairy Tales and Wonder Tales
  (English), 75
Falkner, William C., 165
Fall of British Tyranny, The
  (Leacock), 10–11
"Family Feud, A" (Dunbar), 132–133
Family Instructor, The (Defoe), 18
Fannon, Franz, 267
Fante, 216
Farrison, William Edward, 210
Fasold, Ralph W., 261, 263, 267, 268,
  320 n
Faulk, John Henry, 218
Faulkner, William, xiii, 165–170
Fauset, Jesse, 149
Federal Writers Projects, 201–204, 232
Feigenbaum, Irwin, 263, 267
Female Quixoticism (Tenney), 19
Fenner, Thomas, 68–69
Fetchit, Stepin, 149
Fickett, Joan, 263, 318 n
Fiction. *See* Drama; Novels; Poetry;
  Short stories
Field Techniques in an Urban Lan-
  guage Study (Shuy et al.), 261
Film. *See* Mass Media, film
Fine Clothes to the Jew (Hughes), 186
Fitzgerald, F. Scott, 165
Fleming, Elizabeth McClellan, 40
Flight of the Natives, The (Richard-
  son), 165
Florian Slappey Tales, 152–153
Florida FL Reporter, 263
Folb, Edith A., 249
Folk Beliefs of the Southern Negro
  (Puckett), 208
Folk Culture on St. Helena Island,
  South Carolina (G. Johnson), 209
Folk Music in America (Barry), 204
Folklore. *See* Black American folklore
Folklore Associates, 251
Folklore of the North Carolina Negro,
  The (Brewer), 251
Folks From Dixie (Dunbar), 132–133
Folk-Songs of the American Negro
  (1907, F. Work and 1915, J. Work),
  194

Follett Publishing Co., 240
Ford, Nick Aaron, 281, 282
Ford Foundation, 267
Forrest, Thomas, 9
Foster, Herbert L., 254–255
Four O'Clock Review, 136
Foxx, Redd, 276
Frank, Harriet, Jr., 266
Franklin, Benjamin, 5–6
Franklin, James, 302 n
Fraser, C. Gerald, 270
Free Joe and Other Georgian Sketches
  (Harris), 89
Freud, Sigmund, 251
Frieden, Fannie Haskin, v
Frieden, Samuel, v
From the Desert (Holloway), 150
From a New England Woman's Diary
  in Dixie in 1865 (Ames), 307 n
Frost, A. B., 145, 149
Frost, Robert, 165
Fruit, J. P., 87

Gã, 216
Gabriel Tolliver (Harris), 90
Gambia, xxvi
Garrison, Lucy McKim, 64
Garvey, Marcus, xiii, 148
Gary Post-Tribune, 286
Gay, Eustace, 186
Gehrig, Lou, 201
Gentleman's Magazine, 31
Geographical studies. *See* Black
  English—geographical studies
Georgia Gazette, 7
Georgia Institute of Technology, 229
Georgian, 178
Gershwin, George, 184–185
Gershwin, Ira, 184
Gilded Age (Twain, C. D. Warner),
  103
Gillam, Bernhard, 114
Gillespie, Elizabeth, 217–218
Gillespie, John T., 268
Gilmore, Caroline Howard, 41–42
Gilpin, Charles, xiii, 149, 312 n
Go Down, Moses (Faulkner), 170
Go Tell It On the Mountain (Baldwin),
  235
God Bless the Devil, 204
God Sends Sunday (Bontemps, Cullen),
  239
God Wash the World and Start Again
  (Graham), 242
God's Trombones (J. W. Johnson),
  154–155, 241
Going to Meet the Man (Baldwin),
  235–236

Gola, 123
"Gold Bug, The" (Poe), 32, 35
Gold, Robert S., 246
Goldwyn, Samuel, 184
Gombo Zhèbes (Hearn), 95
Gone are the Days, 240
Gone With the Wind (Mitchell), xiv, 174–180
Gonzales, Ambrose, 109–111, 122, 155, 171, 174–175, 180, 205–206, 207, 211, 250, 315 n
Gonzales, N. G., 110
Goodman, Kenneth, 263, 268
Goophered Grapevine, The" (Chesnutt), 143–144
Gordon, A. C., 109
Gosden, Freeman Fisher, 220–225
Gospels Written in the Negro Patois of English With Arabic Characters, The, 20
Graham, Lorenz, 240–243
Graham's Magazine, 31–32, 61
Grandissimes, The (Cable), 97
Granny Maumee (Torrance), 165
Great God Brown, The (O'Neill), 159
Greeley, Horace, 24, 25
Green, Katherine, 285
Green Pastures, The (Connelly), 156–157
Green, Paul, 162–165
Green Road Housing Development, 283–286
Green Thursday (Peterkin), 171–172, 173
Greenwood Press, 204
Griffin, John H., 163
Griffin, Junius, 247
Griffin, Marvin, 229
Griffith, D. W., 219
Griffith, Mattie, 52–54
Grose, Francis, 6
Gross, Mary Anne, 249
Guest, Charles Boyd, 210
Gullah. *See* Black English—Gullah
Gullah: Negro Life in the Carolina Sea Islands (Crum), 211
Gumbo Ya-Ya (Saxon, et al.), 204
Guy Rivers; A Tale of Georgia (Simms), 39

Haggerty, Sandra, 249, 251
Haight-Ashbury, 247
Hairy Ape, The (O'Neill), 159
Hale, Horatio, 117
Hall, Joseph C., 269
Hall, Robert A., 258
Hall, William S., 285
Hallelujah!, xiv, 219–220

"Hallmark Hall of Fame," 157
Hancock, Ian, viii, 258, 259, 260, 263
Handy, W. C., xiii, 149
Hansberry, Lorraine, 239
Harlem, 148, 149, 230, 235, 236, 247, 265, 301 n
Harlem Renaissance. *See* Black English Cycles—Negro Renaissance; Mass Media—Negro Renaissance Cycle
Harper, Frances E. W., 124–125
Harper & Row, 243
Harper's Magazine, 145, 170
Harper's New Monthly Magazine, 109, 170
Harper's Weekly, xii, 61, 95, 114, 126, 145
Harris, Joel Chandler, xii, xxiii, 78, 79–90, 110, 125, 143, 144–145, 154–155, 178, 179, 182, 196, 231, 250, 308 n; Daddy Jack, 80–83, 89; dialect observations, 83–86; observations by others, 87–88; Uncle Remus, 78–90 passim, 231
Harris, Julia Collier, 79, 178
Harris, Julian, 89
Harris, Lucien, 178
Harris, Mary, 178
Harrison, James A., 116–117, 119, 196
Harrison, Richard B., 149, 156
Hart, James D., 105–106
Harvard University, 194, 272
Haskin, Morris, v
Haskins, Kenneth, 283
Hathorne, John, 3
Hayes, Rutherford B., 59–60
Hearn, Lafcadio, 95–96, 97, 145, 250
Hearst, William Randolph, xxi, 60
Hearts in Dixie, 219
Hecht, Ben, 165
Hemingway, Ernest, 165
Henderson, Elliot Blaine, 150
Henderson, Fletcher, 149
Hepcats Jive Talk Dictionary (Shelly), 246
Heraclitus, xvi
Herskovits, Melville J., xiv, 213–215, 217, 250
Heydenfeldt, S., 118
Heyward, Dorothy, 165, 183–184
Heyward, DuBose, xiii, 165, 180–185
Higginson, Thomas Wentworth, xii, 65–66, 68, 91, 109, 119, 196, 205, 249
His Own Where (Jordan), 243–244
History and Remarkable Life of the Truely Honorable Colonel Jacque, The (Defoe), 17
Hodgson, W. B., 20
"Hogan's Alley" (Outcault), 114

Holloway, John Wesley, 150
Hongry Catch the Foolish Boy
  (Graham), 242
Hoover, Herbert, 222
Houghton Mifflin & Co., 143–144
House Behind the Cedars, The
  (Chesnutt), 144
Houston, Susan, 282
How God Fix Jonah (Graham), 241–
  242
Howard, Sidney, 177
Howells, William Dean, 108, 126–127,
  134
Hughes, Langston, xiii, xiv, 149, 185–
  188, 189, 190, 236–237, 239
Hulik, Katherine, 285
Humble Folks (Henderson), 150
Hurst, Charles G., Jr., 263, 266
Hurst, Fannie, 314 n
Hurston, Zora Neale, 149, 188–192,
  237, 250, 312 n, 314 n
Hutchens, John, 156
Hutter, Gertrude, 281
Hypercorrection, 299

I, Momolu (Graham), 242
Ibo, 216
Iceman Cometh, The (O'Neill), 159
Idle Moments (Davis), 141
Idler Magazine, 103
"If You Think It's Groovy to Rap,
  You're Shucking" (Jahn), 247
Imperial University (Tokyo), 96
"Imports From Africa" (Peterkin), 173
In Abraham's Bosom (Green), xiii,
  163–165
In Splendid Error (Branch), 239
Independent, The, 121, 181
*Industrial History of the United States,
  The* (Davis, G. Jackson), 141
Ingraham, Joseph Holt, 42–43
Ingram, Rex, 149
Intercycles, vii, 24–25, 287–288
Intruder in the Dust (Faulkner), 170
Invisible Man (Ellison), 234–235
Iola Leroy; Or, Shadows Uplifted
  (Harper), 125
Irrelevant English Teacher, The
  (Morse), 274–275
Ives, Sumner, 87–88

Jackson, Giles B., 141
Jahn, Mike, 247
James I, 1
James, Henry, 233
James Towne, 1–2
Janson, Charles William, 25

Jazz: Civil Rights Cycle, 244–246;
  Negro Renaissance Cycle, 192. *See
  also* Burley, Dan; Major, Clarence
Jazz Age, The, 192
Jazz Lexicon, A. (Gold), 246
Jazz Singer, The, 219
Jazz Talk (Gold), 246
Jefferson, Blind Lemon, xiii, 149, 199
Jenifer, George Davis, 133–144
Jes' Plain Black Fo'ks (Henderson),
  150
Jewett & Co., John P., 54
Jewish Tribune, The, 152
Jive, 245–249. *See also* Jazz
Jive Lexicon Analogy Test (Foster),
  255
John Henry (Bradford), 156
Johnson, Charles S., 149, 209–210, 212
Johnson, Georgia Douglas, 165
Johnson, Guion Griffis, 209
Johnson, Guy B., 194, 209, 211
Johnson, James Weldon, xiii, 121, 149,
  185, 241; opinion of dialect, 153–155
Johnson, Kenneth S., 262, 263, 265, 275
Johnson, Lyndon, 230
Joiner, Charles W., 283–287
Jolson, Al, 219
Jonah's Gourd Vine (Hurston), 191
Jonathan Postfree (Beach), 25
Jones, Charles Colcock, Jr., 44–45, 90
Jones, Hugh, 5
Jones, LeRoi, 236, 237, 238
Joplin, Scott, xiii, 149
Jordan, June, 243–244, 281
Journal of American Folklore, 92, 263
Journal of Commerce, 55
Journal of Negro History, 149, 212
*Journal of a Residence on a Georgian
  Plantation, The* (Kemble), 43–44
Judge (magazine), 111–114
Judge Lynch (Rogers), 165
"Jumping Frog of Calaveras County"
  (Twain), 101

Kaimowitz, Gabe, 283–287
Kansas City Star, 286
Kaplan, Arthur M., 152
Kauffman, George S., 156
Kellogg, Theodore H., 117–118
Kelly, William Melvin, 247
Kemble, E. W., 114, 149
Kemble, Frances Ann, 43–44, 145
Kennedy, R. Emmet, 206
Keppler, Joseph, 114
Key, Mary Ritchie, 263
Kilham, Elizabeth, 116
King, Martin Luther, Jr., 228
Kingdom Coming (Bradford), 156

Kinlaw Tales, 110, 111
Kittredge, George Lyman, 194
Knight, Sarah Kemble, 3
Knights of the Horse-Shoe, The
(Caruthers), 30
Knopf, Alfred A., Inc., 186
Kochman, Thomas, 263
Kohl, Herbert, 265–266
Kraft, Charles, 301 n
Krehbiel, Henry Edward, 192
Krapp, George Phillip, 207–208
Krio (Sierra Leone), 260
Krutch, Joseph Wood, 156
Ku Klux Klan, xiii, 219, 263
Kuglar, R. F., 238–239
Kurath, Hans, 278, 316 n

Labov, William, A., 260–261, 263, 264,
268, 270, 273–274, 283
Ladies Home Journal, 176
Lafitte, the Pirate of the Gulf
(Ingraham), 43
*Laguerre, A Gascon of the Black
Border* (Gonzales), 206
Laird, Roland, 272
Language, 258, 316 n
*Language in the Inner City: Studies in
The Black English Vernacular*
(Labov), 261
Language Sciences, 263
"Language of Soul, The" (Brown), 248
Lanier, Clifford, 75–76, 145
Lanier, Sidney, 75–76, 86, 145
Larsen, Nella, 149
Last of the Mohicans, The (Cooper),
26
Lawd Today (Wright), 233–234
Lawson, Edward H., 128
Lay My Burden Down (Botkin), 204
"Lazy Crow, The" (Simms), 36
Leacock, John, 11
Lead Belly, xiii, 196–201
Leblanc, Jerry, 249
Ledbetter, Huddie, xiii, 196–201
Legum, Stanley, 261–262, 263
Legal cases, 282–287
Lehmann-Haupt, Christopher, 279
Leland, John, 5
Lemay, Elizabeth, 155
Lerner, Alan Jay, 306 n
Lester, Julius, 205
Lewis, John, 260
Lewis, Ken, 283–287
Lewis, Nell Battle, 172
Lewis, Sinclair, 165
Lexicons. *See* Black English—lexicons
Lexicon of Black English (Dillard),
279, 308 n

Liars' Bench Tales, 204
Liberia, 241, 260
Liberian Pidgin English, 241–242, 260
Liberty, 256
Library Journal, 238
Life, 256, 266
*Life and Surprising Adventure of
Robinson Crusoe* (Defoe), 18
Light in August (Faulkner), 169
Lincoln, Abraham, 49, 55
Lingua, 263
Linguistic Atlas, 88, 316 n
*Linguistic Correlates of Social Stratifi-
cation in Detroit Speech* (Shuy
et al.), 261
Linguistic Rules, Black English. *See*
Black English—linguistic rules
Linguistics, 263
Linney, Romulus, 239
Linthicum, Richard, 136–137
Lippincott's, xii, 61, 71, 118, 145, 149
Literary Messenger, The, 61
Literature, children's, 240–244
Little, Cleavon, 240
*Living Webster Encyclopedic Diction-
ary of the English Language,* 247
Locke, Alain, 148
Loewe, Frederick, 306 n
Loflin, Marvin, 263, 269
"Logic of Nonstandard English, The"
(Labov), 264
Lomax, Alan, 194–199, 250, 314 n
Lomax, John A., 194–199, 201, 203,
218, 250, 315 n; dialect, discussion
of, 195, 203
London (magazine), 4
"London" (slave), 20
London Evening Star, 312 n
Lonesome Road, The (P. Green), 163
Long Day's Journey Into Night, A
(O'Neill), 159
Long, Huey, 316 n
Long, Richard, 88
Look, 256
Lopez, Thomas R., Jr., 269
Los Angeles: dialect studies of, 261;
Watts riot, 230
Los Angeles Times, 249, 269
Lost Spirituals (Cohen), 193
Louisville Courier-Journal, 155
Loves of the Driver, The (Simms), 37
Low, Samuel, 11–12
Lowenstein, Ralph L., xx
Lower Guinea, 123
Lucy, Authurine, 230
Luelsdorf, Philip, 263
Lyell, Charles, 44
Lyrics of Lowly Life (Dunbar), 126–
127

MacDowell, Katherine Sherwood, 94–95

Macon (Ga.) Daily Telegraph and Messenger, 45, 91

Macon (Ga.) Evening News and Sunday Times, 91

Madamme Delphine (Cable), 98

Magnolia, The, 30, 35, 36

"Mahs' Lewis's Ride" (English), 71

Major, Clarence, 246–247

Majors and Minors (Dunbar), 126, 128

Making of a Statesman, The (Harris), 89

Marcel, 61. *See also* Allen, William Francis

Marcia (Steptoe), 243

Marconi, Guglielmo, 218

"Marse Chan" (Page), 109

Marsh, John, 177, 180

Marsh, Peggy, 176. *See also* Mitchell, Margaret

Martin Luther King, Jr., Elementary School Children *v.* Ann Arbor School District Board, 282–287

Maryland Gazette, 7

Mass Communication, defined, xx–xxii

Mass Communications, defined, xxii

Mass Media
—advertising, xiii, 6–8, 114–115
—Antebellum Cycle of Black English, 23 ff, 158; minstrelsy, 46–50, 215–219; novels, 24–30, 31–41 passim, 50–58 passim; short stories, 31–41; slave narratives, 50–54
—Civil Rights Cycle of Black English, x, xii, xviii, xxi, xxviii, 43, 225–288; Ann Arbor Decision, 283–287; children's literature, 240–244; controversy, 262–282; drama, 237, 239–240; folklore, 249–254; historical background, 227–230; music, 244–246; novels, 231–239
—Colonial-Revolutionary Cycle of Black English, x–xi, xvii, xix, xx, 1 ff, 158, 163, 302 n; classified advertising, 6–8; drama, 8–17; first press in Colonies, 2; novels, 17–20; preliminary studies, 3–8
—controversy in (recent), 262–282
—Cycle Theory, xxix, 287–288; Sixth Cycle, 288
—defined, x, xii
—EPS Curve (Theory), xx–xxi
—film, xvi, 219–220, 316 n; *Gone With the Wind,* 176–180; stereotypes, 216–219
—function of, xxi–xxii, 301 n

—historical base, xi–xvii
—minstrelsy, 218–219
—Negro Renaissance Cycle of Black English, x, xiii–xiv, xxi, 147–225; dialect poetry, 150–151; dialect sermons, 156–157; dialect tales, 151–152, 155–156; drama, 156–165, 183–185; film, 176–180, 218–220; folklore, 188–192; music, 192–201; poetry, 150–151, 154–155, 185, 186 (*see also* Hughes, Langston); novel, 165–183, 188–192; radio, 218, 220–225; slave narratives, 201–204
—newspapers, x, xxi, 6–8; first continuing, 2; "Penny Press," xxi, 23–24
—photography, 218
—radio, 157, 218, 220–224
—Reconstruction Cycle of Black English, x, xii, xiii, xviii–xxi, 59–145, 151, 158; dialect poetry, 71–78, 108–109, 125–143; dialect sermons,, 69–70; ephemera, 114–115; folklore, 79–90, 92–95, 109, 110–111; *Judge* (magazine), 111–114; magazines, 176–225 passim; music, 66–69; novels, 91–92, 94, 96–108, 143–145; poetry, 71–78, 91–92, 124–142; short stories, 90 ff
—stereotypes, 69–70, 71–78 passim, 91–92, 111–114, 150–151, 156–157, 218–225 passim

Mather, Cotton, 3–4, 302 n

Matheus, John, 165

Maxwell, 20

McClendon, Rose, 149

McClure's (magazine), 61

McClure's Syndicate, 103

McDaniels, Hattie, 149, 179, 313 n

McDavid, Raven I., Jr. xxv–xxvi, 36, 264, 268, 278, 316 n

McDavid, Virginia Glenn, 302 n

McDowell, Tremaine, 8, 25–26, 55, 57–58

McKay, Claude, 149, 237

McQueen, Butterfly, 149, 179, 313 n

Media, Messages, and Men (Lowenstein, Merrill), xx

"Meh Lady: A Story of the War" (Page), 109

Mellan, Olivia, 269

Melville, Herman, 30–31

Mencken, H. L., 165, 171, 207, 211, 278

Mende, 216

Mercer, Walter, 274

Merrill, John C., viii, xx

"Merry-Go-Round, The" (Peterkin), 171

Metro-Goldwyn-Mayer (MGM), 219

Michener, Charles, 277

Michigan Legal Services (Detroit), 282–286
Miller, Arthur, 3
Mills, Florence, 149
Millstein, Gilbert, 247
Milwaukee Journal, 248
Mingo, and Other Sketches in Black and White (Harris), 89
Minister's Wooing, The (Stowe), 56–57, 58
Minstrelsy, xiv, 46–50, 201, 218–219, 221–225, 276
"Miss Liza's Banjer" (Davis), 137–139
Mitchell, Henry, 276
Mitchell, Margaret, xiii, 176–180
Mitchell-Kernan, Claudia, 263
Moby-Dick (Melville), 30–31
Model Cities Program (Dayton, Ohio), 280–281
Modern Chivalry (Brackenridge), 18–19
Modern Language Association (MLA), 264
Modern Language Notes, 116–117, 119
"Momma Phoebe" (English), 71–75
Montgomery, Ala., bus boycott, 227–229
Moon for the Misbegotten, A (O'Neill), 159
Moore, Tim, 224
Morris, J. Allen, 36
Morris, Lloyd, 181
Morrow of Tradition, The (Chesnutt), 144
Morse, J. Mitchell, 274–275
Morton, Jelly Roll, 149
Moses, Man of the Mountain (Hurston), 191
Mosquitoes (Faulkner), 166
Mourning Becomes Electra (O'Neill), 159
Mouton, 256
"Mule in the Yard" (Faulkner), 170
Mulebone (Hughes, Hurston), 189
Mules and Men (Hurston), 190
Munford, Robert, 9–10
Munsey's (magazine), xii, 61
Murdock, John, 13–14
Music. *See* Black American music
My Fair Lady (Lerner, Loewe), 306 n
My Special Best Words (Steptoe), 243
Myth of the Negro Past, The (Herskovits), 213–215, 217

NAACP (National Association for the Advancement of Colored People), 148, 149, 153, 173, 185, 224–225, 269–270; eradicationist position, 269–270

NBC, 157, 221–223
Narcisse, Augusta R., 280
Narrative of Solomon Northrup, The, 51, 205
Narrative of William Wells Brown, The, 51, 205
Narratives, slave. *See* Slave narratives
Nash, N. Richard, 184
Nation, The, 61, 119, 156, 205, 277
National Council of Teachers of English, 264, 274
National Era, The, 54
National Urban League, 149
Native Son (Wright), 234
Neale, Walter, 193
Neff, Pat, 197
Negrito, Negro Dialect Poems of the Southwest (Brewer), 250
Negro and American Civilization, The (C. Johnson), 209
"Negro Dialect: Should the Schools Fight It?" (Denton), 267–268
Negro in Films, The (Noble), 316 n
Negro Folk Songs Sung by Lead Belly (J. Lomax, A. Lomax), 194
Negro Folk-Songs (Berkin), 194
Negro and His Songs, The (Odum), 193–194
Negro Myths From the Georgia Coast (Jones), 90
Negro Renaissance Cycle of Black English. *See* Black English Cycles—Negro Renaissance; Mass Media—Negro Renaissance
"Negro Sermon" (Emmett), 70
"Negro Speaks of Rivers, The" (Hughes), 185
Negro in Virginia, The, 204
Negro Workaday Songs (G. B. Johnson, Odum), 194
New American Cyclopaedia, 123
New Orleans Item, The, 78, 95
New Orleans Picayune, 97
New Orleans Times-Democrat, 95, 96
New Orleans Times-Picayune, 156, 286
New Republic, The, 181, 186, 269
New Voyage to Guinea, A (Smith), xxvi
New York Amsterdam News, 245, 270, 272
New York Clipper, 70
New York Evening Post, 7, 84, 219
New York Herald, 24, 47, 135
New York Herald-Tribune, 156, 186, 220
New York Independent, 93
New York Journal, 135
New York New Mirror, 75
New York Review, 265–266

New York Sun, 24
New York Times, 90, 147, 172, 181, 184, 247, 248, 270, 271, 272, 277, 279, 286, 319 n
New York Times Book Review, 239
New York Tribune, 24, 45, 55, 181
New York University, 270
New York World, 155, 156, 172
Newark (N.J.) *Morning Star,* 152
Newell, William Wells, 93–94
New-England Courant, 302 n
Newman, Edwin, 275
Newman, Frances, 181
Newspapers. *See* Mass Media—newspapers
Newsweek, 247, 277
Nichols, Henry H., 268–269
Nichols, Michael, 261–262
Nièpce, Joseph, 218
Nights With Uncle Remus (Harris), 83–85
Noble, Peter, 316 n
North American Review, 118, 305 n
North Town (Graham), 241
Northrup, Solomon, 51, 205
Novels: Antebellum Cycle, xii, 25–31, 54–58; Civil Rights Cycle, 231–239; Colonial-Revolutionary Cycle, xii, 17–20; Negro Renaissance Cycle, xiii, 165–192; Reconstruction Cycle, xii, 70–110, 124–125, 143–145

Oak and Ivy (Dunbar), 125–126
Occurrences of the Times, 12–13
Odum, Howard, 193–194, 250
O'Hern, Edna M., 258
Ol' King David an' the Philistine Boys (Bradford), 156
Ol' Man Adam an' His Chillun (Bradford), 156
Old American Company of Comedians, 13
Old Creole Days (Cable), 97–98
"Old Wine—New Bottles" (Gonzales), 110
Olmstead, Frederick Law, 51
On the Trail of the Negro Folk-Songs (Scarborough), 193
O'Neill, Eugene, xiii, 158–162, 163, 165
Opper, F. B., 113
Opportunity, 149, 151, 173, 185, 186
"Ortymobile, The" (Peterkin), 173–175
Osofsky, Gilbert, 205
Our Singing Country (J. Lomax, A. Lomax), 194
Outcault, Richard Felton, 114, 145, 149
Outlook, 181
Outlook and Independent, 219

PMLA, 264
Page, Thomas Nelson, xii, 87,108–109
Palmer, Marion, 231
Parade, 265
Pardoe, T. Earl, 210–211
Park, Robert E., 212, 301 n
Parks, Rosa, 227–229
Partisan, The; A Tale of the Revolution (Simms), 40
Partisan Leader, The; A Tale of the Future (Sidney), 29, 58
Pathfinder, The (Cooper), 26
Patrick, Thomas W., 270
Peabody, Ephraim, 51
Pedagogy, 61–64, 254–255, 265–276, 280–282
Pederson, Lee A., 262
Peece, Harold, 188
Peet, Creighton, 219–220
Pelham, Richard Ward, 47
Pencilled Poems (Dandridge), 150
Pennsylvania Chronicle, 9
Pennsylvania Gazette, 8
Pennsylvania Packett, 8
"Penny Press." *See* Mass Media, newspapers, "Penny Press"
Perdue, Charles, 205
Perspectives on Black English (Dillard), 279
Peterkin, Julia Mood, xiii, 171–176, 180, 192
Peters, Brock, 184
Peterson, Louis, 239
Petrella, Beatrice, 270
Pfaff, Carol, 261–262
Philadelphia: Black English controversy in schools, 268–269; riots, 230. *See also* Abrahams, Roger D.
Philadelphia Daily News, 268–269
Philadelphia Dollar Newspaper, 32
Philadelphia Evening Bulletin, 268
Philadelphia Herald, 135
Philadelphia Inquirer, 135, 269
Philadelphia Sunday Courier, 32
Philadelphia Tribune, 186
"Pickaninnies" (E. W. Kemble), 114
Pidgin English, 30; defined, 302 n. *See also* West African Languages, West African Pidgin English
Pietras, Thomas, 285
Pilot, The (Cooper), 26
Pioneers, The (Cooper), 26, 136
Plantation Christmas, The (Peterkin), 176
Plantation Echoes (Henderson), 150
Plessy *v.* Ferguson, 60
Plunes (G. D. Johnson), 165
Plymouth, Mass., 1
Poe, Edgar Allan, 31–35

Poems by Irwin Russell (ed. Harris), 78
Poems of Miscellaneous Subjects (Harper), 124
Poet and Other Poems, The (Dandridge), 150
Poetry: Civil Rights Cycle, 250; Negro Renaissance Cycle, 150–151, 154–155, 185, 186; Reconstruction Cycle, 71–78, 124–142
Poitier, Sidney, 184
Polished Ebony (Cohen), 152
Polite, Dennis, 281
Politician Out-Witted, The (Low), 11
Politicians, The; Or, a State of Things (Murdock), 14
Popular Science Monthly, 78, 116, 117
Porgy (Heyward), 165, 180–185
Porgy (Heyward and Heyward), 165, 182
Porgy and Bess (G. Gershwin, I. Gershwin, DuBose Heyward), xiv, 184–185
Portable Faulkner, The (Cowley), 170
Positively Black (Abrahams), 251–253
"Posson Jone" (Cable), 97
"Power of Prayer, The; Or, the First Steamboat Up the Alabama" (S. Lanier, C. Lanier), 75–76
Prairie, The (Cooper), 26
Preminger, Otto, 184
Present State of Virginia, The (H. Jones), 5
Prince of Parthia, The, 9
Proceedings of the American Philological Association, 118
Provincetown Players, 159
Pryor, Richard, 276
Psychology Today, 282
Publication of the American Dialect Society, 263
Puck (magazine), 78, 113, 114
Puckett, Niles Newell, 208
"Pudd'nhead Wilson" (Twain), xviii, 104–108
Pulitzer, Joseph, xxi, 60
Purlie Victorious (O. Davis), 239–240
Putnam, George N., 258
Putnam's Monthly Magazine, 54, 61, 116
Puttin' on Ole Massa . . . (ed. Osofsky), 205
Pygmalion (Shaw), 206 n

"Question of Color, The" (Gonzales), 110
Quinn, Arthur Hobson, 14
Quigg, H. D., 246–247

RCA, 221
Rackey (Culbertson), 165
Radio. *See* Mass Media, Radio
Rafferty, Max, 264–265
Rainbow 'Round My Shoulder: The Blue Trail of Black Ulysses (Odum), 193
Raisin in the Sun, A (Hansberry), 239
Raleigh News & Observer, 172
Raphaelson, Samson, 219
Raspberry, William, 286
Rathbun, Frederick, 68
Ravetch, Irving, 266
Rawick, George P., 204
Read, Allen Walker, 303 n
Recollections of a Southern Matron (Gilmore), 41
Reconstruction Cycle of Black English. *See* Black English Cycles—Reconstruction; Mass Media—Reconstruction Cycle
Red Rover, The (Cooper), 26
Redpath, James, 45–46
Redskins; Or, Indians and Injins (Cooper), 27
Reed, Carroll E., viii, 267
Religion, Black. *See* Black American churches
Religious Instruction of the Negroes (C. Jones), 44
Return to South Town (Graham), 241
Reuter, E. B., 212–213
"Reverend Moakly McKoon" series (Worden), 112
Reviewer, The, 171, 313 n
"Revival Song" (Harris), 308 n
Rhymes, Tales, and Rhymed Tales (Allen), 141
Richardson, Willis, 165
Rider of Dreams, The (Torrance), 165
Riley, James Whitcomb, 116
Riley, William K., 261, 263
Rind's Virginia Gazette, 7
Ritt, Martin, 266
Road Down by the Sea, A (Graham), 242
Roberts, Hermese, 247
Robeson, Paul, xiii, 149, 312 n
Robin, C. C., 24
Robins, Clarence, 260
Robinson, Bill, xiii
Robinson, J., 13, 14
Rochester, N.Y., riots, 230
Rogers, John W., Jr., 165
Roget, Peter Mark, 218
Roll, Jordan, Roll (Peterkin), 176
Romero, C. Gilbert, 272
Roper, Moses, 51

Roving Editor, The; Or, Talks With Slaves in the Southern States (Redpath), 45
Rowan, Carl, 286
Rowlette, Robert, 103
Royall, Anne Newport, 28–29
Rules, Linguistic. *See* Black English—linguistic rules
Russell, Irwin, xii, 76–79, 145
Rustin, Bayard, 270–271

Sacramento Union, 100
Sahdji; An African Ballet (Bruce), 165
Salem witch trials, 3
Sam 'n' Henry, 220–221. See also *Amos 'n' Andy*
San Diego Union, 264
San Francisco Bulletin, 100
San Francisco Call, 100
Sandburg, Carl, 165
Sanders, Isaiah, 208
Sartoris (Faulkner), 165–166
Satanstoe (Cooper), 26
Saturday Evening Post, 152, 170, 176, 256
Saturday Press, 100, 101
Saturday Review of Literature, 172, 286
Saxon, Lyle, 204
Scarborough, Dorothy, 193
Scarborough, W. S., 79, 118
Scarlet Sister Mary (Peterkin), 176
Schneider, Gilbert D., vii, ix–x, 88, 258, 259, 262, 301 n
Schulze, Johann Heinrich, 218
Science (magazine), 118
"Scientific Value of Creole, The" (Hearn), 95–96
Scribner's Monthly, xii, 61, 71, 75–76, 97, 98, 108, 145, 149, 176, 186
Sea Islands, S.C., 61–64, 93, 208–209, 211, 215–217
Second Visit to the United States of America, A (Lyell), 44
Sellers, T. J., 272
Selznick, David O., 179
"Sense and Nonsense About American Dialects" (McDavid), 264
Seraph on the Suwanee (Hurston), 191, 192
Sermons, Dialect. *See* Dialect Sermons
Seward, William A., 55
Seymour, Dorothy Z., 271–272, 273
Shadow of the Plantation (C. Johnson), 209–210, 212
"Shakespeare in Possumville" series (Outcault), 114
Shanker, Albert, 271

Shaw, George Bernard, 306 n
Shearer, Lloyd, 265
Shedd, Mark R., 268
Shelby, Gertrude Mathews, 157–158, 208
Shelly, Lou, 246
Sherwood, A. M., Jr., 219
Short stories: Antebellum Cycle, 31–41; Negro Renaissance Cycle, 150–158; Reconstruction Cycle, 90 ff
Shuy, Roger W., 261, 263, 264, 268, 285
Sidney, Edward William, 29–30
Sierra Leone Krio, 260
"Silhouettes" series (Gonzales), 110, 111
Simms, William Gilmore, xii, 26, 35–41, 48, 57, 108, 180
Simon Wheeler, Detective (Twain), 101–102
Simpkins, Gary, 283
Simple Speaks His Mind (Hughes), 187
Simple Stakes a Claim (Hughes), 187
Simple Takes a Wife (Hughes), 187
Simple's Uncle Sam (Hughes), 187
Simply Heavenly (Hughes), 239
Sinclair, Upton, 165
Sister Jane: Her Friends and Acquaintances (Harris), 89–90
Sixth Cycle of American Black English, xxix, 288
"Sketches in Color" (Kilham), 116
Sketches of Southern Life (Harper), 125
Slang. *See* Black English—lexicons, slang
Slave narratives: Antebellum Cycle, xii, xx–xxi, 50–54, 59, 69, 158, 249; Colonial-Revolutionary Cycle, 201; Negro Renaissance Cycle, 201–205
Slave Songs of the United States (W. Allen et al.), 64
Slavery: abolition, 24, 59–60; first slaves in Colonies, 2; runaway slaves, advertising, 6–8. *See also* Redpath, James; Slave narratives
Sledd, James B., 263, 280
Small, Sam W., 79
Smart Set (magazine), 171, 313 n
Smith, C. Alphonso, 87
Smith, David M., 259
Smith, Ernie, viii, xxviii, 262, 263, 302 n
Smith, Reed, 208, 211
Smith, Riley B., viii, 263, 282
Smith, William, xxvi
Smitherman, Geneva, 283
Smyth, J. F. D., 5
"Snake of the Cabin, The" (Simms), 39

Snuff-Dipping Tales of the Negro (Brewer), 251
Social History of the Sea Islands, A (G. Johnson), 208, 209
Social Stratification of English in New York City, The (Labov), 260
Sociolinguistic Description of Detroit Negro Speech (Wolfram), 261
"Sociolinguistic Factors in the History of American Negro Dialects" (Labov), 259
Sociolinguistic Study of the Pronunciation of Three Vowels in Detroit Speech (Fasold), 261
Soldier's Pay (Faulkner), 166
Some Phrases of Negro English (Sanders), 208
Song of the Boat (Graham), 242–243
Song of the South: Harris, 89, 231; Disney production, 231
Songs of the Cattle Trail and Cowboy Camp (J. Lomax), 194
Sons and Fathers (Edwards), 91–92
"Soul Story" (Dove), 248
Sounding, *See* Black American folklore
South Atlantic Quarterly, The, 121
South Carolina Gazette and Weekly Advertiser, 8
South Town (Graham), 240–241
South-Carolina Gazette, 7
Southern English, discussion of, xxiv
Southern Literary Messenger, 31
Southern Magazine, 105
Southern Quarterly Review, The, 35
Southern and Western Monthly Magazine and Review, 35, 39
Southwest Regional Laboratory for Educational Research and Development, 261–262
South-West by a Yankee, The (Ingraham), 42
Spectator, The, 79
Spencer, Eulalie, 165
Springfield (Mass.) *Republican,* 93
Spy, The (Cooper), 25–26, 27
"Squeak of the Fiddle, The" (J. Allen), 142
St. Helena Island, 193, 209
St. Helena Island Spirituals (Ballanta-Taylor), 193
St. Louis Woman (Bontemps, Cullen), 239
St. Petersburg Times, 274
Stagg, Hunter, 171
Stallings, Laurence, 172
Standard English, discussion of, xv–xvi
Starter, The (Spencer), 165
State, The, 110, 171–173, 205, 206. *See*
also Gonzales, Ambrose
State Fair (Green), 162
State Gazette of South Carolina, 8
Steal Away, 67–68
Stein, Gertrude, 165
Steinbeck, John, 165
Steptoe, John, 243
Stereotype, Black. *See* Mass Media, stereotypes; Minstrelsy
Stevie (Steptoe), 243
Stewart, William A., 259, 263, 267, 268, 277, 281, 282
Stokes Co., Frederick A., 75
Stoney, Samuel Gaillard, 157–158, 208
Stowe, Harriet Beecher, 54–58, 97–98, 103, 125; use of dialect in *Uncle Tom's Cabin,* 55–58
Strange Interlude (O'Neill), 159
Stranger in America (Janson), 25
Strictly Speaking (Newman), 275
Strong Heart (Cable), 98
Study of the Non-Standard English of Negroes and Puerto Rican Speakers in New York City (Labov et al.), 260
Sugar Cane (Wilson), 165
"Sunday's Sinners" (Gonzales), 110
Suwanee River Tales (Bonner), 94
Swahili, 301 n
Sweet talk, 42, 299
Sword and the Distaff, The (Simms), 40
Swords, T & J., 13
Syntactic Structures (Chomsky), 256–257
Syntax, xxvii, 256–257

TESOL Quarterly, 267
Take a Giant Step (Peterson), 239
Tale of the Home Folks in Peace and War (Harris), 89
Tales of Momolu (Graham), 241, 242
Talking Black (Abrahams), 254
Tallant, Robert, 204
Tarone, Elaine, 262, 263
Teaching Black Children to Read (Baratz, Shuy), 268
Tell My Horse (Hurston), 191
Tennessean, The (Royall), 28
Tenney, Tabitha, 19–20, 57
Territorial Enterprise, 100, 309 n
Texas Review, The, 151
Theatre Arts, 156
Their Eyes Were Watching God (Hurston), 191
Theory of Verbal (or Language) Deficiency, xxv. *See also* Black English—theories, Deficit

"Thick Lips Theory." *See* Black English theories—Deficit
36 Children (Kohl), 265–266
Thomas, Isaiah, 18
Thomson, Peggy, 267
Thurber, James, 165
Tidwell, James N., 104
Tilden, Samuel J., 59–60
Time, 172, 201, 267, 277, 286
Times (London), 259
Tinker, Edward Laroque, 97
Tinnie, Gene, 261–262
To Be a Slave (Lester), 205
Tom Sawyer Abroad (Twain), 103
Toomer, Jean, xiii, 149, 165
Torrance, Ridgley, 165
"Tote," 118–119
Town, The (Faulkner), 170
Train Ride (Steptoe), 243
Transformational Grammar Theory, xxxvii, 256–257
Travelers' Commentaries: Antebellum Cycle, xii; Colonial-Revolutionary Cycle, x–xii, 4–6
Trial of Atticus Before Justice Beau, for a Rape, The, 10
Triumph of Love, The (Murdock), 13, 14
Trouble in Mind (Childress), 239
"True Story, A, Repeated Word for Word as I Heard It" (Clemens), 99–100
Tucker, Nathaniel Beverly, 29–30, 58
Turner, Darwin T., 188, 190
Turner, Joseph Addison, 79
Turner, Lorenzo Dow, xiv, 190, 213, 215–217, 263, 316 n
Twain, Mark. *See* Clemens, Samuel
Twi, 216
"Two Runaways" (Edwards), 91

UPI, 246–247, 282, 285
U.S. News and World Report, 286
"Unc' Edinburg's Drowndin' " (Page), 109
"Uncle Caleb" (Russell), 76–77
"Uncle Cap Interviewed" (Russell), 76
"Uncle Gabe's Sag Saws" (Worden), 112
"Uncle Gabe's White Folks" (Page), 108
"Uncle Jim's Baptist Revival Hymn" (S. Lanier, C. Lanier), 75–76
Uncle Remus, 50, 79–80, 83, 84, 86, 89, 90, 93, 177, 178, 250. *See also* Harris, Joel Chandler
Uncle Remus and His Friends (Harris), 85

Uncle Remus, His Songs and His Sayings; The Folk-Lore of the Old Plantation (Harris), 84–85
Uncle Remus' Magazine, 89, 90
Uncle Remus Stories (Harris), 89, 231
Uncle Remus Tales (Harris), 93
Uncle Tom's Cabin (Stowe), 54–58, 97
Uncle Tom's Cabin (film), 219
Uncle Tom's Children (Wright), 234
Underground Railroad, 68
Unified Theory, 287–288. *See also* Black English Cycles
United Brethren Publishing House of Dayton, 125
United Federation of Teachers, 271
United Press International (UPI), 246–247, 282, 285
United States, courts: District Court (Eastern District of Michigan), 282–286 passim; Supreme Court, 60
United States history: abolition, 24; antebellum era, 24 ff; civil rights era, 227–230 ff, 237; Civil War, 24, 29, 58, 59, 60, 65, 71, 99, 100, 129, 149, 177, 179, 275, 307 n; Colonial-Revolutionary era 1–4; Harlem Renaissance, xiii, 149 ff; minstrelsy, 46–50, 220–225; Negro Renaissance, 149 ff; "Penny Press" era, xxi, 23–24; Reconstruction era, 59–61, 65, 231; Salem witch trials, 3; travelers' commentaries, xii, 4–6
University of Pittsburgh, 229
University of Texas, 194, 314 n
Unvanquished, The (Faulkner), 170
Upshaw, Berrian K., 177
Uptown (Steptoe), 243
Urban Language Study Program, 267
Urban League, 149
"Use of Black English to Help Children Fit in at School is Debated Here" (Fraser), 270

Vai, 216
Van Buren, Martin, 29
Van Duen, John, 165
Van Vechten, Carl, 186
Vanity Fair, 186
Verbal Deprivation Theory. *See* Black English—theories, Deficit
Verbal Deprivation Theory. Black English—theories, Deficit
"Vernacular of the Jazz World, The" (Gold), 246
Victor (RCA), 221

Vidor, King, xiv, 219
Virginia Chronicle, The, 5
Virginia Gazette, 6, 7
Virginia Minstrels, 48
Virginia Press, 141
Voice of the Negro, The, 133
Voices From Slavery (Yetman), 205
Voltaire (Green), 162
Von Hoffman, Nicholas, 247
Voyage to Demarary, A (Bolingbroke), 25
Voyages Dans L'Interview de la Louisiane (Robin), 24

WAPE. See West African languages, West African Pidgin English
WEBH, 220, 221
WGN, 220, 221
WMAQ, 220, 221
Wade, Ernestine, 224
Wagner, Jean, 137
Waldron, J. A., 111–112
Wales, James A., 114, 145, 149
Walker, Kenneth, 248
Waller, "Fats," 149
Walser, Richard, 8–9, 19
Walt Disney Productions, 89, 231
Ward, Artemus, 56, 101
Ware, Charles Pickard, 64
Warner Brothers, 157, 219
Warner, C. D., 103
Washington, Booker T., 148
Washington Post, 247, 248, 267, 273, 281
Washington Sunday Star, 272
"Washington's Second Language" (Thomson), 267
Water Is Wide, The (Conroy), 236
Waters, Ethel, 149
Watts, 220, 230
Watts, Richard, Jr., 156, 219–220
Weary Blues, The (Hughes), 186
Weaver, John H., 283–287
Webster, Noah, 118
Weekly News-Letter, 7
Weevils in the Cotton (Perdue), 205
'Weh Down Souf (D. Davis), 141
"W'en Dey 'Listed Colo'ed Sojers" (Dunbar), 129–130
Wendell, Barrett, 194
Wes-Kos. *See* West African languages, West African Pidgin English
West African languages: Bantu family, xxviii, 262, 287; Bini, 216; Ewe, 216; Gã, 216; Hamito family, xxviii, 287; Ibo, 216; Krio (Sierra Leone), 260;

Liberian Pidgin English, 242–43, 260; Mende, 216; Semitic family, 287; Sierra Leone Krio, 260; Twi, 216; Vai, 216; West African Pidgin English (Wes-Kos), ix, xvi, xxvii, 2, 3, 4, 5–6, 12, 14–15, 24, 41, 63, 88, 241–243, 257–260, 262, 287–288, 301 n; Yoruba, 216; Wolof, 259
West, William W., 272
Westbrook, Colston, viii, 259–260, 262, 263
Western Publishing Co., 89, 231
"When Malindy Sings" (Dunbar), 130–132, 137
White, Lucy, 165
White, Newman I., 194
White, Walter, 149
Whitlock, Bill, 47
Whitney, Anne Weston, 121
Whose Town? (Graham), 241
"Why the Alligator's Back Is Rough" (Harris), 80–83
Wife of His Youth, and Other Stories of the Color Line (Chesnutt), 144
Wigwam and the Cabin, The (Simms), 36
Wilkins, Roy, 286
Williams, John G., 122–124
Williams, Spencer, 224
Williamson, Juanita, 262, 263
Wilson, Flip, 276
Wilson, Frank H., 165
Wilson, Woodrow, 108
Wings on My Feet: Black Ulysses at War (Odum), 193
Wirth, Thomas, 114
Wisner, George, 24
Witchcraft Delusion in New England, The (Drake), 3
With Aesop Along the Black Border (Gonzales), 206
Wolfe, Thomas, 165
Wolfram, Walter A., 261, 263, 268, 281, 282, 302 n, 320 n
Wolof, 259
Woodcraft (Simms), 40
Woodson, Carter G., 149
Woofter, T. J., 209
Word in the Brazos, The; Negro Preacher Tales From the Bottoms of Texas (Brewer), 250–251
Worden, A. T., 112–113
Work, Frederick J., 194
Work, John Wesley, 194
Works Project Administration (WPA), 201. *See also* Federal Writers Project
Worser Days and Better Times (Brewer), 251

Wright, Richard, xvi, 232–234, 237
"Write On" (*Milwaukee Journal*), 248, 249

Yamacraw Island, 266
"Yellow Kid, The" (Outcault), 114
Yemassee, The (Simms), 39–40
Yetman, Norman R., 205

Yorker's Strategem, The (Robinson), 13, 14
Yoruba, 216
Your Fiery Furnace (Green), 163

Zero copula, 291–292
Zero possessive, 292
Zimmerman, Eugene, xii, 111, 113–114, 145, 149